YOUR SCHOOLS AND MINE

By

P. ROY BRAMMELL

DEAN, SCHOOL OF EDUCATION
UNIVERSITY OF CONNECTICUT

THE RONALD PRESS COMPANY   NEW YORK

Library of Congress Catalog Card Number : 52–6201

PRINTED IN THE UNITED STATES OF AMERICA

DEDICATION

To Naomi, Helene, and Homer,
sharers in the adventure of translating education
into better living

To C. B. Gentry,
counselor and friend

And to the Education Staff
of the University of Connecticut,
inspiring coworkers in the field of education

PREFACE

This book is intended to serve as an introduction to education for all who seek a thorough understanding of the American school system. Designed primarily as a first book in education for college students, it will also provide an orientation in education for all readers who want information about the school's place in our society. Whether used as a text in professional education courses or read by civic-minded citizens for the information it contains, the book should be helpful in dealing with local educational problems.

It is the purpose of the book to look at American education in its broader setting and scope. How do our schools tie in with the founding and preservation of our beloved nation? What are they trying to do? How are they organized, administered, and supported? What is their program of studies? Who goes to school, and how does the school adjust to the conglomerate mass it serves? How shall we go about improving our education and judging its outcomes? How can we cooperate in our communities to make our schools really public? What about the people who work in our schools? What are the issues today that form the educational battle front for every citizen? So the questions go. Careful thinking on matters such as these ought to help in clarifying the purpose of American education and in giving background for the wise solution of school problems.

Throughout the book the reader will often discern easily the viewpoint of the writer. This is intentional; but it is not so arranged in order that the judgments of the writer shall necessarily be accepted. Good books, like good teachers, encourage people to think for themselves on debatable issues. This book, accordingly, presents at the close of each chapter a few statements of definite positions on educational topics discussed in the chapter. Instructors in college classes can select from these topics assignments for written work or class discussion to bring out arguments for and against the stated positions.

The author will welcome the personal reaction of any of the readers of this book to any of the statements which it contains. Precautions have been taken to avoid factual inaccuracies in discussing American schools. Statements of opinion on educational policy are invited, however, whether or not they happen to agree with the views expressed in the book.

Acknowledgment is gratefully given to all who have shared in bringing this book to completion and to publishers who have allowed certain materials to be quoted.

P. ROY BRAMMELL

Storrs, Connecticut
March, 1952

CONTENTS

CONTENTS

YOUR SCHOOLS
AND MINE

Chapter 1

BACKGROUNDS TO AMERICAN EDUCATION

Our Heritage of Freedom

1. Value of an Overview of Backgrounds

If education is thought of as man's personal development and his adjustment to and control of his environment, then it has been going on for a long time. It has not always involved schools and teachers as we know them today, and certainly it is not limited even now to the program conducted by the school. Man in his development has had quite an ordeal of experiencing. As time has gone on, he has moved from adjustment to adjustment, has awakened to his world, and has evolved his institutions. He has become less and less submissive to his natural environment and has sought, with considerable success, to control it. He has been less successful in controlling himself.

The problems of education stem from these problems of the race: from man's seeking to push back his horizons, to learn and do, to dream and to be free. We of this time are a part of this stream of struggle, of searching and finding, of loss and gain. Although conditions have changed with time, fundamentally man has not changed much in a good many hundred years. Many of his problems of today send their roots deep into the past, and many of his ambitions, centuries old, have not yet been realized. It will be profitable briefly to glance backward and gain a perspective. In so doing we shall be able better to understand the unfolding nature and role of education, to place our present education in its proper relationship, and to establish the origins of some of our present problems and trends. We shall also see some of the influences immediately affecting early American education.

2. Ancient Patterns

The Rigid Primitives.—Primitive societies were simple and severe. The people were buffeted by storm and beast and imaginary spirits, all designed, as they supposed, to destroy them. Life was a struggle, in the rough, for survival. Fear stalked constantly. As

3

ways of slaying the beasts and providing shelter and safety were discovered, they were severely taught and diligently learned. Imitation of the old by the young was complete. Survival, perhaps, depended upon it. As a result, the authority and domination of the old over the young was the rule. Law and ritual, simple indeed, were rigorously observed. The youth became a man when the law and ritual and the skills of the tribe were observed and mastered. Conformity was necessary. Education was, for the most part, the transmittal of the status quo.

In most sections of the world today, man is far removed from many of the conditions and necessities of primitive life. Man, breaking his primitive bonds, has slowly learned to control his environment, to adjust himself to it, to free himself from it. Mastery displaces bungling; confidence displaces wonder and fear. Conformity and domination as means of stark survival are no longer necessary; indeed, they may today prevent survival. The life and problems of one generation in our times differ in significant ways from those of another. Education for adjustment more than for conformity is now necessary. And yet, in large portions of the world where the conditions of primitive living are gone and where man ought to be free, education and, indeed, government, itself, are agents of conformity and domination, road blocks in the path of man's progress to freedom. Primitive education is not limited to primitive times.

The Creative Greeks.—The Greek story is not altogether one of creativeness. In this connection Sparta and Athens present an interesting contrast. The Spartan philosophy and practice were primitive. The primary goal was military might. Conformity to the will and purpose of the state was required. Individuals, to count, must fit into a mold, must accept and sponsor purposes they themselves had not helped to determine. Actually, at times, if Spartan infants gave no promise of contributing to the military strength of the state, they were "exposed" on the hills, the defenseless prey of beasts and weather. Education for boys was training for war; for girls, the rearing of warriors. Sparta was developed and was smothered in the straitjacket of war, barren of the lasting arts of peace. Nothing creative had been born to survive.

Athens, too, had her problems of survival, and she trained well for her defense. In so doing she resisted attack and established herself as a strong city state. But she did more than that. She recognized the capacity and right of free individuals to think for themselves, to serve the state in many ways beyond the military. Special status could be gained through education. Individualism flourished. The glories of art, literature, and philosophy came to equal and surpass those of war. In fact, attention became so devoted to personal pursuits that the solidarity of the state weakened because of a lack of loyalty and of an unwillingness to set aside personal interests when the common good required it. The world has not seen the equal of the Golden Age of Greece in the fruits of the human mind going its own pleasurable, personal way. These personal pursuits were no defense, however, against the military jealousy of Sparta and the conquering hosts of Macedonia and Rome. In the midst of glory was weakness. Birth of one sort seemed to mean death of another. Or is it necessarily so?

The story of Greek civilization points up one of the most difficult problems in education. Does the suppression of individualism by the state, as illustrated by Sparta, lead to destruction? On the other hand, does education in line with individual interests and capacities, as illustrated by Athens, lead to social and political disintegration? Does the parade of history show the downfall of nation after nation that ruthlessly dominated its people? Does it show also the downfall of nations whose people, surfeited in personal gain and pleasures, abandoned the sacrifices and loyalties which bind them together in strength? Is the primary responsibility of education, clear in the evidence of history, that of educating for both individual development and social responsibility? Can it be done? America and all democratic nations are betting their lives on the proposition that it can and must be done.

The Routine Romans.—The Romans were great systematizers and organizers. They were less creative and more practical than the Greeks. They institutionalized much of the Greek culture, but they were choosy. Oratory, for example, which paid off in practical ways, was more important to them than speculative philosophy. They were builders of tangible things. They developed and codified laws. They were basically wise and open-minded in the use of resources, including people, in developing the empire. Extensive use was made of the Greeks in the Roman schools. The people of conquered countries were treated kindly and early absorbed into citizenship. The expansion of the Roman Empire was rapid. The task of organization was immense. The Roman rose to it.

But if Rome rose to the task of developing an organization for the empire, she fell short of developing in the people the lasting loyalties and sacrifices that would make the Empire solid. The weaknesses of Greece appeared. New peoples, generously taken into citizenship, were accepted but neglected and did not become citizens at heart. After many years, flabby expansionism and humanity in the rough met on the northern borders. The Romans lost. By 476 A.D., invading groups had crisscrossed the Empire. Lusty peoples, diamonds in the rough, out of whom Western nations were to evolve, plundered and destroyed much of what Rome had organized and built. Then they settled down to be at home. The institutions of organized society deteriorated and crumbled under the awkward hands of the barbarians. All but one—the Church.

3. Light and Struggle

The Little Fire.—"Behold, what a great flame a little fire kindleth." When Christ was born at Bethlehem, the known world was almost all within the Roman Empire. Approximately 500 years were to elapse before the Empire would crumble before the barbarians. The emperors of the flourishing kingdom came to be so great and powerful that they took on the rank of gods and were worshiped by the people. In such surroundings, a gospel of "one God, and him only shalt thou serve" would fare badly. The idea of "a kingdom not of this world," through which man could find his happiness and security rather than through submission to his rulers in this world, was bound to cause trouble. The early Christians were persecuted and scattered. But they preached nevertheless. It was as though a nest of fire had been blasted into surrounding tinder. People followed the Christians because they held out hope for the common man; he in his humility was important; his soul was worth saving. All who would come must humble themselves, because only in humility could the soul grow and the conditions of harmonious living develop. Here was the doctrine of individual worth embedded in a religious faith. Here were the seeds of democracy, the chance for all to be vindicated "by their works" rather than by their status in life. This was the beginning of an era in which the life resources of all men, great and small, could be used in solving the problems of human living. In time emperors came, humbling themselves. The Church, following the inclinations of the Romans, developed within the Empire a tremendously strong organization; so strong that its status at that time has been described as "a state within a state." It grew up in a society that had felt strongly the influence of Eastern individualism but had developed on its own part vigorous institutionalism. When the Empire fell, the Church survived. What would be the turn of the future, and of education? Would it be institutionalism, limiting the orbit of individual thought and freedom, or would it be individualism, in which institutions are agencies of free men, perfecting and protecting their progress?

The Dominant Church.—During the time from the birth of Christianity to the fall of Rome, the Church established itself. It is well that it did. Otherwise it could not have withstood the disintegration accompanying the barbaric invasions. Inevitably, however, the Hellenic eastern portion of the empire and the Latin West drew apart, forming the Greek Catholic Church and the Roman Catholic Church. The Western church, which was to affect the New World more directly than the Eastern church, rejected the learning and language of the East. The reading of "pagan" authors was forbidden, and the Greek language was forgotten. Schools were established for the training of church leaders. In the East these leaders sought to reconcile Christianity and Greek philosophical thought and to build them into an acceptable system of theology. In the West, however, Greek culture was rejected, and the Church leaders, following the old Roman penchant for organization, fairly walled themselves in behind a strong church with a rigid dogma. This dogma was vigorously defended against all comers. The Church in the West regulated the religious life of its members and taught them such things as it felt they should know. Formal education was limited almost entirely to priests and monks. The Church demanded complete loyalty. The ways and learnings of this world were to be rejected. Salvation is beyond the grave. Save your soul and accept as your lot the conditions of present living. Only through unquestioned acceptance of the teachings and requirements of the Church could salvation be assured. Monasteries were established where groups could remove themselves almost completely from the influences of the world. Such was the picture when the bearded footmen from the North and East surged in and the Dark Ages settled down over Europe. Could it be that the Church, too, would require man to yield himself, or would it help him find himself?

New Horizons.—With the barbaric invasions western Europe came under the heel of conquerors vigorous and towering but crude and uncouth. They took over the control of the cities, lands, and government, but they did not know how to run them, or even how to use the organizations and procedures already developed by the Romans. They could plunder and sack, but they could not rebuild. The god of war they worshiped and followed, but when the pillage ceased and they were in command, they could neither order and conduct a civilized society, nor would they permit others to do so. Europe bogged down for about 700 years of Dark Ages. But at no time was every-thing lost, and in due time light would reappear.

Charlemagne and Alfred. Charlemagne is a brilliant flash on a dark page. By about 750 A.D., things had become so bad in Europe that illiteracy developed even among the priesthood. In 768, Charlemagne came to the throne in Frankland. By the end of his reign in 814 he had, with the aid of Alcuin, chided and scolded the priests into improving themselves, had established schools, extended the benefits of learning to vast new numbers, and had himself become the most eager scholar in the schools of his kingdom. Alred the Great tried to do the same thing in England a little later. But both of these efforts, however brilliant they were in very dark surroundings, did not endure. Additional invasions and plunder again set the clock back.

Education for Chivalry. The wisdom of the Church in dealing with the barbarians was a hopeful thing. Adaptations to the nature and interests of these unrefined people were made, but the authority and dignity of the Church were preserved. As time went on chieftain after chieftain was converted and, at times, large numbers of followers with them. With the development of feudalism, a system of education known as chivalry and centering around the castle of the noble-man, rather than around the cathedral or monastery, was developed in cooperation with the Church. The education of the youth from page to squire to knight culminated in an oath "to defend the church, . . . and to shed his blood, even to its last drop, in behalf of his breth-ren." Such things as riding, swimming, archery, fencing, hunting, whist or chess, rhyming, and, indeed, fighting received religious sanc-tions. These, after all, were the things to which these rugged people were best adapted at that time. If the Church could inject a religious loyalty into this type of activity, so much the better. The recipients of this kind of education became the knights of the Crusades.

The Mohammedans in Spain. The prostrate Roman Empire was beset not only by rugged peoples from northern and eastern Europe but also by Mohammedans from the Near East. This group, during the seventh and early eighth centuries, overran a good portion of the Hellenic eastern end of the Empire until they were checked in Asia Minor. They then moved westward across northern Africa, crossed into Spain, and were finally stopped at the great Battle of Tours, 732, in what is now France. Defeated at Tours, they moved back across the Pyrenees into Spain and settled down. It is impossible to predict what the result would have been if they had won at Tours, what the mixture of Teuton, Latin, and Semitic, of Christian and Mohammedan, would have produced. It might not have been too bad, because the Mohammedans were quick learners. They absorbed much from the Hellenic culture of the East and brought it over into Spain. It may be that their adaptation to Christianity and their effect on the western Church would have been satisfactory. As it was, pushed back into Spain, the doors of western Europe were closed against them and the Church forbade contact with them. But there they were, just over the mountains, developing educationally, agriculturally, scientifically, and philosophically to such an extent that the curious of Europe, including the curious of the Church, had to slip down and take a look. Human curiosity is hard to control, can scarcely be commanded.

The Mohammedan movement, as referred to above, included the conquest of the Holy Land. Christian Europe did not like that. In time, therefore, great bands of Teutonic Knights, diamonds with only a little polish and with a religious zeal driving them into conquest, set out to recapture the birthplace of Christianity. These were the Crusaders.

The Crusades. A breach in the hard wall of unsuspecting Western Europe now appeared. A nation or a region cannot have large numbers of its people leave its borders, dwell with other peoples, contact other practices and points of view, and get a taste of material advantages in other places, without being affected. Straight into the nest of "paganism" went significant numbers of people, contacting not only "heathen" Greek learning but Moslem learning as well. The Western European, capable of the utmost growth and development, sweating and freezing and dying on the rugged roads to Palestine, was nevertheless starting the tide of bond-breaking that would produce the New World. The Crusades initiated much change in Western Europe affecting her commerce, land system, cities, and education, and particularly her thinking. A new middle class grew up. Feudalism cracked. Trade and industry, with accompanying guild training, developed. Gadgets and spices from far-away places were sold, symbolic of new horizons of thought and experience. The institutions of medieval society were witnessing the inevitable and explosive beginnings of man working and thinking for himself.

Dividing the Emphasis.—The Renaissance is important not so much for its "revival of learning" as for the effects of the revival. How would the people of Europe, beginning now to work and think for themselves, react to the ancient writings? Naturally these manuscripts came first into the hands of the clergy and a few other intellectuals. They searched them for their portrayal of the language, culture, and thought of the past. They accepted them as models of form, authoritative, "classics." This was narrow humanism: the adaptation made by Western institutionalism. But this could not satisfy the masses. As the life and thought of the ancients became known to the common man, he quickly used them as springboards to his own times and problems. This was broad humanism: the irresistible adaptation made by the masses. Christian individualism, therefore, seemed now to take its place over against Christian institutionalism. Thus the emphasis divided: a kind of rigidity and formalism based on the Roman emphasis on organization and authority against the concerns of living, the here and the now, man's status under his institutions and within his environment. Aspects of this division, of institutionalism versus individualism, authority versus reason, and insight versus experimentalism, have come down sharply to our own time. They are reflected on every hand in our education.

4. Appraisal and Action

With the sense of personal worth gained through the interpretation of Christianity, and with the awareness that peoples in other times had met their problems in many ways, the Western European began to evaluate his environment and his institutions. He would no longer endure tribulation and submit to authority as the price of eternal life. As he looked around him, he did not like all that he saw. His government, his natural environment, even his church restrained his urge for self-development, for freedom. A new voice seemed to become articulate: Make your world and your institutions serve you and implement your reaches to freedom, not dominate you. Action came swiftly and on various fronts.

The Protestant Reformation.—The rigid institutionalism of the Church came under attack in Europe. As countless thousands raised their heads, and, above all, as they began to read, they insisted that Christ had come to the common man, that his immediate followers in Galilee had experienced his inspiration and leadership at first hand before the Church as an institution was ever established, and that any man, confessing Christ, although he would be aided by the Church, was not limited to the Church in gaining religious experience. Rigid institutionalism, even in religion, would not do. The individual, through his own reading of the Bible and through prayer, could grow in spirit. He need not accept without question the interpretation of those in religious authority. Growth, change, and discovery are as possible in religious living and religious interpretation as in any other area of living. Man must not yield all his thoughts and questions and interpretations in this area to an authoritarian institution but must discover for himself that "the kingdom of heaven is within you." Thus the Protestant groups arose, reflecting in religious matters the individualism of the East. They arose primarily in the home regions of the Germanic tribes. Personal reading of the Bible was emphasized. Reading schools, therefore, were everywhere encouraged by the Protestants.

A Counter Reformation took place in the Catholic Church. The Church now vigorously trained leaders to counteract Protestant teachings and to regain Protestant lands, and in time it encouraged reading for the masses, as had not been done before. But the education of the masses was not for the purpose of personal search for religious experience. It was rather for education in Church doctrines; and the Church exercised rigorous limitations as to what could be read.

Thus we have the spectacle of great masses, members of a common Christian faith, dividing on whether the Church is to dominate or implement their religious experience.

As the reform groups became organized and as their theologies were established, they fell into precisely the old rigidities of organization and control against which they had rebelled. So Protestant groups within Protestant groups appeared. However, the attitude of all the Protestant groups concerning the relationship of the individual to the institution in religious experience remained fundamentally different from that of the Catholic Church.

The Development of Scientific Inquiry.—As man began to forsake the other worldliness of the past and to turn attention on his own world, past and present, he became interested in understanding and controlling his natural environment. Scientific inquiry arose, crude at first but fruitful. Important discoveries concerning the ways of nature in earth, sky, and sea, and in man himself, came along. In some cases these discoveries conflicted with the teachings of the Church, and the discoverer, with his data in his pocket and a new world in his heart, bowed to the authority of the Church and recanted. But the search went on apace. Goaded by his curiosity and his capacity to learn, and following systems of inquiry that rejected authority and opinion, man made discoveries which fairly altered his world and changed his conditions of living. This spirit of inquiry has not limited itself to the natural world. It and its methods have engulfed the institutions of society as well. In the minds of many, the primary task of the school is to press this open-minded search for the most serviceable solution to all our problems.

The Rise of Democratic States.—Western man acted on another front when he looked around and discovered that governments, too, were tyrannical, thwarting the development of his potential for self-development and self-control. Here again, the institution was to serve, not dominate, man; to implement, not restrict, his freedom. Democratic states, basing government on the consent and ingenuity of the governed, were the result.

5. RELEASE TO FREEDOM

These cross-currents in Europe gave rise to much despotism, fighting, and dreaming. The Church and existing governments, to say nothing of disputes between them, did not calmly countenance uprisings against their authority. Wars, especially exhausting religious wars, ensued. Cruelest force was used against dissenters. Small wonder then that when the explorers, sharing man's urge to know his world, discovered America, multitudes of determined eyes turned westward. America was the promised land of freedom where human worth would transcend human institutions. Here they would go, not only to escape the boiling pot of Europe, but to build a society in which political and social and institutional barriers to freedom did not exist. Freedom to work and worship under one's own choice and conscience would be observed. And this is the blessed essence of America: freedom. The full blossoming is slow. Contrary forces and institutions following these pioneers into this land must not be allowed to thwart the right of all our people to think and act in conscience on social, political, economic, and religious matters. The obligations to preserve freedom and use it wisely are great. Education has a stellar role to play.

What Do YOU Say?

NOTE—Statements of definite positions on some of the topics discussed in the foregoing chapter are given below. These are intended to focus attention on current school problems and to stimulate expressions of original thinking in your written work and class discussions. A similar section of topical statements follows each of the succeeding chapters.

1

There has been a pronounced growth in the power of institutionalism in this country during recent years. There is danger that many people may thoughtlessly accept and promote this institutionalism without realizing that the basic freedoms which our nation has nurtured are being violated.

What do YOU say?

2

All of man's institutions and beliefs, as well as his physical environment, are a proper study for the doubtful or inquiring mind. It is a proper function of the school to assist in making such inquiry as valid and unbiased as possible.

What do YOU say?

3

What points in this chapter do you particularly support or take issue with?

Chapter 2

THE DEVELOPMENT OF EDUCATION IN AMERICA

Evolving Schools for Our Own Needs

The early settlers in America were overwhelmingly Protestants. They were, for the most part, middle-class, well-educated, self-thinking people. Their primary purpose in coming to the New World was to gain religious freedom. Even the earliest Catholic settlement, in Maryland, was made up of "persecuted English Catholics who obtained a charter from Charles II, in 1632." The Anglicans, adherents of the Church of England, were not, of course, persecuted. They sought material gain in the New World, but they, like other groups, brought with them distinct points of view and practices with reference to education.

1. BORROWED FORMS

Along the Atlantic Seaboard.—So far as education is concerned, the Colonial period in American history presents little that was not borrowed from the old countries. Let us look first at the backgrounds of these people and how these backgrounds were reflected here.

Origins of the Settlers. The three outstanding Protestant groups in Europe from which our early settlers came were the Lutherans, the Calvinists, and the Anglicans or English Episcopalians. All were the product of long years of growing reaction against a church that had attempted to maintain medieval authority and dogma in a world becoming modern. Each group encouraged education. They were different, however, in their beliefs as to where the responsibility for education rested. The Lutherans viewed education as a means to personal salvation, but they were quite willing that the authority of the state be added to that of the church in seeing to it that children were taught. The Calvinists held essentially the same point of view as the Lutherans, but they put it into practice and in Geneva achieved cooperation of church and state in educational matters. These groups, interested in education for religious purposes, were not fearful of civil authority. In fact, they viewed it as desirable that the state should require the kind of education they envisaged. Matters were different among the Anglicans. This group placed the responsibility for education on the home. If parents themselves were unable to teach their children or could not afford to secure tutors, then it became the religious duty of others to help in providing some learning for their children. The pauper or charity schools of England resulted, and it is likely that the charitable or religious accompaniment to these schools underlies the practice of exempting private schools from taxation.

Transplanted Backgrounds. The settlements along the Atlantic seaboard stemmed primarily from these Protestant origins. The Puritans in New England, Calvinistic in background, had been oppressed by the state church in England. They sought brief refuge in Holland, then came to America, bringing along the Calvinistic idea that the state through its legal authority should require the education of children, in ways, to be sure, sanctioned by the church. This idea materialized early in New England.

In 1642 and 1647 the Massachusetts Colonial Assembly passed laws requiring the education of children and the establishment of schools. Specifically the Law of 1642, although it did not require the establishment of schools, did require that parents or masters should teach children to read. Inspections were made by town officials and fines were imposed when the law was disobeyed. This law was not too effective, and the Law of 1647 was soon forthcoming. The new law required the establishment of schools. Every town that had 50 householders must engage a teacher of reading and writing and make provision for his wages. Every town that had as many as 100 householders must provide, in addition, a school for the preparation of youth for the university. Such laws would not only serve religious purposes, but, as had been learned in England, they would prevent the growing-up of illiterate, untrained citizens who might easily become threats to the security of the state. At any rate, in New England the principle was early established that the state, independent of home and church, can require that children be taught. This concept in due time spread over our country and lies at the root of our present state school system, involving the separation of church and state.

The early settlers in the southern colonies were predominantly Anglicans. These Englishmen held to the same philosophy of home responsibility for education that they had adhered to in England.

Hence private, tutorial education developed in the South. Some of the wealthier families sent their children back to England for schooling. Certainly the Colonial assemblies of the South did not enact laws concerning education similar to the Massachusetts Laws of 1642 and 1647.

The middle colonies were settled by numerous groups with varying backgrounds. Hence, there did not develop a typical pattern such as developed in New England and the South. Numerous Lutheran sects, Scotch-Irish Presbyterians, Dutch Calvinists, Catholics, Anglicans, and others were all there. "Neither New Jersey, New York, nor Pennsylvania may be said to have developed any colonial educational policy aside from that of allowing private and parochial effort to provide such schools as seemed desirable." [1] The numerous Protestant groups that settled Pennsylvania "all believed in the necessity of learning to read the Bible as a means to personal salvation, and all made efforts looking toward the establishment of schools as a part of their church organization. Unlike New England, though, no sect was in a majority; church control for each denomination was considered as most satisfactory; and no appeal was made to the state to have it assist the churches in the enforcement of their religious purposes." [2]

Thus in Colonial America we see in education strong private, Protestant parochial, and state influences. Such a situation would not foster the greatest unity and freedom in the New World. If a new nation should be born, a problem in relationships would arise.

Types of Schools Transplanted.—Early American schools, on all levels, were copies of European schools. English patterns were followed for the most part.

Elementary Schools. On the elementary level, various types of schools were developed. Parish schools, after European models, were developed, especially among Lutherans and Quakers. Dame schools, often with teachers of the meagerest preparation, emphasized reading and spelling. Writing schools gave special attention to writing and reckoning. As dame schools and writing schools tended to combine, there resulted the schools for the three R's—"Readin', 'Ritin', and 'Rithmetic." Charity and pauper schools, after the English type, were developed here, particularly in the middle and southern colonies. Apprentice schools, also, copying but expanding somewhat the English pattern, came in early. Apprenticing was of two kinds, voluntary and compulsory. Under the former a boy from a family of independ-

[1] E. P. Cubberley, *History of Education* (Boston: Houghton Mifflin Co., 1920), p. 371.
[2] *Ibid.,* p. 369.

ent means chose his trade and sought out a likely master who was willing to instruct him. Under the latter the orphan boys and the boys of the poor "were bound out by town officials to masters willing to take apprentices under the provisions of the poor law." Often boys who were bound out were exploited and their education was neglected.

Other types of elementary schools such as the infant schools and monitorial schools were established around 1800. Both had English backgrounds. The infant schools originated with a manufacturer, Robert Owen of Scotland, who wished to do something for the children five, six, and seven years old who were apprenticed to him for nine years. He instituted an informal kind of education for them and for children as young as three years. In the hands of other leaders the infant schools became more formal, and in this country they became preparatory schools for the developing public schools which required reading and writing for admission. In this country the infant school became the primary school, displaced the schools for the three R's, and became the primary department in our public school system. The monitorial schools were based on the work of two Englishmen, Andrew Bell and Joseph Lancaster. This system made use of selected pupils who were taught their lessons by the teacher and each of whom in turn taught about ten other pupils. Large numbers of pupils could therefore be handled by one teacher. The method was cheap and in some ways effective. It spread rapidly until about 1830 and then waned just as rapidly.

Secondary Schools. The Latin grammar school was the first type of secondary school in this country. At the time of the founding of the colonies it was one of the most important schools in England, and it came over to us little changed in form or content. As its name implies, it emphasized Latin. The boys studied Greek toward the close of the grammar school course, and they received some instruction also in numbers and English. Certainly, however, the mastery of the ancient languages received much more attention than the mastery of English. These schools were strictly college preparatory. Their curriculum, therefore, contained whatever the colleges required for admission. They were not suited to the multiform needs of the youth of the New World but served instead the needs of a selected group that wished to prepare for the Christian ministry. The Latin grammar school remained in ascendancy until about the Revolutionary War. By that time a greatly Americanized secondary school, the academy, had begun rapidly to take over.

Colleges. The early colleges, too, followed European patterns, particularly English patterns. Harvard College, founded in 1636, was modeled after Cambridge and adhered exceedingly closely to the European subject patterns. In fact, "The instruction in the new college was a combination of the arts and theological instruction given in a medieval university." William and Mary, founded in 1693; Yale, in 1701; and Princeton, in 1746, all closely resembled Harvard, except that William and Mary had drawn more on Oxford precedents than on Cambridge precedents. All were interested in training ministers; all were rigid in their discipline; all placed great faith in the power of the classics; and none worried at all about the New World's need for leaders in areas beyond the Christian ministry.

Religious Purpose Throughout.—The driving force back of the establishment of schools in this country was religion. After all, these settlers, mainly Protestant, had come here for religious freedom, and they believed sincerely that every man should read the Bible and experience religion for himself. The school was the handmaid of the church; and even the state, as it legislated in New England concerning education, was serving the church.

This religious purpose applied to the schools at all levels. The Massachusetts Law of 1647, which required the establishment of common schools in the towns, prefaced the provisions of the law as follows: "It being one chief project of the old deluder, Satan, to keep men from the knowledge of the Scriptures, as in former times by keeping them in an unknown tongue, . . . that learning may not be buried in the grave of our fathers in the church and commonwealth, the Lord assisting our endeavors—It is therefore ordered . . ." The New England Primer, severe in its Puritanism, was almost ruthless in the manner in which it plied little children with duty, death, devil, and damnation. The salient purpose of the Latin grammar school was to fix in boys the rudiments of Latin, the revered language of the church, so that they could enter the colleges and prepare for the ministry. The early colleges, as stated before, had no other purpose than to train preachers. Thus the early schools were founded predominantly for religious purposes; a pattern, however, that would greatly limit their services. As the New World people, free in their work and worship, discovered their educational needs, they would see to it that institutions rendering broader services were provided.

General Educational Conditions in the Colonies.—For the most part the general educational conditions of the Colonial period were none too good. This should not becloud the fact, however, that the colonists had many other raw problems to meet, that they were fresh from their antecedents abroad, and that time would be required to ripen their basic beliefs into indigenous institutions and practices.

Class and Privilege. It should never be supposed that democratic conditions in education have existed since our Colonial beginnings. Although the Protestant philosophy made it urgent that every individual learn to read, this did not carry beyond the barest essentials of learning. Neither did this philosophy solve the problem of adequate financial support for even the common schools. The economic and social status of the family figured in education just as it had figured abroad. In fact, boys attending Latin grammar schools and colleges were commonly grouped on the rolls and seated in chapel according to the occupations of their fathers. Furthermore, the restricted nature of the program in the institutions above the common schools made these schools useful to only a selected few.

Teachers and Salaries. Actually the teacher situation was better at the very beginning than later. As has been said, the first settlers were middle-class, well-educated, purposeful people. The ministers among them were strong leaders and became the teachers in the new communities. It was no idle concern of the colonists that they establish schools for the training of leaders who could carry on when their present ministers should "lie in dust." Very likely the Latin grammar schools commanded the services of the best teachers of the time. The colleges, too, had good people, but few were needed. For about fifty years the president of Harvard did all the teaching, and at the end of 200 years a staff of half a dozen was still able to carry the load. But, down in the dame schools and in the other schools where the rudiments were taught, the situation was poor. As these schools increased in number, good teachers were not always available to take charge. Furthermore, there were no licensing regulations as we know them today, and no institution gave attention to the training of teachers. Most teachers were checked rather carefully by the town fathers as to their religious qualifications, and, these being satisfactory, they were then permitted to teach the children "as much as they are capable to learn and he capable to teach them within the compas of this year." The result was not always the best.

The pay of the teacher was low. Even the first president of Harvard never received over sixty pounds a year during his fourteen years of service. The remuneration received by other teachers can well be imagined. Often also there was no money for teachers and compensation was given in such things as wood, hay, and foodstuffs.

Board and room were an important part of the teacher's pay, and parents frequently fed and slept the teacher for periods of time determined by the number of children they had in school. In general, the status and salary of the teacher were so low that distinctly inferior education resulted.

Curriculum and Methods. The curriculum of all the Colonial schools was very much limited. This applies to the schools on all levels. These limited programs reflect the limited purposes of the times. Again, religion was paramount. Reading, writing, simple numbers, the learning of a trade, and, above all, instruction in the catechism and the Bible were the chief concerns of the common schools. The Latin grammar schools were working with boys expecting to go on to college as preparation for the ministry. The colleges, therefore, made very clear what should be taught in these schools. Cubberley quotes the admission requirements of Harvard in 1642 as follows: "When any Schollar is able to understand Tully, or such like classical Latine Author *extempore,* and make and speake true Latine in Verse and Prose, *suo ut aiunt Marte*; and decline perfectly the Paradigms of *Nounes* and *Verbes* in the Greek tongue: Let him then, and not before, be capable of admission into the Colledge." [3] In 1745 Yale's requirements stated: "That none may expect to be admitted into this College unless, upon Examination of the President and Tutors, They shall be found able Extempore to Read, Construe and Parce Tully, Vergil, and the Greek Testament; and to write True Latin in Prose and to understand the Rules of Prosodia, and Common Arithmetic, and Shall bring Sufficient Testimony of his Blameless and inoffensive Life." [4] The similarity of these statements, divided by a hundred years, is striking. Clearly, Latin and Greek were at the heart of learning in the Latin grammar schools. The colleges, only nine in number before the Revolutionary War, continued from where the Latin grammar schools left off. The ancient languages, including Hebrew, and the Bible received greatest emphasis. Logic, ethics, and composition were also important. Argumentation was greatly stressed, and mathematics only a little. Toward the end of the Colonial period some of the rigidities began to give way, but the religious, classical purpose remained dominant throughout.

Classroom methods reflected the stern Puritanism of the time. Discipline was severe, and much time was consumed by the teacher

---

[3] E. P. Cubberley, *Public Education in the United States* (rev. and enl. ed.; Boston: Houghton Mifflin Co., 1934), pp. 30–31.
[4] *Ibid.,* p. 30 n.

in administering corporal punishment. Even college students were flogged. Whipping posts were common. Methods as a careful study and practice of adjusting instruction to the nature of learning and the needs of individuals was unheard of. The school day was long. Everybody got tired. The fearful religion taught and the stern measures of the teacher could not prevent restlessness and misbehavior. "A boy has a back; if you beat it he understands."

Buildings and Teaching Equipment. Early buildings were rough and poorly constructed. Heat and light were inadequate. Some were too small and terribly crowded. The New England winters were especially troublesome. The teacher worked with the barest necessities. Such things as good blackboards, supplementary books and materials, sufficient paper, maps, and other teaching aids were far in the future. When some of these things did begin to come in they were of the crudest sort. The Bible, the simplest of textbooks, the horn-book, and later slates and paper made up the essential materials.

Support. Although our forefathers demanded their schools, and although in New England the Colonial assemblies enacted laws requiring the establishment of schools, provisions were not made for their adequate support. In many sections local communities were required to have schools, but they were left to their own devices in raising money for their support. As may be imagined, devious methods were used. Gifts, produce, taxes, lotteries, and grants were used. The rate-bill, of English origin and destined to become one of the most difficult practices to eliminate, was very common. Under this plan parents were assessed for school support in proportion to the number of children they had in school. Often if available funds from other sources ran out before the school term was over, parents were asked to pay "rates," based on the number of children they had in school, to finance the remainder of the term. Rates, of course, encouraged absenteeism and they were hard on poor parents, but they contained a concept of justice which only the development of the idea of free, tax-supported schools could overcome. Naturally, instability in the support of Colonial schools resulted in an uneven quality of education.

Rapid Development in Needs, Slow Adjustment in Program. As the colonies grew, their needs expanded. Up the rivers and over the mountains went the settlers. Communities multiplied. Cities developed, and commerce increased. Lands were limitless, and farming flourished. Lawyers and businessmen and doctors and teachers and leaders of all sorts were needed. Yet the borrowed forms and content of education remained pretty much intact. The Latin grammar schools and the colleges could not see themselves as obligated to train the young people of the New World for the essential work and services of the New World. The religious-classical tradition held fast. How far out of line could educational needs and services become?

2. IRRESISTIBLE IDEAS

It is well to remind ourselves here that the people who settled the colonies were imbued with high purposes. Colonization for gain, of course, developed; but the fundamental drive was a desire for freedom. Religious freedom was perhaps outstanding at first, but the little independent farms, the little businesses, the trades, the very right to move on to a new stake were exciting expressions of the individual making his own choices and directing his own affairs. Schools were demanded so that each could realize the personal religious experience so earnestly sought by the Protestants; but, in addition, all should learn so that in the new land each could think for himself, express himself, and evaluate his institutions. Domination of the individual by his environment and his institutions must not develop. Man's thought and institutions must serve and free him. These irresistible ideas, born out of struggle in Europe, lay as rock under the feet of the colonists. We shall see in the next section that they survived the long years of Colonial hardship and came slowly but surely into tangible fruition.

3. NATIONAL AND EDUCATIONAL UNITY

It was 156 years from the landing of the Pilgrims to the signing of the Declaration of Independence. As history goes, this is a short time, but in that time many people had come to these shores, transplanting here the same problems that have confronted societies everywhere. Would the people in the New World cling to the great ideas that had brought them here? They did.

The Political Revolt Against England.—As the colonies grew, establishing their governments and tapping the wealth of the New World, they became more and more significant to the mother countries. Their ideas concerning the management of their own affairs and the enjoyment of the freedoms they came here to secure did not always square away with those of the controlling governments abroad. These disagreements became so severe that open revolt against England resulted. This was our Revolutionary War, a war against practices which seemed again to reduce man to the role of servant to his government, without chance to share in considerations that might lead to a change in his status. The revolt was successful, and the colonies were cut loose from England.

Effect of the War on Education.—Education, poor enough before the Revolution, was set back drastically by the war. Naturally, in a country that had not yet become accustomed to the systematic support of education and had not yet fitted the school into its important role, war would deal a cruel blow to education. The interest and energies of the revolting colonies were turned to the winning of the war. Money was not available for schools. Enrolments dwindled. College buildings were frequently used for war purposes. Teachers were scarce. Nathan Hale left his job as a teacher to join the fight for freedom. Workers and soldiers and farmers were needed. The school would have to wait.

Democratic Government Without Democratic Experience or Institutions.—One of history's greatest examples of following through on a faith that had not yet been shown to be practicable took place following the Revolutionary War. The new developing nation, true, as it were, to the oppressed thousands in Europe who had looked this way for freedom, established a government which was to depend upon the individual citizen for its wisdom, growth, and durability. Government that based its authority and evolution on the consent and development of its people was established. It did this without vivid precedents, either here or abroad, which showed that such a government could be successful. It is a miracle of faith that our forefathers established such a form of government without the experience or the institutions to maintain it. Here was a faith, newly stated, which was to shape new institutions more than to reflect old institutions. Certainly the school had not cultivated the soil for democracy. It was not until well *after* the establishment of the new government that the great movement for the education of the masses in free schools developed. The government, depending upon the individual's potential for its strength, would have to have the assistance of institutions in which that potential was developed.

Evidences of Leadership and Action.—The thinking of many of our leaders at the time of the founding of our national government is clear on the relationship of education to the new government. Cubberley quotes some of these leaders as follows: [5]

[5] *Ibid.*, pp. 89–91.

Thomas Jefferson:

Above all things, I hope the education of the common people will be attended to; convinced that on this good sense we may rely with the most security for the preservation of a due degree of liberty.

If a nation expects to be ignorant and free in a state of civilization it expects what never was and never will be. . . . There is no safe deposit (for the functions of government), but with the people themselves; nor can they be safe with them without information.

George Washington:

Promote then, as an object of primary importance, institutions for the general diffusion of knowledge. In proportion as the structure of a government gives force to public opinion, it is essential that public opinion be enlightened.

James Madison:

A satisfactory plan for primary education is certainly a vital desideratum in our republics.

A popular government without popular information or the means of acquiring it is but a prologue to a farce or a tragedy, or, perhaps, both. Knowledge will forever govern ignorance; and a people who mean to be their own governors must arm themselves with the power which knowledge gives.

John Adams:

The instruction of the people in every kind of knowledge that can be of use to them in the practice of their moral duties as men, citizens, and Christians, and of their political and civil duties as members of society and freemen, ought to be the care of the public, and of all who have any share in the conduct of its affairs, in a manner that never yet has been practiced in any age or nation. The education here intended is not merely that of the children of the rich and noble, but of every rank and class of people, down to the lowest and the poorest. It is not too much to say that schools for the education of all should be placed at convenient distances and maintained at the public expense. The revenues of the State would be applied infinitely better, more charitably, wisely, usefully, and therefore politically in this way than even in maintaining the poor. This would be the best way of preventing the existence of the poor. . . .

Laws for the liberal education of youth, especially of the lower classes of people, are so extremely wise and useful that, to a humane and generous mind, no expense for this purpose would be thought extravagant.

These, and others like them, gave expression to educational needs which had not yet been met. Statement after statement reveals a reaction against the narrow and privileged nature of the education of the past and envisions an education of the future that will be appropriate and available to all. Thus the early thinking took shape as our national lines were formed.

And the thinking on the national level began to yield results. It was early translated into action that set the pattern for the future. The Ordinance of 1787 to govern the great national domain lying between the Mississippi and Ohio rivers stated that: "Religion, morality, and knowledge being necessary to good government and the happiness of mankind, schools and the means of education shall be forever encouraged." This encouragement by the federal government became tangible in this territory and in all other public domains out of which subsequent states were formed, in the nature of land grants for the maintenance of schools. Approximately 150,000,000 acres of public lands have thus been given to the states for educational purposes. Although the constitution of the new democracy, adopted in 1789, did not mention education directly, it nevertheless expressed concern for the "general welfare," which could hardly disregard education. Evidences of leadership and action at the federal level thus came early, and they have continued until now. In fact, federal action has at times seemed a necessity when existing state governments and educational institutions have acted too slowly in meeting educational needs.

Classism Overthrown in Government.—It should not be imagined that with the adoption of the Constitution the new nation had become completely and suddenly democratic. There were still many forces of privilege and class in the country. The Bill of Rights was added to the Constitution as a guarantee to the individual of certain rights and privileges. Even in top government circles there were those who had no confidence in the masses and stood for a strong central government run by people who had been chosen and educated for leadership posts. For a time it was actually uncertain whether we would have government by the people or by the few. However, the presidential election of 1828 seemed to settle that question. In that year the common people chose a common man, Andrew Jackson, for President. A new era had begun. The idea that only members of a certain class or those trained in a certain manner could hold positions of responsibility was rejected. Now the intellectuals and the sons of intellectuals became people like all the rest, and if they were to hold high public posts they would have to convince their fellow-citizens that they were worthy of such confidence. Classism in government had been overthrown.

Classism Overthrown in Education.—It has already been pointed out that the democratic concept was actually launched in government before it was launched in education. The demands of the new nation, including the requirements of the new government for an informed people, came to the schools faster than they were willing to accept them. The forms and content that had been borrowed from Europe persisted with only slight modifications until the Revolutionary War.

Borrowed Forms Become Inadequate. As the nation settled down to the tough task of implementing its ideas and making itself work, its educational needs became apparent. At first considerable confidence was felt that the existing schools might do the job. The existing Latin grammar schools and colleges, however, were special schools serving a special class. The common or elementary schools were not organized, staffed, or supported to carry the tremendous project of mass education which loomed ahead. Changes on all levels were due; and they came.

Changes in Elementary Education. With the establishment of democratic government, a new reason developed for educating the individual. To the old religious reason was now added the political reason. One should learn to read not only as a means of saving his own soul but also as a means of forming opinions, of judging the policies of others, of becoming a well-informed citizen on a hundred fronts. He should also be able to write and figure, to express himself to others and conduct his own business. Everyone should learn. "A general diffusion of knowledge" was in the public interest. Existing schools, however, bore the private tradition. They were never really public schools. Even in states where the civil authority had been called on to legislate requiring the establishment of schools, the state had not designated how the schools were to be supported. Furthermore, the diverse ideas in the New England, middle, and southern colonies about responsibility for education had never been harmonized. The "battle for the free schools," centering in the period 1825–50, was the result. Suffice it to say here that this battle achieved for America a system of tax-supported, free, nonsectarian common schools. No longer would the common school in any section of our country have to depend on the uncertain attitude or generosity of a church; on doubtful gifts, lotteries, and income from scanty school funds; or on any other of a number of forms of financial support. The recency of the complete winning of this battle for public support is striking. Some people now living in regions where the private tradition was strong can remember the time when the state finally passed a law requiring local communities to tax themselves sufficiently so that schools could be maintained without recourse to such things as the old rate-bill, which, of course, had made educational opportunity dependent in part on the economic status of parents. At any rate, by the middle of the nineteenth century, our country had established a pattern of public schools which, as our leaders had said, was the necessary foundation for our democracy. Curriculum expansion, of course, accompanied this shift from private to public support, from church to state control. The school was no longer an agency of the church; therefore it could not be used for sectarian purposes. Modern elementary school subjects developed. Public elementary schools became graded from the primary level through the eighth grade. The common, free schools were here. Democracy now had the means for the "general diffusion of knowledge."

Changes in Secondary Education. The limitations of the Latin grammar schools led to the rise of the academies in this country. Whereas the purpose of the Latin grammar schools had been strictly preparation for college, the academies added a second purpose— namely, preparation "for the ordinary business of life." Benjamin Franklin's Academy at Philadelphia, which opened its doors in 1751, was probably the first real academy in America. "English" studies, conducted in English and intended to prepare youth for more effective participation in the pursuits of the New World, took their place alongside the study of the classical languages. The expression "alongside" is significant, since both programs were present. As time went on, in fact, the older college preparatory function of the academies became again predominant and they fell into the same errors of nonadjustment that the Latin grammar schools had been guilty of. Entrance requirements prescribed by the colleges were more influential than the requirements of community living in determining their programs of studies. The public could not forestall this development, since the academies were private institutions, controlled by boards of trustees, and not directly subject to the public will. The Americanized academy did much good in popularizing secondary education, introducing new subjects, assisting in teacher education, and acting as a transition school to the public high school. Its growth was rapid following 1750, and from about 1825 until the Civil War it supplied most of the secondary education in this country. In 1850, 263,096 pupils were enrolled in 6,085 such schools. By about 1840 a new kind of secondary school, supported by public taxation and subject to public control, had been forced into existence by the determination of the academies to stick to the patterns dictated by the colleges rather than adjust to the common needs of their pupils, most of whom would never set foot on a college campus. This new institution was the public high school.

The first public high school was established in Boston in 1821. By 1860 over 300 such schools had been established. Their growth, as may be supposed, was rapid. Here at last was in prospect a school at the secondary level which would give attention to launching vast numbers of young people directly into the pursuits and responsibilities of citizenship and community living. There was reason now, with the development of practical studies in the secondary school, to discard the idea that secondary education was only for the few. It was for the many also. Why shouldn't secondary education of the new kind be as common for all as the education in the common elementary schools? And so it seemed on the way to becoming when a Mr. Stuart in Kalamazoo, Michigan, in 1872, called the whole process into question. This was the well-known Kalamazoo Case. Mr. Stuart contended that the action the city had taken by voting additional taxes for the support of a high school was illegal because the new school was not a "common school." He therefore sued to prevent the collection of the additional taxes. After all, reasoned Mr. Stuart, only the common schools where everybody attends are eligible for tax support. The high school is a higher institution and attended by only a few. It is therefore a class school, not a common school, and cannot draw its support from general taxation. Much was at stake here. If Mr. Stuart's contention should hold, then a serious damper would be placed on the enthusiasm which was surrounding the public high school. The case went to the Michigan Supreme Court. Chief Justice Cooley, who wrote the decision, said in part:

We content ourselves with the statement that neither in our state policy, in our constitution, nor in our laws, do we find the primary school districts restricted in the branches of knowledge which their officers may cause to be taught, or the grade of instruction that may be given, if their voters consent in regular form to bear the expense and raise the taxes for the purpose.

Clearly, from the decision, any community in Michigan that wanted to could tax itself for the support of secondary schools as well as for elementary schools. Each community could decide for itself how much education it wanted to make common and available to all. The decision in the Kalamazoo Case set an important precedent. It was a kind of green light for the developing public high school, and subsequent to it the securing of a secondary school adjusted to the needs of the masses and supported by taxation was speeded up in thousands of communities.

Changes in Higher Education. The higher institutions did not escape the surge of demand for education in line with the requirements of the new nation. As stated before, these schools had changed little in their general purpose and program up to the Revolutionary War. Nor were they to be easily budged after the war. As the new nation developed, there was great need for trained people. College programs limited mainly to the religious-classical pattern were hardly adequate. And yet, education of a professional or vocational nature was so against the prevailing concept of collegiate respectability that in spite of genuine pressures very little real adjustment was made. The pressure persisted. The public wanted and needed college-trained people to staff the essential activities and services of the new nation. Colleges were considered important agencies in shaping the new nation. Indeed, comment began to arise stating that the existing colleges represented class interests and that they were aristocratic in nature. If the nation were to be in fact democratic, it was argued, perhaps higher institutions under public control would be desirable. This type of thinking, along with the unwillingness of the existing institutions to expand adequately their purposes and programs, resulted in the demand for public higher institutions. At first considerable effort was made to change certain existing private institutions into state schools. In 1810, Massachusetts, which had certain relationships with Harvard, tried to exercise added controls. In 1865 Harvard broke off all connections with the state. Yale also resisted the efforts of Connecticut to increase public control. Virginia tried without success to take over William and Mary. Pennsylvania was rebuffed in its effort to draw closer to the university. The best-known case is the one involving the State of New Hampshire and Dartmouth College. New Hampshire wished to change Dartmouth into a state institution. Daniel Webster defended Dartmouth against such action by the state. The case went to the United States Supreme Court, and in 1819 the decision was handed down that the charter of the college was inviolate. The states, therefore, were not to succeed in their efforts to transform private institutions into public. The effect of these efforts, particularly of the Dartmouth decision, was to increase the number of both private and public higher institutions. If a private interest group could secure a college charter, it could rest assured that that charter would stand. If the states were to have higher education adjusted to the public need and will, new state-supported institutions would have to be established. The Morrill Act, frequently called the Land Grant Act, which was passed in 1862 by the federal government, and which provided for the establishment of higher institutions in which agriculture and mechanic arts would be taught, is a manifestation of the same public pressure for higher institutions in which education in line with the nation's needs would be offered.

Thus the varieties and uncertainties of education which attended the mixture of church-home-state controls during Colonial times were judged a poor foundation for the new democracy. The basic transition in education between the Revolutionary War and the Civil War was from old forms with the religious-classical pattern to new forms with the citizenship functional pattern; from private controls to public controls; from "class" conceptions to "mass" conceptions. Classism in education, in theory at least, was now overthrown; and no individual, because of his social, economic, or religious status, would be denied the privilege of developing whatever talents he had been blessed with. In education, as in government, the individual would have his chance. Society itself would buy this chance for him.

The Goal Becomes Clear.—It is exceedingly important to realize that the transitions in government and education sketched above did not occur suddenly and are even now incomplete and imperfect. However, the theory and general framework for democratic government and for a system of public schools underlying that government did take shape. A kind of national and educational unity had been achieved. The thinking of the mass of the people as demonstrated by the laws passed concerning elementary, secondary, and higher education was amazingly consistent. However, much time would have to elapse before the pattern could become well developed. This was especially true on the secondary and higher levels. Also it must be remembered that the system of public schools took its place alongside the private schools. The country had no interest in abolishing private schools. The democratic right of these institutions to exist was never questioned; and, as is known, thousands of such schools are in operation today, some of which had their beginnings in Colonial times. But the goal became clear. Government based on the intelligent participation of every citizen was sought. A system of schools devoted to the education of the citizen along cooperative, nonsectarian, classless lines was also sought. The present result is a system of public schools extending from the kindergarten through the graduate school, paralleled by thousands of private schools that may maintain their own programs so long as they prepare youth wisely to use their privi-

to discharge their responsibilities in our society.
enough for all. Education in line with the capacity of
each individual to think and learn for himself and to cooperate effectively with his fellows of whatever background, color, or creed is the
important thing. Clearly, out of the old countries had come a new
nation; and out of the old schools had come new schools.

4. Division and Setback

The new government established by our federal Constitution did
a pretty good job of applying the principle of individualism to the
states that constituted the Union. States that had in effect been independent nations before were now joined together in a federation so
generous in the powers it granted to the member states that they in
turn drew up their own constitutions with accompanying bills of
rights. As time went on, the tendency in certain states was to emphasize the federal or central aspects of the Union while in other states
the emphasis was on the aspects of state independence. Each state
had its own economic, social, and political problems, and in some
cases these differed drastically. Some of these problems bore a
national significance, touching upon great principles of human freedom. The practice of slavery in the South seemed to many to negate
the very nature of our government, to say nothing of the specifics in
the Bill of Rights. When the federal government attempted to correct these abuses, a group of states stood on the principle of State
rights in dealing with such matters and seceded. Our Civil War, or
the War between the States, was the result. The forces of the Union
prevailed; and the states that had officially declared themselves out of
the Union would abrogate such action and, in due time, return.

The new nation, not yet of an age reached by many individuals,
was terribly set back by the war. The promising progress that had
been made toward getting ourselves on our feet economically, politically, educationally, and internationally was seriously impeded. Again
all material and human resources were thrown into the conflict and
pretty well used up. Schools, which did not contribute as directly
then as now to success in war, were woefully neglected. This neglect
was more critical in the South than in the North. School support
practically vanished, especially in the South; enrolments fell off, and
many schools were closed; college development stagnated; effective
direction of existing schools deteriorated; and special school funds
and endowments which had aided greatly in the maintenance of
schools were used for war purposes, especially in the South.

The catastrophe of the war might not have been so great if Reconstruction had been wiser. The plan of reconstruction which was devised by President Lincoln was set aside after his death, and a North-dominated congress set up a plan which completed the process of bleeding the South. The region was sacked of its remaining economic wealth and of its spirit. If difficult and continuing problems arose concerning the restoration of the economic resources of the South, the recovery of momentum by the South in tackling its own problems, and the re-establishment of rapport between North and South, the North had only itself to blame. The period, however dark, was not without an occasional bright spot. One of these was the establishment by broad-thinking northerners of educational foundations or funds to give assistance in making available to southerners, both white and Negro, the advantages of education. But tremendous educational problems, continuing to this day, arose. These included:

a) The re-establishment of an economic base to support education
b) The securing of school buildings to take care of the pupil load, including new groups eligible for education
c) The development of schools and school programs adapted to the needs of a Negro-white population
d) The maintenance of adequate schools in communities where the children, mainly Negro, came from families that could contribute little to the support of schools
e) The elimination through education of attitudes rendered obsolete by changed conditions
f) The achievement of equal educational opportunity among all groups

As our country picked up the broken pieces following the War between the States, and as the states again constituted themselves for cooperation within the Union, the progress of the nation, which had been so rudely interrupted, could be resumed.

5. TIDES IN AMERICAN LIFE

The period from the Civil War to the early part of the twentieth century was one of great development. A few of the important accomplishments of the period, with the briefest of comments, are noted here. All were directly related to education.

Completing the Territorial Unity of the United States.—The process of admitting newly organized states to the Union was not completed until 1912, when Arizona and New Mexico were brought in. In fact, the process is likely to continue until Hawaii and Alaska have attained statehood. We are still completing the task of securing boundaries and organizing for responsible government.

Agricultural Expansion.—Agricultural developments following the Civil War were rapid and far-flung. Vast areas came under cultivation, and every covered wagon that disappeared over the horizon was a project in individual freedom. Land was cheap and good, and it returned to the farmer vast quantities of meat and grain.

Industrial Expansion.—Industrial expansion accompanied agricultural development. Natural power, wasting on our rivers, was put to use. Factories multiplied. Hundreds of manufactured items, large and small, intended to increase man's comfort and to help him do more work with less effort, appeared in the market-place. Here, too, as in agriculture and business, the spirit of individualism ran high. The laissez-faire concept prevailed.

Science and Invention.—Inventive genius and the know-how necessary to put inventions to work underlay the Industrial Revolution. Of what use was it to invent steam engines, cotton gins, and telegraphs, or to discover the uses of electricity if these inventions could not be developed into railroads, textile mills, communications systems, and light bulbs? Science, too, discovered new ways of releasing and transforming raw materials into products that would increase man's health and happiness.

Immigration.—During the hundred years from 1825 to 1925 approximately 35,000,000 immigrants came to this country. Up to about 1880 these people were primarily northern and western Europeans; since that time they have been predominantly southern and eastern Europeans. Each region has supplied about half of our immigrants. They were attracted here for many reasons; but primarily for reasons of religious, political, and economic freedom.

Growth of Cities.—Industrial concerns required the concentration of large groups of workers. Many immigrants went to work in our factories. Cities grew rapidly, accommodating the factories and marketing the products of our vast agriculture. They would also have to supply the government, transportation, protection, education, and other services necessary in any area where a large number of people lived.

Business and Commerce.—The marketing of vast amounts of farm products and manufactured goods underlay rapid expansion in business and commerce. Also, the marketing of services and protection demanded by the people, such as water, telephones, fuel, and insurance, became important. Monopolies raised their heads.

Transportation and Communication.—A vast network of roads, railroads, ship lines, canals, and telegraph and telephone lines tied our nation together and linked us with other countries. Our isolated frontiers became known and accessible.

Wealth from the Earth.—Mining developed. The earth yielded much wealth in useful and precious minerals. Coal supported the age of steam. Oil resources were tapped.

Status of Labor.—Workers who had no enterprises of their own, but who earned their livelihood by working for others, felt the same right to freedom that the farmers and the owners of mills or businesses had demanded for themselves. Employed workers were not to be exploited. They were not property. They were entitled to decent homes, wages, health and educational advantages, and the protection and services of the community, the same as anybody else. Labor organizations arose, secured a voice in the determination of their working conditions, and raised the status and influence of the labor group in society.

Status of Women.—It is rather surprising how long the idea persisted in this country that man was superior to woman, that the education of girls should be limited to homemaking, that only men should vote, and that entrance to a host of vocations should be open only to men. But the great movement toward the freedom of the individual could hardly pass the women by, especially after some of the supposed superiorities of men had been disproved. Why free the slaves and keep women in bondage? The results are known. Women came rapidly into their own, securing equal rights in education, at the polls, in vocations, and in many other ways.

International Stature.—With the great unification and development achieved by this country, culminating, in a way, in the Spanish-American War, international stature was achieved. Actually within a hundred years our country had passed from doubtful beginnings, through internal crack-up, to unity and international prominence.

All the developments noted above, and more, too, directly affected education. The demands of such a teeming nation on education would greatly influence school practices and points of view. We shall turn to a brief consideration of some of these changes and tendencies.

6. Expanding Our Education and Giving It Emphasis

Multiplied educational needs stemmed from our rapid national development. Effort was made to meet those needs. Certain tendencies in purposes and programs also appeared.

Growth in Number and Types of Schools.—We have already referred to the opening-up of vast new territories in our country until after the turn of the twentieth century. Great population increases occurred during the same time. These called for thousands of new schools. Furthermore, the developments referred to in the section above called for new kinds of specialized education for workers and leaders. As a consequence, new types of schools arose and new subjects were introduced into the existing schools. Vocational, technical, and professional education expanded greatly on both the secondary and higher levels. Part-time and continuation schools and education suited to the needs of adults arose for those who needed and wanted further training but could not pursue their studies on a full time basis in a regular school. Vocational training for girls developed. Labor took its position in support of public schools and the vocational movement.

Agriculture, Mechanic Arts, Business.—The swing toward education in line with the nature of the times is clearly illustrated in the growth and acceptance of the federal government's program of support for education in the fields of agriculture, mechanic arts, and business. Obviously agriculture, industry, and business underlie our economy, and here the bulk of our young people leaving school find their work. In 1862, it will be remembered, the federal government passed the Morrill or "Land Grant" Act, providing for the establishment of colleges in which agriculture and mechanic arts would be taught. In 1887 the Hatch Act was passed, providing funds for the establishment of experiment stations in the land-grant colleges. With the finest of consistency, the government, in 1914, passed the Smith-Lever Act which authorized funds for extension services in agriculture and homemaking to rural people, through which the findings of the experiment stations could be broadcast and their application encouraged. States accepting benefits under the Smith-Lever Act had to match federal funds with state funds. In 1917 the Smith-Hughes Act was passed. Here the government extended its support to vocational education in secondary schools, in agriculture, vocational-industrial studies, and homemaking. Land-grant colleges were also given support for the preparation of teachers in these fields. Again, the requirement that states match federal appropriations was applied. More recently, in 1937, the government enacted the George-Deen Act which extended federal benefits to secondary education in the distributive occupations. The George-Barden Act of 1946 increased federal aid to all these programs; that is, in agriculture, vocational-industrial education, homemaking, distributive occupations, and teacher education.

One of the most significant aspects of the above series of acts by the federal government was the projection downward into the secondary school of federal aid for vocational education. Most secondary school pupils would not, of course, go on to college. They would, on the other hand, go directly into jobs, and this type of education would fit them more effectively into these areas of work so basic to our material progress. Acceptance of this aid has been widespread, and the annual enrolment in these federally aided classes now stands at better than 2,500,000 pupils.

Compulsory Attendance.—Compulsory attendance at school, as we know it today, is a recent development. Although there was an aspect of compulsion to attend Colonial schools, it was not until 1852 that Massachusetts passed the first modern compulsory attendance law. Twenty-five additional states and territories had passed such a law by 1890, and not until 1918 did the last state, Mississippi, make the practice complete for the nation. The lateness of compulsory attendance legislation illustrates the lag in adjusting practice to accepted theory. We were clear in our democratic theory that the individual's participation in government and in the running of his own affairs should be made more effective through education. In practice, however, it was a long time before we established educational minima for our people in the form of attendance requirements. Compulsory attendance laws have, of course, been closely associated with child labor laws. The first child labor legislation in the states preceded the first modern compulsory attendance legislation. To some extent, in the early stages, child labor legislation forced compulsory attendance legislation. Nonworking children could hardly remain idle. As time went on, compulsory attendance laws became more widespread and more demanding as to the number of years that should be spent in school and in the required number of school days during the year. As the compulsory attendance age moved upward, employer and home pressure secured provisions whereby children, under certain conditions, could secure permits to go to work even though they had not reached the permissible school-leaving age. On the whole, the tendency in our country for the age of beginning employment to rise has eliminated any serious conflict between employment needs and compulsory attendance laws. In fact, it is more than likely that the permissible school-leaving age will have to be raised in order to eliminate the idleness gap between school-leaving and job-taking.

Mass Education Extended Upward.—The rise in compulsory attendance ages, together with the adjustment of secondary education to life needs, projected mass education upward. Furthermore, it will be remembered that the decision in the Kalamazoo Case cleared the way for communities to provide secondary education at public expense if they wanted to. They wanted to; and all over the nation increasing thousands of young people continued their education beyond the elementary grades. As secondary education became better adjusted to the needs of the times, the educational requirements of job-taking were raised. The percentage increase in enrolments, especially in the secondary schools and colleges, mounted rapidly. The level of education of the mass of Americans attracted attention throughout the world.

Scientific Study of Human Behavior.—Around the beginning of the twentieth century the scientific study of man and his relations to his fellows took on seriousness and system. Psychology and sociology came into their own. Knowledge was gained steadily about the nature of child development, learning, and the effects of environmental conditions on the individual. The modern testing movement began about this time. Education had now begun to study the individual, to adjust the program of studies to him, and then to measure his achievement.

The Cost Mounts.—With more schools having broader programs for more people for greater lengths of time, the costs of education naturally increased proportionately. Many buildings and teachers were required. An increasingly varied program called for more equipment and supplies. Most American communities, providing the funds through public taxation, found that the expenditures for education exceeded those for any other public service.

Job Specialization in Education.—As would be supposed, specialized jobs in the field of education arose, first in the cities, later in other areas. In the city, for example, the magnitude of the educational enterprise made the integration of program and coordination of effort on a city-wide basis desirable. This gave rise to the position of superintendent of schools. Twenty-nine cities had created such a position by 1870. Problems of finance, curriculum, staff, community relations, and other matters were all interrelated, and a strong leader and supervisor was needed. Other positions requiring specialized training arose rapidly, such as special supervisor, child study specialist, curriculum specialist, director of testing, director of guidance and counseling, specialist in the education of special groups including the handicapped, specialist in certain subject fields, business director, health worker, and so on. As the problems in rural education came to the fore, specialized training in that field developed. Education came to be one of the country's biggest businesses. It also dealt constantly with the difficult area of human development and adjustment. The services of the ablest and the best-trained people were needed.

"Laissez Faire" Reflected in Education.—The urge for freedom which has been so conspicuous throughout the history of America supported the doctrine of noninterference which characterized our development. The individual demanded to be let alone in the conduct of his home, his farm, his factory, his business affairs, his religion, and his franchise. It was up to him to make his own way in a society where everybody else was intent on the same thing. Competition was keen. If things didn't go well in one community, there was always the lure of other work in other places. Education was greatly stressed for its relationship to "getting on." The material benefits of schooling were paraded before the young. Large charts appeared in many school corridors purporting to show how much an elementary school graduate, a high school graduate, and a college graduate could expect to earn. A new measuring stick for education appeared. How applicable is education to my problems? How much will it get me?

"What Knowledge Is of Most Worth?"—In 1859, Herbert Spencer, an Englishman, published an essay entitled "What Knowledge Is of Most Worth?" Spencer approached the problem systematically. Education, he said, ought to be for "complete living." Knowledge is useful to the extent that it contributes to preparation for complete living. Of all knowledge, a knowledge of science, he said, was most useful as preparation for the activities and needs of life. Spencer did not, of course, discard other learning, and he wrote other essays on other aspects of education. He merely placed science on top of the heap.

Science and Vocationalism.—Spencer's reasoning suited the mood of America. His influence here was great. This country, experiencing great material progress, found it easy to accept the science-vocational emphasis. New subjects appeared in the curriculum. New scientific, vocational, and technical schools were organized. To be sure, many other emphases remained in education, such as religious, citizenship, liberal, and classical; but America had now brought to education a powerful new practical, materialistic standard.

7. New Awakenings

It Looked Good; but It Wasn't Good Enough.—At the beginning of the twentieth century, America was doing all right. Our doctrine of free enterprise, coupled with the natural resources and youthfulness of the country and the quality of the people, resulted in a host of outstanding developments. We seemed to be on the threshold of comfort and luxury. In fact, the more we got of material things and individual freedom, the more we seemed to want. In the minds of many, freedom meant personal privilege, limitless opportunity, and a minimum of rules. The education of all was stressed so that each could compete more successfully. Specialization in education arose, as over against broad general education. Since most youngsters would not remain in school beyond the age of sixteen or eighteen, this specialization moved downward into the secondary schools. As a nation we were proud. We were ahead of the world, and we had done it ourselves. However, education in international understanding and cooperation did not accompany our attainment of international stature. We were isolationist. Internally we were humming. We were producing many more things in ever-increasing quantities. Here the immigrant, his son, and his grandson had the opportunity to experience the freedom and comforts he had so long hoped for. It looked pretty good; but it wasn't good enough.

New Concepts of Social Responsibility.—America's frontier conditions could not last indefinitely. As the areas between the Atlantic and Pacific were traversed and occupied, compactness developed. The chance to "move on" declined. Frontiers of a new sort appeared. Problems of adjustment arose to replace in good part the older problems of escape. We must now live together, ever closer together, and with many more people. These people, like us, were free; but the old interpretations of freedom would not always work under newer conditions. New concepts of social responsibility arose. After all, one could not very well view the other fellow as being in one's way. All had an equal right to be here; and perhaps one's welfare might even be wrapped up in the welfare of another. Advantage-taking should not be permitted. Our government became more and more a referee, and asked the people to set up more and more rules for playing the game of democracy in ever-tightening quarters. Social legislation began to appear.

The idea of developing social responsibility through education has always been present in America, but it was at pretty low ebb early in the present century. However, some voices were heard. The work of John Dewey stands as a great awakening in this connection. Dewey was certainly not opposed to the scientific-vocational developments in education. In fact he was a careful experimenter himself. But perhaps his greatest contribution was to give the initial great emphasis in this century to the idea that the school is the place where children should not only learn about their life and times, but should actually live those aspects of social cooperation and sharing that will be projected forward by them to effective social responsibility in later life. Other educational leaders, thinking along similar lines, quickly joined in to give expression and demonstration to this new emphasis in education. This group was not rejecting individualism in education—the idea that the school should study the child, adjust its program to his nature and needs, and try to lead him into appropriate work in society. It accepted individualism in education, but it added the idea of education for social responsibility through schools democratically conducted. We had learned the lesson of ancient Greece. A democracy must, through education, develop the potential of individuals; but it must also, through education democratically conducted, establish in those individuals habits of voluntary cooperation and sacrifice for the common good, which are the keystones of social solidarity and strength.

Too Little, Too Late.—One cannot hold America responsible for the outbreak of two great world wars within a period of twenty-five years; however, this country must assume its share of responsibility for continuing to think and speak in terms of "let the rest of the world go by" long after the world had become so interwoven that the price of freedom in any nation was freedom in all nations. We had not, as has been said, accompanied our march to the forefront of nations with a corresponding emphasis on international understanding and cooperation. Our movement in education toward social responsibility, including international responsibility, was just getting under way. We had not even yet really tackled the job of promoting better intercultural relations within our own country. We, and the world, were a little late. Nations that knew freedom relaxed to enjoy it and were slow to realize that in other parts of the world freedom was losing. In a world where all men have the capacity to be free, and where the gifts of freedom can no longer be kept from the enslaved, freedom and slavery cannot exist interminably together. In the one case, the forces of enslavement seek, through aggression, to bring others under their domination; in the other case, the forces of freedom rise in the hearts of men to throw off the oppressor. In the meantime, violent clashes occur. Education has operated, and will operate, primarily in the area of how people think and feel about these matters.

8. Double Disaster

The two great world wars of recent years have had the effect of suddenly hurling nations out of their isolationist bailiwicks into an open arena where they must now play the game of world-making together. By their own ships, books, radios, sports, planes, commerce, movies, diplomacy, charity, education, and argument they have broken down the artificial barricades of national boundaries. It is unfortunate that the rules for the new game could not have been developed in time to keep it orderly. The readiness and opportunities of peoples for freedom are uneven. Much thinking and experiencing with reference to the nature and responsibilities of freedom are necessary before freedom can be successfully implemented. Not all people have had this opportunity. In fact, in some quarters the policy of government has been to channel the thinking of the people into lines of acceptance and conformity rather than to encourage open-minded investigation and reforms in line with the thinking of all. Education has frequently been called upon to defend an established position rather than to train minds to think straight and honestly on all matters and to evaluate all conditions and institutions in the light of the best evidence.

The effectiveness of education as a means of molding the thinking and attitudes of an entire nation is nowhere better demonstrated than in the aggressor nations of our time. After the first World War a considerable effort was made by leading educators to have the potential of education harnessed for internationalism by giving it prominent status and support in the organization and activities for peace. The effort was none too successful.

When during the interval between wars, the educators of the world talked about large-scale international exchange of students, a strong international office of education, consistent teaching of democracy and international goodwill, men in positions of power seldom paid attention. . . . Education for world citizenship was merely a title for a book; it was never accepted as a goal for statesmen in the real world. Education was relegated to a secondary position in peace by most of the world's political leaders.

By most of them—not by all. As the years went by there came to power one group that saw with fearful clarity that the effectiveness of all social planning is based upon education. These were the rising leaders of the modern dictatorships. For their wicked purposes, they lavished on education and youth almost unlimited attention, prestige, solicitude, and resources. They regimented the mind and militarized the spirit of their youth before they dared to build them weapons of war.[6]

Our own nation, finding it hard to give up "rugged individualism" at home, reverted to it in our foreign relations after the first war. We rejected the League of Nations, considered the world "safe for democracy," and in an amazingly short time awoke to find that the peoples and resources of nations left to their own devices had again been molded for war. The forces of education and propaganda within nations were found to be more powerful than international organizations in determining the events of history. Surely international organizations for peace would in the future realize that agencies other than diplomatic agencies are at the heart of the people, and the potential of these agencies for developing the conditions of peace in the minds of men must be used and supported to the full.

9. It May Work

Throughout the foregoing pages we have traced in broadest terms the development of our nation from meager but hallowed beginnings, through turmoil and phenomenal growth, to a position unsurpassed in free education and democratic government. During that time the school has constantly served the people, bending its purposes to their purposes, its program to their needs. At times it has seemed too removed, too narrowly classical and religious; at other times it has seemed too materialistic, overspecialized, and vocationalized. At all times it has served the cause of individual freedom, from its early religious philosophy to its more recent specialized training for success in a competitive society. It has made the discovery of late that its great emphasis on understanding and developing the individual must be paralleled by an equally important emphasis on education for social responsibility and cooperation. It has also discovered that the freedoms we seek to preserve and develop in this country are the rallying cries of all mankind. We are, in a very real sense, at the head of the human parade; and others look to this nation to give leadership in the achievement of those rights to think, act, work, learn, speak, and

[6] Educational Policies Commission, *Education and the People's Peace* (Washington, D.C., National Education Association, 1943), pp. 8–9.

worship, honestly and without fear. Isolationism is swallowed up in the compactness of the world. Internationalism has come. Education at home must include education in international understanding and the mutual sharing of ideas, developments, and problems. Education, if it rises to its opportunity, will include, but go beyond, personal development, specialization, cultural appreciations, adjustment to externals, and leadership-followership and will promote straight thinking, mutual understanding, discovery of the common ground, and the development of techniques of cooperative thinking and acting. Larger goals, to include the welfare of more people, are looming. Our individual, small-group, nationalistic goals have to be modified; they need not be given up, but they must be adapted to the conditions and goals of a rapidly changing world. The essence of freedom has not changed; the environment of freedom has.

> Freedom's gains have altered freedom's state;
> But freedom's changes on the outward part
> Must not molest the freedom of the heart.

It is in this setting of internal and international relationships to freedom, of man in relation to himself, his fellows, his environment, and his institutions that the problems of education in America now chiefly reside. If the potential of education and of other agencies dealing with the mind and motives of men can be utilized effectively, peace and freedom will come. It may work.

What Do YOU Say?

1

It is a good thing in a democracy to extend mass education upward. Our society should give assistance to superior students who are interested in pursuing further studies but who would otherwise be unable to continue their education beyond the free schools.

What do YOU say?

2

Our higher institutions constitute the weakest link in our school system in adapting educational programs and practices to the needs of our democracy.

What do YOU say?

3

We stand in need throughout our entire school system of making education for moral and social responsibility as tangible and useful as education for employment in the specialized occupations.

What do YOU say?

4

What points in this chapter do you particularly support or take issue with?

Chapter 3

THE AMERICAN IDEAL OF EDUCATION

Establishing Our Own Goals

1. CHANGING TIMES AND CHANGING EMPHASES

It should be remembered that at no time in our educational history has the school served any one purpose exclusively. However, at numerous times the school, responding to the prevailing interests and developments in society, has shifted from one major emphasis to another. The previous chapter traced some of the changes in American life and thought which brought about changes in the aims and offerings of the school. A brief listing of some of the outstanding emphases that have stood out in American education will provide a setting for a fuller consideration of purposes and points of view in education today.

Religion.—For a good many years the schools of our country turned all instruction to religious ends. The school served the church. Teachers were checked more carefully on their religious qualifications than on their mastery of subject matter or their ability to teach. The religious emphasis began to subside when the growth of the colonies required education for participation in a large variety of jobs and services. It was definitely eclipsed with the advent of the public schools, although it still predominates in some church-controlled schools.

Culture.—The emphasis on "culture" in our education concentrated more in higher institutions than in elementary and secondary schools. The liberal-cultural tradition was brought over from Europe and became the forte of the colleges after their religious emphasis began to wane. The secondary schools also served this tradition in so far as they were controlled by the colleges. In schools where the cultural concept predominated, great resistance was given to the inclusion of vocational-professional studies.

Knowledge.—The expression "knowledge is power" has greatly influenced our education. It didn't matter so much what was known, just so knowledge accumulated. Such an attitude would, of course,

45

permit the perpetuation in the curriculum of time-consuming but rather fruitless studies. Spencer's answer to his own question, "What knowledge is of most worth?" helped to destroy the concept that just about any knowledge would do.

Mental Discipline.—The idea that pupils ought to study certain subjects because of what they presumably do to the mind has been present for a long time in our education. For a time psychology, through its discussion of the "faculties," supported this idea. However, many people have clung to certain subjects as useful for "mental discipline" long after psychology itself exploded the notion that any subject possesses any magic in this regard. To be sure, all subjects are a mental exercise, and some call for different kinds of thinking than others do; but it would be hard to show, for example, that a foreign language is superior to shorthand as a means of mental development. Again, the doctrine of mental discipline became the defense of some subjects in the curriculum that were hard to justify on more practical grounds.

Occupational, Adult Preparation.—The idea that education ought to prepare for adult living flourished particularly during the great American upsurge following the Civil War, and it continues now. For a long time, however, a great mistake was made. Children were asked too often to consider adult problems and to learn content that might be "useful twenty years from now" but had few uses for the present. Children's conduct and interests were judged by adult standards. Actually, much of our vocational education today, which extends far down the educational ladder, deals with adult problems. This is hard to avoid. One cannot object to such preparation for adult life, but serious consideration must be given to the problem of whether or not the child has the ability or the disposition to project himself forward beyond his years.

Child Nature.—The "child-centered school" was a kind of counteremphasis to education for adult living, without denying, of course, the validity of the latter. The difference lay in permitting the child to indulge in interests appropriate to his age and to deal with problems associated with his own living. If this were done step by step to adulthood, and if the child established the habit of approaching ever-broadening problems honestly, his preparation for adult living would actually be more effective than if he were required to deal with adult problems and be judged by adult standards before his years justified it. The "child nature" emphasis in education also countered strongly the concept of mental discipline. The nature and needs of children now took precedence over content. Extensive studies in child development accompanied the emphasis on child nature.

Social Living.—The needs of the child, referred to immediately above, were social as well as personal. He should grow in his ability to adjust to social problems. He should know his community, and also be able to cooperate skilfully with his classmates and others in real community living. The "community-centered school" was the result.

Learning the Ways of Democracy.—During recent years great emphasis has been placed on the interpretations of democracy and on education for democratic living. The eclectic nature of education is stressed. Balance is sought. Above all, people are considered more important than subject matter. Their personal development and social relationships have become as definitely the problem of the school as their mastery of any content. Such a goal absorbs and expands all other goals. Its central position in American education will be observed as the present chapter unfolds.

2. Some Contemporary Statements of Objectives

There have been many recent statements of objectives embodying the emphasis on democracy referred to above. Most of these statements have come out in the last thirty-five years. They bear a striking similarity. Let us content ourselves, therefore, with two statements which deal directly with the schools and one statement having broader applications but inseparably linked to education.

Cardinal Principles of Secondary Education.—In 1918, the Commission on the Reorganization of Secondary Education, appointed by the National Education Association, issued a small but important bulletin entitled, *Cardinal Principles of Secondary Education.* The commission attempted an analysis of the essential activities of an effective citizen in a democracy, and then formulated objectives to guide the secondary school in educating for democratic living. The seven objectives are:

1. Sound health knowledge and habits
2. Command of fundamental processes (reading, writing, arithmetic, and oral and written expression)
3. Vocational efficiency
4. Good citizenship
5. Worthy home membership

6. Worthy use of leisure time
7. Ethical character

The cardinal principles constituted one of the earliest and best statements in which the focus of the secondary school was turned more upon youth and their needs in the modern world and less upon the perpetuation of a curriculum dictated largely by the colleges. The wisdom of the principles was recognized so broadly that they became a kind of ideal pattern for all levels in education. They reflected the point of view and practice of John Dewey, which had already taken firm hold in the elementary schools. Their translation into practice in the secondary schools, however, was faltering at first, gaining momentum only as it became clear that students with good native ability graduating from high schools which served these objectives did quite as well in college as students of comparable ability graduating under the more rigid academic patterns. The high schools were slow to launch themselves upon programs of education dedicated to the overall needs of youth, even though only about 15 per cent of their graduates would ever go on to college. At any rate, the cardinal principles pointed up the contemporary emphasis on the vital relationship of education to the requirements of democratic living. They reflected clearly the trend in educational thought in this country following the first World War. They have been in essence restated many times by subsequent writers.

Objectives of the Educational Policies Commission.—One of the most carefully worked-out statements of objectives for American education is that of the Educational Policies Commission of the National Education Association, presented in 1938. The commission's objectives are presented in its report entitled *The Purposes of Education in American Democracy.* Four primary concerns of education are presented by the commission as follows:

1. Development of the learner
2. Home, family, and community life
3. Economic demands
4. Civic and social duties

On the basis of these concerns, four groups of educational objectives are identified. These are:

1. The objectives of self-realization
2. The objectives of human relationship
3. The objectives of economic efficiency
4. The objectives of civic responsibility

One of the virtues of the commission's report is the extent to which it details these objectives, giving clarity to the fundamental things the commission was concerned with, and making easier their translation into appropriate studies and activities. The report breaks down the above groups to include the following objectives:

1. THE OBJECTIVES OF SELF-REALIZATION

The Inquiring Mind. The educated person has an appetite for learning.
Speech. The educated person can speak the mother tongue clearly.
Reading. The educated person reads the mother tongue efficiently.
Writing. The educated person writes the mother tongue effectively.
Number. The educated person solves his problems of counting and calculating.
Sight and Hearing. The educated person is skilled in listening and observing.
Health Knowledge. The educated person understands the basic facts concerning health and disease.
Health Habits. The educated person protects his own health and that of his dependents.
Public Health. The educated person works to improve the health of the community.
Recreation. The educated person is participant and spectator in many sports and other pastimes.
Intellectual Interests. The educated person has mental resources for the use of leisure.
Esthetic Interests. The educated person appreciates beauty.
Character. The educated person gives responsible direction to his own life.

2. THE OBJECTIVES OF HUMAN RELATIONSHIP

Respect for Humanity. The educated person puts human relationships first.
Friendships. The educated person enjoys a rich, sincere, and varied social life.
Cooperation. The educated person can work and play with others.
Courtesy. The educated person observes the amenities of social behavior.
Appreciation of the Home. The educated person appreciates the family as a social institution.
Conservation of the Home. The educated person conserves family ideals.
Homemaking. The educated person is skilled in homemaking.
Democracy in the Home. The educated person maintains democratic family relationships.

3. The Objectives of Economic Efficiency

Work. The educated producer knows the satisfaction of good workmanship.

Occupational Information. The educated producer understands the requirements and opportunities of various jobs.

Occupational Choice. The educated producer has "selected" his occupation.

Occupational Efficiency. The educated producer succeeds in his chosen vocation.

Occupational Adjustment. The educated producer maintains and improves his efficiency.

Occupational Appreciation. The educated producer appreciates the social value of his work.

Personal Economics. The educated consumer plans the economics of his own life.

Consumer Judgment. The educated consumer develops standards for guiding his expenditures.

Efficiency in Buying. The educated consumer is an informed and skilful buyer.

Consumer Protection. The educated consumer takes appropriate measures to safeguard his interests.

4. The Objectives of Civic Responsibility

Social Justice. The educated citizen is sensitive to the disparities of human circumstance.

Social Activity. The educated citizen acts to correct unsatisfactory conditions.

Social Understanding. The educated citizen seeks to understand social structures and social processes.

Critical Judgment. The educated citizen has defenses against propaganda.

Tolerance. The educated citizen respects honest differences of opinion.

Conservation. The educated citizen has a regard for the nation's resources.

Social Applications of Science. The educated citizen measures scientific advance by its contribution to the general welfare.

World Citizenship. The educated citizen is a cooperating member of the world community.

Law Observance. The educated citizen respects the law.

Economic Literacy. The educated citizen is economically literate.

Political Citizenship. The educated citizen accepts his civic duties.

Devotion to Democracy. The educated citizen acts upon an unswerving loyalty to democratic ideals.

The comprehensiveness of the above objectives is apparent. They contain goals applicable on all levels of education. Their influence continues unabated.

The Social-Economic Goals of America.—In 1932 a Committee on Social-Economic Goals of America was set up by the National Education Association. This committee was asked to propose desirable social-economic goals for America, and to "indicate the materials and methods which the schools of the nation should use to attain these goals." The committee issued a tentative report in 1933 and in 1937, in cooperation with numerous subcommittees, it issued a full report entitled *Implications of Social-Economic Goals for Education.* The goals as set forth here are taken from the 1937 report. Brief annotations are given:

1. *Hereditary Strength.* The development of rich personalities and the achievement of social betterment depend upon the improvement of the innate strengths and capacities of individuals.

2. *Physical Security.* Innate capacities should be conserved and developed through adequate medical attention, nourishment, and safety.

3. *Participation in an Evolving Culture Through Skills, Technics, and Knowledges.* The individual should develop those skills, technics, and knowledges which will make him able to share in the activities of agencies that play a part in selecting and transmitting the culture of the race, such as the family, the church, the school, the library, the newspaper, the radio, and the workshop.

4. *Participation in an Evolving Culture Through Values, Standards, and Outlooks.* Such values, standards, and outlooks as will harmonize self-interests and social interests, critical attitudes and constructive attitudes, should be developed in all individuals.

5. *An Active, Flexible Personality.* Individuals should be guided by intelligent purposes, should express their individualities freely but unselfishly, should be able to adapt to new situations, and should be able to cooperate enjoyably with others.

6. *Suitable Occupation.* Individuals should be aided in entering and succeeding in a congenial life work through guidance, training, placement, and advancement.

7. *Economic Security.* Economic conditions that underlie the development and happiness of the individual should be available to every person.

8. *Mental Security.* Every individual is entitled to information that is dependable, untainted by the devices of commercialism and propaganda.

9. *Freedom.* The conditions of freedom, consistent with human dignity and with the freedom of others, should accrue to all.

10. *Fair Play.* Equality of opportunity must replace special privilege. Honest concern that others have their full chance must replace selfishness and advantage-taking.

In a very real sense the publication of the social-economic goals represented a landmark in American education. Here goals for the larger society of which the school is a part were considered. The implication, pointedly taken, is that society and the schools are inseparable; that one cannot succeed in its aims without the aid of the other; that both must have aims if both are to progress; that mutual isolationism which has been too prevalent in the past must go; and that both the school and the nation are concerned about the same thing— the development and happiness of people in a democratic order. The fundamental similarity between the social-economic goals for our society as a whole and the two lists of objectives for the school is impressive. With the publication of goals for the nation and the detailing of what the school could do to help in realizing those goals, we had set a new standard for education that was stirring and vital, and one that would cause much uneasiness when applied as a criterion to the curriculum of the schools of the nation.

Many other lists of educational objectives could be enumerated here. They would, for the most part, duplicate the spirit and detail of the lists presented. It will be profitable at this point to turn to a consideration of objectives as they apply at the various levels of education.

Objectives in Relation to Grade Levels.—Again, many statements of objectives have been published pertaining to pre-elementary, elementary, secondary, higher, and postgraduate education. A general summary of such statements is presented on page 43. No claim is made to completeness in the summary; and the assignment of certain objectives to certain grade levels to show their cumulative nature will raise many objections. However, the summary does make available in short compass a fair relationship of objectives to grade levels. The list should be read from the bottom up.

In examining the summary, one should remember that for any grade level, all the objectives listed below it pertain to it also. The exception here is in the vocational phases of education. Other exceptions may be argued, but, again, hope is expressed that the summary may serve the purpose of seeing the objectives in meaningful relationships. It may be too much to expect, but it is not too much to hope, that the student in a higher institution, having been introduced to the areas of learning and experience indicated for the earlier levels, will continue an active interest, participation, and improvement in those areas. Otherwise, education is not the growth experience that it ought to be.

CUMULATIVE EDUCATIONAL OBJECTIVES

Higher institutions, including graduate education

20. Assumption of leadership responsibility for the implementation in society of commitments understood and adhered to
19. Contribution to knowledge
18. Vocational specialization (professional)

Junior College

17. Philosophy of life
16. General education (intelligent survey of areas of human knowledge: the common ground of thought and appreciation basic to mutual understanding, unity, and progress)
15. Vocational specialization (semiprofessional)

Senior High School

14. Ethical character
13. Techniques of effective personal action and cooperative action
12. Understanding and use of the scientific approach to problem-solving
11. Understanding of civic responsibilities
10. Establishment of worthy leisure-time activities
9. Elementary vocational specialization (including college preparation)

Junior High School

8. Self and society (including worthy home membership)
7. Vocational exploration

Elementary

6. Self and the physical world
5. Fundamental processes (in the more traditional sense)

Common to all levels: pre-elementary through adult and graduate education

4. Creative expression
3. Instruction and practice in self-thinking and group thinking
2. Effective social understanding and participation
1. Physical and mental health

A tendency for the objectives to pile up somewhat at the senior high school level will be noted. This is not surprising. It doubtless reflects our realization that most of our youth will not continue in school beyond the senior high school, and it points up our desire to prepare them as adequately as possible for successful living in a democracy. If compulsory attendance should some day include the junior college grades, then some of the objectives now assigned to the senior high school might be moved into the junior college. Vocational specialization, for example, would quite likely be delayed.

Attention should be called to one other important aspect of the objectives. The writer has taken the privilege of rephrasing some of the objectives and adding one or two of his own to emphasize the participation-practice aspect of school experience and, above all, the need for developing the spirit and techniques of cooperative action and the willingness to assume responsibilities in line with the growth of insight. Objectives 2, 3, 4, 12, 13, and 20 pertain to this. In connection with number 20, it seems right to expect that college graduates, having had the advantages of much education, will do more than go into communities and earn a living. These communities have a right to expect them to be leaders active in matters important in community life. In fact, the whole ring of educational objectives on all levels sounds this note of sharing in community living beyond job-holding. It appears at times that the present emphasis on specialization in higher institutions tends to defeat this purpose.

Objectives Stated in Terms of People.—It is worth pointing out again that recent statements of educational objectives are phrased in terms of people, their development, needs, desirable attributes, and responsibilities in our kind of society. This is good. It does not necessarily follow, however, that the organization of our schools and the nature of the studies and activities found in them have been made to serve the objectives. There still exists a tremendous gap between accepted objectives and their fulfilment in practice. In many schools it will be found that the accepted objectives are in terms of people, but the organization and practices are in terms of subjects. Clearly, however, American schools are more and more breaking down meaningless rigidities and are bending school subjects and activities to the needs of the people they serve.

3. Evolving a Point of View

It is an excellent thing to know what others have considered to be the goals of education in our country. It is important also, however, that each should think for himself concerning these matters and evolve some points of view that are meaningful because they are personal. It is the purpose of this section to suggest a simple approach which may be helpful in thinking about educational purposes and programs in this kind of country. A few considerations are important.

Characteristics of Democracy.—This country is a democracy. It is not perfect, of course; but the democratic ideal guides the thought and practices of all loyal individuals and institutions, including the school. Democracy is the starting foundation, the assumption, the commitment in education. Two or three simple but important aspects of democracy should be understood and remembered by all.

The Individual. Democracy accepts and nourishes the Christian concept of individual worth. It gives reverence to human personality. It holds all institutions responsible to develop and not thwart the capacity of human beings to grow into an understanding and wise use of freedom. Democracy insists that each individual have his chance to develop. But it also insists that, having had such an opportunity, the individual act as a responsible person, willingly cooperating with others for the common good. Democracy is a philosophy of individualism; but, rightly conceived, it places on the individual tremendous responsibility to conduct his life and affairs without injury to others and in a way that will promote the welfare of others. Reverence for the individual must be present in every relationship and action involving a single person or involving millions of persons. This attitude is hard to maintain in some of our relationships involving large numbers, but until we secure and maintain it, we are imperfect in our practice of the democratic ideal.

Groups. A democratic society is an association of free individuals, cooperating willingly, developing into their best selves, agreeing mutually on rules to govern their relationships, but forever retaining the right freely to discuss those rules and share in their modification. Organizations and institutions in a democracy are expressions of cooperation among individuals. Individuals are free to belong to groups, but they have a sacred obligation not to surrender to any group their duty as free men to think, speak, and act in conscience. There will be times of stress in a democracy when the accepted freedoms of individuals will have to be curtailed. There will be times also when government will have to establish rules and penalties to correct abuses. One of the chief problems of a democracy is to educate all groups, and all individuals, voluntarily to conduct their affairs for the benefit of all so that regulations and controls by government can be held at a minimum. Such governmental curtailments, ideally, will be known to be temporary; and they will be democratically evolved. Temporary curtailments that violate basic freedoms are dangerous. They form the defense of some of the most despotic governments of our time. In a democracy the right of individuals to be free is more basic and sacred than the right of groups to be free. This denies the right of groups to violate the basic freedoms of the individual, and it denies the right of the individual to surrender his freedoms to a group. Furthermore, groups within our society form around certain interests. Individuals are free to promote certain interests by belonging to certain groups. However, these special interest groups must see to it that their goals and methods do not violate the goals and methods of the society that permits and encourages their existence. When groups use the privileges of a society to undermine that society, they are subversive; and when they seek their ends against other groups without reference to the larger goals, they are acting to pull down the whole house on their own heads. On the other hand, if all groups believe in a democratic society, they may fight vigorously among themselves along lines of special interests, but they will come up side by side when the society that gives them their freedom is threatened.

In Process. Democracy is constantly in process; it evolves continuously; it is forever becoming. It is this process of becoming, of being subject continuously to study, modification, and improvement by responsible individuals that is so much more important than the forms of democratic government. Democracy is not a stereotype. It cannot be drawn on paper. To be sure, it has its government, its institutions, and its patterns of living, but all of these are products of the people themselves, and they will change and improve as the people change and improve. Progress is assured as long as the process is maintained by honest people.

It is important, then, that the citizens of a democracy have clear concepts concerning the nature and position in society of the individual, of groups, and of the evolutionary process.

Studying the Individual.—If the individual is so important in a democracy, then the schools of a democracy must make every effort to understand him and make his education most appropriate for him. In this connection, three simple questions should be asked by every school worker, or, for that matter, by anyone associated with children and youth. If these questions are kept in mind, our dealings with the individual are likely to be more intelligent and helpful.

What Is He Like? If anything is demonstrated today by biology, psychology, sociology, and other studies, it is the fact of individual differences. The school that operates in the spirit of democracy will realize that these differences exist and will attempt to discover the real equipment, background, and needs of each pupil. Every classroom teacher who receives a group of new youngsters in the fall will seek first to discover them and then to cooperate with them in their learning, in terms of their individual situations. The seventh grade English teacher will not start off by explaining "how much of what" seventh grade English is, and that success or failure will be measured in terms of that standard. Rather, the teacher will immediately do the human job of finding the gifted and the dull, the special interests of each, and the degree of achievement in the subject thus far. He will find that some pupils come from homes where a foreign language is spoken, others from homes of fine English usage with good home libraries. Attitudes, aptitudes, parental influences, health conditions, and a hundred other things will be found to differ; and these are the things which will determine the pupil's accomplishments in the class. If instruction is given in the light of these differences, much more progress will be made than if an artificial standard for all is fixed. Democratic education requires such a discovery of the individual prior to the school's determining programs or standards for him. Adjustment in terms of the individual will, of course, be continuous. Many of the activities of the modern school will be recognized as an effort to get the answer to the question "What is he like?" The psychological and achievement testing, important aspects of the guidance program, the work of the school social worker, and the health examinations of pupils are illustrative. The answer to this question, imperfectly secured at present, is nevertheless the first step in bringing education into line with the democratic ideal.

What Do You Want Him to Become? In a democracy no one makes the mistake of trying to define the perfect individual and then urging everyone else to become like that. No one even urges a person to become like a friend, to ape an ideal. No wise teacher or parent keeps urging upon one child the virtues and achievements of another, insisting on a kind of copy-cat living. This is not to deny the influence of the ideal, the hero, or of their fellows upon the lives of youngsters; but it is to deny that any value exists in the artificiality of the stereotype and the demand that one copy the attitudes, interests, achievements, and conduct of another, imaginary or real. Such an insistence would be the renewal of the old externally determined molding process. Democracy insists that individuals become what in terms of their own potential they ought to become. The influence and inspiration of others will be used in the development of this potential, but these others must never be substituted for it. In no other way can democracy ever realize the best contribution of each person. Democratic education, therefore, having discovered the individual, will be consistent and see to it that his school experiences are in line with his capacities and needs, helping him to become what, by gift, he ought to become.

What Are His Characteristics at Various Stages of Development? The adjustment of education to the individual should be continuous. This will necessitate the continuous study of the individual so that the wisest adjustments can be made. Much is already known about individual development. We know, for example, that changes come gradually. One doesn't change from a child to an adolescent, or from an adolescent to an adult, over night. Some outward manifestations of these changes may seem sudden, but the basic processes involved in change have been going on for a long time. Furthermore, in physical development the body structure and the organs are not always abreast. The carcass may get ahead of the heart. Similarly, physical development and emotional, social, and intellectual development are not always abreast. Types of activities and interests vary, too, at different stages of development. At one time boys seem to be interested only in sports and physical activities, and in vocations that suggest action—aviator, cowboy, policeman. At this time girls are definitely in the way, to be avoided and even abused. But a very few years change all that. Social interests develop; vocation is looked at differently, and attitudes toward girls change too. Girls have their developmental characteristics the same as boys. It is these basic, natural characteristics to which education must ever attend. The coach or physical director who does not know the physical characteristics of youth at various stages of development, and who does not adjust his physical activities accordingly, should not be permitted to continue in his position. The English teacher who does not adjust his reading program in terms of the characteristic interests of pupils at various ages is missing the mark. Tact is also necessary in planning social events appropriate to various age groups. Much more could be added; in all of it, however, the importance of the principle clarified by John Dewey is apparent. The school experience of the child should not be determined basically by what he may do or need when he is an adult, but by what he is like and ready to take as he progresses through the school. He will be a better-educated, better-adjusted citizen if he is so treated.

Studying Society.—Democracy's fundamental interest in the individual requires attention to the society in which he moves as a free person. The study of the individual's relationship to others and to the institutions of society, his harmonious fitting into community living, and his voluntary acceptance of the responsibilities of citizenship in a free country are as binding on the school as the study of the individual. If the individual and society are understood by the school, the former developed in terms of his potential and the latter sponsoring and benefiting by that development, we may begin to approach a solution to the problem which was pointed up in our study of ancient Athens. As we look at our society, the same simple questions, with slight variations, can be asked that were asked about the individual.

What Is It Like? The society and the communities of which the schools are a part, and into which individuals will enter when they leave the schools, must be understood. This ranges all the way from an understanding of the salient features of democracy to the type of jobs that are available in a community for the graduates of that community's high school. Policy-making boards, administrative personnel, every classroom teacher, and the community itself should see to it that the program of the school evolves in relation to the local community, and to the larger communities which radiate out from it. This means that community surveys and continuing studies will be made to gather information on which the school's offering and activities and its classroom instruction can be based. It is hardly wise to limit the high school program to college preparatory and commercial subjects in a community that is mainly agricultural or industrial. Similarly, the nature and needs of the community ought to be reflected in the health work of the school, in science, in the work in problems of democracy, and, for that matter, in mathematics and foreign languages. Adaptations of this sort will not be limited to local conditions. All school personnel need a clear understanding of the nature of democracy itself and skill in adjusting the content and conduct of their work to serve democratic ends. The important point here is that if we are to make such adjustments well, we must get as good and accurate an answer as we can to the question of what our society, including the individual community, is like. This we do so that the adjustment of the individual to that society and his effectiveness in bettering it can be improved.

What Do You Want It to Become? Since a democratic society is the association of free individuals thinking and acting in conscience and cooperating honestly for the common good, it follows that that society cannot be pegged or described. Its essential characteristic is its change, growing out of its effort to follow the lead of individuals and groups who have studied it freely and have had ideas that were accepted by others, who, however, were free to appraise, attack, or support those ideas before accepting them. It is this process of change, the sometimes bungled implementation of the honest thinking of responsible people, that characterizes a democratic society. And that is the way we want it to remain. The incomplete answer, then, to our question is that we want our society to become, not a stereotype, but what in fact it will become when it encourages and implements the honest thinking of individuals motivated not only by personal interests but by the general welfare as well. This should not be

thought of as a concept removed from reality. It ought to be operative in the conduct of business, in the program of every organization,
in government, in school administration, in the home, and in the
classroom. School administration, for example, has too long been
guilty of not encouraging or permitting the expression of ideas from
staff members and students concerning the conduct of the schools.
The concept of an evolving society denies the philosophy of domination and blind conformity in government, in the school, or in any
other human relationship.

What Are the Cooperative Techniques Basic to Its Improvement?
This is one of the most crucial questions about our society that could
be asked. We have said before that many people in our country have
failed to grasp the significance of their responsibilities in a democracy
and have thought lopsidedly about opportunities, rights, noninterference, "getting ahead." Education itself has contributed to this attitude. Under such conditions the largest good cannot possibly come
to our people, even to such persons themselves. Within the next few
years in American life we shall probably see either a voluntary shift
by individuals to the acceptance and practice of greater social responsibility, or the imposition of controls intended to protect the oppressed
from the advantage-taker. Education would make an endless contribution to freedom if the children and youth in school who will be the
citizens and leaders of tomorrow could be brought to understand the
nature of democracy, the importance of their own contributions, and
the demand that each must now make on himself to work with others
rather than to maintain himself against others. Let us be more specific. Take an ordinary group discussion on a controversial issue in
this country. What is it like? It is too frequently an indulgence of
the right of individuals to express and defend their own points of
view, an experience in the fixation of ideas. Let us be clear. It is the
right of these individuals thus to express and defend themselves; but
somewhere in such a discussion surely the participants could be put to
work on the job of finding out whether or not there was any common
ground on which all could stand, some area of agreement which might
lead to further agreement and become at last a basis for group action.
Is group discussion intended to be a sounding-off process, or should
it get somewhere? Is it time in the evolution of our society to seek
out and emphasize our agreements as well as our differences? One
could easily remark here on the failure of the churches to make the
contribution they ought to make in this regard. It doesn't ring true
for a priest, a minister, or a rabbi to harangue the nations for non-

cooperation and to pray for the time when all shall "dwell together in peace" and then to preach and practice noncooperation among themselves. Democracy cannot continue to exist unless more and more effective ways of living together are discovered. To the school will fall more than its share of the responsibility for developing habits of cooperation among the young.

There are definite things the school can do in this regard. The selection and conduct of games and activities can be made to break down barriers of intolerance and narrowness. The teacher in the classroom can make assignments that call for group effort and can see to it that pupils with various backgrounds cooperate in these groups. When differences of opinion are aired among pupils in the classroom the teacher can insist that each pupil shall state the other fellow's position to the other fellow's satisfaction before he takes issue with it. And so the list would grow. The point here is the need to establish early the habits of cooperative thinking and acting which, continued and translated on the adult level, will guarantee the steady self-improvement of our society. The development of such cooperative techniques in our democracy will forestall the necessity for compulsion in government, a forestalling earnestly to be sought. Thus a premium is placed on the cooperative participation of the individual in the betterment of his community and nation. The techniques by which he can best cooperate to that end have yet largely to be developed. The urgency is to develop them speedily and to make them a part of the growth and experience of all citizens. So far as the schools of a democracy are concerned, the establishment through school experience of such habits and attitudes must become an essential addition to the mastery of any traditional educational content.

At the beginning of this section it was suggested that although it is good and useful to know educational objectives as they have been stated by others, it is even more important that we evolve a point of view of our own. This discussion has suggested the approach of (a) understanding a few simple but fundamental aspects of democracy, (b) studying carefully the individual whose personality is held in such high esteem in a democracy, and (c) studying the society in which the individual is nourished and upon which, in company with others, he reacts freely and constructively. With these understood, the position of the school in fulfilling them becomes clearer to all— teacher, parent, citizen; and the school's endless influence can be seen as it feeds into society well-developed people who know how to cooperate for the common good.

4. OTHER FEATURES OF THE AMERICAN IDEAL

The Whole Individual.—There was a time in the history of our schools when it was believed that the individual was, as it were, a collection of blocks, any one of which could be separated at will and shaped and polished as desired. This idea was supported for a time by the "faculty" theory of psychology, which held that the mind was not only separate and identifiable from other aspects of the personality, but that the mind itself was divided into certain powers or "faculties" which were capable of independent development. There was, and is, widespread insistence that the school should be concerned only with intellectual development, and not with other features of total personality. Psychology has long since changed its position; it now emphasizes the totality of personality, the ever-present blending and interaction of all experiences to produce, at any moment, the individual. People cannot be taken apart and put together again like jigsaw puzzles. They are organisms having many functions, each function affected by and affecting all other functions continuously.

Children do not take their minds to school and leave their emotions, bad teeth, and social embarrassments at home. Furthermore, their success in intellectual pursuits is not determined solely by intellectual capacity. The effect of physical health on school success is, of course, known. Emotional disturbances based on unstable home conditions, low economic status, and indulgence in practices considered immoral have similar effects. So do social maladjustments, religious conflicts, and vocational indecision. The whole personality comes to school; and even if the school were interested only in maximum intellectual development, it would have to give attention to the whole personality to achieve that end. The fact is, however, that the school, because of its determining character in our society, must be concerned to infuse into society not only good intellectuals but good people. Democratic schools are concerned with fully developed, responsible people. The curricula, activities, even the graduation requirements of the schools are beginning to reflect this larger responsibility and purpose. Democracy is not served well by its high schools, for example, if graduation requirements and the selection of the valedictorian are based solely on intellectual achievement. How shall we profit if our valedictorians, academically superior, are inexcusably weak, morally, physically, socially, ethically, aesthetically, and vocationally? Of course no one claims that all our valedictorians are thus warped. The fact is emphasized, though, that such warping can happen if only intellectual development is aimed at.

The interest that the school must have in the full development of the individual is complementary to the work of other agencies in our society. No one contends that the school will now take over the responsibility for the full development of everybody and all other agencies can close shop. The facts are that the school has had to take on some of its responsibilities because other agencies have failed to do their part or accept their fair responsibility in providing the activities and leadership necessary to the balanced development of youth. The school will view with extreme satisfaction forward-looking programs of youth development in home, church, theater, press, or anywhere else; and it will cooperate to the full in making them successful. The public school, however, cannot permit these agencies to promote their specialized interests within it. It has its own job to do, which, if well conceived and practiced, transcends differences of family, race, religion, or color and seeks the type of personality integration and development in pupils which will result in cooperation with others.

Going Beyond Traditional Content.—If the school is to be concerned with the well-developed individual and his constructive participation in society, then it will have to be willing to introduce new content, experiences, and activities which will be helpful in such development. If it is desirable for the citizen to be cooperative as well as to know mathematics, then the school must give the pupil experiences in cooperation as well as experiences in mathematics. The skilful mathematics teacher can accomplish this admirably. If it is important that the good American be tolerant as well as know the history of his own country, then the teacher must provide for the fair exchange of opinion on controversial issues as well as teach the facts and events of American history. If it is important to our way of life that all people use wisely their ever-increasing leisure, then the school ought to seek to establish interests and activities that will carry over into postschool life as desirable leisure-time pursuits. If physical health, social poise, and vocational decision and preparation are aspects of the fully developed person, then the school should attend to them as well as to subject matter of the more traditional sort. The foregoing type of reasoning indicates pretty well the origins of such objectives as the seven cardinal principles referred to on page 47. When we began to look beyond subjects as such and began to view education in terms of people, the old content became inadequate and new types of content and experiences became necessary. The first concern now is the human concern. The successful adaptation of youth to their world involves more than the mastery of subject matter. It involves habits of straight thinking, self-reliance, responsibility, good workmanship, tolerance, cooperation, alertness, fair play, emotional stability, freedom of thought, and action in line with the common good. The acquisition and use of these habits should concern us quite as much as the acquisition and use of learnings in mathematics, mother tongue, or anything else. The school is to do more than perpetuate a curriculum; it is to help people develop fully and live constructively. Albert Einstein put it this way:

Sometimes one sees in the school simply the instrument for transferring a certain maximum quantity of knowledge to the growing generation. But that is not right. Knowledge is dead; the school, however, serves the living. It should develop in the young individuals those qualities and capabilities which are of value for the welfare of the commonwealth. But that does not mean that individuality should be destroyed and the individual become a mere tool of the community, like a bee or an ant. For a community of standardized individuals without personal originality and personal aims would be a poor community without possibilities for development. On the contrary, the aim must be the training of independently acting and thinking individuals, who, however, see in the service of the community their highest life problem.[1]

Functional Emphasis.—A great deal of emphasis is given today to the fact that education must yield results in a difficult world, beyond producing some kind of strange elevation of the mind. Whatever is done or required on any level must be shown to be the best use of time in terms of the realities of living. Any content that cannot stand the test of comparison with other likely content in contributing directly to the great educational objectives must be supplanted by that which is more fruitful. Time was when it was unthinkable in some of our institutions to deal with such mundane matters. But that time is past. People, and the world in which they live, are now the springboard. Education will not seek to remove young people from their world or transport them disconnectedly to other times; it will seek to make them more effective in *their* times, using content and activities, remote or immediate, which are best adapted to that end. It used to be the philosopher's privilege to remove himself, as it were, into the upper air to speculate on things far out of reach of the common man. Today it is different; he may go up all right, but he must also come down with something that contributes to better personal and social living, better business practices, and better government. The school

[1] Albert Einstein, "Some Thoughts Concerning Education," *School and Society,* XLIV, 590.

has too long thought and taught subjects, without relating those subjects pointedly to life, and without abandoning them if there were
other more life-significant activities that could be put in their place.
A. N. Whitehead addressed himself to this problem, as follows:

> The solution which I am urging, is to eradicate the fatal disconnection of
> subjects which kills the vitality of our modern curriculum. There is only
> one subject-matter for education, and that is Life in all its manifestations.
> Instead of this single unity, we offer children—Algebra, from which nothing
> follows; Geometry, from which nothing follows; science, from which noth-
> ing follows; History, from which nothing follows; a couple of Languages,
> never mastered; and lastly, most dreary of all, Literature, represented by
> plays of Shakespeare, with philological notes and short analyses of plot and
> character to be in substance committed to memory. Can such a list be said to
> represent Life, as it is known in the midst of the living of it? The best that
> can be said of it is, that it is a rapid table of contents which a deity might
> run over in his mind while he was thinking of creating a world, and had not
> yet determined how to put it together.[2]

It is important to note that Whitehead was not arguing for the
eradication of subjects, but for the eradication of the "fatal discon-
nection of subjects" from "Life, as it is known in the midst of the
living of it." The teacher is duty-bound to make these connections;
if he cannot, or if he cannot do it sufficiently to justify the time
requirements of his subject in the school, then the welfare of youth
hard pressed in a swift-moving world calls for the modification or
elimination of these subjects.

This principle of connectedness with life is not remote, and the
teacher's application of it should be tangible and real. A fond hope
that somehow learning will transfer to life situations is not enough.
The teacher who has not yet made these vital connections and taught
them is himself living in a kind of vacuum, not much help to students
seeking guides and tools for a good life in a real world full of real
people. Illustrations of "connections" are manifold. The government teacher who projects his instruction beyond the textbook and
gives his students direct observation and experience in community
problems is on the right track. Some schools require students to
alternate periods of study at school with periods of work and study
on the job. Mathematics problems can be drawn from situations
meaningful to any grade level. The teacher who used batting aver-
ages in baseball to get the day-dreaming boy over to his percentage
work knew the value of "connections." Vocational and professional

---

[2] A. N. Whitehead, *The Aims of Education and Other Essays.* Copyright, 1929,
by the Macmillan Co. and used with their permission.

studies, of course, if they are good, make extensive use of real problems and applications. The necessity for all of education, then, is clear. Subjects as we have known them must serve real purposes. They are defensible only as they contribute vitally to living.

Freedom Applied to Groups.—It has already been pointed out that many groups and organizations exist in our society, and individuals may join them at will, but they must not violate the individual's basic freedoms or opportunities. This privilege extended to groups has resulted in the establishment of many schools supported by special group interests. The right of these schools to exist has been upheld many times. More recently, in 1925, the United States Supreme Court held unconstitutional action that had been taken by the state of Oregon requiring that all children of compulsory attendance age attend the public schools. The action by Oregon was held to violate the constitutional right of parents to determine the type of school, including a religious school, their children should attend. However, it should not be supposed that any group can maintain any kind of school it pleases. The society which grants to these groups the right to maintain schools must still insist that children attending them shall not have their basic freedoms and opportunities impaired. Although in most states public officials do not closely supervise or control private schools, action would quickly be taken, including police action if necessary, to close a private school, or a public school, that flagrantly violated the rights and opportunities to which children are entitled. This has not, of course, been a serious problem in America. On the contrary, the record of the private school has not only been satisfactory, but private schools have been at the forefront of many educational advances. Pupils in them have experienced no serious curtailments, unless it be that in some of them the fundamental right to think freely and independently on religious matters has been restricted.

The State and Education.—Whereas the state in our society defends the freedom of the individual and the right of special interest groups to exist, it itself functions in the area of the general welfare. It is nonspecialized. It is above class, promotes harmony among groups, and, above all, does not set class against class. The projects it supports must be defensible in terms of the welfare of all. The state plays no favorites; and special groups with special interests should not expect the state to support their limited causes, morally or financially. More constructively, governmental support at any level, federal, state, or local, should be for projects which cut across special interest lines, promote the common ground of democratic living, and are nondiscriminatory in their benefits. Police and fire protection, public roads, the postal service, public parks, public schools, and many other examples could be cited. Even a federal price-support program must result in benefit to all. Legislation involving labor-management relations must keep uppermost the welfare of the public at large and give no special advantage to either group.

In short, government must maintain the arena within which special interests can compete and maneuver, but at the same time it must stay out of the arena and promote on its part projects intended to elevate harmony above differences, secure just rights and protection for all, and turn freedoms and competition into constructive and not self-destructive channels. Public education is one of these harmonizing, common-ground, equal-benefits projects. Such ends are so important to our way of life that our people have gladly taxed themselves to support institutions that promote them for all. And government, thus supporting the public schools, denies itself the privilege of using its own schools to propagandize in its own favor or promote its special interests. Hence government cannot permit any special interest group to promote itself through public education. It will not, in other words, finance special interests, differences, disintegration, or restricted inquiry. It will finance unity, the common good, unrestricted inquiry. Public schools are not only tuition-free; they are free-inquiry schools as well. They are not restricted to the interests of Democrats, labor, Catholics, whites, Protestants, Republicans, or the American Legion. All of these groups, and many more, constitute the make-up of our society, and as such they are a proper study for the public schools, but they are not a proper control for the public schools. Let us be clear. The right of these groups to exist is defended; their right to the time and funds of public education, for special interest purposes, is denied. It is easy to see what would happen if government funds were available for private education. Every loyal Presbyterian, Catholic, and Jew would insist that his child attend his own religious school. Increased enrolments in private schools would mean increased requests for public funds. The public would finance the disintegration of its own public schools; and all the while, the children in the religious schools would be isolated and taught in terms of differences, and every meeting on the street of the children from these schools would be a reminder of those differences. If religious groups contend that attitudes of cooperation would be taught in their own schools, let them grasp the public school situation as an opportunity to practice the cooperation they preach. It is this kind of cooperative, nonsectarian ethical education that the public school is interested in promoting. The state, then, in terms of support, is neither for nor against private interests; it is for and not against public education, equally free to all, which enlarges the common ground beyond differences, the only fertile soil of democratic progress.

It certainly is not the intention here to give the impression that all private schools are narrow and self-centered. They are not. Some of them, as we have said, have shown the way in educational matters. They have supplied some of the country's outstanding educational leaders.

Their presence in our society demonstrates the freedoms we support, and they will survive or die as they themselves promote those freedoms. Their influence on the total educational scene can be great. But they must maintain themselves. They continue to exist as private schools because of some special interest or limitation they wish to promote or enforce. The state operates in a larger sphere.

Education a Community Responsibility.—With the realization that the individual is a total personality and cannot be taken apart for purposes of education has gone the realization also that the school cannot do the job alone. The school has no monopoly on education.

The pupil's entire life in the community constitutes his education. Community agencies, therefore, are beginning to cooperate to build a total environment that will foster desirable over-all development and will avoid negation by one part of the community of the constructive work done by another part. For example, there is not much point to a community taxing itself to support good programs of health and ethical character in the school if it permits the existence of dives and disease to which youngsters can be exposed at three o'clock in the afternoon. There is good point to such programs if they are supported by clean quarters, good theaters, good recreation activities, and good youth programs in the community. Community councils are springing up across the country intended to encourage the coordination and rounding-out of community efforts to provide an excellent total community environment. These councils are not control agencies. They represent the voluntary cooperation of many groups. They illustrate the growing conviction in our country that the adequate education of youth requires full community cooperation in ways that are tangible and real. This whole development is so important that all of Chapter 13 is devoted to it.

5. Traditionalists, Progressivists, Essentialists

It has already been said, and it cannot be overemphasized, that educational purposes and practices in our country have varied from time to time. However, they have not waxed and waned uniformly. They have existed side by side, varying locally and in separate schools and classrooms pretty much as our teachers, leaders, and citizens have desired. Such diversity, insofar as it reflects the honest indulgence of individual and group thinking, is desirable. It must, however, move toward the fulfilment of the great freedoms and cooperative arts toward which humanity moves.

Some of the differences in purposes and practices which are found in our schools today can be seen in a brief discussion of the traditionalists, progressivists, and essentialists. These groups have been singled out and described by numerous writers. For our purposes here, they are not to be thought of as organizations with presidents and platforms. They are, rather, understandable ideas that might easily get lost if surrounded by too much discussion of idealism, authoritarianism, experimentalism, pragmatism, and the like.

Traditionalists.—The traditionalists hold that certain things ought to be taught in the school because they are true. Truth is everlasting, unchangeable. It has been delivered to certain humans through insight, intuition, revelation, and careful study. These persons and their writings are appealed to as authorities. The "tradition" takes on great importance. Certain studies, also, are held to produce certain outcomes in the mind which make them desirable for all. The teacher, under the traditionalist concept, is authoritarian. He knows best what is good for the pupils, and he sees to it that they learn it. Assignment and drill stand out. The child learns what is selected for him, and is expected to accept the judgment of others that it is good. The school is thus an agency of transmittal, to pass on preconceptions, to perpetuate the tradition, and to condition pupils for the acceptance of authority.

Progressivists.—The progressivists place the child rather than the tradition at the center of the educational stage. Children are to be first understood, and then served by content rather than enslaved by it. The nature of the learner is the springboard. The school will shape its program to the abilities, aptitudes, interests, and needs of those it serves. Pupil participation in determining and evaluating pupils' own learning activities is emphasized. Self-reliance is sought. Freedom is extended so that wise self-direction in the use of freedom can be cultivated. The teacher does not make all decisions beforehand. He cooperates, helps, consults, and seeks to place within the reach of pupils the materials that will make for success as they pursue their own learning. The teacher motivates and assigns in terms of individual differences. Cooperative action among pupils is sought, as well as learning experiences related to the society of which the pupils are a part. The school is not authoritarian; it is an agency of discovery and adjustment.

Essentialists.—The essentialists seem to say that the progressivists went off the deep end; that, after all, there are some things that all children ought to learn, without reference to their differences in intelligence, aptitudes, interests, or vocational intentions. The individual emphasis in progressivism, they seem to say, ran away with the social emphasis. They bring us back hard to the proposition that the school ought to secure in children the mastery of those things and the establishment of those habits that will help them live more effectively within their culture. Certain subjects and activities, then, again become important. They are to be understood and mastered because they are the necessary equipment of everyone who thinks for himself and conducts his own affairs. The teacher sees to it that these things are done. There is a definite control here; but it should be observed that the appeal is not to tradition or to the magic of subjects themselves. The appeal is to the requirements of our times, to the demands of our evolving culture. So the "essentials" are to be made meaningful, attacked, and learned; not sugar-coated and dangled as bait before fastidious youngsters. History is important; and so are the ways of getting along together. The school sees to it that the essentials based on the nature of our culture are mastered; and, while it recognizes the existence of individual differences, it does not excuse any individual from these essentials.

The descriptive statements above are doubtless too sharply drawn. Certainly no person would classify himself as strictly traditionalist, progressivist, or essentialist on the basis of the above statements. As was said before, these are influences at work; they are not organizations. They are all through our society; everyone is affected by them. They are not mutually incompatible, unless, perhaps, the doctrine of authority clashes with the idea of analysis, experimentalism, emergent man. Tradition and inquiry are difficult to reconcile; but difficult only if tradition is inflexible, and if inquiry forgets that tradition is as real in the minds of men as stones and trees. Tradition and dogma, accepted without inquiry, are just as real as an automobile or the Fourth of July. Faith and inquiry, though, go beyond this. They rise above the certainties of life; they are a reaching, an aspiration, growth. They seek for "the substance of things hoped for, the evidence of things not seen." They constitute the ultimate freedom of which man is capable. They are courage, adventure, the magnificent release. Not to take them is to stand, grounded, with strong wings folded. One cannot experience all this if he is suffocated by tradition. Tradition can help if it merely starts him on his upward way. Man, personally, must go on to "grow in grace and knowledge" if he is to gain the perfection of which he is capable. His institutions will give him aid and succor, but he must rise in his spirit above them or he is not free. The mission of his institutions, then, is to fling him upward.

It is contended often that tradition, authority, the unquestioned acceptance of "truth" give us the anchors we need in a teeming world. And anchors are needed, to be sure. But are we true to our own capacities if we permit those anchors to become the intuitions of others, mainly ancients, who were no more or less human than we? On the other hand, we can hardly be stable or secure in our world if we must live always in waiting to see the results of our endless inquiry and experimentation. Must we not now establish a new concept of human progress, one based on becoming, on fulfilment, in which tradition and inquiry are both essential, but both flexible? Tradition and inquiry are incompatible except as they become parts of a larger pattern. The new anchor, then, let us say, is the movement, the improvement, the reach of the race. It is to the perpetuation of this concept of discovery and growth, rather than to the perpetuation of inflexible tradition, that the public school is committed.

6. SOME STUDENT OPINION

It has been exceedingly interesting and stimulating to the writer to follow the thinking of a considerable number of college students with reference to their ideas concerning democracy and the relationship of education to those ideas. The summary presented below is not intended to prove anything. It is intended only to acquaint the reader with student opinion concerning certain matters bearing upon the previous discussions, and it may serve to stimulate the reader to further thinking on his own. It may reflect, also, the shape of things to come educationally if students, as represented in this sampling, take over the direction of our schools.

Within the last five years approximately a thousand college students in three universities, mainly sophomores and juniors, were given a week to prepare a paper dealing directly and specifically with the following leads:

1. As I conceive them, the salient features of democracy are: . . . .
2. If I had my way, we would see more of the following in secondary schools and colleges, in line with education for democratic living: . . . .
3. These are things I have encountered in my secondary school and college experience which I consider out of line with education for democratic living: . . . .

The students wrote their papers before any discussion of the American ideal of education had been taken up in class. Their contributions, therefore, represent their own thinking prior to such discussion and reading. This is not to say that they had not had work in other classes that shaped their thinking greatly. The complete summaries of student contributions cannot, of course, be given. Some related items have been combined, but an effort has been made to retain the intent and language of the original statements. The prevalence of the items among the total contributions is also indicated.

The lead, "As I conceive them, the salient features of democracy are:" brought forth the following responses:

Listed by about 40 per cent or more of the students, in order of frequency, were:

1. Freedom of worship
2. Freedom of speech
3. Freedom of the press
4. Majority rule; popular participation in making all decisions; people retain the supreme power
5. Equality for all regardless of race, color, or creed
6. Equal economic opportunity for all classes
7. Free education for all
8. Freedom of pursuit of happiness
9. Freedom of assembly

Listed by about 25 to 39 per cent of the students, in order of frequency, were:

1. Right to the fullest development of one's capacities and personality; wide diffusion of culture and means essential to the good life
2. Right to safety and security
3. Freedom from want and fear

4. Representative government; checks and balances in government
5. Worth and dignity of the individual
6. Freedom of thought and choice
7. Freedom of work; occupational choice
8. Loyalty to a common ideal; for the good of the whole; brotherhood
9. Right of trial by jury
10. Free elections
11. Private property; individual enterprise; privacy of one's home
12. Freedom to criticize the government
13. Freedom of movement, travel, abode

Listed fewer times, but significantly, in order of frequency, were:

1. Civic responsibilities; active participation in government and social work
2. Continuous progress; nonstatic society
3. Good schools; good teachers well paid; no censorship in education; free access to truth
4. Team work; cooperation; fair play
5. Living independently yet cooperatively; self-reliance and cooperation mutually adjusted
6. Protection of minority groups; equal rights and representation of minority groups
7. Utilization of expert intelligence in the administration of society; active participation of an educated civic body
8. Respect of rights of others
9. Separation of church and state
10. Right of collective bargaining
11. Self-discipline
12. Flexibility of government in power, function, and leadership between local, state, and national units
13. Absence of regimentation

Rarely mentioned were:

1. Tendency toward corruption
2. Inefficiency and slowness
3. Mediocrity
4. Right to go deer-hunting
5. Right to love and marry

The reader will interpret the above lists to his own satisfaction and draw his own inferences from them. He may feel that there are, in general, two types of responses; that is, learned responses and thought responses, the former making up pretty much the first list. This, of course, is not bad in itself if the student has thought for himself and has made sure that the learned items express his own ideas and convictions. The reader may see also another rather clear separation of the items into two groups; namely, those emphasizing rights, privileges, and opportunities and those emphasizing participation, responsibilities, and progress, with the former occurring more frequently. There is much material in the lists for further fruitful inquiry. Let us pass on, however, to the students' ideas concerning the relationship of school practices to education for democratic living.

The lead, "If I had my way, we would see more of the following in secondary schools and colleges, in line with education for democratic living:" brought forth the following responses:

Listed by about 40 per cent or more of the students, in order of frequency, were:

1. Emphasis on present status of American government and current problems; knowledge of the organization, functions, and development of our government, law, and legal procedures; continuous adjustment of education to social needs; more emphasis on citizenship

2. More opportunities for pupils to practice democratic procedures in school and community; practical application of individual skills and talents; emphasis on actual experience; emphasis on practical and current materials; consumer education; more work experience; assignments involving projects outside of school; integration of the curriculum with life situations; closer unity between the school and the community, the school and the home

3. More international understanding and intercultural education; banishment of all religious, racial, and social prejudice

4. Development of self-responsibility and self-control in the individual; sense of competence and adequacy; development of critical attitude in thinking and reading; more problem-solving training; stimulation of self-education and creative work; more attention to motivation and stimulating the desire to learn

5. Recognition of individual differences; development of personality; self-realization; personal well-being; recognition of the worth and dignity of each person

6. Better-trained teachers; better teaching; better instructional materials and methods; curriculum reorganization; adjustment of curriculum to individual needs and abilities; more use of audiovisual aids to learning; teachers' assignments concise and clear;

amount of subject matter assigned proportionate to time allotment; clear-cut, interesting textbooks

7. Learning to get along with others; discovering and working for the common good; more cooperation and group activities; group-affair participation; more student-led group activities; learn the oneness of men

8. Better school support; equalization of educational opportunity; federal aid to equalize educational opportunity; better school plant and equipment; higher teachers' pay

Listed by about 25 to 39 per cent of the students, in order of frequency, were:

1. More concentration on vocational needs to suit each individual; free public vocational education; extension of vocational education and vocational guidance

2. More emphasis on guidance; increased counseling services and staff

3. Closer relationship between teachers and students; more free discussion between students and teachers

4. More student participation in class work; have students and teachers set the standards of teaching together; student participation in curriculum planning

5. More general courses; more elective courses; fairer system of electives; emphasis on teaching basic values; emphasis on general education

6. More extracurricular activities; better play program; better integration of the curriculum and extracurricular activities; education for leisure time; revision of physical activities program with wider participation

7. Truly representative student governments, made to work

8. Better health and safety programs

9. Smaller class size; reduced teaching load

10. Modify present marking system; get rid of current marking system

Listed fewer times, but significantly, in order of frequency, were:

1. Student evaluation of teachers and courses; students represented at faculty meetings; wider use of student opinion in determining discipline; student participation in school management

2. More classes for adults; informal education through all life; more parent education; stimulation of life-long learning

3. Scholarships for students in need of financial aid
4. Consolidation of rural schools; better educational opportunities for rural children
5. Elimination of prejudice among faculty members; elimination of partiality of some teachers for certain pupils; tolerance and fair-mindedness on the part of teachers
6. Practice of the honor system
7. Teaching of awareness of the agencies and methods of propaganda
8. Better selected school boards; more representative school boards
9. More men employed in elementary schools
10. Broader practice of democratic principles by teachers and administrators
11. Improvement or banishment of fraternities and sororities

Rarely mentioned were:

1. Country-wide uniformity in education; more standardization of subject matter; centralized school system under control of federal government
2. Abolish private and parochial schools
3. Lower expenditures in public schools
4. Required reading of classics
5. More emphasis on competitive athletics
6. Compulsory military training
7. Release of teachers using dictatorial methods

The above lists of suggestions for the improvement of our school system are as meaty, profound, and practical as the writer has seen anywhere. Extended observations could be made; let the reader evaluate the items for himself. One remark may be permitted. The lists accomplish the individual and social ends of democratic education in a remarkable manner; they also require that education follow through to applications, to direct tie-up with experience; and they emphasize greatly that education should be a sharing, participating, developmental experience rather than an experience in survival.

The third and last of the leads dealt with by the students was: "These are things I have encountered in my secondary school and college experience which I consider out of line with education for democratic living." This brought forth the following responses:

Listed by about 40 per cent or more of the students, in order of frequency, were:

1. Racial, religious, and social intolerance and discrimination
2. Teacher domination, indoctrination, and regimentation in class; authoritarian teachers; lack of willingness of teachers to allow students to think; superior, infallible attitude of teachers
3. Teacher prejudices; favoritism shown by teachers
4. Curriculum not related to individual needs and present-day living; neglect of applications and practical experiences; failure to bring out practical values of courses; not related enough to government, history, and social and current problems; little practice of democratic living
5. Lack of free expression of views on the part of students; lack of free discussion of controversial issues in class
6. Fraternities, sororities, cliques, sub-deb clubs; coalitions
7. Poor marking system; competitive system in marking; overemphasis on marks; marks not representative of quality of learning

Listed by about 25 to 39 per cent of the students, in order of frequency, were:

1. Overemphasis on formal aspects of education; overemphasis on memorization of materials; too much course prescription; narrow college-preparatory curriculum; unnecessary rules and regulations; teachers teach subject matter, not children
2. Inadequately trained teachers; poor teaching methods; conservatism in teaching; antiquated methods
3. Lack of academic freedom; domination by pressure groups; domination by administrators; banning of textbooks; biased textbooks
4. Neglect of individual interests, needs, and capacities; neglect of bright pupils; neglect of slow pupils; little attention to development of individual personality
5. Formalized and harsh discipline; mass discipline
6. Lack of true student participation in student government and school administration; teacher-dominated student government; teacher influence in class elections
7. Lack of effective guidance and counseling service
8. Differences in educational opportunity; inequality in financial support

Listed fewer times, but significantly, in order of frequency, were:

1. Too large classes; too heavy teaching load
2. Not enough education in group cooperation; getting along with others

3. Not enough school activities; lack of general active participation by students in school activities
4. Censorship of school papers
5. Failure to teach critical thinking; too little liberty and responsibility given to pupils
6. Lack of cooperation among teachers, homes, boards, laymen, church, community
7. Inadequate vocational guidance and preparation
8. Nonrepresentative student government; domination by few in school activities
9. Lack of international and intercultural education; lack of adequate citizenship training
10. Lack of interest by teacher in subject taught
11. Failure to create incentive to work; teachers force pupils to work for them rather than with them
12. Disunity among faculty members; lack of cooperation among departments
13. Cheating
14. Teachers, especially females, restricted by the community with regard to their recreation
15. Teachers practice differently from what they preach

Rarely mentioned were:

1. Swimming pool segregation
2. Restrictions on class cutting in colleges
3. Teaching religion
4. No teaching of religion
5. Not returning tests
6. Teachers have no faith in God or man
7. Professors look into students' transcripts

A few quotations from student papers concerning undemocratic practices will show the tangible, direct-from-experience nature of their contributions.

Many instructors will ask questions on which the answer is entirely a matter of opinion; but if your opinion does not coincide with theirs, then you are wrong. Too many students tend to conform rather than become individuals with ideas of their own.

Some instructors in both secondary schools and college refuse to consider opinions of the students. This results in marking in accordance with how well the student shows that he has accepted the instructor's opinions.

The student is constantly referred to authority as the infallible answer to an issue. For instance, in English courses a certain bunch of authors is considered good whether you think so or not, purely because the teacher has said so without giving any reasons for his choice. In practically every other course, rules and laws are set up which make the appeal to authority a habit, obviously a bad one in a democracy.

It is not democratic to put major emphasis on college preparatory work at the expense of the other students who require training in various fields because their formal education will be terminated at the high school level.

There were few or no courses offered which dealt with the operation of this democracy on current issues. Even those that were taught were mainly of a factual nature and somewhat idealized, thus losing much of their quality and desirability.

My high school student council was subjected to the influence of a dictatorial teacher, and the powers that she left it were so slight that the body might as well have been nonexistent.

First of all in college I found fraternities and sororities. There are various reasons why I consider these out of line for democratic living. They do not further education in any way, and they are very discriminating on religion, personality, looks, and marks. In these organizations one pays for his friends, he doesn't choose them.

Perhaps the most significant defect has been the failure of the school to educate me in terms of my aptitudes and interests. Immediately upon entering high school, I was subjected to a stereotyped, planned curriculum. Not one attempt was made either by the so-called guidance counselor or by any of my teachers to find out in what respect I differed from other students, what subjects I was interested in, what my particular capabilities were, and what ambitions I had.

A male student contributed the following:

We used to have to march out of the building to go home to the tune of the school band. It was something like a "convict" set-up. Beyond this we were watched every time we went out the door by teachers stationed at intervals. One teacher was even stationed at the door of the latrine. She objected if urination did not take place.

7. Tomorrow's Prospect

As one reviews our concern in this chapter with the nature of democracy, our educational goals, the dual role we must play as free but freely cooperating individuals, and the relationship of education to individual development and social improvement, he takes heart in the above responses. Again, the responses are not presented with the idea of proving anything; but the conviction is admitted that it is as important to our future to know what young people think about democracy and education as what professional educators think. All persons, young and old, should think on these matters. Perhaps this presentation will supply a framework for further thinking on the part of many. But a problem remains. The mere fact that these things were written down by a good number of typical college students does not guarantee that conditions will be any better in the future. It is easy to put such things on paper and then say that there is nothing one person can do about them. Personal commitment, therefore, must follow. There will be a thousand chances for the administrator, the teacher, the parent, the taxpayer, the butcher, the baker, and the candlestick maker to do something about the desirable things presented here. This can be done effectively and without turning a community upside down if some of the cooperation demanded in the items is practiced. Clearly, if the understandings, the recognized weaknesses, and the constructive suggestions contained in the above lists are coupled with a personal acceptance for future action, then the prospect for tomorrow's schools, and, in turn, tomorrow's world, is good.

What Do YOU Say?

1

Of all the basic institutions which our citizens promote and around which they rally—e.g., the churches, the schools, the unions, politics, business—the public school is freest of bias and partisanship. It ought, therefore, to be preserved independent of all other agencies, but defended by them, as our great investment in mutual association and free inquiry.

What do YOU say?

2

The central problem of democracy is moral. Principles that are personally adhered to and that establish the dignity of the other fellow and require fair play in dealing with him are necessary. The central problem of the school in a democracy is to discover and develop the potentialities of each person, and to accompany this with commitments and skills in working cooperatively with others.

What do YOU say?

3

What points in this chapter do you particularly support or take issue with?

Chapter 4

SOME ASPECTS OF EDUCATION ABROAD

The School: Instrument of Control or Release

1. LIMITED PURPOSE OF THIS DISCUSSION

Having considered the ideal of education in America, it will be useful to look briefly beyond our own borders at some general aspects of education in other countries. The purpose here is not to detail the organization and curricula of the schools abroad. It is, rather, (*a*) to show the relationship of education to national policy; (*b*) to show some of the developments, problems, and trends in selected countries; (*c*) to review problems associated with the re-education of certain peoples; and (*d*) to introduce the function of UNESCO as an international educational agency. In order to achieve this purpose it will be necessary to exercise considerable selectivity among the nations, and within the available material.

2. THE POSITION OF THE SCHOOL UNDER CENTRALIZED GOVERNMENTS

The advent of modern dictatorships demonstrated as never before the power of the school in shaping the thinking of a complete people. The importance attached to the school in prewar Germany, Japan, Italy, and Russia is known, and the dispatch with which those assuming control took over and made over the schools is also known. No government can expect to stand long which does not have the genuine loyalty of its people. Dictators know this full well. They seek quickly, therefore, to eliminate organizations or persons that would directly or indirectly counter such loyalty, and they seize earnestly upon agencies and persons they believe can promote it. The school is immediately recognized as one of these agencies; and it is especially important because it deals with those who have not yet thought too much for themselves, whose loyalties are yet largely to be formed. The personnel and program of the school are quickly brought into line with national goals, and if distortions of science, economics, history, or psychology are needed to protect and promote these goals, then such distortions are made. These distortions having been made, it becomes additionally necessary that the truth in such matters not be allowed to reach the people; hence rigid controls on textbook materials, radio listening, research, reporting, teaching, and other agencies of thought are imposed. Through controlled education, propaganda, and coercion, the dictator seeks to build up the thought patterns and the attitudes that will support him, and by the same means to discredit and destroy those who would oppose his policies or practices. The school, therefore, becomes a sounding-board of political philosophy and national policy. It becomes an instrument for the perpetuation, not the examination, of ideas. It is the government's agency for thought control. It is not an agency of individual freedom, but an agency of domination, limitation, and submission. It is surprising how successful such educational programs have been, even in countries where human progress has been outstanding. However, if the devices of communication throughout the earth can keep up with the devices of oppression, the capacity of man to want freedom and to use it wisely will surely forestall any long-standing domination of such character.

Not all centralized governments, of course, are dictatorships. In some cases wide central powers are exercised throughout the land, but the government itself is constituted by so many individuals and groups that it is representative in character. As the number of individuals and groups involved in government becomes greater, and as governmental responsibilities extend farther and farther away from the capital, then government becomes more and more representative, more democratic. Conversely, as the number of individuals and groups becomes smaller, and as controls are withdrawn from outlying units and returned to the capital, then government becomes more and more centralized, less democratic. The inevitable outcome of the latter process is dictatorship. Under either process, education is directly affected. In some countries the organization and curriculum of the schools are controlled from the national capital, without the severe limitations and distortions referred to in the previous paragraph. In other cases, local provinces and communities would like nothing better than to be able to break down governmental uniformities and adapt education to local needs. It is extremely difficult for centralized governments not to serve their own special purposes through the controls they hold. The problem and the danger lie in the despotic tendencies of the central government, or, indeed, of the dictator. History has a few examples of benevolent despots; but it has more of grasping, self-centered despots. Mankind in the future is likely to put its faith in its own mass evolution rather than in the disposition of a few people to rule with kindness and generosity. At any rate, under centralized governments the educational quarterback is at the top, and the local schools operate to carry out his signals. Education fares differently under different centralized governments in the extent to which it is permitted to share in evolving the national patterns, and, for that matter, the local patterns. If such participation is on the increase, then that government is releasing its people to self-thinking, to truth, and to freedom. If it is on the decrease, the capacity of the people to think for themselves, to know the truth, and to grow in the constructive uses of freedom is being violated.

3. The Position of the School in Democracies

In democracies, as has been pointed out before, extreme importance is placed on the development and liberation of the individual. Along with this must go the honest recognition by each individual of the worth and rights of other individuals, and the sincere desire to promote their welfare. In a very real sense, the common good in a democracy transcends individual interests; but, most importantly, it does so in the minds and hearts of individuals. They are not coerced. The common good can never be realized progressively and permanently unless individuals freely and cooperatively promote it. Thus, in a democracy, institutions are the devices of free men to preserve and promote freedom through the development of the individual and the establishment of processes and channels through which he can be heard and felt. They do not limit individuals in their free inquiry; on the contrary, they are willing to revise their policies and practices in terms of the impartial findings of free individuals. This kind of action applies, of course, to government itself; and it certainly applies to the school. The school seeks the development of independent-thinking, freely cooperating individuals, the free access to truth in all areas of human experience, and the development of techniques of common action that will preserve the freedom and collective influence of individuals. It is an agency free to seek truth and report it fearlessly. It is supported by government to educate impartial thinkers who in turn may examine, criticize, and control government, changing it as needed in line with the general welfare. In democracies, then, the school is not an agency of thought control reflecting and fostering the policies of the central government; it is, on the other hand, an agency of thought stimulation which is as free to attack problems of national policy as problems of geometry or composition.

4. The Determination of Educational Policies and Practices

Under Centralized Governments.—Since under dictatorships and ordinarily under other forms of centralized government the school is a sounding-board of national policy, it follows that educational policy is determined by government officials. These policies are radiated out to the provinces, cities, and hamlets, and they in turn, without the right of acceptance or rejection, carry them out. The central government often prescribes at least a part of the subjects that must be taught in the schools, and, as may be supposed, indicates the basic content that must be included. Government inspectors circulate freely throughout the country to check up on the fulfilment of government prescriptions within the schools. Frequently, also, only personnel acceptable to the central government may be employed. The local schools, therefore, are instruments of central decisions.

It is important to call attention to one thing further. It should never be supposed that all the educational practices in dictator countries are bad. Many American visitors to these countries have testified to the resourcefulness of teachers, the rebuilding of the curriculum in line with community needs, the attention given to health and physical fitness, and the program of pupil activities which projects out into the community. A great deal of freedom in the area of teaching methods is also noted. These practices should be evaluated and used wherever improvement in education is sought. It must be remembered, however, that in dictator countries these practices must operate within and promote the national policy. Of course those in power are interested in finding more effective ways of indoctrination, so they grant freedoms within the political framework; but they are not interested in granting the freedom to criticize or challenge the framework. Again, educational policies stem from the central government, and educational practices in the outlying regions must support them.

In Democracies.—In democracies educational policies and practices are determined wherever the individuals live and associate together in communities. They are determined at the point of operation. The people who are to be affected by policies, and whose children are to be affected, share in their development. Responsible policy-making boards, therefore, selected by the people and present at the local, state, and federal levels, are found in democracies. These boards, representing the people in many thousands of communities in some countries, determine the quality and character of education in those communities. Many such boards encounter drastic financial limitations. The result, to be sure, is extreme diversity in education among the communities; but democracies are determined to find ways and means of eliminating such educational inequalities among the communities without taking from them their right to shape the policies of their schools. The community will continue to set up the program of study and employ its own school personnel. The democratic approach, therefore, seems clear; that is, better education of all individuals in all communities who in turn will be better able to make wise decisions concerning community schools, and, for that matter, will be able to spend more wisely than anybody else the funds supplied from outside sources if such assistance is necessary. The delegation of the policy-making responsibility to local communities by central and intermediate governmental units is, therefore, characteristic of democracies. This places a premium on the thinking and initiative of multitudes of individuals in multitudes of communities. It is in sharp contrast to the conformities required of local communities under centralized governments.

It should not be supposed that in democracies the central and intermediate governmental units lose all interest in the local communities when responsibility for policy-making and support have been delegated. Quite the contrary. But the relationship is one of leadership, advice, consultation, and helpfulness, not coercion. Financial aid is also often extended, without the demand that local controls be surrendered. Thus the "grass roots" concept persists; which is nothing more than the idea that controls of society ought to remain as close as possible to the individuals who constitute society.

A caution was thrown out earlier calling attention to the narrowness of deciding that all educational practices under dictatorships are bad. Caution should be taken here also not to suppose that all educational practices in democracies are good. The democratic system is subject to all the weaknesses of individuals, and they are manifold. All communities have assortments of people that are sometimes baffling and hard to coordinate into groups for intelligent action. But the democratic system is subject also to all the possibilities of individuals, and they are many. In fact, at this point in the rise of Western man, following his awakening after the Dark Ages, it would be a catastrophe if ways and means could not be found simultaneously to preserve individual freedoms and turn individual motives and achievements to the common good. Democracy, imperfect as it is in its operation, aims to accomplish this. The schools of a democracy have their important contribution to make in bringing about this accomplishment.

5. EDUCATION IN SELECTED COUNTRIES

England.—The Anglican concept of family responsibility for education dominated England for a long time. The private schools were the outstanding schools, serving primarily the children of families who were more fortunately situated economically and socially. A class or "dual" school system developed, with separate educational ladders for the classes and the masses. This separation appeared in the early grades of the elementary school and continued up the ladder. The term "secondary school" commonly referred to a type of school rather than to a level of education. It was very difficult for a pupil to transfer from the schools for the masses, which trained primarily for entrance into nonprofessional occupations, to the schools for the classes, which prepared primarily for entrance into the universities and, in turn, into the professions. The expenditures for education were relatively much higher at the secondary level than at the elementary. Even as late as the twentieth century, in such laws as the Education Act of 1902, the famous Fisher Act of 1918, and the Education Act of 1936, the benefits went primarily to older pupils. During recent years, however, attention has turned strongly to the lower grades, with a continuing interest, of course, in the improvement of education at all levels. With the passage of the Education Act of 1944, England laid "the framework of a reformed national system of education." It is interesting, and perhaps significant, that England's two greatest educational reforms during the present century, the Fisher Act of 1918 and the Education Act of 1944, were made in the midst of war. The two greatest challenges in our time to freedom and democracy may have shown England that education is basic to the preservation of freedom. At any rate, the Education Act of 1944, with subsequent acts for its implementation, has launched England on a program which will eliminate educational inequalities and will make the schooling in the state schools as good as "money can buy outside the state system." Curriculum adjustments have been made also which represent a break with "traditional classicism" and turn England, with head high into the scientific age. Education adjusted to individual differences and to the needs of society is emphasized. Some of the provisions of the all-important Education Act of 1944, which show its sweeping character, are listed below:[1]

[1] Good references on this topic include: Ministry of Education, *The Nation's Schools: Their Plan and Purpose,* Pamphlet No. 1 (London: His Majesty's Stationery Office, 1945); Ministry of Education, *School and Life,* Report of the Central Advisory Council for Education (England) (London: His Majesty's Stationery Office, 1947); Ministry of Education, *The New Secondary Education,* Pamphlet No. 9 (London: His Majesty's Stationery Office, 1947).

1. Primary education covers the years from two to eleven or twelve. Education is compulsory at age five. Primary education will be cared for in nursery schools, infant schools, and junior schools.

2. Secondary education no longer refers to a type of school, but to a state of education. Secondary schools include secondary grammar schools, secondary technical schools, and secondary modern schools. These are to provide for individual differences among pupils. The secondary modern schools will accommodate the majority of pupils.

3. Secondary education must be made available, without cost to the parent, for every child over eleven.

4. From April 1, 1947, attendance is compulsory to age fifteen; and as soon thereafter as the Minister believes it to be practicable, to age sixteen.

5. Secondary schools must be separate from primary schools. (This breaks down the "class"-"mass" ladders.)

6. Detailed minimum requirements for school buildings, as well as such matters as qualifications of teachers and size of classes, are laid down by the Minister of Education in statutory regulations, which apply equally to the schools provided directly by the local education authorities (*county* schools) and to the *voluntary* schools initially provided by a religious denomination or school foundation— in respect of which the authority pays all the educational costs, including the teachers' salaries, and in some cases is now responsible for improvements.

7. Public money is made available under certain conditions to the voluntary schools to help them to fulfil the Minister's requirements and play their part in the new scheme.

8. Every local education authority is now responsible throughout its own area for the full range of education—primary, secondary, and "further" education. Previously there were some authorities responsible for elementary schools only, the secondary schools in the same area being administered by a different authority.

The recent developments in England represent a nation's determination to upgrade and modernize the education of all its people. Great leadership is being exercised at the national level, and considerable national funds are being made available; but at the same time much responsibility for decision-making and support rests on the local communities. The determination seems not to be one of dictating the content of education, but rather of insisting that appropriate education be available to all. To the accomplishment of this end the national government now devotes more leadership and more financial assistance than ever before.

France.—The French people in modern times have been driven by the emotions of freedom; but because of their location, resources, and numbers, they have won and lost freedom with such regularity that they are extremely cautious and nationalistic. They have been hard put to it to preserve status within the cross-currents of international tugs of war. The nation presents an interesting paradox, therefore, of strong sentiments and sacrifices for freedom on the one hand and an unusually strong centralized government on the other. The French people would not likely tolerate the suppressions of a Hitler or a Stalin; but they are quite willing to support a strong central government that avowedly wants to unite France, build a strong national spirit, and make possible the survival of the nation. Education has come under this strong centralization.

When the Third Republic was set up in France in 1870, a state system of schools including primary, secondary, and higher education was established. This continued until the Vichy government was set up during the second World War. A Minister of National Education, with cabinet rank, was at the top. His ministry was subdivided into six divisions, each of which was presided over by a director responsible to the Minister. These divisions were (*a*) Department of Higher Education, (*b*) Department of Secondary Education, (*c*) Department of Elementary Education, (*d*) Department of Accounts and Personnel, (*e*) General Department of Fine Arts, and (*f*) General Department of Vocational Education. Territorially, France was broken down into sixteen educational regions, or academies. Each of these had a rector who was recommended by the Minister of National Education but actually appointed by the President of the Republic. Each academy had a state university. The rector had two advisory councils and he, with the aid of these councils, exercised almost complete control over the schools in his academy, especially over secondary schools and higher institutions. The central government shared some control of the elementary schools with the local prefects. Here, nominally, teachers were appointed by the prefects, but actually appointments and promotions were controlled by the rectors and their councils. Types of schools in the Third Republic included nursery schools, primary schools, advanced primary schools, lycées and colleges, vocational schools, normal schools, and higher institutions. Great uniformity existed throughout the country in the state schools. In the matter of textbooks, for example, the Minister of National Education prepared lists of approved books from which all schools must select texts. Private schools were allowed to exist, but they were subject to government inspection, and government control of the examination system used for transfers and admissions among the schools meant that the curriculum of the private schools was shaped by government policy. The sixteen state higher institutions in the academies were, of course, financed by the state and "systematically regulated."

During the Vichy regime the elementary schools were brought more completely under governmental control. Elementary teachers, who had been chosen by the prefects and approved by the rectors, were now appointed directly by the Minister of National Education. Changes in the training of these teachers in the normal schools also brought them under greater central control. A new emphasis on religious education appeared, and the church gained added influence over public education. This, however, fell off again after the war. The German influence on French education was reflected in the increase in technical studies and in the introduction of anti-Semitic studies and activities.

With the restoration of France and the reconstitution of the Republic, the prewar pattern of education was essentially restored. France certainly did not launch herself upon educational reforms as did England. Certain tendencies toward a breakdown of some of the curriculum rigidities of the past, the separation of church and state, and the adjustment of education to individual and social needs are in evidence, but strong centralization remains and too many inequalities in educational opportunities still exist. Postwar cross-currents of democracy, fascism, and communism have delayed the establishment of a stabilized central government which could give its attention to long-term matters. Perhaps as such a government evolves we may see evolving with it a pattern of education geared directly to the freedoms that France herself fought so earnestly to establish in the Western world.

Sweden and Denmark.—Let us be content here to mention only one general characteristic of education in Sweden and Denmark, which has been influential far beyond the borders of those countries. This has to do with the manner in which these countries have broken with tradition so far as time and content of education are concerned. Education is planned to meet the needs of the people rather than to perpetuate a tradition. Consequently, the schools are always accessible to the people of the community. The farmer, the skilled laborer, or the housewife are served by the community school as certainly and as directly as the child who is of compulsory attendance age. Great emphasis is placed on cooperatives and effective participation in them.

Much of the vocational, technical, continuation type of schooling is in effect. Furthermore, the people of the communities seem to have developed the habit of using these "people's schools." There is no hesitation. Many activities of a social and cultural nature are also centered in them. These countries have given a clear demonstration that education, if it takes its cue from the needs and interests of the people, can become a rewarding, lifelong experience.

Russia.—The story of Russian education is one of the most interesting, and in some ways the most magnificent, of all time. Backwardness and near-barbarism survived in Russia long after the advent of modern nations in Western Europe. As late as the establishment of our American democracy following the Revolutionary War, Catherine II, a benevolent despot in Russia, was trying to do something to dispel some of the darkness of illiteracy and subservience that engulfed the people. During most of the eighteenth century, she and Peter the Great before her, both despotic in their power, strove to swing a great people into line with Western learning and progress. Their efforts were in good part nullified by an antiquated land system and by the domination of the Eastern Greek Church, which was more interested in seeing the people subservient and obedient than learned and free. Such education as existed prior to the Revolution of 1917 was not for the masses. About 80 per cent of the Russians are reported to have been illiterate at the time of the Revolution. Educational opportunities had been restricted to certain classes who could afford the costs and were willing to accept the restricted, largely church-controlled curriculum. Early in the twentieth century, Russia seemed suddenly to realize that she was behind in a race for which she had admirable resources; and she was in an urgent hurry to catch up. She sought to assemble the skills of all nations for a rapid development of her human and natural resources, with which she was bountifully supplied.

The Revolution of 1917 threw off the yoke of czarism, feudalism, and churchism; and Russia launched another great experiment in the earth. The Communist doctrine became the doctrine of a sovereign state. The day of the proletariat had come. But he and his millions of laboring brethren were ignorant and subdued. How could they function as intended in a Communist state? They could not. Hence the "temporary" dictatorships and terrible disciplines in Russia while the people, presumably, are being prepared to manage the Communist state in some way not yet made clear. Since the Revolution was a "mass" revolution, the education of the masses loomed large under the new regime. Many laws have been passed concerning the establishment and support of schools, and their content, conduct, and personnel. Miracles have been performed in changing a predominantly illiterate population into a predominantly literate one in one generation. The types of schools are very close to the usual pattern in other nations—nursery schools, kindergartens, elementary schools, junior secondary schools, senior secondary schools, and higher institutions. All schools are state schools; private schools are prohibited. Compulsory attendance extends only through the elementary school, but pupils are encouraged and often helped to go on through the secondary schools and higher institutions. Education is free through the junior secondary school. In all schools and on all levels, education is political in purpose. In order to fulfil this purpose the central government supports the schools, determines the curriculum, supplies the textbooks, controls the teachers, and promotes youth organizations and activities to supplement the work of the schools. Before 1943, boys and girls attended all schools together; in that year, however, boys and girls were segregated in the secondary schools. The argument was given that through segregation education could be conducted better to prepare boys and girls for their proper functions in society. This seemed to counter somewhat the former concept of equality between the sexes. In fact, numerous writers point out that in recent years education has tended to become more conservative and restricted. The teacher enjoys high status in Russia. Those who are outstanding in their work and are especially effective in generating enthusiasm for the Communist state are given special governmental recognition. The school, in short, is the state's primary means of propagandizing itself favorably with the young, and propagandizing the non-Communist world unfavorably. The state will succeed in this mission so long as an educated Russian people are shielded from the free exchange of thought, discovery, and inquiry on an international basis. If, however, the agencies of international communication and education pierce the shield, an enlightened Russian people will surely require for themselves the status that enlightened people are entitled to.

It is not necessary here to discuss the Russian satellite states as examples of the subservience of the school to the Communist doctrine. The story of what has happened in satellite countries concerning such matters as school and university control, purging of school personnel, destruction of library books, curriculum revision, and control of textbooks is known to all. Again, the regime seems determined to divert whole peoples from the broad path of how to think to the narrow channels of what to think. In man's long climb out of darkness, this flash from the East is not likely by these tactics to extinguish the steady light of the West. Communism, with its present tactics, has come too late to command the loyalties of people who know what freedom in democracies means; the story may be different with other peoples who have not yet experienced those freedoms.

China.—Education in China for several thousand years reflected a philosophy of life that minimized material advantages and emphasized inner peace through the stoic acceptance of things as they were. Such formal education as existed was limited to a very small minority of the people, the vast majority being illiterate. The absence of a desire to improve conditions through education, the disorganized character of the vast country, the many dialects, and the inaccessibility of great rural areas because of poor transportation facilities prevented any real educational improvements. Furthermore, the responsibility for education rested mainly on the family; and for hundreds of years families had neither the interest nor the means to do more than perpetuate the status quo. During the nineteenth century China began to establish trade relations with the West. Not only goods but ideas entered her ports. The early twentieth century witnessed also the departure of a goodly number of Chinese students for study in other countries. As these educated people returned and assumed responsibilities in China, the vast people began to think in new terms about the status of the nation and the education of the people. Educational leaders in other countries were brought to China to give counsel concerning the establishment of a school system to serve all the people. With the establishment of the Chinese Republic in 1912, therefore, plans were laid not only for a new political framework but for a new educational system as well. The American school system became the principal pattern. Part VII, Articles 131–138, of the Constitution of the Republic, dealing exclusively with education, contained the following provisions:

Article 131.—The educational aim of the Republic of China shall be to develop a national spirit, to cultivate a national morality, to train the people for self-government and to increase their ability to earn a livelihood, and thereby to build up a sound and healthy body of citizens.

Article 132.—Every citizen of the Republic of China shall have an equal opportunity to receive education.

Article 133.—All public and private educational institutions in the country shall be subject to State supervision and amenable to the duty of carrying out the educational policies formulated by the State.

Article 134.—Children between six and twelve years old are of school age and shall receive elementary education free of tuition.

Article 135.—All persons over school age who have not received an elementary education shall receive supplementary education free of tuition.

Article 136.—In establishing universities and technical schools the State shall give special consideration to the needs of the respective localities so as to afford the people thereof an equal opportunity to receive higher education, thereby hastening a balanced national cultural development.

Article 137.—Educational appropriations shall constitute no less than fifteen per cent of the total amount of the budget of the Central Government and no less than thirty per cent of the total amount of the provincial, district, and municipal budgets respectively.

Educational endowment funds independently set aside in accordance with law shall be safeguarded.

Educational expenditures in needy provinces shall be subsidized by the central treasury.

Article 138.—The State shall encourage or subsidize the following persons or enterprises:

1. Educational enterprises established by private persons within the State, with a high record of achievement.
2. Educational enterprises for Chinese citizens residing abroad.
3. Those who have made academic or technical inventions and discoveries.
4. Teachers who have good records and long service.
5. Students who achieve high scholastic attainments and show good conduct but are unable to receive further education.[2]

After the adoption of this constitution, China started a systematic drive to fulfil the provisions concerning education; but the goals concerning such things as mass education, adequate school financing, supplementary education for illiterate adults, the development of higher education, and national subsidization of worthy persons and enterprises, although nobly conceived, fell far short of realization. Up until 1937, when the war with Japan broke out, progress had been satisfactory. In 1935, a compulsory education law, aimed at the elimination of illiteracy and applied to both children and illiterate adults, was put into operation. Although this effort, along with others in the field of education, was greatly set back by the Japanese war, the

[2] U. S. Office of Education, *Education in China Today,* Leaflet No. 69 (Washington, D.C.: Government Printing Office, 1944).

Chinese people held on tenaciously during the war to their educational ambitions. The war, however, was most disrupting and exhausting. The migration inland of whole institutions with their faculties and student bodies and their families, the terrible economic inflation, the oppressions of the invader, and the infiltration of various ideologies are well known. The national government, conceived at first along democratic lines, exercised, of necessity, great centralized powers.

By the close of the war in 1945, this centralized control seemed to have become a habit, and the Nationalist government under Chiang Kai-shek resisted coalition movements which might have united the people. Education was not neglected, but it was controlled and censored beyond all previous intention. Private schools were allowed, but their teachers had to be trained in government-controlled higher institutions. In fact, all higher education was under the national government. Vocational education was strengthened. Although the government subsidized Chinese students studying abroad, it hoped to withdraw such aid and make China self-sufficient through the development of excellent universities with research and graduate programs. The progress of Communist arms into China from the north changed the entire picture. The future is now a great question. Many Chinese, including many students, experiencing a decline in economic and political security under the Nationalist government, have accepted Chinese communism. If there could be such a thing as a continuing "Chinese communism," the result might not be disastrous. If, however, Chinese communism is a front for Russian communism, the result will be a distortion of freedoms such as that experienced in other satellite countries. The school will become one of the chief agencies of propaganda and thought control. On the other hand, it may be that the centuries-old habits of the Chinese people to pursue a family, small-community life and to find their peace in intellectual and spiritual independence will not bend easily to the Communist dominations. The future history of all mankind will doubtless be greatly affected by the turn of the tide in China.

India.—India, like China, has had a long, nonprogressive history. For centuries she lay dormant, swarming with people who were satisfied with the barest existence, and who endured with amazing silence the ravages of famine, disease, and economic destitution. For a good while she proved commercially profitable to Great Britain. Her contacts with the Western world, as in China, produced a slow awakening; and in time, they were to result in demands for national status. These demands were granted by England in 1947, when India became an independent nation. Achieving national solidarity among a people 85 per cent illiterate is a task which concerns the new nation greatly.

India, which has taken its place in the comity of free nations of the world, has to march forward in every field of her national life with alacrity, but you will agree that none of these fields is as important as the educational field. At present, the percentage of literacy in India is only 14.7, that is, out of every 100 nearly 85 persons are totally illiterate. . . . If we are unable to make arrangements for the primary education of about 30 million of our children, all our nation building schemes will, *ipso facto,* become valueless. The only way out, therefore, is to try and lift millions of these children from the depths of neglect and ignorance immediately.[3]

Minister Azad also detailed the following six items which should receive immediate attention in India:

1. Establishment of a National Museum where Indian philosophy, literature, and art may be preserved
2. Provision for fundamental research work, government-subsidized, not only in the sciences but also in the humanities
3. The preparation of a Guide for Teachers for the new scheme of education; "While the Central Government do not wish to impose uniformity, but to leave the greatest possible margin of freedom to the Provinces, there should be some indication of the general lines on which this education is to be imparted.

   "The question of preparing some kind of a generalized curriculum may also be considered. Any fixed curriculum has the tendency of imposing rigid uniformity and, therefore, the preparation of this curriculum should be undertaken with the greatest possible care."
4. Grants to educational experimental institutions "without waiting for the time when the results of such experiments have been verified . . . the Government should come to the help of the institution at the initial stages so that lack of funds may not hinder the institutions from carrying out their experiment."
5. The development of archeological studies in India
6. The promotion of mass education, using all available means, including radio and the film

India stresses the importance of "the development of a national mind." For many years loyalty to England was emphasized; loyalty to India must now be substituted. Group and class divisions within

[3] Statement by Maulana Abul Kalam Azad, Minister for Education, Government of India, quoted in *India Information,* XXII, 101.

the country must also be eliminated. The main hope for achieving this is mass education. Prior to independence a small, educated "intelligentsia" held themselves very much aloof from the masses. The masses need education in their own languages, which are numerous throughout the country. The status of missionaries and their schools is now a lively problem. The attitude of the new government to date has been one of gratitude for what they have done, and its future policy is not likely to be one of abruptness or harshness.

The lack of trained teachers is perhaps the most serious problem of all. Much attention has therefore been focused on the establishment of new institutes for teacher education. The emphasis on technical education reflects India's desire to develop herself industrially. However, if the Gandhian philosophy prevails, this industrialization will be subservient to the social welfare of the many, and will not become the means to great wealth for the few. The Indian temperament calls for religious instruction, but, so far as education is concerned, the new government is more interested in having it placed on a broad base in the public schools than narrowly sectarianized in private schools. Religious education should lead all groups to harmonious living through the establishment of accepted principles for all. India still looks to other nations for much help in education. She plainly admits that her educational, industrial, and technical future will be determined largely by what her scholars studying abroad bring back home. The government considers the scholarships granted for foreign study as "sacred trusts" to the students receiving them. One of the very noticeable emphases in the educational plans of India is that on research and experimentation. C. Rajagopalachari, Minister for Education before Azad, put it this way:

I hope the Government of India and the Universities will give a charter for experiments to all responsible earnest men and women in the field of education. That is the only way, by trial and error and actual experiment, that this great task of education can be achieved in our country. The method of imposing one uniform method from above and refusing to encourage any variation will not do hereafter and our requirements will not be in that manner.[4]

For guidance along lines of educational research and planning, the government has set up a Central Advisory Board of Education. This body to date has been extremely influential. Its recommendations, usually in published form, carry great weight, albeit the board is carefully constituted as advisory. In short, the pattern and spirit of edu-

[4] Statement by C. Rajagopalachari, former Minister for Education, Government of India, quoted in *Indian Information*, XX, 94.

cation in India seems to be more democratic than in China. India has spoken out clearly on several fronts against centralization in the national government. The government wishes to help, but it exercises leadership without domination. Great stress is placed on research and experimentation; and this spirit of inquiry is attested to in the number of students studying abroad. The spirit and example of Gandhi, which sought the elimination of classism in India and the extension of opportunities to all, have carried the desire for unity and coalition to the point where national stability seems likely. To date, resistance to Communism has been certain and intelligent. If China should become Communist-dominated, the importance and difficulties of an Indian democracy can be realized. Thus the peoples of the ancient East have with startling suddenness taken their places in a one-world arena where the issue of domination and acceptance versus freedom and moral challenge—for the whole world—must be resolved.

South American Countries and Mexico.—Prior to the nineteenth century the South American countries were colonies much as our American colonies were. Spain was the mother country to most of them, although Brazil was a Portuguese colony. The educational patterns from the mother countries predominated. Schooling was routine memorization, the classics were emphasized, the dogma of the Roman Catholic Church received much attention, and discipline was harsh. The education of the masses was neglected. Protestant influences were, of course, weak. Illiteracy was high. Early in the nineteenth century these countries acted on a smoldering desire for reform, freedom, and the opportunity to receive an education. They were greatly encouraged by the success of the American colonies against England. Their revolutions were successful; but they immediately found themselves faced with problems which are still unsolved. A system of schools for the education of the masses had to be established. The position of the church with reference to education had to be resolved. The raising of money to support the schools was a difficult problem. The training of teachers and the securing of adequate school supervision were also serious problems. However, by the enactment of fundamental school laws, mainly since 1900, these countries have made significant inroads on illiteracy and have evolved systems of schools ranging from preschool levels through the university. On the whole, the central governments have retained extensive powers for the determination of educational policies, the building of the curriculum, the development of supervision, and finance. The control of the church over education has been reduced. More recently, significant advances have been made in technical, agricultural, and general education. However, the education of the masses is still at a low level; and limitations such as the multiplicity of dialects, difficulties of transportation, low economic ability of the people, and general apathy do not bode too well for rapid improvements. At present in South America the pattern of domination by the central government prevails. Some responsibility is shared with the local units, particularly as concerns support, but for the most part the decisions are made at the national capital and spread throughout the country. It remains to be seen whether or not these countries, as mass education develops, will delegate to the people more and more control over their local institutions, including the school.

Mexico's educational development has followed more closely the pattern of the South American countries than that of the United States. In recent years, however, Mexico has outstripped most of her neighbors to the south in the vigor with which she has gone about the task of upgrading her people. Extensive land and educational reforms have been instituted since about 1911. The illiteracy of approximately three-quarters of her people has concerned the Republic; and thousands of schools, primarily in rural districts, have been set up by the central government. These schools teach more than reading and writing; they are central agencies in the communities for the improvement of agriculture, health, and home conditions as well. The commanding influence which the Roman Catholic Church exerted over education in Mexico was ended by the central government in its new constitution of 1917. All private schools were brought under the supervision of the government. The government made certain large companies responsible for the education of the children of their employees, but this education must bear government inspection and supervision. In the fight against illiteracy, the school was not to carry the whole load. By government decree, every person who could read was enjoined to teach another who could not. The result has been outstanding. Mexico, in brief, under the leadership of a "Socialist" government, has implemented educational reforms with striking success. Her methods and the content of her education have broken with tradition. She now scrutinizes American education carefully and adopts practices suited to her purposes, instead of withdrawing and resisting American influence as before. At the present rate, if the disposition to explore possibilities and adopt good practices continues, she will doubtlessly make advances that this country might well emulate. The present move in the direction of making rural education serve rural people in a broad manner is a case in point. Mexico, along with many other nations which now support the democratic principle, will have to solve the problem of centralized versus local control when her people have become interested in and educated for the direction of their community affairs.

Canada.—Although education in the older provinces in Canada was patterned at first after practices in France and England, it early came under the influence of American practices, particularly those in New England. The idea that education is the responsibility of the state soon began to supplant the old-country idea of church-family responsibility. At about 1850 the trend toward state responsibility became dominant; and the Dominion Act of 1867 placed the control of education in the provinces, much as the states in the United States exercise like control. Under provincial control, public education has developed steadily. Democratic, mass education, in which the social or economic position of the family does not determine the educational opportunity of the children, has been the goal. Canada definitely outstripped the mother country, England, in eliminating a "dual system" that maintained separate educational ladders for the classes and the masses. At present the elementary and secondary schools are predominantly public schools. In 1947, in all the Canadian provinces with the exception of Quebec, there were approximately 40,000 pupils enrolled in private elementary and secondary schools. This was about 2 per cent of the enrolment in public elementary and secondary schools in the same provinces. Quebec has more private elementary and secondary schools than the other eight provinces combined, but their enrolment does not substantially change the ratio of private school pupils to public school pupils throughout the Dominion. At the college level the situation is different. There are many private colleges and universities in Canada. During recent years steady growth in public higher institutions has been made, but this growth has not kept pace with the development of public higher education in the United States. In recent years there has been a great deal of administrative consolidation among higher institutions. Also, the classical, academic tradition has given way sufficiently to permit the introduction into the colleges of a great deal of vocational, technical, and professional work. Professional education, for example, is even now securing its first firm hold in higher institutions. At the secondary level the same shifts are in process. A great deal of vocational-technical training is now available; but, even so, a much higher percentage of secondary school pupils in Canada enroll in the classical subjects than is true in the United States. Clearly, however, there has been in Canada for a long time a movement to change elementary and secondary schools "better to serve their communities." Some practices of long standing with strong traditional attachments, such as the emphasis on academic subjects and the great dependence on the examination system, have given way more slowly than in the United States; but changes are continuous, and the careful nature of the Canadian has made these changes defensible.

Canada, like all other countries, has troublesome school problems. For example, the status of rural education is relatively bad. The tenure of rural teachers is conspicuously low compared to that of urban teachers. Other factors related to effective learning are seriously absent in the rural schools. This situation is not different from that found in the United States. Teachers' salaries in Canada are low also. In this connection, in several of the provinces, and especially in the cities, the average salary of men teachers is frequently $1,000 more than that of women teachers. Finally, Canada has permitted a great deal more of church influence in the schools than is true in the United States. This applies to public schools as well as private.

Withal, however, the school systems of Canada and the United States are greatly alike. The principle of decentralization of control is operative in both countries; equalized educational opportunity is emphasized; adjustments to bring education in line with the needs of the times is sought; and emphasis on education for independent thinking and responsible action is present throughout. The existence of many common conditions and problems and of goals common to both countries has resulted in more cooperative action than is found between the United States and any other country. The border is no barrier when mutual problems require mutual conferences, studies, and exchange of opinion.

General Observations.—A few items stand out in the above discussions of education in selected countries. The same items would be noted if additional countries were included. There is a great movement throughout the earth to eliminate illiteracy and extend education to the masses. This applies not only to countries like China, India, Mexico, and Russia; even in England great strides are being made to go further in the direction of equalizing among all classes the opportunity to receive a good education. There is a widespread development in technical and vocational education. This is a natural accompaniment to the desire of the nations to develop their economies, become more and more self-sufficient, and have something to sell abroad. The traditional, classical, memoriter type of studies are giving way on a wide front and are having to make room for studies that deal directly with the welfare and development of the nations. In all countries the training of qualified teachers in sufficient numbers is a crucial problem. The extent to which teacher education, and all higher education, is under the control of the central government is noteworthy. Financial support is, of course, a universal problem. Religious bodies are in general exerting less control over education, mass education being achieved outside the churches. Forever present to determine the fortunes of freedom in the future is the relationship of the central government to the policies, program, and personnel of the school. In some countries centralized control over such matters is complete and rigid; in others there is much delegation of responsibility for decision-making to the local units. It is worth pointing out here that mass education and excessive centralized control are not compatible. The nations that now promote mass education and at the same time, as a matter of government policy, distort facts and deny freedom are likely placing too much faith in their ability successfully to propagandize their people and shield them from outside influences. The trend of human history since the Crusades is not likely suddenly to be reversed.

6. Re-education in Germany and Japan

Prior to the second World War, the governments of Germany and Japan were, of course, highly centralized. The schools served completely the will of the government. In the war these governments were overthrown and the countries were occupied by the victorious powers. Immediately there arose a multitude of problems associated with the rebuilding and redirection of the occupied countries, not the least of which was the problem of re-education. The ambitions, methods, and narrow nationalism which characterized these countries prior to the war had to be uprooted and new concepts, motives, and procedures substituted. Education, differently organized and to new purposes, had to be developed. It will be helpful briefly to note educational conditions in Germany and Japan before the war, and then to indicate certain postwar developments.

Education in Prewar Germany.—Germany led the way among modern nations in making education serve the interests of unity and development among the people. At first this was quite liberal in character, but the Prussian concept of state domination soon turned education to authoritarian ends. State controls radiated throughout the school system. The school was the chief agency of the German "culture." Pride, loyalty, and faith in military power were intense. After about 1850 individual freedoms were seriously curtailed; discipline and obedience were stressed; state regulations established uniform patterns of education; individual initiative was discouraged; formalism prevailed; and the freedom of teachers was curtailed in all schools. Out of all this there evolved a hard, unified, highly nationalistic German state, convinced of its own superiority and confident beyond reason in its arms. The first World War changed all this. German arms were beaten. Confidence in the military was shaken. German superiority was challenged. In fact, the idea of equality, democracy, and international good will took vigorous root in Germany. The Weimar Republic was the result. This flash of democratic spirit was genuine. It appealed especially to German youth; and it might have succeeded if the arrangements for peace had been more wisely conceived and managed. Events again happened swiftly. While the tired, neglectful victors assumed that the world was now "safe for democracy," new leadership was active in Germany, rallying the people around the old concepts of glory, superiority, and power. The story of the rise of Hitler's dictatorship is known. Again education, drastically purged, became a subservient arm of the central government. The schools devoted themselves to the concepts, methods, and propaganda of naziism. The country had a well-organized school system that functioned effectively. Elementary education was public and free. Secondary and higher education were optional and were, in general, limited to the upper classes. Enrolments in secondary schools and higher institutions were purposefully limited. Too many trained, thinking leaders are not desired in a dictatorship. Much emphasis was placed on physical education and technical education for the masses. Many youth organizations under state direction were also formed. The "party line" was all important. The training of party leaders was carefully attended to. When the people had again been psychologically conditioned for conflict, and when the materials of war had been sufficiently stockpiled, Hitler produced the incidents that ignited the second World War.

Education in Prewar Japan.—Japan entered the modern phase of her national development about 1850. This paralleled the development of her world trade relations. A latent country promptly responded to the stimulus of these contacts with marked ambition, pride, and determination. In 1871 a Department of Education was organized within the government "for the control of the educational affairs of the whole country." In 1872 a Code of Education was promulgated, modeled on the French system, which set up the ladder of elementary, secondary, and higher schools. In 1890 an Imperial Rescript on Education was issued, which established, "once and for all," the educational policy of the country. The closing paragraph of this rescript contains the following sentence: "The Way here set forth is indeed the teaching bequeathed by Our Imperial Ancestors, to be observed alike by Their Descendants and the subjects, infallible for all ages and true in all places." Plainly, education was controlled by the state. "The main principles regarding the nature and objects of schools, their scholastic terms, curricula, organizations, entrance qualifications, qualifications for teachers, equipment, means of meeting the expenditure, tuition fees, etc. are prescribed by Imperial Ordinances."[5]

There was some delegation of responsibility to local administrations, but it was more for the purpose of carrying out central decisions than of originating policy at the local level. The government controlled textbooks and the certification of teachers. Youth Schools for Social Education were established in 1935. These occupied the spare time of youth beyond the elementary school and were a kind of continuation school for technical and "cultural" learning. The government was greatly concerned about the thought life of the people, as well as their health and physical fitness. As in Germany, the schools served directly the purposes of the state; and they were highly instrumental in creating the national spirit which launched Japan on a series of aggressions. Her successes in China were the prologue to her spectacular entrance into the second World War.

Re-education in Germany.—When Germany was defeated in the second World War, her people emerged from dictatorial controls under a National Socialist state to controls exercised by the occupying powers of England, France, Russia, and the United States. These new controls varied greatly in character. We shall confine ourselves here to the re-education policies of the United States.

The democratic ideals of the United States made it inevitable that drastic changes in the policies, controls, objectives, and content of education in Germany would be made. As opposed to the old patterns of domination-submission, restricted learning, and emotionalized indoctrination came decentralization, freedom of thought, and the development of individual responsibility for the common good. Many

[5] Department of Education (Japan), *A General Survey of Education in Japan* (Tokyo: The Department, 1937).

controls had to be exercised at the start, denazification was attempted, but the ultimate goal was intelligent, free, self-direction. This country was urgently desirous of proceeding wisely. A careful study of the over-all problems, and a well worked-out plan of action were required. The best judgment of many people was sought. In line with this, in 1946, a United States Education Mission was sent to Germany to study the situation, cooperate with occupation authorities and German leaders, and prepare a report, with recommendations. The report [6] of the mission provided the foundation for the subsequent approach to problems and for action. In the October, 1947, issue of *School Life,* Bess Goodykoontz summarized the principal recommendations of the mission.[7] These recommendations, condensed, are as follows:

1. Keep all children together for six years in the elementary school, not divided according to sex, social class, race, or vocational or professional intentions.
2. Unify secondary schools and make them tuition-free, providing for vocational and professional differentiation within the schools, rather than by establishing separate schools.
3. Center the curriculum on pupil needs, make it a democratic experience, and break down rigid academic tradition.
4. Change the content and form of the social science curriculum, making it contribute more to democratic citizenship.
5. Provide for democratic *living* in school through cooperative class projects, classroom committees, discussion groups, school councils, student clubs, community service projects, etc.
6. Revise vocational education to promote effective citizenship as well as technical skill. Additional time will be needed in this program for social studies and cultural subjects.
7. Avoid stereotyping the curriculum through the preparation of textbooks.
8. Encourage the re-establishment of teachers' organizations for the study of problems and the upgrading of the profession.
9. Establish and properly staff guidance services for all students.
10. Provide good educational-recreational programs for preschool and school-age children, as part of the regular school services.
11. Improve teacher education and elevate the status of the elementary teacher in relation to the secondary school teacher.

[6] U. S. Department of State, *Report of the United States Education Mission to Germany,* U. S. A. Publication No. 2664, European Series No. 16 (Washington, D. C., U. S. Government Printing Office, 1946).
[7] Bess Goodykoontz, "United States Education Mission Report," *School Life,* XXX. 10–13.

12. Develop programs of research and experimentation in the universities for the improvement of both elementary and secondary education.

13. Promote demonstration schools in which democratic education is practiced and where preservice and in-service German teachers can observe.

14. Encourage and subsidize the exchange of teachers and students with the United States.

15. Strengthen general education in the universities and introduce extraclass activities that will give practical experience in the processes of democracy.

16. Secure responsible advisory bodies of representative citizens to advise faculties of universities in making their curricula more responsive to changing conditions and needs.

The spirit and proposed action of the above recommendations are reflected in the principles furnished by our military government in January, 1947, to local school authorities as guides for the formulation of their educational objectives and plans. These principles became the essence of a directive issued in June, 1947, entitled *Basic Principles for the Democratization of Education in Germany.* The principles are as follows:

Equal educational opportunity for all; free tuition in all public schools; free textbooks and materials and school maintenance grants for those in need of aid; compulsory school attendance for all from six to fifteen years; compulsory part-time education from fifteen to eighteen years; elementary and secondary to mean two consecutive levels, not two different types or qualities of instruction; schools to lay emphasis upon education for civic responsibility and a democratic way of life through both curriculum and school organization; promotion of international good will and understanding through curricula; provision for professional education and vocational guidance; provision in all schools for health supervision and health education; teacher education to be on a university level; safeguarding of educational standards, where the constitution permits establishment of interdenominational and denominational schools side by side; a democratic school administration sensitive to the wishes of the people.[8]

Our military government, above all, is not trying to establish and administer an inflexible educational pattern. Continuous help is sought. Specialists in various areas such as testing, school administration, curriculum, and teacher education are brought from the United States to serve as consultants to occupation forces and to

[8] *Education and Religion,* Report of the Military Governor, U. S. Zone, Military Government of Germany, May 1, 1946–April 30, 1947, No. 22.

German leaders. Progress is positive but slow. The curriculum is still too traditional and academic. School plants and equipment suffered heavy damage from the war. Only about 15 per cent of pupils enter the secondary school and about 5 per cent graduate. Habits of conformity under the prewar regime lead to considerable uncertainty and bungling now. The teachers are mainly older persons without the know-how or inclination enthusiastically to redirect education along democratic lines. American authorities report that "teacher education remains the most significant problem in the reorganization of German education." The cross-currents of influence and propaganda resulting from the four-power occupation prevent stability and concerted, long-time planning. Withal, however, the German response to the freedoms and responsibilities which the American type of education emphasizes is encouraging.

Re-education in Japan.—The national ambitions and the school system in Japan before the war were in many regards similar to those in Germany. There were a strong national spirit, highly centralized governmental controls, and a program of education that produced citizens who did humble obeisance to those in power. The person and ancestors of the Emperor were held in great reverence. Authority was accepted. It would be a long step from all this to equality of opportunity, independent thinking, and responsible action for all. Japan, in defeat, presented an occupational problem quite different from that of Germany. The psychology of the people seemed to be different; their acceptance of the occupying authority was complete; and they seemed open to follow the lead of the United States. Furthermore, only one occupying nation was in control. This, of course, made possible a unity and continuity of action which was lacking in Germany.

During the same year, 1946, that a United States Education Mission was dispatched to Germany, one was dispatched to Japan also. The Japanese mission spent several weeks in Japan and produced a report,[9] with recommendations, that set forth approaches to educational reform. The report concentrated on six areas, namely, (a) the aims and content of Japanese education, (b) language reform, (c) administration of education at the primary and secondary levels, (d) teaching and the education of teachers, (e) adult education, and (f) higher education. Brief summaries of the Mission's findings under these headings follow:

[9] U. S. Department of State, *Report of the United States Education Mission to Japan*, U. S. A. Publication No. 2579, Far Eastern Series No. 11 (Washington, D. C.: U. S. Government Printing Office (1946).

Aims and Content of Japanese Education. Decentralization of the educational system, to eliminate regimentation and to develop freedom and resourcefulness among teachers, is necessary. The curriculum should be broadened and set up with the aid of teachers. Attitudes and motives basic to democratic living should be developed and practiced in the program and activities of the school. Textbooks more objectively written and making greater use of current materials will have to be written. Research in higher institutions is emphasized. Health instruction, physical education, and vocational education are stressed.

Language Reform. A drastic reform of the written language is recommended. An inordinate amount of the time of pupils is consumed in learning the characters. The written language now constitutes a serious barrier to children, and denies to them the learning in many other fields that they ought to have. Some form of Romaji is recommended. A commission composed of Japanese scholars, educational leaders, and statesmen, to initiate, direct, and coordinate the program of language reform is also recommended.

Administration of Education at the Primary and Secondary Levels. "Control of the schools should be widely dispersed rather than highly centralized." The Ministry of Education, formerly all-powerful, should provide technical aid and professional counsel, but its direct control over local schools should be greatly curtailed. Educational boards at the local and prefectural levels, elected by popular vote, are recommended. They would approve schools, license teachers, and select textbooks. Compulsory, tax-supported, coeducational, tuition-free education to cover nine years of schooling is proposed. The 6-3-3 plan of school organization is recommended. Private schools should not be disturbed, but minimum standards should be maintained so that transferring students would not be penalized.

Teaching and the Education of Teachers. "Teaching methods emphasizing memorization, conformity, and a vertical system of duties and loyalties should be modified to encourage independent thinking, the development of personality, and the rights and responsibilities of democratic citizenship." Normal school education will have to be modified, and in-service programs for the re-education of teachers developed. The period of teacher education should be extended to four years, providing for both general education and professional education. Programs of advanced and graduate studies for teachers and administrators should be developed.

Adult Education. Adult education can be fostered "through parent-teacher activities, evening and extension classes for adults, and the opening of buildings to a variety of community activities." Central public libraries with branches are recommended. Forums and discussions should be fostered in community organizations such as professional societies, labor unions, and political groups.

Higher Education. Higher institutions should pioneer in free thought and inquiry, and should extend their opportunities to the many. General education should be strengthened. Government control should be practically nonexistent. Economic and academic freedom for faculties is stressed.

Financial aid should be extended to promising students. Women should enjoy the same opportunities as men. The improvement of education in the professions is recommended. Research and library facilities should be extended.

A report in August, 1948, from the General Headquarters of the Supreme Commander for the Allied Powers in Japan indicates numerous actions that have been taken to implement various aspects of the Mission's report. For example, the Education Law of 1947 called for course of study revisions from authoritarian procedures to modern participatory procedures, based on the interests and abilities of pupils and the needs of society. Also, the Board of Education Act of 1948 provided for the establishment of boards of education in all prefectures and in six cities by November, 1948, and in all other communities by November, 1950. These boards will assume functions previously carried out by the national government. The 6-3-3-4 plan of organization is in operation, and compulsory education to include the ninth year went into effect in 1949. The process of decentralization of educational administration, of educating all for responsible self-direction, and of relating education more closely to the problems of daily life goes on at a gratifying rate. All this is a far cry from policies and practices before the war.

The Problem of Leadership Toward New Goals.—It is apparent that in both Germany and Japan, where postwar policies differ so greatly from prewar policies, a period of compulsion will have to transpire. If reversions are to be prevented, old practices and attitudes will have to be uprooted and others substituted. Effective leadership toward the new goals is sorely needed. In this connection it is extremely significant that the American policy has been one of seeking to evolve this leadership among the native peoples. Temporary administrators have had to be used, but their job is more specifically to train native administrators than to perpetuate themselves in authority. Certainly our government does not believe that American dispensers of a kind of "packaged democracy" can be effective in Germany and Japan. Local leaders, developed through patient and sincere helpfulness, must evolve. American controls and guidance may have to continue until a generation of children trained in the democratic atmosphere of the new schools becomes adults and takes over leadership positions. This is the sure way; and it is also the lasting way if the new leaders have been challenged to think things through for themselves rather than to accept new practices without question.

The Problem of Youth Familiar Only with the Circumscribed Education of the Regimes.—The fears that were so sharp at the close of the war concerning what youth, fanatical in their loyalty to their defeated leaders, might do, seem to have diminished. It is quite true that youth who have known no other gospel than the gospel of the dictator and have been fanned to a fury by emotionalized propaganda are at sorry ends when their cause is lost. Let no one suppose that the immediate result of a disastrous defeat is a heart-felt and sudden adoption of the victor's modes of thinking and acting. However, these same youth have youth's advantages: the time and resilience necessary to adjustment. If they encounter patience and sincerity among those now in control, and especially if they are urged to think long and hard on the great problems of human progress, they can hardly remain in their adulthood the circumscribed individuals they would have been under the old dominations. Some, perhaps a goodly number, will never give up the old fire and ambition. It is important, therefore, that they do not come into positions of educational responsibility. Vigilance will have to be maintained until this generation is gone. But vigilance need not be oppression or domination. While time slowly eradicates the biases born of direct experience with dictatorships, it must also build in the minds and hearts of new generations, through direct experience with democratic practices, the understandings and motives that promote peace and good will. The potential of the school in this connection is inestimable. It will be a sorry day for our world if that potential is not used to the full.

The Relationship of Education to Other Factors.—Satisfactory progress in the re-education of Germany and Japan cannot be expected if other factors are unsatisfactory. What we say and teach about democracy in the new education must be demonstrated in our other relationships. What we say about a genuine regard for the other fellow, helpfulness, concern for the common good, and opportunity to think and act constructively must be borne out in our efforts to secure economic stability, decent housing, clothes, seeds, machinery, and the granting of freedom as rapidly as it results surely in the development of responsible self-direction. Education, therefore, is only a part of a vast project in the redirection of human relations; a project which seeks to play the game in a different manner. Education is important, but it is not single; it can contribute much, but it cannot succeed alone.

7. UNESCO [10]

In looking back upon the arrangements for international cooperation and peace following the first World War, many people feel that
too much confidence was placed in top-level organization and diplomacy and that not enough attention was given to the development of
international understanding and good will among the vast peoples of
the earth. Following the second World War there was an articulate
demand for provision in the new world organization of agencies that
would further such understanding and mutual approach to problems
among the people of all nations. The primary agency for this purpose, organized as a specialized agency within the United Nations, is
the United Nations Educational, Scientific and Cultural Organization. The significance to world peace of the down-to-earth thinking
of the masses on a world-wide scale is emphasized in the preamble to
the constitution of UNESCO, which is given here in its entirety.

THE GOVERNMENTS OF THE STATES PARTIES TO THIS CONSTITUTION ON
BEHALF OF THEIR PEOPLES DECLARE

that since wars begin in the minds of men, it is in the minds of men that the
defenses of peace must be constructed;

that ignorance of each other's ways and lives has been a common cause,
throughout the history of mankind, of that suspicion and mistrust between
the peoples of the world through which their differences have all too often
broken into war;

that the great and terrible war which has now ended was a war made possible by the denial of the democratic principles of the dignity, equality and
mutual respect of men, and by the propagation, in their place, through ignorance and prejudice, of the doctrine of the inequality of men and races;

that the wide diffusion of culture, and the education of humanity for justice
and liberty and peace are indispensable to the dignity of man and constitute
a sacred duty which all the nations must fulfil in a spirit of mutual assistance
and concern;

that a peace based exclusively upon the political and economic arrangements
of governments would not be a peace which could secure the unanimous,
lasting and sincere support of the peoples of the world, and that the peace
must therefore be founded, if it is not to fail, upon the intellectual and moral
solidarity of mankind.

[10] An excellent reference of brief compass, and written for "the ordinary citizen
everywhere" is the bulletin entitled *UNESCO and You*, prepared at the Secretariat
of the United States National Commission for UNESCO (U. S. Department of
State Publication No. 2904, 1947). The material for this section is drawn primarily
from this bulletin.

The purpose of UNESCO as set forth in its constitution is clear and challenging:

. . . to contribute to peace and security by promoting collaboration among the nations through education, science, and culture in order to further universal respect for justice, for the rule of law and for the human rights and fundamental freedoms which are affirmed to the peoples of the world, without distinction of race, sex, language, or religion, by the Charter of the United Nations.

UNESCO has assumed the task "of helping the individual citizen everywhere to understand the problems of building the peace and to use his personal energies toward solving them." Its "primary target area is the individual mind." It seeks to establish the foundations of world unity through science, education, and culture. It has far-reaching projects of its own, but it cooperates with many other agencies, groups, and individuals both inside and outside the United Nations. UNESCO's organization contains the general conference, the executive board, and the secretariat. The secretariat is divided into eight program sections, as follows: education; natural sciences; social sciences; philosophy and the humanistic studies; arts and letters; libraries; museums; and the mass media of film, radio, and press. Activities and projects are of three general kinds: (a) large-scale, UNESCO-wide projects in which all the program sections participate; (b) separate activities of the eight program sections; and (c) continuing activities intended to become regular features of UNESCO's work. Some UNESCO-wide projects that involve all eight of the program sections are reconstruction and habilitation; fundamental education; education for international understanding; and the Hylean Amazon Institute, to study the resources of the Amazon Basin and coordinate research into the problems of living in tropical areas. The extent to which education is recognized as an international problem is apparent from the above. When President Truman signed the measure authorizing the entry of the United States into UNESCO in 1946, he said: "The Government of the United States will work with and through UNESCO to the end that the minds of all people may be freed from ignorance, prejudice, suspicion and fear, and that men may be educated for justice, liberty and peace. If peace is to endure, education must establish the moral unity of mankind."

Several of the nations which are members of UNESCO have established in their own countries commissions which are advisory to the government and to the delegates to UNESCO's general conferences. These commissions also serve "as a connecting link with national groups in matters relating to UNESCO." In the United States this body is the United States National Commission for UNESCO. It was authorized in July, 1946. Its membership may not exceed 100 persons, carefully chosen to represent educational, scientific, and cultural matters on the national, state, and local levels. This is the group whose duty it is to contact and motivate large numbers of groups and individuals within the country, permeating society with the objectives and proposed activities of UNESCO. Educational organizations and leaders find in the national commission an opportunity to take their place and make their influence felt in the world movement for peace through understanding. In turn, the commission has been able, through the cooperation of hundreds of thousands of educational workers, to place before millions of children in the schools and parents in the communities the purpose and program of UNESCO. Again, the primary aim and problem is to reach through and stimulate thought and discussion where individuals meet in classrooms, civic clubs, labor organizations, parent-teacher groups, churches, card parties, forums, and a hundred other places.

The UNESCO program has had the virtue of tangibility. It is more than thinking; it is acting as well. For example, some of the educational reconstruction needs for 1947—needs that every individual can share in meeting, and that will be urgent for several years to come, include the following, summarized from UNESCO publications:

1. *Educational Materials.* Common school supplies for such countries as Greece, Yugoslavia, Poland, Hungary, Austria, China, Philippines, Japan, and Ethiopia: pencils; notebooks; rulers; drawing paper; chalk; pen nibs; blackboards; laboratory equipment and supplies; audio-visual equipment, including projectors, films, radios, phonographs, records, and cameras; office equipment of all types; special equipment for medical, dental, agricultural and vocational education; recreational and athletic equipment of all sorts, including educational toys

2. *Publications.* Technical, scientific, professional books and periodicals (particularly those published since 1939); standard literary classics in all languages, historical works; standard reference books; current textbooks at all levels but especially for universities, teacher training institutions, technical institutions, and secondary schools; collections of art reproductions; maps, especially outline maps

3. *Fellowships, Scholarships, Study Grants.* Needed in all fields but especially those in which marked advances were made during the war years. Particularly urgent are fellowships similar to the abandoned UNRRA fellowships whereby mature specialists deprived during the war of contact

with their fields of learning are provided with refresher training to permit them to conduct training programs on their return to their native lands

4. *International Voluntary Service Projects.* Sometimes known as educational work camps; these involve opportunities for young Americans to join with youth of other lands and with local citizens in rebuilding schools and other public institutions in the devastated countries

5. *Graduating Class Memorials.* A Class Memorial Project has been set up to permit the classes graduating from elementary schools, high schools, and colleges to make contributions to international educational reconstruction. A certificate suitable for framing will be awarded each class entering the project.

It would be difficult for any school child or any adult in the United States not to find something in the above list of needs which he could personally do to further the cause of world reconstruction. Action on these tangible, immediate needs can be the beginnings of a habit of interest and helpfulness which is precisely the prerequisite to international good will and cooperation. Thus UNESCO, great in its design and character, penetrates through to each individual. It can be the agency that gives blood and life to the top-level political and economic arrangements of the United Nations. If its purposes can become operative in the world, we shall see the substitution of broad internationalism for the narrow nationalism encountered so generally in our time.

What Do YOU Say?

1

The proper acceptance and support of education as a means to international understanding and cooperation have not been forthcoming. The political, economic, military, and philanthropic efforts in behalf of world peace will fail unless the power of education is used to promote understanding and good feeling among the masses of the world.

What do YOU say?

2

Mass education and highly centralized governments are incompatible. Learning and the desire to think and act freely go hand in hand. The means of international communication are too powerful to permit any nation to insulate its educated people against outside influences.

What do YOU say?

3

What points in this chapter do you particularly support or take issue with?

Chapter 5

THE ORGANIZATION AND ADMINISTRATION OF AMERICAN EDUCATION

Our System: What It Is and Who Runs It

1. PURPOSE AND SCOPE OF THIS CHAPTER

The concern of this chapter is to gain a general knowledge of the organizational structure of American education. As the organization becomes clear, functions and activities associated with various parts of the structure will also come to light. Certain problems of interrelationship involved in the organization and administration of our schools are sure to arise and command attention. Some note needs to be taken also of the place and influence of nongovernmental agencies in the conduct of our schools.

As the structure and administration of our schools are clarified, the need for making our educational practices conform more closely with our educational ideals will become apparent.

2. GENERAL STATEMENT

The evolution of ideas and practices in the colonies and the policies evolved subsequently by our federal and state governments have produced in this country an educational system in which our federal government, for all practical purposes, has no control over the organization and conduct of our schools. Furthermore, the responsibilities resting upon the state legislatures have been delegated in good part to local school units. This is in striking contrast to the strong centralization so frequently encountered in the nations discussed in the previous chapter.

The Tenth Amendment to our federal Constitution, which was ratified in 1791, states that "powers not delegated to the United States by the Constitution, nor prohibited by it to the States, are reserved to the States respectively, or to the people." Since control over education was not thus "delegated to the United States by the Constitution" nor prohibited by the Constitution to the states, authority and responsibility for the development of public education were therefore invested in the states. The federal government has not passed our fundamental laws concerning education. The states have done this, independent of one another. The state legislatures, therefore, and not the United States Congress, set the pattern. Congress, by the Tenth Amendment, gave over any such direct responsibility to the states. The state legislatures have in every case assumed this responsibility and have provided for the establishment of a system of public schools. Each state has passed the fundamental laws governing public education throughout the entire state.

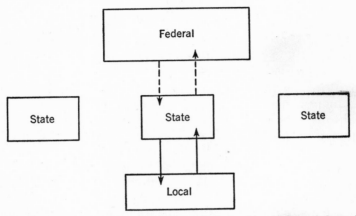

Figure 1. Authoritative and Nonauthoritative Relationships in School Organization

Figure 1, in which the solid and dotted lines represent authoritative and nonauthoritative relationships, puts the matter simply. The relationship between the federal government and the states, because of the Tenth Amendment, is voluntary, cooperative, nonauthoritative. The relationships between the states and the local units within them are direct and authoritative. The federal government, having passed the responsibility for education on to the states, cannot in turn make authoritative demands on the states; hence, the return line from the states is a dotted line. For example, the United States Office of Education can request educational data from the states, but the states are not obliged to furnish them. The states, on the other hand, having assumed the responsibility for education, and having organized a state public school system, bear an authoritative relationship to their local subdivisions and can require cooperation in numerous ways; hence, the return line from the local units to the state is a solid line. The present voluntary relationship between the federal government and the states could be changed only by a change in our federal Constitution. It would be possible, for example, to adopt a provision that would add education to the powers "delegated to the United States by the Constitution," such as the coinage of money and the control of interstate commerce. Such an action would be drastically out of line with the freedoms and responsibilities this nation wishes to establish among its people, and it is not likely, therefore, that it will ever happen.

Let us look further into aspects of our education at the federal, state, and local levels.

3. THE FEDERAL GOVERNMENT AND EDUCATION

It is not to be supposed that, because our federal government passed on the basic responsibility for education to the states, it is therefore uninterested in education. The history of federal interest and participation in education is as old as our federal government itself. In fact, many people insist that the federal government is obliged to be concerned with education, since education is obviously an aspect of the general welfare. The "general welfare" clause in the preamble to our federal Constitution seems to indicate that our federal government willingly bound itself to an interest in and responsibility for education, although through the Tenth Amendment it excluded itself from the control of education in the states. Let us review a few of the evidences of federal interest and participation.

Evidences of Federal Interest and Participation in Education.— No effort is made here to present a complete list of federal activities in education. Rather, selected items, intended to be illustrative, and distributed over the history of our country, are presented.

The Northwest Ordinance. Two years before the adoption of our federal Constitution in 1789, the Confederation adopted the Northwest Ordinance for the government of the new national domain north of the Ohio and east of the Mississippi rivers. With reference to this region, the Ordinance declared that : "Religion, morality, and knowledge being necessary to good government and the happiness of mankind, schools and the means of education shall be forever encouraged." The federal government made this encouragement tangible by giving to the new states the sixteenth section of each township for the maintenance of schools within the township. These land grants were not outright gifts for the purpose of promoting education, but were made in exchange for the exemption of federal lands from taxation by the new states. It is significant, however, that schools were designated as the beneficiaries of these grants. Sufficient interest in education was present to prevent any other agency from being named beneficiary. The precedent set in the Northwest Ordinance of granting federal lands in the new states for schools was continued, and the grants were increased, until the last of our forty-eight states was admitted to the Union in 1912.

Statements of National Leaders. National interest in education is admirably reflected in the statements concerning education that have been made by our national leaders. The reader is referred here to the quotations on page 24 of statements by leaders in the early days of our national life. Since that time a steady stream of pronouncements concerning the significance of education to our national welfare has been forthcoming from our leaders and statesmen.

Educational Requirements Imposed on New States. As the pattern of land grants to education became established through experience, the federal government became more extensive and forceful in stating the educational conditions which must be met before statehood would be granted. There was good reason for this. In the first place, the government wished to eliminate the abuses associated with the handling of the earlier grants. Furthermore, the larger grants to the states more recently admitted naturally led to a desire for careful state management; and finally, the close relationship between the education of the people and the success of our democratic government became more and more apparent as time went on. It is not surprising, therefore, that the federal government extracted from the states last admitted to the Union more guarantees concerning education than from the states first admitted.

The Morrill Act of 1862. The Morrill Act, commonly known as the "Land Grant Act," is a landmark in the story of the relations of the federal government to education. In this act, and in subsequent related acts, the government demonstrated its ability to translate its interest in education into action, and at the same time indirectly to chide existing colleges for their failure to keep up with the needs of the times. With our great agricultural and industrial expansion bursting upon us just prior to our Civil War, we had great need for research, leadership, and teaching in those fields—a need not met in the existing colleges. Through grants of land and subsequent money grants, the government secured the establishment of "A. and M." colleges which would administer to that need. The money grants have increased through the years, and aid has been extended to other vocational fields. These items were discussed in greater detail on pages 35 and 36.

The United States Office of Education. In 1867 the federal government recognized the fact that a good many services to education might be rendered at the national level if some sort of central office or department were established. Accordingly, in that year, Congress approved the establishment of a Department of Education, without cabinet rank, "for the purpose of collecting facts, statistics, and information as to schools and school systems which would aid the people of the different states in the establishment and maintenance of efficient school systems and otherwise promote the cause of education generally throughout the country." [1] In 1868, the new department was reduced to an "office," the salary and staff of the Commissioner of Education were cut, and a highly significant and promising project was cruelly deflated. Since that time, under serious limitations, the office has nevertheless supplied valuable information and leadership to the schools of the nation. At no time has there ever been a demand to make it any more than an effective service agency. Most persons interested in the expansion of its staff and services are not interested in making it an agency of educational control. During recent years a strong demand has risen to lift it from its submerged position within the Federal Security Agency to a position more in line with its significance and one in which it can exercise greater leadership and speak for itself in the councils of government. More specifically, the American Association of School Administrators in 1951 recommended that the Office of Education be made an independent governmental agency, under the control of a policy-making board of laymen appointed by the President and confirmed by the Senate. This board, if the recommendation were carried out, would select the Commissioner of Education, who would be the board's executive officer and would preside over the Office of Education.

Special Groups and Institutions. The federal government is directly responsible for the education of persons in all American possessions and territories, including the District of Columbia. There is no single type of organization, program, or control which is applied in all these regions, and there is considerable variation among them. Although our government is directly responsible for education in the

---

[1] E. P. Cubberley, *Public Education in the United States* (rev. and enl. ed.; Boston: Houghton Mifflin Co., 1934), p. 740.

territories, it has nevertheless delegated to territorial governments a good deal of responsibility for educational matters. This includes responsibility for the financial support of the schools. These governments are not equally able or disposed to meet existing educational problems. The education of Indians is also the responsibility of our government. Numerous government schools for Indians are maintained, but extensive use is also made of the public schools, the government paying the tuition charges for Indian children who attend. The children of government employees billeted in foreign countries are also the educational responsibility of the federal government.

The government also maintains complete educational institutions when such are necessary to the fulfilment of its obligation to the people. The national defense, for example, justifies the maintenance of such institutions as the United States Military Academy at West Point, founded in 1802; the United States Naval Academy at Annapolis, founded in 1845; and the United States Coast Guard Academy at New London, founded in 1876.

Special Agencies Arising from Urgent Conditions. There have been times in our national life when unusual conditions have necessitated unusual action. The great depression of the 1930's is a good example. During that time millions of people were unemployed, money was scarce, and thousands of youth were out of school and out of jobs. It was generally recognized that we were in a national crisis; but state and local governments, themselves hard hit financially, did not feel able to provide emergency measures. The presence in our society of a large number of youth who were out of work and out of school was especially critical. The Civilian Conservation Corps, established in 1933, and the National Youth Administration, established in 1935, were organized by the federal government to relieve this situation. The CCC gave employment to several million youth in work that was mainly out-of-doors and related to the conservation of our natural resources. Favorable comment has often been made concerning the health aspects of the program and the manner in which youth were removed from urban centers at an age when idleness and purposelessness might have bred trouble. The CCC was terminated in 1942. The NYA, clearly a relief agency, provided work for both in-school and out-of-school youth. Restrictions that were fairly rigid at first concerning the relief status of students and their parents became more lenient as time went on. By the time the NYA was discontinued in 1943, it had aided over two million students in our schools and colleges, to say nothing of the larger out-of-school group.

Both the CCC and the NYA were administered by federal authorities. They were financed almost entirely by federal funds. Both were concerned with education. As time went on, the educational program and services available through the CCC and the NYA expanded rapidly. School subjects were made available, even including frequently the traditional academic subjects; faculties were employed; guidance and counseling services were set up; and buildings and supplies were provided. In fact, occasionally the regular public schools found themselves close neighbors to federal schools in which the school costs were paid by the federal government and the pupils, as it were, being assisted by the NYA, were paid to attend.

This situation, of course, drew much criticism from the public school people of the country and from much of our general population as well. It was clearly hostile to our belief that our schools should not be under the direction of our central government. Furthermore, it seemed quite certain that large amounts of money were being wasted that could have been saved if the government had seen fit to use and strengthen regular educational facilities rather than establish duplicate facilities. If government funds had been utilized through regular channels, the schools would have been strengthened at a time when they needed it desperately; and they would not have been weakened by a diversion that not only divided the funds but created considerable apprehension as well. However, there is another side to the case. There were many people in leadership positions in the states and communities who were blissfully and tenaciously asleep during the depression. It is not likely that we ever would have had these federally directed programs of education if our states had alerted themselves to the emergency, evaluated their needs in terms of doing the right thing for youth, clarified these needs to the federal government, and presented well-developed plans for the use of federal funds. Our states did not do this. Rather, they seemed to assume that doing something about a depression was the responsibility of the federal government; and they stood ready to complain if federal activities seemed to encroach on local prerogatives.

The bugaboo of federal control is not likely to assume alarming proportions in this country if the states and local communities will forerun the federal government in analyzing youth needs, in making clear their need for financial help if they cannot carry the load alone, and in presenting wise plans for the use of whatever aid may be accorded them. The idea of support without control, which is the right and democratic way, can hardly become operative until such forethinking is engaged in at the local level.

Examples of federal interest in education during urgent times could be multiplied. During the depression the government also set up the Public Works Administration (1933) and the Work Projects Administration (1935). Under these agencies a great deal of much-needed school building was done. Later on, in 1941, when defense activities had thrown large numbers of workers into war production centers, the government passed the Lanham Act. This act gave government assistance to communities that were unable through their own resources to provide the additional schools, equipment, recreation centers, and child care centers which were needed. In some communities a feeling arose that government officials were too independent in administering the act, not cooperating closely enough with local school officials in such vital matters as the planning and construction of school buildings. It can be said in summary, however, that the government's interest and participation in education have not waned in times of stress. Independent government action, or the use of existing educational channels, or the wise combination of both has been the continuing problem.

Educational Activities in Federal Departments and Bureaus. Numerous departments and bureaus in our federal government carry on educational activities. These activities range from simple projects to programs of graduate study such as that found in the Department of Agriculture. The Treasury Department conducted during the war extensive stamp-selling and bond-selling projects, in cooperation with thousands of schools. The State Department administers extensive programs, including international exchange of students and staff members. The "Voice of America" is also a tremendous educational project involving mass media. Educational activities in regions under our military occupation are administered by our Department of the Army. The Bureau of the Budget has its educational activities and personnel. The Federal Security Agency, of course, has the United States Office of Education within its jurisdiction.

Government-School Cooperation During Wartime. Everyone is familiar with the vast wartime responsibilities assumed by America's schools, at the suggestion of the federal government and in cooperation with it. Very early in the war, school and college leaders from all over the country were assembled and were told of ways the schools could assist in the war effort. These activities ran the gamut of highly specialized training in our colleges and universities, technical training of all sorts, preinduction training in our secondary schools, release of students for part-time work in war production plants, victory gardens, scrap drives, junior Red Cross, teacher assistance in numerous projects, and a hundred others. In fact, at no time in our national history has the government leaned so directly and so heavily on the schools for the performance of important emergency services.

Educational Benefits to Veterans. One of the finest examples of our government's interest in education is the educational benefits it extended to veterans of the second World War. These benefits were implemented mainly through the Servicemen's Readjustment Act of 1944. Any veteran who served at least ninety days in the armed forces prior to July 25, 1947, was entitled to one year of education plus the amount of time he spent in actual service, not to exceed four years. He had to start this program within four years of his discharge and complete it by July 25, 1956. The government not only made payments direct to the veteran while he was in school, but also to the institution in which he was enrolled. For an unmarried veteran these payments amounted to approximately $1,500 per year. For married veterans, and married veterans with children, it was more. Benefits also extended beyond traditional schoolwork to on-the-job training and rehabilitation activities. The government's generosity in this connection was matched by a general seriousness of purpose and excellence of achievement on the part of participating veterans that were outstanding.

Importance Attached to Re-education in Occupied Countries. During the war, education officers were among the first to follow the fighting troops into regions and cities wrested from the enemy. The importance of maintaining normal community activities, including the operation of the schools, was recognized. The interest of our government in making education play a vital part in the postwar adjustment of the people in occupied countries was indicated in the discussions of re-education in Germany and Japan in the previous chapter. This program is carefully staffed and planned on a long-time basis. The Department of the Army has sought to obtain among civilians the people who are best qualified to make the organization, conduct, and content of the schools in these countries effective agencies for peace.

Progress Toward Federal Aid to the General Education of All the People. During recent years the federal Congress has been more and more disposed to favor legislation proposing significant grants of federal money to the states for the improvement of elementary and secondary education. Up until now, government funds have supported vocational education, or educational projects of a specialized character. The government has not supported education on a "general welfare" basis. It appears certain that with the ironing-out of a few problems connected with the administration of federal grants, such aid for general education will be forthcoming. National polls have repeatedly shown this to be the desire of a majority of our citizens.

Special Committees and Commissions. At numerous times in the past our federal government has caused committees and commissions to be set up to study special educational problems and make recommendations concerning them. Frequently our presidents have taken the initiative in these matters and have named the personnel of the study groups. The White House Conferences on child welfare, of which there have been six since 1909, are a good example. In 1929 President Hoover set up the National Advisory Committee on Education to explore the problem of the relation of the central government to education. In 1936 President Roosevelt named an Advisory Committee on Education to investigate the same problem, but the scope of the study was broadened. More recently, in 1947, the President's Commission on Higher Education made an extended report, with recommendations, concerning the status, needs, and likely future developments in higher education in this country. Such studies would not, of course, have originated if persons in high position in our federal government had not been interested in education and had not honestly sought to steer a right course concerning it.

It is easy to see from the foregoing brief discussions that the interest of our federal government in education is of long standing and has not waned in recent years. In fact, that interest is probably keener now than at any other time in our history. There seems to be a sincere willingness on the part of the federal government to lend significant financial support to general education in the states without requiring the centralization of controls at the national level. This relationship can be maintained if the leadership and planning at the state and local levels are such as to command confidence at the national level.

Major Areas and Characteristics at the Federal Level.—It will be useful to summarize briefly some of the larger areas and general characteristics of the federal government's activities in education.

Major Areas. Most of the government's educational activities are comprehended under the following headings:

1. The United States Office of Education
2. The program of vocational education; stemming from the "Land Grant" Act and subsequent acts, with expansions. (Although the administration of these acts falls within the U. S. Office of Education, the program, because of its unity and significance, deserves special mention.)
3. Education in areas under federal jurisdiction
4. Education in specialized institutions, such as the military and naval academies
5. Educational activities in federal departments and bureaus
6. Educational benefits to veterans, administered by the Veterans Administration
7. Educational activities in occupied countries

Some of the above activities are on a more continuing basis than others. The last two, for example, although they are large projects within themselves, may be expected to reduce and close out within a few years. On the other hand, other activities, such as federal aid to general education and aid to a seriously lagging school building program, are likely to be added.

Major Characteristics. The following general characteristics seem to apply to educational activities carried on at the federal level:

1. They are on the basis of assistance, not control. This is largely true even in areas of federal jurisdiction outside the United States.
2. They are cooperative, not directive. The participation of states and institutions in the development of plans for federally aided vocational education and the cooperative arrangements between the government and the schools during wartime are examples of this.
3. They are special, not general. This characterization would have to be modified if federal aid to general education were to be approved.
4. They are investigative and advisory. The investigative and informative function of the U. S. Office of Education and the work of the presidents' commissions illustrate this.
5. They are scattered and piecemeal, not integrated. The high degree of autonomy and independence enjoyed by federal departments, bureaus, and agencies has resulted in the development of a good many uncoordinated activities.

Federal Court Decisions.—The influence of the federal government on education has also been felt through federal court decisions. These decisions have in some cases restrained the states in certain matters and in other cases have required the states to take certain action. In every case federal court action has been taken only at points where state policies, either by commission or omission, seem to place basic constitutional provisions in jeopardy. Between 1789 and 1948 the Supreme Court handed down twenty-five decisions on education. Fourteen of these were rendered between 1928 and 1948.[2]

The Supreme Court upheld the inviolability of charters when in 1819 it restrained the state of New Hampshire from making Dartmouth College a state institution against its will. It upheld the constitutional guarantee of freedom of religion when in 1943 it restrained local or state school authorities from requiring all pupils to salute the American flag. It prevented undue restraint on private interests in education, including churches, when in 1925 it declared unconstitutional an Oregon law which stated that all children in the state between eight and sixteen years of age must attend public schools. In this case the right of the state to set minimum standards which must be observed by private schools was not questioned. In 1948, in the McCollum Case, the Supreme Court upheld the principle of the separation of church and state when it denied to churches the use, under certain conditions, of a part of the regular school day for sectarian religious instruction in public schools. In 1948 the Court enjoined the state of Oklahoma to extend to qualified Negroes educational opportunities in public higher institutions—an implementation of the right of all citizens not to have their constitutional rights denied because of race, color, or previous condition of servitude. Federal court action, therefore, has not sought to shape the organization, administration, or content of education within the states; it has, however, spoken out clearly when the relationship of school practices to constitutional law has been called into question.

Selected Problems.—Let us close our discussion of the federal government and education by listing a few related problems which are prominently before our people today and are likely to occupy our attention for some time to come. The list is only a starter. The reader will think of numerous problems that ought to be added:

1. Does education as an aspect of the general welfare merit greater federal attention and support?

[2] Ward W. Keesecker, "Supreme Court Decisions Affecting Education," *School Life*, XXXI, 4–7.

2. Should there be greater integration and coordination of the educational projects carried on under the jurisdiction of the federal government?

3. Should there be a national board of education, stemming from the federal government as state and local boards stem from state and local governments, to consider the interests and appropriate activities of education at the federal level?

4. Should the United States Office of Education be removed from the Federal Security Agency and have its status, and the status of the Commissioner, elevated?

5. Should it be the policy of our federal government whenever possible to work through existing public school channels in attempting to improve the education of all the people?

6. Is the federal government ever justified in instituting independent educational projects basic to the general welfare, particularly when the states do not take the lead in analyzing their needs and presenting plans for the wise use of federal aid?

7. Would increased federal support to education, in which the government acted on its obligation to the general welfare, necessitate any basic modification of our long-standing pattern of state control, stemming from the Tenth Amendment?

4. The States and Education

State Responsibility.—It has already been made clear that it was the responsibility of the several states in this country to enact the basic laws establishing the public school systems. This responsibility was accepted and acted upon. It will be remembered, also, that when the Tenth Amendment was approved in 1791, we had not yet even begun our "battle for the free schools." As the free school idea took hold in this country, becoming generally accepted around 1850, the states one by one set up state-wide public school systems. They did this at their own pace and in their own way. The new states admitted to the Union, although they had to reassure the federal government with reference to certain things concerning education, took their own good time to pass the legislation necessary for the establishment of a real system of public schools. In fact, the states even now are continuously passing laws affecting education—its organization, financing, administration, personnel, and so on. This is their privilege—and, above all, their responsibility. The state legislatures in our forty-eight states are the primary determiners of the nature of our public school systems. They are independent of one another. No two states need have like systems; and no two states are alike in all respects. Such autonomy among the states has, of course, resulted in numerous differences, but they are primarily differences of detail. There are also many similarities, based upon common interpretations of democracy and of the position the school ought to hold in relation to the people. On the whole the states have felt that, although they would be completely within their rights if they retained in the state capital the complete running of all the public schools, they ought nevertheless to delegate much responsibility to the people in the communities. A good many of the basic laws in the states, therefore, dealt first with the setting-up of an organization for education and then with the delegation of much authority and responsibility to the newly established local units. One should not lose sight of the fact, however, that local responsibility, even the existence of the local units themselves, is a result of state action; which, again, emphasizes the fact that it has been, and will be, the province of the state legislatures to determine the over-all nature and organization of education within the states.

In setting up state-wide public school systems where local units with responsibility and authority were provided, the legislatures had to provide an organizational framework at both the state level and the local level. There would be at the state capital a state-level organization to deal with state policies, carry out responsibilities assigned to it directly by the legislature, represent the state in relation to the local units, and administer educational projects that were supported by the state and were outside local jurisdiction—such as state teachers colleges, state trade schools, special schools for the blind and deaf, and so on. It is the primary concern of this section to consider this state-level organization. The next section will deal with local-level organization.

Although there are numerous differences among the states in their state-level organization for public education, three major provisions are nevertheless typical among them. These can be said to describe in general the American pattern at the state level. They are: a state board of education, a chief state school officer, and a state department of education. Let us consider each of these in turn, briefly.

State Board of Education.—The first effective state board of education was set up in Massachusetts in 1837. By 1840 eight states had state boards; and by 1860 sixteen had made provision for them. This was precisely at the time when the states were establishing state-wide public school systems and were beginning to weld the many local school units into some kind of coordinated whole. In numerous states the early state boards were pretty much fiscal and clerical in character, set up to administer state school funds and gather the information necessary for their distribution. But such was not the case in Massachusetts and Connecticut. Horace Mann and Henry Barnard became the secretaries of the state boards in these states, and under their leadership these boards became powerful influences for the study and improvement of education. The legislatures, having set up the boards, received in turn the excellent and sometimes startling reports of the secretaries, which presented the facts concerning the schools and made recommendations for corrective legislation. The state boards, under their leadership, took the initiative in formulating far-reaching policy and did much to awaken the conscience of the people with reference to education. Since their time many states have established state boards. In some instances the boards have been limited in their powers and functions so that their influence has not been great. Even now, among the forty states having such boards, the range in powers and duties and in opportunity to exert real leadership is tremendous. Without doubt, however, the power and influence of state boards have been on the increase during recent years.

Three methods of securing members of the state board of education are most common. They are: by granting ex-officio membership, by election, and by appointment. Ex-officio membership means that one is a member of the state board by virtue of holding some other office such as governor or president of a state institution. This is generally recognized as poor practice and is slowly diminishing. The second method, the election of state board members by popular vote, is rare. Colorado adopted such a plan in 1948, as did Texas in 1949. Opinion in general seems not to favor this plan, although the recency of the action in Colorado and Texas may indicate a new trend. Many observers would wish to remove these boards having long-term policy-making responsibilities as far as possible from direct political influences. This is not to say that Colorado and Texas may not have found a way to do this and still elect their board members. More state board members receive their positions by the third method, appointment, than by any other means. Such appointment is most commonly by the governor. Some boards, of course, are made up of both appointive and ex-officio members. There is much opinion favoring appointment by the governor, without confirmation by any body such as the state senate. This fixes responsibility, and eliminates such "buck-passing" as, "I had to appoint someone I knew the senate would confirm" or "We can confirm only those whom the governor recommends." In Utah and Washington some state board members are elected by school board conventions.

There seems to be general agreement that the state board should be small, numbering five to nine members. Sizes now range from three members in Mississippi and Oregon to twenty-one in Texas. Also, terms of office should be relatively long. For example, if the governor appoints the state board members, their terms should definitely outlast his. Members, of course, are staggered in their appointments. This, it is believed, tends to minimize political considerations and makes it unlikely that any governor will ever appoint a majority of the board.

State board members should be lay citizens of demonstrated good ability in thinking and managing, with a profound desire to see the public schools of the state meet the needs of the children of the state. They should be willing and able to spend time and energy in studying educational problems and attending board meetings. They should serve without pay, although their expenses arising from their services to the board should be paid from state funds. Their jobs are in no sense a lazy pay-off for past political activities nor "front" positions for basking in public esteem. They are hard, inconspicuous, public-service jobs; and they are of tremendous long-time consequence.

The duties of the state board of education are many. The following are illustrative:

1. To review the policy of public education within the state and make recommendations to the state legislature concerning it
2. To represent the state in its many relations with the local schools in such matters as the disbursement of state funds, the application of school building regulations, the administration of school transportation, the certification of public school personnel, and school supervision and accreditation
3. To select a commissioner of education who is a professional expert capable of making recommendations concerning state educational policy
4. To provide the commissioner with an adequate staff for the proper performance of his duties.
5. To adopt policy concerning the conduct of institutions under its direct charge
6. To conduct studies on a state-wide basis when such studies are useful in establishing state policies and in improving services to the public schools

7. To seek to coordinate public education within the state, and to encourage all school units in activities pointing toward self-improvement

8. To cooperate with all units of the state system in supplying leadership and expert counsel and services

9. To prepare and justify budgets basic to the essential activities and services of the board

10. To establish regulations concerning certain matters when this responsibility has been assigned to it by the legislature

Additional comment needs to be made about the last item immediately above. Very often the state legislature wishes to have certain educational practices adopted but does not wish to set up all the regulations associated with their implementation. It will frequently pass on to the state board of education the responsibility for drawing up those regulations. For example, the legislature may pass a law saying that all public school teachers must be certified; but it will usually add: "the regulations concerning certification to be drawn up by the state board of education." So it will go with school building regulations, the authorization and accreditation of schools and colleges within the state, and so on. This, of course, gives such regulations the force of law and again sharpens the necessity of having on the state board members who will act carefully and wisely in such responsible matters.

Chief State School Officer.—A few of the states do not have a state board of education, but all of the states have a chief state school officer. In states without state boards, many of the duties ordinarily assigned to the board fall to the chief state school officer. It might seem at first that this would be a satisfactory arrangement, but it is not. It is generally agreed that public education is much better served if a strong, devoted board having policy-making powers represents it before the people and in the state legislature than if a single spokesman represents it. Furthermore, it is not the disposition of the American people to place broad, policy-making powers within the hands of an individual. In general, therefore, chief state school officers, whether they be associated with state boards or not, are more administrative and supervisory than legislative in their functions.

The first state school officer was authorized by New York in 1812. By 1840 such a position had been provided for in eleven states. By 1860 thirty-two states had made like provisions. Again, as in the founding of state boards, the establishment of this office closely paralleled the winning of the battle for free public school systems. As state after state took action to establish state-wide public school systems, it was quite natural that a need would be felt for policy-making boards and supervisory officers at the state level.

The most common method of securing a chief state school officer is through a general state election. This applied in twenty-nine states in 1950. In thirteen other states appointment was made by the state board of education and in six other states by the governor. When the office is filled by appointment, the title of "Commissioner of Education" is usually assigned; when filled by election, "Superintendent of Public Instruction" is the common title. Appointive officers have higher average salaries and longer average tenure than elected officers. Much can be said in support of having the commissioner appointed by the state board of education, without confirmation by any other person or body, for an indefinite term, and at a salary that will attract the best qualified people in the country. If the salary is adequate, if the tenure is long enough to permit following through on long-term policies, and if accountability in office is centered in a responsible, nonpolitical state board, it stands to reason that the job can attract good personnel. If these conditions do not exist, it stands to reason also that good personnel will not be attracted to the job or, if once in it, cannot render their best service. Continuity of leadership in evolving and implementing educational policies and practices is fundamental to a stable, improving school system.

The chief state school officer is essentially the executive officer of the state board of education and its professional expert. It is better to have one such expert, the best to be had, than to arouse professional disputes by having several professional educators as members of the board; hence the strong recommendation that state boards be made up of outstanding lay citizens devoted to public education. Professional educators in the state are usually glad to cooperate with the state board in special ways, but their services as members of the board are not needed if the caliber of the commissioner or superintendent is what it ought to be.

The duties of the chief state school officer vary greatly among the states. The following, however, are typical:

1. To act as the executive officer of the state board of education for the administration of state policy in education
2. To supply to the state board facts and expert opinion regarding problems before the board
3. To become familiar with the needs of public education in the state and make recommendations to the state board for meeting them

4. To suggest to the state board needed school legislation
5. To act as liaison officer between the state board and the public schools of the state
6. To act as general supervisor of the public schools of the state, seeing to it that minimum requirements are met and needed information is supplied to the state
7. To provide leadership among educational groups in the state for the continuous improvement of the school system
8. To request the employment of personnel adequate to carry out the policies of the state board
9. To prepare the budget of the state department of education and of other projects and institutions for which he may be responsible
10. To interpret school law to the state and receive and decide disputes that fall under his jurisdiction

Obviously, the chief state school officer holds one of the most important positions in the state. His influence extends from the councils where far-reaching policies are formulated to the last child in the remotest classroom. He is at the forefront in interpreting public education to the people and in adjusting education to the requirements of a democratic nation.

State Department of Education.—We have already seen how the state board depends upon the chief state school officer to put into operation the many policies of the board and to carry out responsibilities assigned to it by the legislature. Plainly, the commissioner or superintendent cannot personally perform all of these duties, or be an expert in all matters under his supervision. For example, the state board will hold him responsible for the administration of certification requirements adopted by the board; but he cannot possibly personally examine the college transcripts and carry on the correspondence connected with the thousands of requests for certification that come in. He must have a certification officer to do this work. Similarly, he will be held responsible for the collection and use of data, sometimes involving attendance data on hundreds of thousands of children, which will be used as a basis for the distribution of state money to the public schools of the state. He can hardly personally assemble all these data and make the necessary computations. He must have helpers to do this. So it goes with school building regulations, supervision and leadership in the schools at all levels, legal ramifications, research studies, and a hundred other matters. Competent, expert helpers are needed. This corps of helpers, essentially the staff of the chief state school officer, constitutes the state department of education. In some states this department employs hundreds of highly qualified people who perform services of the greatest significance and which reach directly to local school and community personnel. In other states the staff is woefully small, and its activities have to be mainly clerical in nature and confined largely to the offices of the department.

Recent years have witnessed the development of strong pressures to expand the staffs and services of the state departments. Great emphasis is also placed on the adoption of salary schedules that will attract top-notch people to these staffs. The state department should not be a place of refuge where mediocre people find pleasant work and where the last few years before retirement can be spent in peace, removed from the harassments of "kids" and budgets and town meetings. Finally, there seems to be a growing realization that state departments are primarily and properly agencies of service and leadership as related to the public schools and not primarily agencies of dictation and control. The service of supervision must be rendered, but it is still a service. Minimum requirements established by the state must, of course, be met. But the matter of checking on minimum requirements is far less important than the matter of stimulating local groups to be interested in their school problems and then cooperating with them in finding solutions that seem reasonable to them and that make use of their own best thinking. The state department, therefore, ought to be staffed to do not only its administrative, interpretative, and supervisory duties but also its consultative and leadership duties. Most states fall far short of such staffing. State department budgets are usually much too small. If it could be demonstrated to the people in our states that enlarged staffs would mean more adequate services and leadership and not undue centralization of control, then staff expansions might be more readily approved.

State Court Decisions.—In most states the laws concerning education that have been passed by the legislatures are enough to form a good-sized book. Most of these laws are noncontroversial and deal with rather routine matters. In other cases the laws are not interpreted uniformly and give rise to controversies. The courts are then appealed to, and the decisions of the courts influence school practices as surely as the laws themselves. In fact, whole patterns of school practice have been determined by such decisions. For example, in the instance of the Kalamazoo Case, which was discussed on pages 28 and 29, certain citizens in Kalamazoo, Michigan, felt that the law which authorized taxation for the "common schools" did not cover taxation for the support of high schools, and they brought suit to restrain the school board from collecting taxes for that purpose. The state Supreme Court, which received the case, might have ruled these citizens correct and not been judged unreasonable in so doing. It ruled instead that it is up to the local community to decide for itself how much education it wishes to make available or "common" through tax support. The effect of this decision in and beyond Michigan is well known. Judgments by state courts concerning the intent of law, responsibilities under the law, and rights and privileges within the law are numerous. On the whole, the courts have been strong defenders of the public schools, ruling that they are agents of the state and not of the local communities, and maintaining an autonomy for them that is admirable. This is not to say that the public schools are secure. In Connecticut, for example, it still remains to be seen whether or not the town boards of finance, set up by state law during the depression for economy purposes, have destroyed the fiscal autonomy of the town boards of education. Some court decisions have been rendered in connection with disputes between boards, but satisfaction has not been given. It is earnestly to be hoped in regard to such relationships that we shall not take steps that will cause us to lose the gains of a hundred years ago when we won the "battle for the free schools." The power and influence of the courts in directing the course of the future can hardly be overestimated.

5. SUBSTATE OR LOCAL UNITS AND EDUCATION

Principle of Delegated Responsibility and Authority.—The state, as we now know, is the unit basically responsible for public education in this country. Each state had complete freedom in setting up its public school system as it pleased. It could run everything and pay all the bills from the state capital if it wanted to. It didn't want to. Rather, the states chose to break themselves down into smaller sub-units and delegate to these units much responsibility and authority. These units, it must be remembered, are parts of the state system. They are state schools, administered locally. It is as though the state said: "We will let the people in District Number 28 run that part of our state school system." In this manner the schools have become local only in the sense that permission is granted to the local community to manage state school affairs. The primary responsibility of the local board of education, and of other public school personnel, is to the state. It is the privilege of the state, if the legislature will pass the laws, to change or even abolish the local units, regulate their monetary matters, and determine their courses of study, without even consulting them—except as they are represented in the state legislature. The point is, the states have followed the pattern of setting up subdivisions of themselves and endowing them with a great deal of authority that is, nevertheless, recallable.

Many of the states' school laws pertain to the conduct of education in the local units. Some of these laws are mandatory, and the local units must conform to them, as when the state passes a law stating that no public school teacher in the state shall receive less than a stated minimum salary. Other laws are permissive; that is, local units may do certain things if they want to, but they don't have to, as when a law is passed permitting, but not requiring, local units to make the kindergarten a part of the tax-supported school program.

Types of Local Units.—There are many types of local units within the states. They are all characterized in general by the presence of boards or committees of education which have general jurisdiction over the schools in each unit. Also, tax levies for school support are made for each unit, and tax receipts are disbursed on a unit-wide basis. A common classification of local units is as follows: (*a*) county and parish; (*b*) town and township; (*c*) district; and (*d*) other special types, such as city and consolidated districts of many kinds.

County and Parish. Of the types listed above, the county or the parish is ordinarily the largest in size. This type is more prevalent in the southern states than in any other section of the country. It has many points in its favor. It permits better coordination of school-work, broadens the tax base, and presents a better supervisory situation. It also ensures that school problems and plans for improvement will be considered on a county-wide basis, thus making it less likely that certain poor communities will remain inferior and neglected in relation to other communities within the county.

Town and Township. When local school units in a state are set up on a town or township basis, it merely means that all the public schools in each town or township are under the jurisdiction of one board of education, and school taxes are collected and distributed on a town-wide basis. The township as a school unit suggests, properly, that the boundaries of the school unit are the boundaries of the surveyed township. The fact that in many states the federal government gave a section of land in each township for public education tended at least to suggest the township as a local school unit. Unlike the township, the New England "town" did not have the benefit of the surveyor's chain. Town boundaries were sometimes weirdly distorted. Sometimes these boundaries make sense today; other times, none at all. It is worth pointing out that whereas the surveyor's lines are important for the identification and exchange of property in this country, they have no particular virtue in determining the boundaries of local school units. School boundaries should, on the whole, conform to natural community boundaries; and school buildings should be located at the community's center. The recent legalization of "community districts" in some states carries with it this important social implication. At any rate, in some states the town or township, smaller than the county, is the unit of local public school control.

District. States organized on the district system may be thought of as having continued the breakdown process beyond the county and the town and having set up smaller districts as the local units. In some states there are thousands of these small districts to which the state has delegated the authority and responsibility for public education. In tens of thousands of cases, pieces of land less than five miles square, often with very sparse populations and possessing little taxable wealth, represent local organization for the principal support and control of the schools. In some states, therefore, local school units are typically very small; in others, somewhat larger; and in others, quite large. One might obtain a fair idea of relative sizes by saying that dozens of counties make hundreds of towns, and hundreds of towns make thousands of districts.

Special Types. Although our states may be described in general as having county, town, or district systems, it is also true that, within the states, laws have been passed authorizing many other types of districts. For example, schools now in villages that are under the supervision of the town or county may become independent school districts when the population of the village grows to a certain size. City districts thus come into being. Authorization is also given for the formulation of all kinds of new districts through consolidation. Hence, most of our states have a rather large assortment of types of local school units. Added to the basic pattern are the special types set up within and among communities through permissive legislation enacted by the state. It has been estimated that, taking the states together, close to 150 different types of districts have been authorized.

Trends in Local-Unit Reorganization.—Three trends in local-unit reorganization deserve to be mentioned.

Larger Local Units. For a good many years the consolidation movement in this country has been strong. When consolidation takes place, two or more school units take advantage of a permissive state law and form a larger consolidated unit. The newer consolidated schools are almost without exception better schools than those they replaced. Conditions of financial support, educational program, school activities, teaching staff, school supervision, and school plant are usually greatly improved. Although the results of consolidation have been generally good, many people feel that changes have come too slowly. Occasionally a state will achieve a sweeping change by going, let us say, to the county system; however, it should be remembered that going to the county system will not necessarily eliminate a lot of ineffective schools that ought to be eliminated. The change may simply mean an administrative change. The fundamental job of consolidation which will result in better schools may still go undone. At any rate, one of the trends during recent years has been the establishment of larger local units, mainly through consolidation initiated at the local level. Between 1929 and 1948, the number of one-teacher public schools in the United States decreased from 149,282 to 75,096.

District Lines Following Community Lines. Communities tend to be "naturals"; that is, the community center has a natural "drain-off" of people from all directions. The people gravitate to the center. They find there, on the whole, the things they need. It is handy. It is reached more easily than other places. A river or the top of a ridge may be the natural dividing line between it and another community. In the minds of many people this "naturalness" of a community ought to be reflected in the establishment of school district boundaries, making sure, of course, that schools of an effective size are secured. If it is convenient for a family to go to a certain center to buy supplies, to go to church, and to be entertained, it is also convenient for them to have their children attend school there. The best roads, too, will probably lead to that center. Some of the district lines that reach over the mountain and pick up a child who ought to remain over the mountain for school purposes would be better arranged if the community idea were adopted. The idea is gaining some headway, slowly.

Wide-Area Attack. The results of consolidation initiated at the local level are not always entirely satisfactory. It is quite possible, for example, that pin-point consolidations throughout a state will leave numerous small areas isolated without much hope of ever being included in a consolidated district and without the resources to have good schools of their own. It is not well to have such schools become fixed on the educational landscape. One way of preventing this is to attack the problem of district reorganization on a wide-area basis, say state-wide. This is an approach that has gained considerable momentum during recent years. The movement has had opposition, mainly from people who think of the public schools as "local" in the strict sense of the word. Others, however, who realize that local school units are subdivisions of a state system, see it as the duty of the state to make sure that local-unit reorganization is wisely done.

Reorganization Before Equalization.—We shall see in the next chapter that during recent years the states have been giving more and more financial help to local school units. In fact, in some states well-worked-out equalization plans have been put into effect. These plans usually specify a minimum amount of money that must be spent annually on every pupil in the public schools of the state. Each school community is to place a reasonable assessment on its taxable property and spend a reasonable percentage of its tax income for public education. If this is done and the amount of money available for education is not sufficient to pay the minimum per-pupil expenditure, then the state will help the community by contributing enough state funds to make the minimum required expenditure possible. The important point here is that before such equalization plans are put into operation, the state should make sure that it does not pour large quantities of money into maintaining schools that ought, by all reasonable standards, to be discontinued. It is quite possible through equalization to perpetuate weak, ineffective schools that have little chance of ever being able to provide really good education. In fact, these are precisely the schools that can present the best case for equalization in terms of financial need. It is the state's obligation so to arrange its local subdivisions that equalization funds will support only good schools. This is in no sense a violation of the principle of local control. It is an effort on the state's part to place under local control only schools that are equipped to do a good job.

The Democracy of the Adult and the Democracy of the Child.—The devotion of local citizens in this country to their local institutions is well known. The local school, which they have controlled and supported, is frequently an object of special affection. This is most admirable; and under no circumstances should we weaken the bonds of unity growing out of close association in our small communities, where, after all, the final test of democracy is made. Occasionally, however, loyalty to a struggling local school can become far-fetched and misplaced. The adults of the community may feel that it is their right by the American tradition to keep and to control the local school. The schoolhouse is in poor repair, the enrolment is down to almost nothing, money to keep things going is hard to raise, and each year the teacher moves on to a better job; but the school "belongs to us." For many, many years the smoke from the chimney has spiraled lazily into the frosty morning air and the bell at noon has signaled the farmer home to his plate and beaker. Father went to school here, and so did grandfather. It is our right to keep it. Our children will make out all right. This, in a rough way, is the democracy of the adult. But it may very easily come into conflict with the democracy of the child. It may even represent a stubborn denial to the child of his right to a decent educational opportunity. If it is clear that this is happening, then no amount of devotion to a beloved landmark in the community should keep the adults from making arrangements that will give to the children the educational advantages essential to their proper development. This is the democratic right of the child. The argument here is not for a step-by-step surrender of local controls to ever larger units until complete state control results. It is, rather, for the continuation of local control; but, emphatically, local control associated with local schools that are efficient and that give to all pupils the advantages they are entitled to.

The Interest of All the People.—The American principle of delegation of authority and responsibility to the states and, in turn, to the local units, places a heavy obligation on the people in the local units. The American system will succeed or not in the same measure as people discharge their responsibilities to the local schools. The people in a local community need to realize that they are stewards of a part of a state school system and that they can continue to be that if they acquit themselves well. It is as though the local group said to the state: "We appreciate your willingness to place this part of your school system under our jurisdiction; we are interested in good schools for our children and will strive continuously to make the public schools in this community the best possible." In this manner the public schools become what they ought to be: schools "of the people, by the people, and for the people."

Local Boards of Education.—One of the most direct ways the people of a local unit have of influencing the local schools is through the election of a board of education. In some communities, to be sure, board members are secured in other ways than by election; for example, through appointment by the mayor. Before this can be done, however, the state legislature must authorize it. In an overwhelming majority of cases, school board members are elected by the voters in the units they serve. Voters will also have opportunities beyond the election of the board to determine the character and quality of their schools, both directly and indirectly. Some matters will be presented for a vote to the people. Ordinarily, however, these will come first as direct recommendations from the board of education; hence the importance of selecting a good board is apparent.

Duties of the Board. The local board of education is the policy-making group for the local schools. There are certain state laws and regulations that it must observe; but beyond these it may develop the schools as it pleases and as it can. It is this situation that makes the local board, in the judgment of many, the most important controlling group in our whole school system. This group is responsible for such matters as the following:

1. Approving a budget for the operation of the schools, and directing how it shall be spent
2. Determining whether or not new areas of instruction may be added to the school program
3. Employing all school personnel, for the performance of duties clarified and understood
4. Establishing salary schedules for all school personnel
5. Authorizing the payment of bills
6. Deciding whether or not certain issues shall be placed before the people, such as whether or not new buildings should be constructed
7. Adopting regulations concerning such things as the use of school buildings and grounds for community purposes, the transporting of pupils, and the duties and responsibilities of school officers
8. Evaluating the effectiveness of the schools and their personnel

The list could be lengthened. The fundamental nature of the items is apparent.

Legislative, Not Executive. It is important to point out again that the functions of the local board of education are legislative and policy-making in character and not administrative. For example, when the board hires a new staff member, it must know that it is hiring this member to perform certain services, such as, let us say, the teaching of music. This does not mean, however, that the board will follow through with the administrative task of determining the teacher's class schedule, assigning the activities to be directed, and judging the competence of the teacher's work. Responsible administrative and supervisory officers will be employed by the board to follow through on these things. So it will go in many other matters. The basic decisions will be made by the board; their execution will be left to the professional school personnel. Some boards and administrative officers have done an excellent job of setting down in black and white their appropriate duties and relationships. This fosters confidence and understanding, eliminates much duplication of effort, and creates, through the fixing of responsibility, assurance that the real jobs connected with the smooth running of the schools are going to get done.

Nature of the Board. It is generally agreed that members of local boards of education should be lay citizens, competent, interested in making the public schools of most use to the children and the community at large, and willing to work at the job. No funny notions about social or professional standing, marital status, religious or political affiliation, sex, property-holding, childlessness, and so on should be allowed to deprive the community of the services of people who would make excellent board members. Tenure on the board should be relatively long, not less than three years. Boards should be small, but not necessarily all the same size. In tens of thousands of small districts, a board of three members is large enough. Other districts, such as large cities, should have more, but probably never more than seven or nine. The board should be kept small enough to transact its business as a committee of the whole. Special assignments will be given to individuals and small subcommittees, but this represents a division of labor and in no sense relieves any other member of his share of responsibility in making decisions on all matters.

Again, local board members are operating a segment of the state's school system. It follows, therefore, that legally their primary responsibility is to the state and not to the voters who elected them. This may seem to place the board between the horns of a dilemma, but it does not. Obviously the state wishes the local boards to conduct good schools in their communities. This gives the board full opportunity, at one and the same time, to be good representatives of the state and to bring into being in the community the good schools desired by the people.

Local School Organization.—Organization for education within the local units ranges from a very simple to a very complex thing. Figure 2 shows the simplest arrangement, which, incidentally, is found in thousands of local districts. The people elect a board of education, which hires a teacher, who teaches the pupils. This simple organization applies, of course, to local units that have only one school with one teacher. If there are enough pupils to require the services of two teachers, then administrative officers begin to bob up, for in some states the law requires that in such a school one of the teachers must be designated as principal or head teacher. If the school has several teachers, a principal who can coordinate and improve the work of the school must be employed. If the local unit has several schools, each with a principal and a corps of teachers, then coordination among the schools is necessary, and a superintendent of schools is employed. A

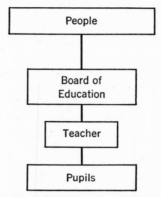

Figure 2. Simplest Organization for Education in Local Units

local school system having these added functionaries is illustrated in Figure 3. This same basic pattern, further expanded, is followed in the organization of the complex city school system. In such a system certain aspects of the total program are so important and far-reaching that the superintendent needs special assistants to be responsible in those areas. He cannot possibly handle all matters himself. For example, the business management involved in a large system is tremendous. Millions of dollars are handled. The management of supplies, purchases, salaries, debt services, and the like must not be inefficient or tardy. Hence a special assistant to the superintendent, sometimes designated as the business manager, is employed. Also the job of keeping the necessary records on all the pupils, a tremendous job in a large system, is sometimes assigned to a special assistant. An assistant who will be in charge of research studies is sometimes named. There may also be an assistant in charge of curriculum planning and revision on a system-wide basis. And certainly there will be one in charge of instruction at all levels, who, in turn, will have helpers expert at the elementary and secondary levels, and in special subject fields. The work of the principals and teachers will be coordinated by the assistant in charge of instruction. The other assistants will have a considerable corps of helpers, but the division of instruction will be the most expansive and the most important. This is not to detract from the importance of the others, but their programs are justified, in fact, only as they contribute to the welfare of the children in the classrooms.

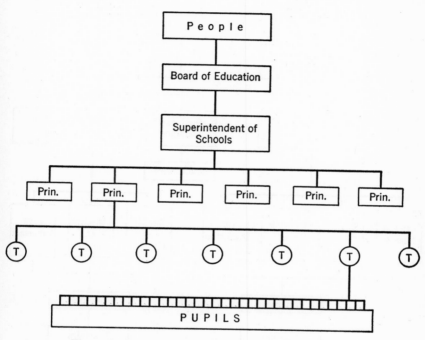

Figure 3. Organization in Local Units of Moderate Size

Unit and Multiple Control. The matter of all branches contributing to the welfare of the children in the classrooms gives point to the emphasis placed today upon integration and coordination in school administration. If such coordination is to be achieved, the school system will need one coordinating head, the superintendent of schools, and will not set up two or more independent heads who deal directly with the board of education. When a school system has a single administrative head who coordinates the work and activities of the entire system, it is said to be a "unit control" system. If there are two heads of equal authority, each dealing directly with the board of education, the system is said to have "dual control." If there are more than two such independent heads, the system is operating under "multiple control." Figure 4 illustrates the unit and dual situations. There seems to be no question in the minds of students of school administration as to which of the three types of control is the best. School systems will experience less confusion and will be able to progress more unitedly toward accepted goals if "unit control" is practiced.

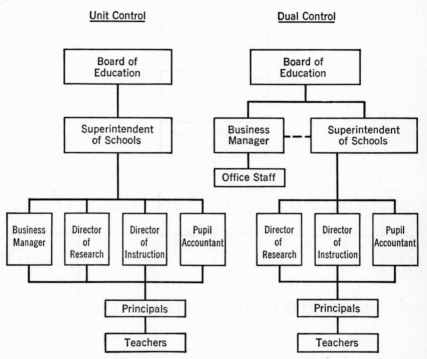

Figure 4. Unit and Dual Control in Local School Administration

Interrelationships Among Local Personnel.—Our description thus far of the American school system makes it clear that it is at the local level where the effectiveness of our education is primarily determined. One of the most important factors that will determine the effectiveness of the local schools is the interrelationships among local personnel. This, of course, is not limited to school personnel but includes everybody in the community. A few of these interrelationships ought to be emphasized.

The People and the Board of Education. The most important single official action that the people of a community can take with reference to education is the election of a board of education. This should concern them mightily, and they ought to be careful. Many writers who wish to emphasize the importance of this choice insist that board members should be chosen in a special election. In this way the people are able to dissociate the choosing of a governing board for their public schools from the political cross-currents of a general election. Furthermore, the people ought to be interested in the doings of the board once it is chosen. The board should welcome and stimulate this interest. It is a good practice to have the people understand that they are welcome to attend board meetings. After all, the board is determining policy for public, not private, schools; and the public, which supports the schools, should be urged to keep in close contact. Alert boards will cultivate this relationship as a means of securing public support for policies they believe will improve the education of the children. Frank and continuous contact between the people and the board can help to establish popular confidence in the board, without which real leadership cannot be exercised.

The Board and the Superintendent of Schools. Brief reference was made to the relationship of the board and the superintendent when the functions of the board were described on pages 140 and 141. The superintendent of schools, like the state commissioner of education, is the executive officer of the board under which he serves. He is the board's professional expert, and he should supply to the board the best available information and opinion on problems that arise. He should, therefore, be in a position to make wise recommendations concerning school policy. The board will or will not adopt his recommendations. Theirs, it will be remembered, is the policy-making responsibility. If the board adopts his recommendations, it therewith places upon him the responsibility for carrying them out. He is employed to do this. As the board's professional expert, he should do the professional job. It is at this point of discriminating between legislative and executive functions that trouble sometimes arises between boards and superintendents. The board, for example, ought to adopt policy concerning the minimum qualifications and salaries of teachers; but it ought to leave to the superintendent the professional job of finding and recommending qualified persons whom the board may hire and of determining the job assignments of these people in the school system. A superintendent who makes a diligent search to find qualified candidates for a coaching job, and brings into a board meeting one or two names of people whom he recommends for employment should not have to endure the shock of having a board member present the name of a surprise competing candidate who, for that matter, may be employed, thus setting aside the professional service the superintendent was employed to render. Similarly, the board will authorize the purchase of science equipment for the school system, but it will hardly designate the classrooms in which individual microscopes are to be placed. It needs to be pointed out that whereas the board hires the superintendent as its professional expert and executive officer, it is still responsible for appraising his effectiveness on the job. It needs to be emphasized also that if the board finds that it has an ineffective superintendent on the job, it errs inexcusably if it begins to perform his administrative duties for him. It acts with dignity and caliber if it proceeds in good form to find another executive who can supply the professional leadership needed. Let us refer again to the desirability of boards and superintendents working out in writing a clarification of the proper functions and responsibilities of each. If this is done and observed, both will come closer to an effective discharge of the duties placed upon them by the state and by the people of the communities they serve.

The Superintendent and the Principals. The good superintendent will do his best to recommend for principalships only persons who understand the proper goals and techniques of democratic education and who can work harmoniously with teaching staffs. If he succeeds in this, his primary obligation to individual schools is met, for then he ought to let such persons alone to do the good jobs of which they are capable. He will always be available to assist, guide, and coordinate the work of all the principals so that all the children in all the schools will receive a good education; but he will remain the general supervisor and coordinator and not become the administrator of a given school himself. Sure enough, he is responsible for recommending to the board persons who will be good principals. If, however, he gets a bad one, he should recommend that he be replaced by a better person, and not take over the duties himself. This sometimes becomes an especially serious problem in some small school systems. For example, a good many superintendents are in charge of systems that have several elementary schools and one high school. The superintendent's office is frequently in the high school building; or, for that matter, in one of the elementary school buildings. He does not have separate administrative offices. When this is the case, he may find it hard at times not to step in and assume certain administrative duties and give certain directions in the school where he is situated, when he feels that things are not going well enough. It is probably a good practice, when it is possible, to locate the superintendent in offices outside the school buildings.

The superintendent and the principals, like the board and the superintendent, should work out a clear understanding of their duties and relationships and then act accordingly. Much responsibility should be delegated to principals and they should be given commensurate authority. They should be consulted on matters pertaining to their schools, such as the selection of candidates who are to be recommended for jobs in their schools, the drawing-up of budgets for educational supplies and equipment, and the determination of the educational program best suited to the needs of their communities. Principals will, in turn, cooperate in every way possible with the superintendent and other general officers associated with his staff in making their schools good schools in a good system.

The Principals and the Teachers. It used to be argued that the principle of delegated responsibility in connection with local school control ended with the school principal. He was placed in a building to be in charge. The teachers' job was to instruct and not to administer. The principal "ran" the school; the teachers were fortunate if they had a good principal and unfortunate if they didn't. But times have changed. Today principals and teachers cooperate in making all aspects of the school, including its administration, as effective as possible. The good principal delights in working with committees of his staff not only on problems connected with instruction but on administrative problems also. He will doubtless evolve a better system of traffic control or of pupil activities or of guidance services if he enlists from teachers, and pupils, all the help he can get. Furthermore, although principals and superintendents are employed to be the professional supervisors and administrators of the schools, they will, if they seek a maximum of strength and democracy in the operation of the schools, go beyond the professional staff and secure the judgments of qualified people in the community on school problems. They will not give over the responsibility for decision-making on professional matters to lay people; but they will use lay people as sources of ideas and information that will help them make wiser decisions in their own areas of responsibility. Teachers who work in schools where the principals turn to them for serious participation in planning and directing the educational program are almost certain to develop interests and loyalties that will be manifested in better services to the children.

Administrators Versus Teachers. Although in many communities in the United States the relationships between administrators and teachers are excellent, we should not suppose that they are satisfactory everywhere. There is a distressing tendency among our teachers to feel that, when one of their number is advanced to an administrative position, he is now on the other side of the fence. He has, as it were, deserted the ranks. He has suddenly come to represent the voice of authority of the board of education and no longer represents the teachers. He seems now to stand between the teachers and the board, defending the board against the teachers. Saddest of all, some administrators by their actions justify these feelings. They seem to revel in the exercise of authority and they fairly bask in the dignity they assign to higher rank. They will not jeopardize their administrative posts by urging upon boards of education the adoption of measures intended to improve the working conditions of the entire staff. It can without question be shown that in some communities teachers' groups have been formed to sponsor before the board of education reasonable matters that by all means should have been sponsored by the superintendent of schools but were not. In some cases, teachers' strikes are as much against ineffective school administrators as anything else. It is not too much to say that if local school administrators do not wish to have local teachers' organizations replace them as contact agents with the board, they must learn how to cooperate better with teachers and continue to be the teachers' best voice before the board. Teachers, in turn, can mightily strengthen the hands of an administrator who is sincere and fearless in his effort to improve the schools.

If the above situation is somewhat sharply drawn, it is because the writer believes that the "critical point" with reference to the future solidarity of the profession of education lies in the area of administrator-teacher relationships. Schism here will permit the introduction of influences that can change the nature and purpose of public education. Stated positively, unity here, and the development of techniques of cooperative action, can secure for education the independent voice and service it ought to have and keep.

The Welfare of the Learner as the Common Ground. Schools are conducted, of course, for learners. There would be no need to hire teachers if it were not for learners—or to build school buildings, or have superintendents, or elect boards of education. There is no justification of school taxes, or chalk, or salary schedules except in terms of learners. The school program, plant, and personnel have the welfare of learners as their central aim; and this aim is big enough to command the best services of all. The interrelationships of all school workers and patrons take on unity around this aim. Each sees his own work and the work of others as important in achieving it. Furthermore, when anyone shirks his duty or does less than his best, or when people who ought to know how to work together do not, the inescapable victims are the learners in the classrooms. As we contemplate the operation of the multiplied thousands of our local schools, we return again to the clear conclusion that the object of primary importance is the individual child, and around him we build and justify our educational enterprise.

6. Federal-State-Local Interrelationships

Let us recapitulate briefly here for purposes of reorientation.

The United States has stayed far away from any semblance of a centralized federal school system like that found in many other nations. The tradition of our federal government, however, is not one of no concern for education; it is, on the other hand, one of interest and assistance. Our government early placed the responsibility for the organization of a school system on the individual states. Our people have favored this, and the states have organized such systems; but we still hold that our federal government has an obligation to education as an aspect of the general welfare. It should therefore aid the states if the need for its help can be demonstrated, using as channels for its aid the systems it has asked the states to establish.

Our states have established their public school systems and are constantly passing additional laws affecting them. They organized local units that are subdivisions of the state system and delegated to these units much responsibility for the direction and support of the local schools. Of late years there has been a considerable tendency for the states to increase their support of the local schools and a lesser tendency to increase their control.

On the local level the people are very jealous of their public schools. They tend too much to see the schools as strictly local rather than as parts of a state system, and they resist "interference." However, they are coming to see and accept their more distant relationships, and they seek more and more to be good stewards of the state. The quality of education in the local units varies greatly.

In general, the American pattern is one of delegated control, until the last citizen in the farthest hamlet is reached. We have been inclined to place in the citizen's hands the responsibility for the direction and support of the schools in his community. Delegation, however, has not meant abandonment. Responsibility for the quality of education in the remotest community continues to be felt by state and federal governments. These governments are inclined to say: "Mr. Citizen, you have done well, within the resources at your disposal, in making your part of our schools effective; keep up the good work, and here's some money to help you make our schools better." Our educational faith, therefore, has been placed in the local community and in the common man; and the common man, sensing the greatness of his calling, swells with good feeling and good resolution as his state and federal governments place real confidence in him.

7. Relationship Between Control of Education and the General Education of All the People

The typical American soldier of the first World War was found to have an education at about the sixth grade level. The general education of our armed forces during the second World War was at about the tenth grade level. In November, 1947, the Bureau of the Census of our Department of Commerce estimated that in April of that year,

The median number of school years completed by persons in the younger age groups (20 to 29 years old) was about 12 years, representing the completion of high school. This level represents an increase of about four years of schooling over that reported by the population who completed their schooling a little more than a generation ago (those 55 to 64 years old). The general pattern among adults of a higher educational level at successively younger ages reflects the historic trend toward more and more schooling.[3]

In other words, our young people (twenty to twenty-nine) who have had fewer years in which to get an education have more education (twelve years) than our older people (fifty-five to sixty-four), who have had more years in which to get an education, but who actually have less (eight years).

The general education of our people is clearly rising. It is quite likely that by 1965 the average years of schooling of persons becoming thirty years of age will be fourteen or better. The future certainly will see new generations of youth coming into adulthood with more and more education. These citizens will, of course, make up our local communities; and if their education has been at all effective, they should be better and better equipped to think straight, act cooperatively, and deal wisely with problems of local and general concern. It seems, therefore, that state and federal governments should not find it hard to place more and more confidence in the people at large.

[3] Bureau of the Census, *Educational Attainment of the Population: April, 1947,* Series P-20, No. 6 (Washington, D. C.: U. S. Government Printing Office, 1947).

It simply is not consistent to parallel a general upgrading in education with increased centralization of control. Local units will always, of course, have to recognize state and federal responsibilities to education and make proper adjustments to both. Similarly, states will realize that there are federal responsibilities to which they must adjust. But the adjustments will be the result of cooperative action, not coercion. The arrow of confidence, reflected in the decentralized control of education, will point outward from the central government, through the states, to the local units. It certainly should not point inward toward centralized control, indicating a withdrawal of confidence at a time when our people are more and more able to discharge greater responsibilities. The great urgency of education in a democracy is to give youth the background and experiences through which they can develop into responsible citizens, skilled in thinking and acting personally and cooperatively for the general good, and not drilled in the art of submitting to the thoughts and authority of others. If democratic education can achieve this, then these people, in the communities where they live, ought not to be denied the acceptance of responsibilities that they are prepared to assume. Government that educates its people for responsible citizenship and then withdraws that responsibility is inconsistent. To the extent that it withdraws from the people the responsibilities they are able to discharge, it is undemocratic. The assignment of responsibilities in line with the ability to discharge them breeds confidence and good feeling and induces growth. Education for responsibility accompanied by failure to grant responsibility breeds feelings of futility and actual mistrust. The workings of a democracy must be so ordered that the best in every person will be challenged and used. On this basis, local control holds the best promise for the future.

8. The New Concept of Leadership

During recent years a new concept of educational leadership has become articulate in this country, and much effort is now being put forth to put it into practice. This concept came into sharp focus after the second World War, when American education looked in on itself and found a disturbing amount of the very thing we had fought to eliminate in this world—dictatorship. We were surprised to find so great a gap between the democracy we had talked about and the democracy we practiced. Our schools were conducted too much on an authoritarian basis. Administrators made the decisions; teachers accepted them. The principal conducted the faculty meeting, made the announcements, and assigned all responsibilities. Administrators were responsible for the running of the schools; why shouldn't they "run" them? "If you're not happy here, move on. We expect our teachers to cooperate with us." Textbooks were chosen in the central office; curriculum changes originated there. Teacher rating was imposed from above. Parents were not welcomed at school. The board of education would not admit patrons to its meetings. The state department of education issued courses of study that must be followed in all the public schools. It was strong on inspection and accreditation. The legislature passed laws requiring the teaching of certain subjects in the schools. Worst of all, the teachers in the classroom were dictators. Learning seemed to be a teacher-telling and pupil-conforming process. Fear and dogged routine thwarted the development of normal, healthy personalities. These conditions were not universal; but as we looked around we found them all too prevalent. Fortunately we have recognized that such practices are not compatible with our democratic ideal, and we are doing something about it.

The new concept of leadership rests squarely on the democratic insistence that every individual counts. His mind and personality are to be respected. He is capable of ideas that deserve to be heard. Under this concept the leader is not the director, keeping others "in line" with his way of doing things. He is, rather, one who knows how to motivate, to challenge, to stimulate all who are associated with him. He sees clearly the major goals and problems of his enterprise, and he is skilled in organizing his helpers around them. He has a keen sense of coordination, causing all activities to contribute to the achievement of major ends. He honestly admits that he does not know all the answers; and he knows full well that he has people on his staff who are just as good thinkers as he is. He seeks to tap ideas wherever he finds them; and, above all, to cause those who have been barren of ideas to generate a few. His primary task is to be big enough himself in the concept of his job and skilled enough in his dealings with people that their finest abilities will be turned to constructive ends. He no longer feels that he will lose status if he does not furnish all the ideas. He takes on status as he becomes a genuine leader, demonstrating faith in people and stimulating them cooperatively to move forward on the solution of vital problems. Thus the federal government places at the disposal of the states its resources of counsel, leadership, and funds without its coercion. It respects the ability of the states to deal intelligently with their own problems, and it urges them to attack them. The states, in turn, work for "grass roots" improvement. They refrain from recalling to themselves the direct responsibility for educational planning and direction which they have delegated to the local units. They stay on hand to assist and stimulate and coordinate, but they do not coerce. The local leadership enlists the wit and services of all in making education the experience in cooperative action that it ought to be. And again, above all, the new leadership must permeate the classroom. If education will practice the democracy it preaches, our youth will experience and establish the patterns of conduct that are basic to the preservation of the freedoms we cherish. Without such leadership and such cooperative action, we shall surely have lived an obvious lie.

9. Nongovernmental Agencies and Education

There are many agencies in this country not a part of the public school system which greatly influence education. It is impossible, of course, to discuss them all. The following are illustrative and will serve to emphasize the many forces that bear upon education in a free society.

Professional Associations.—Professional associations may be thought of as organizations whose membership is drawn from educational workers, and whose purposes deal with some aspect of professional education. There are hundreds of such organizations. Some serve broad purposes within the profession and some concentrate on narrow fields. The largest and most comprehensively organized professional association is the National Education Association. In May, 1950, it had a membership of 453,797 and twenty-eight different departments, to say nothing of a large number of committees, commissions, councils, and divisions. Some of its departments have several thousand members and include such organizations as the following: American Association of School Administrators; American Educational Research Association; Association for Supervision and Curriculum Development; National Association of Secondary-School Principals; National Council for the Social Studies; Rural Education; Audio-Visual Instruction; Classroom Teachers; American Association for Health, Physical Education, and Recreation; and American Association of Colleges for Teacher Education. The influence of this powerful organization on American education can well be imagined. All of the forty-eight states also have state associations and hundreds of local associations. The local associations are ordinarily affiliated with the state associations, and all of the state associations are affiliated with the NEA. The American Council on Education is another far-reaching, influential professional organization. The American Education Fellowship, the John Dewey Society, and a host of others hold conferences, conduct studies, and publish materials that exert a wide influence.

Accrediting Associations.—Accrediting agencies may be national, regional, state, or local in their scope. Individual institutions, such as state universities, sometimes accredit also. National accrediting bodies deal ordinarily with professional education in various fields. Some of these agencies are the American Bar Association, the American Medical Association, the American Dental Association, the American Association of Colleges for Teacher Education, the American Association of Schools of Social Work, and the National Association of Schools of Music. So it goes for chemistry, engineering, architecture, forestry, journalism, pharmacy, business, and other subject fields. The regional accrediting associations, which, by the way, give much more attention to secondary schools, are the following: Middle States Association of Colleges and Secondary Schools, New England Association of Colleges and Secondary Schools, North Central Association of Colleges and Secondary Schools, Northwest Association of Secondary and Higher Schools, Southern Association of Colleges and Secondary Schools, and Western College Association. Not all of these associations are equally rigid in their standards for membership. In numerous states the state department of education acts as an accrediting agency.

The important point about accrediting associations is that they set up standards which must be met before membership can be obtained. Such matters as school plant, equipment, endowment, curricula, requirements for graduation, qualifications and teaching load of staff members, school records, efficiency of instruction, and school organization and administration are dealt with. The far-reaching nature of these criteria is apparent. Membership in a strong accrediting association carries considerable advantage and prestige with it, hence schools are ambitious to be accredited. This has served as a powerful stimulus to school leaders to bring their institutions up to requirements. The standards of the associations, clearly set down in published form, have been the chief yardstick and weapon of many local school administrators in their efforts to secure improvements in the schools. However, this process can be carried too far. Accrediting associations can become the very negation of the type of local initiative for which we have argued all along. There is not much point to our objecting to federal and state control of our public schools if we turn around and permit them to be controlled by private accrediting agencies. A college president or dean often finds that he is more an implementer of externally imposed curricula and standards than a leader of his staff in studying the basic goals of education and suiting the curriculum to the purposes of the institution. Furthermore, there is a strong tendency for schools that are accredited to become self-satisfied and to feel that all is well so long as they do not lose their accredited status. The eye of the school, therefore, is on external forces; on the fulfilment of standards that will be checked faithfully by the inspectors when they arrive. The coercive element in accreditation at present cannot be gainsaid.

Accrediting associations, exerting, as they do, tremendous influence, need to examine their manner of operating and judge it by democratic standards. If this is done it may be that coercion and inspection will give way to leadership and cooperation. The representatives to the associations will be welcomed as consultants and helpers and not feared as inspectors and checkers. These organizations, if they will, can replace a kind of superexistence above the schools with a stimulating, cooperative, human relationship with the schools. One does not argue, therefore, for the elimination of these organizations any more than he argues for the elimination of the state department of education; but he does argue, as in the case of the state department, that they ought to wield their power more for leadership purposes and less for control purposes. This is exactly the direction taken by the North Central Association of Colleges and Secondary Schools when it initiated the cooperative study of secondary school standards which came out with materials for the evaluation of secondary schools. These materials, above all, were to be used by the schools themselves; and they have become the basis for self-study and self-improvement in thousands of schools. This is a service of leadership.

Educational Foundations.—There are a good many foundations in this country that include educational projects in their support programs. Some of them have extremely large endowments and have expended large sums of money for the promotion of education in one form or another. Mention of a few of the better-known foundations will give some conception of the influence they exert.

One of the earliest of the educational foundations was the John F. Slater Fund, established in 1882, to aid in providing normal school and industrial education for Negroes. In 1902, the General Education Board was established, and received an initial endowment of $129,209,167 from John D. Rockefeller. To date the board has expended approximately $300,000,000 for the promotion of education "within the United States of America, without distinction of race, sex, or creed." The activities of the board have been concentrated somewhat in the South, and close cooperation with state departments of education has been maintained. Mr. Rockefeller also gave $182,814,480 for the original endowment of the Rockefeller Foundation, set up in 1913. The purpose of this foundation is "to promote the well being of mankind throughout the world" through the advancement of knowledge. Its international character is noted. To date it has expended approximately $400,000,000. In 1905 the Carnegie Foundation for the Advancement of Teaching was founded, with an endowment of $10,000,000 given by Andrew Carnegie. This foundation has spent over $50,000,000 to date "to do and perform all things necessary to encourage, uphold, and dignify the profession of the teacher and the cause of higher education." Mr. Carnegie also contributed $125,000,000 as the original endowment of the Carnegie Corporation of New York, established in 1911. This organization has expended over $200,000,000 for the "advancement and diffusion of knowledge and understanding among the people of the United States and the British Dominions and Colonies." Special emphasis is placed on the discovery and application of new knowledge. The Julius Rosenwald Fund was set up in 1917 with an endowment of $20,000,000 to aid in the general improvement of Negro education, mainly through school buildings, libraries, and consolidation. Mr. Rosenwald specified that the entire fund, principal and interest, must be used up within twenty-five years after his death. He died in 1932, and the fund was closed out in 1948. The Mary Louise Curtis Bok Foundation, with an original endowment of $12,500,000, was set up in 1931 for the "support of music and musical education, support and promotion of fine arts, science, scientific research, invention, discovery, or general education." In 1937 the W. W. Kellogg Foundation was established "to promote the health, education and welfare of mankind." Already it has spent approximately $25,000,000 for this purpose, and its activities have expanded from local and regional projects to projects of national and international scope and consequence. More recently the Ford Foundation has been established. The exact amount of its endowment has not been announced, but it is presumed to be larger than for any other foundation of its kind. The five main areas to which it will give attention initially are: the establishment of peace, the strengthening of democracy, the strengthening of the economy, education in a democratic society, and individual behavior and human relations.

No comment is needed to convince the reader that foundations such as these, with their resources of money, expert leadership, and publication facilities, affect our education in a significant manner.

Pressure Groups.—For most people, the matter of pressure groups and their relation to education comes much closer home than do the activities of professional associations, accrediting associations, and educational foundations. Pressure groups can and do operate on the grand scale, but they also operate in individual communities and on individual schools. The National Association of Manufacturers may seek to influence the content of American textbooks in the social studies, and the DAR can organize a drive to have Latin III rather than health education added to the local high school curriculum. Religious lobbies put the pressure on in Washington, D. C., and they also put the pressure on in Centerville. Whatever their scope of activity, pressure groups are a potent force in American education.

There are many pressure groups, such as the PTA, labor groups, religious groups, patriotic organizations, veterans organizations, farmers' organizations, civic groups, business and manufacturing concerns, government agencies, educational organizations, political groups, and so on. Frequently they have no intention of operating as pressure groups and do not realize it when they do. Let us make two points clear.

Pressure groups should not be discounted as bad in all respects. The interest they take in the schools, even for selfish ends, is an open recognition on their part of the potentialities of the school. No educational leader would wish to have all the groups listed above suddenly decide to have nothing to do with the schools. If he is a skilled leader, he will welcome these group interests and democratically turn them to unselfish ends if he can. Resistance to them means misery. An honest effort to absorb narrower group interests into larger school purposes may succeed. This is not to be interpreted as "giving in" or "giving up" to pressure groups. Many of the ideas and suggestions of pressure groups are not selfish at all. They are good ideas, and they promote the general welfare of the pupils and the community. It goes without saying that the good leader will accept good ideas wherever he finds them.

Information about pressure groups is legitimate content for our public schools; content prepared by pressure groups, by which they propagandize their special interests, is not. In public schools the pupils are students of society, and should examine with equal open-mindedness all the organizations that constitute it. The public school stands between them and bias, bigotry, pressure, and propaganda; and it must insist that the teacher and the teaching materials promote intellectual honesty and broad understandings.

Private Research and Writing.—It goes without saying that the private thinker and researcher, working in the seclusion of his own study or laboratory and free in this great country to publish openly the results of his studies, has a profound effect on our education. Historically this has been the primary basis of progress. Only recently has the public subsidization of research taken on significant proportions.

10. RECAPITULATION

In the preceding pages we have sought to draw a simple and accurate outline of the place of the federal, state, and local units in our school organization and administration and to show certain relationships among them. Emphasis has been given to a democratic type of leadership which motivates and coordinates rather than dominates. We have insisted that it is inconsistent in a democracy to have greater centralization of control parallel a general rise in the education of all the people. Brief attention has also been given to some nongovernmental agencies that are influential in determining the nature and quality of our education.

What Do YOU Say?

1

It ought not to be necessary for the federal government to organize federally supported schools that compete with existing public schools or duplicate their programs.

What do YOU say?

2

Each state has the obligation to study and redistrict its local schools so that the best arrangement for school children and the best use of local resources can result. It is wiser to approach this problem on a state-wide basis than to hope it will be solved through voluntary arrangements among local districts.

What do YOU say?

3

Education concerns all the people; and everyone should be actively concerned with it. Any school superintendent or principal who insists that the schools are his responsibility and that he will supply all the ideas and decisions ought either to learn and practice the art of promoting wide interest and participation in school affairs or be relieved of his job.

What do YOU say?

4

What points in this chapter do you particularly support or take issue with?

Chapter 6

THE SUPPORT OF SCHOOLS IN AMERICA

Buying What We Believe In

America has presented a most interesting situation with respect to the support of education. Our record is one of amazing neglect and inadequacy; but it also contains examples of a fine capacity to act when the schools are threatened. Our fundamental belief in education has not been reflected in an adequate support of education; but when public education following the second World War was shown to be in real danger of disintegration, the radio, press, pulpit, and other agencies came to its support with telling vigor. The result was not fruitful enough, but the evidence that our people appreciate the central position of the school in our society and are not willing to see it deteriorate is most encouraging. It gives some hope that in the future the support of education will be a little more in line with the relative value of its services.

1. How Much Is Spent?

Expenditures for public schools in this country have ranged from about three to about five billion dollars a year during the last few years. The second World War caused some reductions, particularly in capital outlays, but total expenditures during the war did not sag greatly. Column 10 of Table 1 on page 164 shows the total expenditures for public education since 1920. There are, of course, additional expenditures for private schools.

The relationship of the total expenditures for public education and the national income shows considerable variation during the last few years. In 1929, just prior to the great depression, when the national income was eighty-three billion dollars, our expenditures for public education were $2,316,790,000, or about 2.7 per cent of the national income. In 1932 the national income dropped to forty billion dollars, of which about 5.2 per cent was spent for public education. By 1943 the national income had reached approximately 150 billion dollars, but the amount spent for public education was the same as for

1929, or 1.5 per cent of the 1943 total income. In 1948 the percentage was still approximately 1.5, and in 1950 it was about 2 per cent. This, incidentally, compares badly with educational support in England and Russia since the war.

Some students of school finance in this country estimate that our total expenditures for education ought not to be less than about 5 per cent of our national income. If this had held in 1950, when our national income was better than 200 billion dollars, our expenditures for public education would have been about eleven billion dollars instead of about five billion.

2. What Is It Spent For?

The customary classification of educational expenditures gives an excellent idea of what educational funds are spent for.

Classification of Expenditures.—Mort and Reusser, in their book entitled *Public School Finance*,[1] not only classify school expenditures but illustrate expenditures under each class, as follows:

1. General control
   Business administration
     Board of Education
     Secretary of board
     School elections
     School census
   Educational administration
     Superintendent's salary
     Superintendent's office, clerical
     Superintendent's office, supplies

2. Instruction
   Supervisors
     Salaries
     Supplies
     Clerical
   Principals
     Salaries
     Supplies
     Clerical
   Instructional service
     Teachers' salaries
     Instructional supplies
     Free textbooks

3. Auxiliary agencies
   Library salaries
   Library supplies
   Transportation salaries
   Transportation expense
   Lunchroom
   Tuition to other districts

4. Coordinate activities
   Compulsory attendance
   Medical service
   Nurses' salaries
   Dental service

5. Operation of plant
   Salaries
   Janitor's supplies
   Fuel, water, light
   Power

6. Fixed charges
   Insurance
   Rent

[1] By permission from *Public School Finance* by Paul R. Mort and Walter C. Reusser. Copyright, 1941, by McGraw-Hill Book Co., Inc.

7. Maintenance of plant
  Upkeep of grounds
    Labor
    Materials
  Upkeep of buildings
    Labor
    Materials
  Upkeep of service systems
    Labor
    Materials

8. Capital outlay
  Purchase of land
  Improvement of land
  Construction of buildings
  Improvement of buildings
  Construction of service systems
  Improvement of service systems
  Furniture
  Instructional apparatus

9. Debt service
  Bond redemption
    Current funds
    Sinking funds
  Bond interest
    Current funds
    Sinking funds
  Temporary loans
    Payment
    Interest

Mort and Reusser point out that each of the above classifications can, of course, be itemized much further. Furthermore, in small school systems, some of the classifications may be combined, such as "operation of plant" with "fixed charges" and "auxiliary agencies" with "coordinate activities."

The principal classes of expenditures used by the United States Office of Education, as indicated in Table 1, are as follows:

1. Administration
2. Instruction
3. Operation of plant
4. Maintenance of plant
5. Auxiliary agencies
6. Fixed charges
7. Debt service
8. Capital outlays
9. Summer and adult schools

The similarity between the classifications used by Mort and Reusser and by the United States Office of Education is apparent.

The data in Table 1 show some very interesting facts concerning educational expenditures since 1920. For example, the effect of the war on capital outlays is clearly portrayed in column 7. From a high of 370 million in 1930, expenditures fell off to a low of fifty-three million in 1944. Increases after 1944 were slow until about 1947. The accumulated backlog of needed school building construction represents one of our serious educational problems today. In 1948 the

Office of Education estimated that it would take $450,000,000 a year for ten years to make up past shortages and meet annual needs in capital outlays. Columns 3 and 4 show how increasingly costly it was to keep a plant going that remained substantially the same between 1942 and 1947. Several items, such as administration, instruction, auxiliary agencies, and fixed charges, have maintained a steady, uninterrupted rise since 1920, in spite of the war. Summer and adult schools suffered a severe slump between 1940 and 1942 and have got back to 1940 levels only recently. Interesting relationships between some of the columns could be pointed out, such as that between capital outlays in Column 7 and interest payments in Column 8.

Attention should be called briefly to the relatively large amount spent for instruction. This is as it should be. Numerous writers insist that from 65 to 70 per cent of all expenditures should go for instruction. This will vary at different times, of course, for a given school system; but unless the average over a long period of years is about this amount, something is a little out of line. An analysis of the data in Table 1 reveals that, for the country as a whole, instructional costs from 1920 to 1940 were about 60 per cent of the total costs. After 1940 this percentage rose to about 65 per cent in 1946. Since then, because of the great rise in capital outlay, the percentage has returned to about 60. Actually, all of the other items of the budget should be seen in a supporting relationship to instruction. In the last analysis, all educational expenditures must be able to be defended in terms of learners.

Meaning of the Budget.—The school budget represents the financial arrangement for the implementation of the educational program. It certainly should be viewed as a means to an end, and not the most important item in school matters. The fundamental approach in education should not be: "Will the budget permit it?" but rather, "What is the program we should have in our schools, and how can our budget be best adjusted to provide the largest possible part of that program?" If a local board of education finds that its financial resources will not buy the educational program that local pupils need, it should not contend weakly that "We don't have the money; our children must do without." The board has the moral obligation, based on the rights of children, to seek assistance beyond its own resources, in regional, state, or federal arrangements, that will make possible the opportunities the children under their charge are entitled to.

TABLE 1

EXPENDITURES FOR PUBLIC SCHOOLS *²

Year	Administration	Instruction: Including Instructional Supplies and Expenses	Operation of Plant	Maintenance of Plant	Auxiliary Agencies	Fixed Charges, Including Teacher Retirement	Capital Outlay	Interest Payments	Summer and Adult Schools	Grand Total of School Expenditures
	1	2	3	4	5	6	7	8	9	10
1951–52....										
1949–50....										
1947–48....	169.99	2,571.53	356.62	169.53	336.68	190.31	412.46	76.33	27.67	4,311.17
1945–46....	132.89	1,853.91	270.28	101.25	213.61	135.47	111.04	76.92	11.44	2,906.85
1944–45....	117.34	1,696.32	251.50	91.21	197.62	113.00	76.13	86.78	8.72	2,638.66
1943–44....	110.63	1,590.63	238.77	77.32	169.52	106.45	53.85	96.80	8.58	2,452.58
1942–43....	102.79	1,502.42	219.38	71.01	145.06	87.07	68.76	102.94	8.63	2,308.09
1941–42....	101.46	1,457.87	209.78	78.86	138.95	80.71	137.55	108.78	8.70	2,322.69
1939–40....	91.57	1,403.28	194.36	73.32	129.14	50.11	257.97	130.90	13.36	2,344.04
1929–30....	78.67	1,317.72	216.07	78.81	101.99	50.26	370.87	92.53	9.82	2,316.79
1919–20....	36.75	632.55	115.70	30.43	36.38	9.28	153.54	18.21	3.27	1,036.15

* In millions; continental United States.
² Adapted from *Statistical Circular*, Circular No. 241, May, 1948, Federal Security Agency, Office of Education, Washington, D. C. Also *Statistical Circular*, Circular No. 270, March, 1950.

Also, a place in the budget should not necessarily fix an activity in the educational program. Sometimes a kind of priority is attached to activities that have been previously provided for in the budget. However, a high school with limited funds that has supported a program of military science, for example, and is now convinced that a good program of health and physical education would serve the student body better, should find no difficulty in shifting funds to the new program. In other words, educational matters should take precedence over financial matters. The budget is to reflect, not direct, the educational program. Finance officers in educational institutions, therefore, are primarily implementers, rather than determiners, of educational policy.

3. Are Costs Rising?

Educational costs are rising, and for good reason. A few of the more obvious causes are noted here.

Increased School Enrolments.—During the period from about 1930 to 1945 the total enrolment in our public elementary and secondary schools dropped from 25,678,015 to 23,299,941. Table 6, page 229, presents the data. Since 1945 there has been a pronounced increase, particularly in the elementary school. In 1949 the total enrolment had returned to 1930 levels, and predictions based on birthrates call for an enrolment of at least twenty-eight million in 1953 and thirty million in 1956. These figures do not include enrolments in private schools or higher institutions. According to estimates, therefore, we shall have an enrolment increase of about seven million pupils in the public elementary and secondary schools between 1945 and 1956. Clearly, such enrolment increases affect educational costs. More pupils require more teachers, more buildings, more transportation, and more school supplies.

Increased Teachers Salaries.—We are not only employing more teachers in our schools, to take care of increased enrolments; we are also paying them better salaries. The average salary of teachers throughout the country for the 1945–46 school year was $1,995. Two years later, for 1947–48, it was $2,639. In 1950–51 it was estimated at $3,080. There are roughly a million teachers in the country. Hence, the expenditure for salaries in 1950–51 was roughly a billion dollars more than in 1945–46. Salary increases will likely continue, thus serving further to increase educational costs.

Increased Costs.—One of the reasons for the slowness in school building construction since the war is the glaring increase in building costs. Similar increases apply to all kinds of school supplies and services. If a million dollars prior to the war would buy a three-story school building, it would buy two stories of the same building after the war. In a single year after the beginning of the war in Korea, school building costs rose about 25 per cent. Under these conditions, some boards of education, eager to build much-needed buildings, have tried to get along with existing facilities, waiting for cost reductions that seem desperately slow in coming. However, other school supplies and services cannot be delayed. The children are on hand. The schools must go on. Increased costs must be met.

Reduced Purchasing Power of the Dollar.—In 1951 a dollar would buy about 55 per cent as much as it did in 1940. Or, in 1951, it would take about $1.80 to buy what $1.00 would buy in 1940. A school system that has an increasing number of pupils can hardly cut back on its school supplies and services; hence, it must raise the additional dollars necessary to buy the same things that fewer dollars would have bought a few years before.

Expansion of Educational Services.—Our schools, more than ever before, are being asked to provide a program that gives attention to the well-rounded development of youth. For example, physical and health education, vocational education, and education for the wise use of leisure time are considered quite as important now as the traditional academic subjects. Also, schools are being asked to do more for youth during more hours of the day and more months of the year. After-school recreational activities and summer playgrounds and camps are coming in most rapidly. The year-round school is no longer the impractical thought of an idle dreamer. Furthermore, schools are serving everybody in the community much more than they used to. Adult education is on the upsurge. The school, in fact, is being looked to by our society to perform many services that were completely foreign to it a generation or two ago. It all costs money.

Addition of Grades 13 and 14.—It begins to look now as though our states are in the process of adding the thirteenth and fourteenth grades to our system of free, tax-supported schools available to all youth. In other words, youngsters can go two years beyond graduation from high school without having to enter tuition institutions. Not every high school, of course, would add two years to its curriculum; but a regional public junior college would be within bus range of every youth who wished to continue his education at public expense. States like Washington and California are moving rapidly in this direction. It is a well-known fact that educational costs are higher at the higher grade levels than at the lower grade levels. The cost of adding the thirteenth and fourteenth grades to our public school system can therefore be appreciated.

Education Appropriate to All.—The people of this country know very well that the job of education is not complete when school buildings, desks, and buses have been made available to all children. Education must be appropriate to all as well as available to all. If this is done, pupil-teacher ratios are going to have to decrease, guidance and counseling services are going to have to increase, school curricula will have to change, much equipment will have to be added, clinical and testing services will have to expand, and so on. These, too, will add to school expenses.

The above items, and, of course, many others, all contribute to greater educational costs in America. These increases cause no alarm to persons whose first concern is the human concern; and whose urgent desire is to improve society through the steady improvement of its people.

4. How Much Is Needed?

It would be foolish to suggest a specific amount of money that the United States ought to spend annually on public education during the next several years. Economic conditions are too variable for that. Under present conditions, assuming that the program implied in Section 3 above were to be financed, we should perhaps be spending about ten billion dollars annually. If dollar values should go down, more dollars would be needed, and vice versa. Since the demands on education remain relatively constant, as represented by such things as the number of pupils enrolled and supplies and transportation required, some means should be found of maintaining educational support at satisfactory operational levels as economic conditions change. It is perhaps more fruitful to suggest again that about 5 per cent of our national income ought to go to public education. This is certainly not an exorbitant proportion, and it is definitely below that found in some other countries. Experience seems to be accumulating to show that 5 per cent of our national income will just about provide the educational program and services our people want their public schools to provide.

5. WHERE DOES IT COME FROM?

Money for public schools comes, of course, from public taxes. We have seen before that the public, as represented by government, is concerned with education at the federal, state, and local levels. All three of these levels of government have taxing powers; and all three can, and do, raise tax money for the support of public schools.

Federal, State, and Local Sources.—It will be remembered that the history of responsibility for public education in this country is one of delegation from federal to state to local agencies. This responsibility has carried with it the obligation to support the schools financially. Hence, for many years the local communities have been the chief source of tax income for public schools. As the costs of education have increased, however, and as local communities have been less and less able to meet these costs, assistance has been given by the states to the local units. The proportionate amount of support from federal sources is exceedingly small, and has changed very little over a long period of time. Of the $2,322,697,688 spent for public schools in the 1941–42 school year, 66.6 per cent came from local taxes, 31.6 per cent from state taxes, and 1.8 per cent from federal taxes. In 1949–50, the percentages had changed to 55.8, 41.8, and 2.4 respectively. These data are shown in Table 2. This, of course, is for the country as a whole. The situation varies greatly in individual states. For example, in 1949–50 the state of Delaware raised only 8.2 per cent of public school money from local taxes, whereas local taxes made up 92 per cent of public school funds in Nebraska. State support comprised 89.6 per cent in Delaware and only 5.9 per cent in Nebraska. Federal support ranged from 0.7 per cent in Missouri to 6.4 per cent in Nevada.

One significant trend among these sources of support is noticeable; that is, there is a definite increase in the percentage of the total funds that comes from the states. The states' share increased from 15 per cent in 1920 to 30 per cent in 1940 and to 41.8 per cent in 1950. It should not be supposed that as state percentages have increased, the actual amounts spent by local and federal units have decreased. This certainly is not the case. Although federal amounts have increased only slightly, local amounts have increased substantially. Only the proportions have changed. Local resources, however, have been used to the limit in many places. Hence, the increased costs of education in recent years are being taken up more and more by state funds. We shall see later that the states, too, have unequal resources, and that the federal government should see to it that increased educational costs do not mean that in some states and communities the children will be deprived of decent educational opportunities. The financial responsibility for education, like our interest in education, is joint, involving federal, state, and local resources.

There seems to be rather general agreement among school administrators in this country that the primary support of public education should never pass from the local communities. One frequently encounters the suggestion that, on the whole, state and federal support should not carry more than about 50 per cent of the load. The objective here is retention of the American tradition that the schools belong to the people. This will most surely occur if local communities really show an interest in and make some sacrifice for their schools. However, here again the controlling idea in any given situation should not be to preserve a certain support relationship. It ought to be, rather, the adjustment of those relationships so as to provide good educational opportunities to all of America's children.

Different Types of Taxes.—As revealed in Table 2, at present a little more than half of the income for public schools comes from taxes on real property, such as lands, buildings, machinery, household goods, livestock, automobiles, and so on. It also happens that most of the money for other public services, such as police and fire protection, government, and streets and roads, comes from the same source. In recent years the number and cost of public services have steadily increased. Tax people tell us that real property in some cases has become overtaxed. People with wealth, observing the heavy tax on real property, are inclined to limit their real property holdings. Nevertheless, our people still seem to want to buy more and more services through taxation. It follows that new sources of tax income are being sought to finance public services. Wealth other than property holdings is being tapped through such taxes as income tax, corporation tax, severance tax, and inheritance tax. Such taxes as sales taxes, luxury taxes, liquor and tobacco taxes, and gasoline taxes are levied widely on the general proposition that people buy things in proportion to their ability to buy them, and are thus fairly taxed. At any rate, when public costs, such as those for education, mount, sufficient taxes must be levied to pay the bill. Additional types of taxes have come into use.

With reference to public education, not just any kind of tax will do. If luxury taxes were earmarked for education, and hard times should dry up the sale of luxuries, where would the schools be? The

TABLE 2

REVENUES FOR PUBLIC EDUCATION BY STATES, 1949-50 [3]

State	Total Revenues	Per Cent Federal	Per Cent State	Per Cent Local	Per Cent from Property Tax (State, Local)	Per Cent from Other Revenues (State, Local)
Alabama	72,543,888	1.5	75.8	22.7	25.1	74.9
Arizona	32,362,812	1.5	36.0	62.5	63.4	36.6
Arkansas	43,717,000	5.1	62.7	32.2	32.5	67.5
California	393,773,566	1.4	53.4	45.2	44.3	55.7
Colorado	47,537,679	1.3	21.9	76.8	77.8	22.2
Connecticut	61,377,187	1.4	22.8	75.8	74.4	25.6
Delaware	12,179,941	2.2	89.6	8.2	8.7	91.3
Florida	93,993,470	1.2	53.4	45.4	42.9	57.1
Georgia	78,499,842	5.4	67.7	26.9	28.4	71.6
Idaho	20,668,038	2.1	25.7	72.2	65.2	34.8
Illinois	312,545,452	1.1	18.9	80.0	80.9	19.1
Indiana	146,089,552	1.4	39.4	59.2	58.9	41.1
Iowa	102,084,854	1.6	17.6	80.8	80.8	19.2
Kansas	74,602,797	1.4	18.5	80.1	81.3	18.7
Kentucky	63,100,428	4.5	38.5	57.0	58.5	41.5
Louisiana	95,419,819	5.9	67.4	26.7	26.4	73.6
Maine	26,137,500	2.3	27.6	70.1	65.6	34.4
Maryland	72,057,837	1.3	40.0	58.7	58.9	41.1
Massachusetts	145,501,619	1.1	18.2	80.7	79.9	20.1
Michigan	243,867,474	1.2	57.6	41.2	38.6	61.4
Minnesota	105,000,000	1.9	46.6	51.5	48.1	51.9
Mississippi	38,384,744	6.3	51.7	42.0	42.9	57.1
Missouri	104,000,000	0.7	38.8	60.5	48.6	51.4
Montana	25,280,682	4.2	28.9	66.9	69.0	31.0
Nebraska	39,537,417	2.1	5.9	92.0	93.5	6.5

State	Total Revenues	Per Cent Federal	Per Cent State	Per Cent Local	Per Cent from Property Tax (State, Local)	Per Cent from Other Revenues (State, Local)
Nevada	6,959,075	6.4	36.9	56.7	57.1	42.9
New Hampshire	14,957,624	2.4	6.5	91.1	92.6	7.4
New Jersey	178,418,784	0.9	19.1	80.0	78.7	21.3
New Mexico	26,935,862	1.9	84.7	13.4	14.4	85.6
New York	530,850,000	1.0	46.7	52.3	48.7	51.3
North Carolina	127,566,626	3.1	78.1	18.8	13.6	86.4
North Dakota	24,402,850	1.4	26.9	71.7	63.0	37.0
Ohio	260,400,000	1.2	36.4	62.4	61.5	38.5
Oklahoma	73,709,285	2.7	42.9	54.4	32.6	67.4
Oregon	75,714,257	1.3	28.6	70.1	71.0	29.0
Pennsylvania	323,995,051	1.0	37.6	61.4	56.4	43.6
Rhode Island	21,404,430	1.9	18.7	79.4	80.0	20.0
South Carolina	51,889,189	4.4	64.0	31.6	28.6	71.4
South Dakota	21,728,131	1.9	13.0	85.1	80.7	19.3
Tennessee	80,672,708	3.5	63.3	33.2	28.2	71.8
Texas	314,489,908	2.2	49.9	47.9	51.8	48.2
Utah	33,502,962	1.9	53.1	35.0	60.3	39.7
Vermont	10,695,600	1.6	31.7	66.7	66.7	33.3
Virginia	81,185,127	2.6	40.7	56.7	53.2	46.8
Washington	104,826,855	2.9	68.5	28.6	29.5	70.5
West Virginia	65,408,539	4.1	62.4	33.5	35.0	65.0
Wisconsin	102,460,000	1.5	22.6	75.9	75.8	24.2
Wyoming	14,661,310	1.8	44.6	53.6	64.0	36.0
Total revenues	4,997,097,771					
Averages for the nation		2.4	41.8	55.8	55.0	45.0

[3] Adapted from *State and Local Public School Finance Programs, 1949–50*, prepared by U. S. Office of Education, Washington, D. C., in cooperation with state departments of education, the Council of State Governments, and the University of California.

same would hold for several other types of taxes. The fundamental character of education in our society requires that the support of education be on the most continuing and certain basis possible. In general, this principle is being observed by the states as they seek to find new sources of tax income for public schools. More specifically, the income tax is frequently used to supplement the property tax. The sales tax has been used increasingly of late, but many feel that it cannot be as equitable in its application as an income tax. Of course property taxes and income taxes will reflect good times and hard times, but of all the types of taxes they are perhaps the most dependable and continuous.

Another principle of taxation is coming into play which has a direct bearing on education. This principle states that primary public services should have primary claim on tax income. This is the principle of relative values. Taxing authorities in the forty-eight states are facing up to the problem of whether or not all projects for which public money is spent are of equal importance, or if some are more important than others. If some are more important than others, then they should have prior claim on public funds. In the application of this principle, the public schools have no fear of losing status. California, for example, established, then lost, and now seeks to establish again the specification that in disbursing state funds, the costs of public education should be met first.

6. The Problem of Unequal Ability to Secure and Maintain Good Schools

It is a troublesome thing, in a society that emphasizes fair play, to witness a situation in which a community, because of its poor, hilly lands and lack of wealth, must get along with the poorest of schools, while another community, a half-dozen miles away in a fertile valley, with its railroad and mills, can furnish the finest kind of education for its children. It is also disturbing to realize that one of our forty-eight states can spend 1.5 per cent of the income in the state for education and get about $57.00 per pupil in return, while another state can spend the same percentage and get over $190.00 per pupil. There are tremendous inequalities in the ability of communities within the states to secure and maintain good schools. The same is true among the states.

Inequalities Within the States.—Many people do not realize that in some communities in some states as little as $10.00 per pupil per year is spent on education. In the same states some communities, without any greater effort, will spend ten or fifteen times as much per pupil. For the country as a whole, in 1946–47, the top 10 per cent of school children were in schools costing $185.00 or more per pupil; the bottom 10 per cent were in schools costing $50.00 or less per pupil. No state is without its extremes. For example, New York, the state that had the highest current expenditure per pupil in 1946–47, about $230.00, still had a range in expenditures among local units from just over $50.00 to about $325.00; in the same year the range in Minnesota was from about $35.00 to about $335.00; in Connecticut, $75.00 to $250.00; in Georgia, about $10.00 to $125.00; in Texas, $20.00 to $200.00; in Wyoming, $30.00 to almost $300.00; and in Mississippi, about $10.00 to $100.00.

It stands to reason that at any given time in a given region a decent education will cost about so much per pupil. If communities fall below this, it simply means that those children are being denied their just privileges because of accident of place of birth. A few years ago it was proposed, on good foundation, that no school in the country should spend less than $70.00 on each pupil per year. Later the estimate went up to $100.00; and in 1948 the National Education Association proposed a minimum of $200.00. It has gone up since. There are hundreds of communities within our states now operating their schools on less than $20.00 per pupil per year, to say nothing of $200.00. In 1946–47 only about 7 per cent of all the pupils in the country were in schools spending as much as $200.00 per pupil per year. Half were in schools spending less than $100.00. The fact of differences in educational support within the states is, therefore, apparent.

One should caution himself here not to be too merciful with all the local schools that have a hard time financially. In the previous chapter considerable emphasis was given to the fact that a good many ineffective schools ought to be eliminated through a careful reorganization of districts. No amount of local reorganization, however, is likely to solve completely the problem of inequality in the ability of local units to support their schools.

Inequalities Among the States.—Inequality among the states is just as glaring as within the states. This is strikingly portrayed in a bulletin published in 1948 by the National Education Association, entitled "Still Unfinished—Our Educational Obligation to America's Children." This bulletin also reveals the differences within the states presented in the paragraphs immediately above.

In 1946–47 all the school children in Massachusetts and New Jersey attended schools that spent more than $99.00 per pupil per year on current education expenditures. The national average was $99.00. In six states, Alabama, Arkansas, Mississippi, North Carolina, South Carolina, and Tennessee, better than 90 per cent of the children attended schools that spent less than $99.00 per pupil. In five additional states, Georgia, Idaho, Kentucky, Virginia, and West Virginia, better than 80 per cent of the children attended schools that spent less than $99.00. In the same year, 1946–47, current expenditures per pupil in Arkansas and Mississippi were about $45.00. In California they were about $165.00; in Illinois, $150.00; in New Jersey, $185.00; in New York, $230.00; and in Alabama and Kentucky, just under $50.00. It goes without saying that $45.00 per pupil per year cannot buy the same quality of education that can be bought for $200.00 per pupil per year. Such drastic inequalities of support among the states constitute one of the most serious problems in school finance.

Effort and Yield.—A look at the differences among the states in the amounts spent for education causes one to wonder immediately if the low states may not be shirking on the job. Why doesn't Mississippi try as hard as New York does? And Arkansas could equal California if it only tried! The Biennial Survey of Education in the United States for 1944–46, published by the U. S. Office of Education, gives some interesting data on this point. The percentage of income in a state spent for schools is used as a measure of effort. Yield is indicated by the expenditures per child in average daily attendance. This is an accurate indication since public schools ordinarily spend all their funds annually and do not build up reserves. Data on these items for fourteen states are presented in Table 3. It is clear for the states paired in the table that the lower yield was not the result of lower effort. Mississippi actually tried harder than New York and got $44.80 per pupil in return. New York, with less effort than Mississippi, got $194.97 per pupil. Illinois made an effort equal to Alabama's and got three times as much money per pupil in return. West Virginia made a substantially greater effort than Michigan but fell definitely short of Michigan in yield. The data seem to show that if all the states made an equal effort in the support of education, the differences in school expenditures would be even greater than they are now. One must explain the differences among the states, therefore, more in terms of financial ability than in terms of effort.

TABLE 3

EFFORT AND YIELD IN EDUCATIONAL SUPPORT [4]

States	Per Cent of Income in State Spent for Schools, 1943–44	Expenditures Per Child in Average Daily Attendance, 1944–45
New York	1.52	194.47
Mississippi	1.64	44.80
California	1.31	163.38
Arkansas	1.53	60.26
Connecticut	1.22	159.50
Kentucky	1.71	80.94
New Jersey	1.74	198.33
North Carolina	1.91	68.91
Illinois	1.47	169.02
Alabama	1.50	56.93
Michigan	1.46	127.73
West Virginia	2.47	93.18
Washington	1.31	159.78
Georgia	1.30	64.92

7. EQUALIZATION

Equalization is intended to eliminate some of the vast inequalities referred to in the sections above.

The Principle.—Ordinarily equalization suggests money to most people. True, money is involved in equalization plans, but there is a fundamental ideal underneath. That ideal is our democratic insistence that every child in the land is entitled to a decent educational opportunity. Equalization plans attempt to translate that ideal into practice, at least to move in the direction of the ideal. Opponents of equalization plans cannot limit themselves to financial matters; they must face up squarely to the rights of the children in a democratic nation.

Furthermore, equalization does not mean "equal." If equalization on a national basis were to come, it would not mean that all the states would then spend equal amounts per pupil. These plans have always

[4] Adapted from *Still Unfinished—Our Educational Obligation to America's Children* (Washington, D. C.: National Education Association, 1948).

established a minimum or floor, usually based on per pupil expenditures per year, below which no state or school system could go. Expenditures, therefore, are equalized up to a minimum; and any school or state that can do so is urged to exceed the minimum. A minimum floor is established, but no maximum ceiling. Equalization, then, is not intended actually to "equalize." It is concerned with the minimum floor; and this floor should be placed at an amount sufficient to secure for every child an education of reasonable quality. Schools that can should exceed the floor and make the best possible education available to the children in their charge.

How It Works.—If a state wishes to adopt an equalization plan, it will very likely proceed somewhat as follows: A minimum expenditure per pupil per year will be fixed for all the public schools of the state. Different amounts may be fixed for elementary and secondary pupils. Effort will likely be made to secure uniform assessments for taxes on property throughout the state, and tax rates will have to be considered. At least assessments and tax rates will have to be properly equated. Then a percentage may be set which is the part of local tax receipts that must be spent for education before state aid can be requested. If this percentage of local taxes reaches the per pupil minimum set for the state, then that community would receive no state aid. If it did not produce the minimum, then the state would make up the difference between the receipts and the minimum required. Communities are urged to exceed the minimum as they can.

Obviously, before a state can help its needy communities, it must collect taxes for this purpose. Naturally enough, it will be the wealthier communities that will contribute most of these taxes. This means that the wealthier communities will not only support their own schools on a high plane but they will also help support the schools in poor communities. This is precisely what equalization means: getting the money from where it is, and spending it where it is needed. The same applies whether the plan is national, state, or local in scope.

The Common Objection.—There is an attitude which seems always to come to the front when equalization plans are being discussed. It is the attitude that "our wealth is our own"; that in some strange way all the wealth in a city, for example, originated within the city limits. The city will be interested greatly in roads that will make it convenient for people in the outlying communities to come in and spend their money; but too frequently it is not interested in contributing any taxes for the support of schools in those communities. The fallacy of the idea that "our wealth is our own" is, of course, apparent. Every village is sustained by the surrounding neighborhood. Far-flung neighborhoods support cities and states. Our great insurance cities, for example, collect wealth from all over the nation. The same for commercial centers, grain and livestock centers, and so on. Some regions even import temporary help during certain seasons to aid in the production of wealth. When the crop is in or the job is done, these people then go back home. Certainly, no center is nonregional in its wealth; and yet, when proposals for educational equalization come along, very selfish interpretations of wealth are sometimes encountered.

Educational Effects Are Not Localized.—It makes very good sense to many people to contend that if all roads lead to Middletown, then Middletown ought to be concerned with conditions at the other end of those roads. From here will come the people who will walk her streets, take her jobs, and in general determine the character and quality of her life. If these communities are equipped to produce good people, then Middletown need not worry; if they are not, then no amount of worry will save Middletown. It has been demonstrated clearly in recent years that if education is maintained at a high standard in these communities, Middletown will not only have nice people coming in, but she will also grow wealthier because these people will demand more things that Middletown can supply.

The same principle holds on a national scale. Bad educational conditions in any state in the Union affect the whole Union. The bulletin entitled *Unfinished Business in American Education,* published by the National Education Association in 1946, supplies data pertinent to this point. Table 4 is adapted from data taken from that bulletin. The first column in the table shows a group of ten states in which more than half the population was born outside the state. Obviously these people had to come in from somewhere. Our immigration laws make it unlikely that they came in primarily from other nations. For seven other states in the same column, 15 per cent or less of the population was born outside the state. These states were producing a much greater proportion of their own people. Perhaps also they were producing more children per unit of population than the first group of states. If this were true it would tend to indicate that a lot of the "outsiders" going into the first group of states were coming from the second group. The second column of the table shows that the birthrate in the second group of states is definitely higher than in the first. The second group of states is doubtless feeding hundreds of thousands of people into the first group. And what kind of people are they? Data were presented in Section 4 of this chapter to show that the southern states in general spend far less on education than other sections of the country. Presumably this would result in a more poorly educated people. This seems to be borne out in column three

TABLE 4

DATA RELATIVE TO THE NONLOCALIZED EFFECTS OF EDUCATION [5]

State	Per Cent of Population Born Outside the State	Ratio of School-Age Children (5–17) to Total Population, 1939–40 (U. S. Average Index Equals 100)	Per Cent of Selectees Who Signed Their Registration Cards With an "X," May to September, 1941
Nevada	67	83	0.25
California	64	78	0.25
Wyoming	63	104	0.25
Oregon	59	86	0.25
Washington	58	86	0.25
Arizona	56	115	1.6
Colorado	55	100	0.25
Idaho	55	110	0.25
Montana	53	99	0.25
Florida	51	99	4.7
New Jersey	43	90	0.50
Oklahoma	42	115	0.70
New Mexico	41	128	1.7
Connecticut	40	90	0.25
New Hampshire	39	96	0.50
Rhode Island	37	96	0.25
Delaware	37	92	1.0
South Dakota	36	112	0.25
Michigan	36	98	0.25
New York	35	86	0.25
Louisiana	15	115	9.2
Georgia	13	120	11.0
Kentucky	13	120	3.3
North Carolina	11	130	7.0
Alabama	11	127	8.2
Mississippi	11	127	13.6
South Carolina	10	132	13.5

of the table where percentages of selectees who signed their registration cards with an "X" are given for twenty-five states. The percentages are highest for the southern states. It appears, therefore,

[5] Adapted from *Unfinished Business in American Education* (Washington, D. C.: National Education Association, 1946).

that the states with the poorest education and the lowest standard of living have the highest birthrates, and many of their people are moving on into the wealthier states. This being the case, the wealthier regions ought vitally to be interested in the educational, social, and economic conditions of the poorer regions.

Proposed Federal Aid.—The democratic justice of every child's receiving a good education, the obvious inequality among the states in their ability to provide good education, and the realization that low standards in any region affect the whole country have brought a surge of demand that the federal government provide aid to the needy states. Efforts in this direction have been made for a good many years. Realization seems to be near. Popular polls in recent months have repeatedly shown that our people favor such aid. Numerous organizations and groups have worked for its adoption. Several things, however, have operated to slow it down.

The Problem of Federal Control. We have noted repeatedly that this is a country of decentralized control in education. For many years we have guarded our localism jealously. For some reason also we have assumed that control of education inevitably accompanies support of education. It is this assumption that has delayed federal aid to education more than anything else. We simply are not willing to have the federal government control our schools. However, federal aid to schools is needed terribly. Hence, the idea of federal aid without federal control has arisen. When we are sufficiently convinced that such an arrangement is possible, we shall doubtless have federal aid. To doubt the workability of such a scheme is to doubt democracy itself. We have already had something to say about government in a democracy delivering responsibility to the people as rapidly as they are qualified to assume it. The qualification of our people increases with time, if our democracy is any good. The central government has no monopoly on virtue or ability. Federal support with local control is feasible and workable.

It ought to be pointed out here that the bills before the U. S. Congress which have proposed federal aid have safeguarded the country against federal control. This can be shown best by quoting Section 2 of the Educational Finance Act of 1951, House Bill 915, of the Eighty-second Congress. It should be remembered that this was proposed legislation that did not pass. Section 2 follows:

Section 2. Nothing contained in this act shall be construed to authorize any department, agency, officer, or employee of the United States to exercise any direction, supervision, or control over, or to prescribe any requirements with respect to any school, or any State educational institution or agency, with respect to which any funds have been or may be made available or expended pursuant to this Act, nor shall any term or condition of any agreement or any other action taken under this Act, whether by agreement or otherwise, relating to any contribution made under this Act to or on behalf of any school, or any State educational institution or agency, or any limitation or provision in any appropriation made pursuant to this Act, seek to control in any manner, or prescribe requirements with respect to, or authorize any department, agency, officer, or employee of the United States to direct, supervise or control in any manner, or prescribe any requirements with respect to, the administration, the personnel, the curriculum, the instruction, the methods of instruction, or the materials of instruction, nor shall any provision of this Act be interpreted or construed to imply or require any change in any State constitution prerequisite to any State sharing the benefits of this Act.

In a bulletin published in July, 1946, entitled *One Hundred and Sixty Years of Federal Aid to Education,* the National Education Association summarized in part by saying : "Our national experience proves that federal control follows federal aid only when authorized in the law and that federal control does not thus follow when the law forbids." If and when a federal aid bill is enacted containing a provision like Section 2 above, it is not likely that the bugaboo of federal control will ever raise its head.

Reasonable Federal Limitations. It is not to be expected that if the federal government gives substantial financial support to education, there will not be some areas in which it will be the duty of the government to specify certain reasonable limitations. It would be negligent otherwise. Some of these limitations have also served to delay the passage of federal aid legislation. Four such reasonable limitations are noted here.

It is reasonable for the federal government to ask states that receive federal funds to set up a research bureau in the state department of education if one does not already exist. The assumption here is that states with such bureaus are likely to be better informed about their educational conditions and needs than states that do not have them. Federal funds, therefore, are likely to be more wisely spent.

It is reasonable for the federal government to require that federal funds for education shall be spent in the states to the equal benefit of all children in the public schools. It is imperative, of course, that the government not violate its own constitutional guarantees to all citizens by supporting discriminations within the states that commit such violations. Our government would be lax in its duty if it did not safeguard the children on this count.

It is reasonable for the federal government to specify that federal funds shall be spent in the states for the support of public schools only. Any other position would seem to violate the basic national principle of the separation of church and state. It is a roiling of the issue to talk about public funds for private-school transportation but not for private-school teachers; for nonreligious textbooks, but not for religious textbooks. The very existence of the private school demonstrates a special interest on its part sufficiently different from the public school to cause it to maintain itself separately. If the federal government contributes in any way to the support of these schools, it is financing their special interests, most of which are religious.

The recent proposal to permit the states to spend federal money in this matter the same way they spend their own state money seems to be a compromise of principle which could result in the public's actually financing the disintegration of its own public school system. Nothing here, of course, is meant to challenge the existence, the usefulness, or the contribution of the private schools; but they ought to maintain themselves completely free of public support. The federal government should set a decisive example by keeping its financial support unequivocally in line with national ideals.

It is reasonable for the federal government to say that the states and communities may not reduce state and local funds for public schools because of federal aid. In other words, federal funds may not be substituted for state and local funds; they are to be in addition to them. In this way, federal aid would in fact represent educational upgrading and not the mere maintenance of the status quo.

Such limitations as those above are considered reasonable when equalization at the federal level is considered. The primary goal of the entire proposal, of course, is to have the federal government discharge its obligation to the general welfare as embodied in the right of every child to a good education. The above-mentioned Educational Finance Act of 1951 carried the idea in its opening paragraph: "A bill to authorize the appropriation of funds to assist in reducing the inequalities of educational opportunities through public elementary and secondary schools, for the national security and general welfare, and for other purposes."

8. The Relation of Educational Objectives to Educational Support

It cannot be reiterated too often that school funds are a means to an end. The basic question in school finance is not "How much money do we have?" but "How much money will it take to provide the kind of education that ought to be provided?" When we are clear on the kind of education that ought to be provided, then we can with greater enthusiasm employ local, state, and federal resources to secure it.

The facts are that there has been a great deal of educational financing in this country without enough educational thinking. Too often the people in a local community are asked to finance their schools "from afar off." They are not familiar enough with what the schools are doing, and why; and they have not been brought into the councils where consideration is given to what the schools ought to be doing. The American people have a way of getting what they want. If they understand what good education is, and if they want it badly enough, they will get it. The money is abundant. During 1950 we spent approximately thirty-five billion dollars on intoxicating beverages and gambling. The responsibility of educational leaders to help our people really to want good education is obvious.

We ought to remind ourselves again of the universality of educational objectives. They are not different for children in rural schools and city schools, in the North and in the South, in residential areas and across the tracks. Take the seven cardinal principles again: (a) health, (b) command of the fundamental processes, (c) vocational training, (d) citizenship, (e) worthy home membership, (f) worthy use of leisure time, and (g) ethical character. One will hardly say that the health objective applies to the children in the North but not to the children in the South; that vocational training is all right for city children but not for country children; or that any other objective applies to one group and not to another. Similarly for the four great objectives of the Educational Policies Commission: (a) self-realization, (b) human relationships, (c) economic efficiency, and (d) civic responsibility. Do we desire these for one group and not for another? Surely not. Shall we say to any youngster that, because he lives far out in a rural area or happened to be born in a poor state, he does not therefore share in these objectives? Hardly. The over-all task seems clear. We must arrange our school support so that our educational objectives come alive for every child.

9. DISTRIBUTING THE BURDEN

The task of supporting education adequately will be easier if the burden of support is justly distributed. A few considerations seem pertinent.

Supplementing the Property Tax.—Considerable argument can be marshaled for the point of view that no wealth should be immune from taxation for the support of public services. It is not just, in the minds of many, for the holders of real property to carry the whole tax load when wealth in great amounts exists in other forms. Wealth in all forms should be tapped for the public welfare. It is quite possible, for example, for a person of large income to live in a community without holding any property. Local communities ordinarily do not have income taxes; and many states do not. Such a person can easily completely bypass any support of local or state schools, except as some of his federal income taxes might return to the state, if, indeed, a comprehensive plan of federal school support were in effect. It is a well-known fact that in some cases where states that have income taxes lie adjacent to states that do not, a good deal of "colonizing" takes place in the latter. These people should not be permitted to withdraw their wealth from a fair support of public services. The suggestion is implicit here that if one state has a state income tax, so should they all; and public education should receive its fair share of benefits. The broader implication is that more people should share in the support of education through the broadening of the tax base.

The National Approach.—Basic to the idea of a national approach to school support is Section 8 above, which deals with the relation of educational objectives to educational support. [Our educational objectives extend impartially to all persons; our finances must be sufficient to secure them for all.] Without reference to where the money is to come from, we must see to it that no child in the nation is denied an adequate education. If the local community can provide such an education without unreasonable sacrifice, well and good. If the state and local community together can provide it, that, too, is good. If, however, the state and local community fall short, then our national ideal of equality of opportunity should be cause enough for the federal government to come forward with its assistance. Our tradition of local control must not chain us to the error of unsupplemented local support when the quality of future citizens is at stake, especially when local control and outside governmental aid can be so nicely adjusted. Persons in our local communities are, after all, citizens of the nation.

Putting Effort in Proper Sequence.—If we say that we want to control our schools locally, we should also be willing to make a reasonable local effort to finance them. In many communities such an effort will yield funds enough to provide an excellent educational program. In such cases no expectation of outside aid should exist. Communities able to support their schools ought to, and do, take genuine pride in doing so. In this way, whatever resources the state has for local aid will go to communities having the greatest need.

The same principle applies at the state level. If a state has the resources, coupled with local funds, to provide a good education for every child, it should make no effort to obtain federal aid. If federal funds were forthcoming, it would only mean that the children in needier regions were being penalized unnecessarily.

The federal government should, of course, be willing to equalize sufficiently on the national level to guarantee good educational opportunities to every child. If it wishes to make a token appropriation to every state to indicate its interest in and support of public education in general, no objection can be raised. But the bulk of the funds should be distributed on an equalization basis, thus assuring that the money will be used where it will do the most good.

Honest Effort.—If we can bring ourselves in this country genuinely to want our public services, such as education, as we want some other things that we need less but pay more for, we shall have an easy time with our school finance. We spend money more willingly for items we genuinely want than for things we have no particular interest in. Frequently also we spend our money for fanciful things of little worth and then we complain that the cost of things of real worth is exorbitant. Some taxpayers' leagues get themselves into the unenlightened position of supporting such complaints. Common honesty requires that we face up squarely to our public obligation and think ourselves clear of a desire to shirk it. If this were done, complaints would diminish and resources would be ample. Local communities would do more. States would do more. In the minds of many, there is an element of unfairness and irresponsibility in the action of a wealthy state that retains hundreds of millions of dollars within its borders as a result of reductions in federal income taxes, taxes that were paid without much difficulty, and then refuses to provide tens of millions of dollars in state aid to needy public schools. We still have a long way to go in our country in dealing unselfishly with our public services.

Tax Sources.—The problem of what types of wealth should be reserved to federal, state, and local governments for taxation purposes and how heavily each type of wealth may be taxed is too deep for us here. However, it does stand to reason that if a taxing authority, say the federal government, tends to monopolize tax sources so that the capacity of the states and communities to support their public services is impaired, then the obligation of the government to aid the lesser units is clear. It would be possible also for the federal government to dry up income taxes as a source of revenue for the states by placing the federal income tax rates so high that further income taxes by the states would be out of reason. Logically, he who collects the taxes ought to pay the bills. However, it is probably correct to say that our people do not want the federal government to collect all the taxes and pay all the bills. They undoubtedly prefer to reduce federal aid to a minimum, thus permitting the states and the communities to pay the largest possible share of their own bills. At any rate, the problem of interrelationship among taxing authorities bears directly upon the support of public education.

10. A Few Current Concepts or Principles

Let us close our discussion of the support of schools in America by listing a few of the concepts or principles that currently give direction to practices in this field. Such a list will recall some of the things that have gone before, and will serve as a point of departure for further thinking.

1. School support should stand firmly on an intelligent understanding of educational goals.
2. Education is a state function. The state, therefore, is interested in and accountable for satisfactory financial practices in every public school in the state.
3. School finance is a part of public finance. It affects, and is affected by, the community's total load of public services.
4. The control of local school budgets should be in the hands of autonomous school boards responsible for public education. Although such boards should be fiscally free from control by other local governmental boards, they should nevertheless recognize that their financial claim on the community is only a part of

the total claim and should accordingly freely cooperate with other boards representing other public services.

5. [The nature of democracy requires local participation in school support, but not necessarily complete local support.]

6. The burden of educational support should be equalized in line with financial ability and effort.

7. Educational support and educational control are not completely and inseparably joined. State and federal governments engaging in educational equalization are duty-bound to specify reasonable limitations growing out of the state and national welfare.

8. Public schools should be free to all pupils.

9. School funds should be sufficient to extend to all pupils a good educational opportunity.

10. When economy in school finance results in inadequately trained citizens, the economy is false.

11. School finances should be arranged to encourage long-time educational planning.

12. Citizens who finance the schools have a right to an educational program that is flexible and adjusted to the needs of the pupils and the community. School funds should not be used to perpetuate school subjects or activities of doubtful worth.

13. School finances should be managed in accordance with approved financial procedures. The public welfare demands wise handling and full accounting.

14. Persons responsible for the handling of public school funds should be trained in school finance.

What Do YOU Say?

1

Governmental units at all levels in this country are organized to promote the general welfare of the people they represent. Since education is a vital aspect of the general welfare, federal, state, and local governments ought to combine resources whenever and wherever needed to support a good basic education for all our people. It is altogether workable and wise to retain the control of education in the local communities even though state and federal financial aid may sometimes be necessary.

What do YOU say?

2

Educational financing should be geared to the educational program, and not vice versa. When the people of a community, represented by their board of education, find that their local resources will not buy the kind of education the children ought to have, it is their obligation to seek aid and adjustments beyond their own resources in order that the educational program may be made adequate.

What do YOU say?

3

Wealth in all forms should be taxed for the support of public services such as public schools, public roads, and police and fire protection.

What do YOU say?

4

What points in this chapter do you particularly support or take issue with?

Chapter 7

THE AMERICAN EDUCATIONAL LADDER

Reorganizing for Better Service

1. NATURE AND DEVELOPMENT

Nature of the Ladder.—It is quite common, and rather accurate, to think of the school experience of an individual as a climb up an educational ladder. The rungs in the ladder are the grades in our school system. Ordinarily each rung, or grade, occupies a year in the life of the individual. The child who enters the first grade, destined to complete a college education, has a climb of sixteen rungs or grades or years ahead. Figure 5 carries the idea. These sixteen grades, of course, are differently put together in different communities. Even the twelve grades provided in most American communities as free public education are not grouped into the same grade combinations in all communities. Furthermore, in some communities the rungs of the ladder have been made to extend further down to include prefirst-grade experiences; and, of course, graduate education beyond the bachelor's degree is available in many higher institutions. It will be our purpose in this chapter to consider the educational ladder, its development, its reorganization, the problem of interrelationships among the units of the ladder, and pupil progress up the ladder.

Development of the Ladder.—The earliest schools in America were ungraded. Schools such as the reading schools, the writing schools, and the dame schools were supposed to accomplish certain things with the pupils. Anyone who needed the instruction that these schools offered, no matter what his age might be, attended them. Furthermore, one teacher usually did all the teaching; he was all things to all pupils. Enrolments were usually small. This was true also of the grammar schools and the colleges. It will be remembered that the president of Harvard did all the teaching for a good many years. The offering of the school, therefore, was suited to the limited things expected of the school and to what the teacher was qualified to do and had time to do. The curriculum was limited. When a pupil finished it, he was through with that school.

The idea of certain things for certain schools applied, of course, to the early "common schools." The primary interest of these schools was the 3 R's and religion. Certain accomplishments in these fields were laid out for these schools, and all pupils studied these subjects. They were, however, at different stages of achievement. The teacher adjusted to these differences, but without setting up different grades.

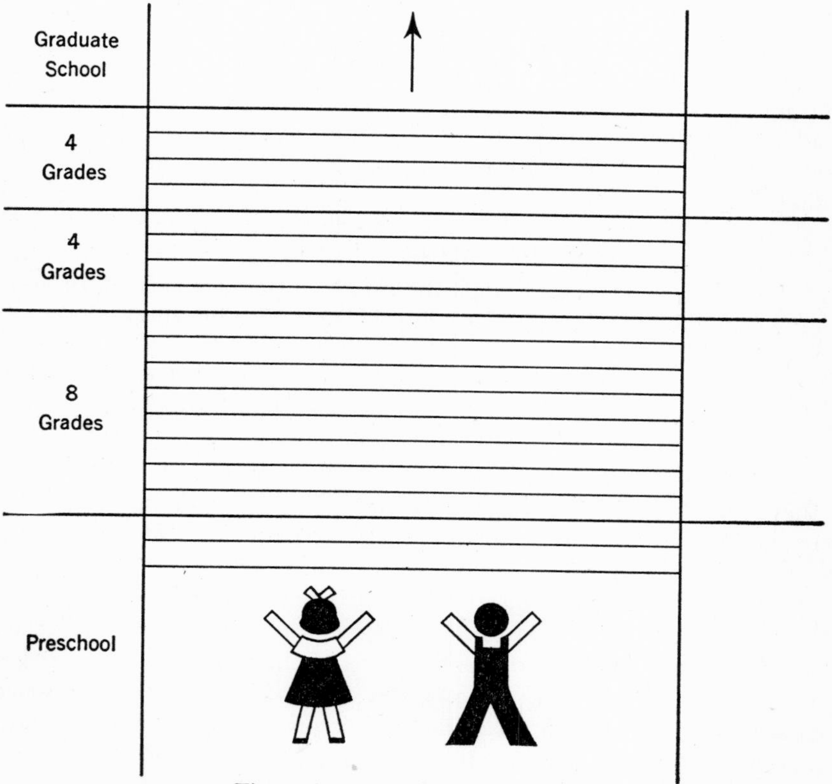

Graduate School

4 Grades

4 Grades

8 Grades

Preschool

Figure 5. The Educational Ladder

The work, it may be said, was greatly individualized. Cubberley illustrates such an ungraded school by citing the report of the Free School Society of New York City for the year 1819. This report details the studies of 1,051 pupils as follows:

297 children have been taught to form letters in sand.
615 have been advanced from letters in sand, to monosyllabic reading on boards.
686 from reading on boards, to "Murray's First Book."

335 from "Murray's First Book," to writing on slates.
218 from writing on slates, to writing on paper.
341 to reading in the Bible.
277 to addition and subtraction.
153 to multiplication and division.
 60 to the compounds of the first four rules.
 20 to reduction.
 24 to the rule of three.

Cubberley comments: "This shows the common American ungraded 3 R's school, taking children from the very beginnings, and advancing them individually and by subjects, as their progress warranted. Such schools were very common in our cities and villages in the early period." [1]

In due time, however, the common schools began to expect that all children coming to them would have had the beginnings of reading and writing. The dame school, the infant or primary school, or some other private school might furnish this beginning instruction. At any rate, the idea of a primary level prerequisite to the common school developed. Also, the common school itself subdivided vertically into a writing school and a reading school. Later on, the reading school was further subdivided into lowest class, second class, third class, and highest class. These were not grades so much as school divisions, and they varied greatly in terms of local buildings and teachers. For example, one school system might have the primary, middle, and high divisions, while a neighboring system might have the divisions of subprimary, primary, intermediate-primary, secondary, grammar, and high. It is important to remember that up to this time individual teachers taught in most of the divisions of the school. In fact, it was common for a teacher to have on one floor of a building a cross section of all the pupils in the school, while on the floor below or above another teacher also conducted classes at all levels, and in all subjects.

As school enrolments grew, the system of having each teacher virtually conduct an independent school became cumbersome and ineffective. Some relief was given when assistants or "ushers" were employed to conduct classes for the teachers. This led to the building of small recitation rooms off the large room of the teacher or "master."

The graded system actually appeared, however, when supervision came in and the schools of a community were looked upon as a single school system. As Cubberley states it: "The third and final step in the evolution of the graded system was to build larger schools with

[1] Elwood P. Cubberley, *Public Education in the United States* (rev. and enl. ed.; Boston: Houghton Mifflin Co., 1934), pp. 303–4.

smaller classrooms, or to subdivide the larger rooms; change the separate and independent and duplicate school on each floor, which had been the common plan for so long, into parts of one school building organization; sort and grade the pupils, and outline the instruction by years; and the class system was at hand." [2] Along with this, of course, went reductions in the range of teacher responsibilities. With the growth in the number of subjects taught and the expansion of the public school to include the high school, teacher specialization on the elementary or secondary level naturally followed, as well as specialization within certain content areas. When the graded system became complete, teachers could even be given only one grade to handle if local conditions made such an arrangement seem advisable. By about 1860 such a graded system had been established in all the northern states. Much remained to be done in adapting instruction to the graded pattern and in establishing subject sequences, but the rungs of the ladder had been put into place and the older subdivisions had lost most of their meaning.

2. TYPICAL ORGANIZATION OF THE LADDER

Variations in Pattern.—Although by about 1875 our country had pretty well accepted the idea that our public schools should provide twelve years, or grades, of schooling, local communities were still free to organize those grades into whatever combinations they chose. If one community wanted to set up an eight-grade elementary school and a four-grade high school, well and good. Perhaps in one state or region this might be the pattern, whereas somewhere else a seven-five combination was preferred, or even a seven-four. Certain experimental schools might try other combinations. The decentralization of the public schools in the United States, as would be expected, made it unlikely that a uniform pattern would develop. And it did not. For example, the South made more use of the seven-five and the seven-four patterns than did the North. All of these patterns, of course, as time went on, would have to stand the test of experience and experimentation.

The Typical Pattern.—Although the organization of our educational ladder did not follow a uniform pattern, nevertheless one pattern became much more common than any other. This was the 8-4 plan, consisting of an eight-grade elementary school and a four-grade high school. At the beginning of the twentieth century this pattern

[2] Cubberley, *op. cit.*, p. 311.

was so predominant that our country could be described as following the 8-4 plan. This is still the typical organization today, although experience and experimentation have brought about a good many

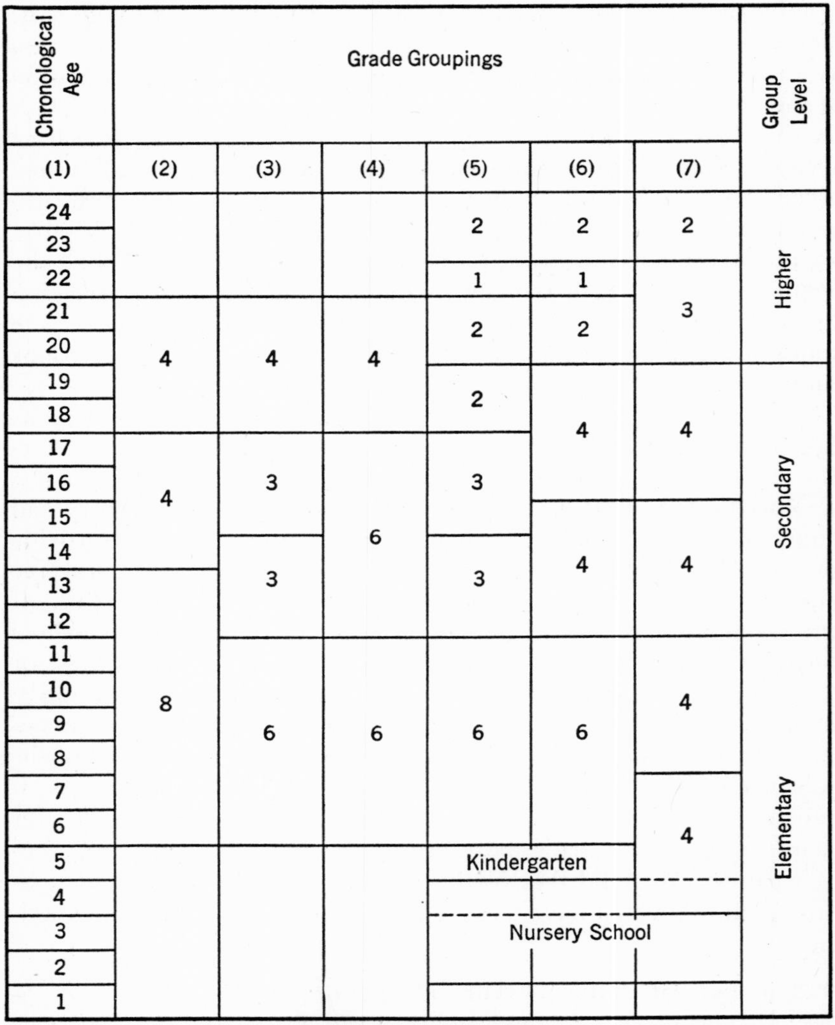

Chronological Age	Grade Groupings						Group Level
(1)	(2)	(3)	(4)	(5)	(6)	(7)	
24				2	2	2	Higher
23							
22				1	1		
21	4	4	4	2	2	3	
20							
19				2			Secondary
18					4	4	
17	4	3		3			
16							
15			6				
14		3		3	4	4	
13							
12							
11	8					4	Elementary
10		6	6	6	6		
9							
8							
7						4	
6							
5				Kindergarten			
4							
3				Nursery School			
2							
1							

Figure 6. Grade Combinations in the Educational Ladder

modifications. We shall deal with those in due course. It is worth while to add that in 1900 the typical college in this country was also a four-grade institution. This type still predominates today, although reorganization at the college level is also in process. We have, then, an 8-4-4 organization of the ladder as the typical structure around 1900. Let us use this as our basic point of departure for further discussion.

Figure 6 is a useful condensation of much that can be said about the ladder and its reorganization. It does not, of course, show all the patterns that can be found in the country today; and it does not attempt to establish any historical sequence among the changes. However, if one studies it from left to right one will get a good idea of changes that have been introduced and proposed. Look at it carefully. Familiarity with it will add much to the discussions in the next few pages.

Column (1) in Figure 6 indicates the age in years of the individual. Column (2) shows the typical 8-4-4 set-up that we have already described. As is known, the ordinary child starts the first grade at approximately six years of age. State regulations as to when he must attend—and local regulations as to when he may attend— of course affect this. Many boards of education say that no child may begin the first grade in September who will not be six years old before the first of January. This regulation is frequently contested by parents in school systems where there are no kindergartens. At any rate, the child who is six when he starts the first grade will be about fourteen when he finishes the eighth grade. He will finish high school at about eighteen, and college at about twenty-two. His sixteenth birthday, the permissible school-leaving age in many states, will fall midway in his high school career.

Shortly after 1900 reorganizations of the 8-4 school pattern began to appear. Effort was made to correct weaknesses that had long been discussed and to establish new grade combinations that would group pupils more effectively.

3. Reorganization at the Elementary Level

Objections to the Eight-Year School.—The early advocates of a change in the eight-year elementary school were able to cite two or three weaknesses in it that could not be shrugged off.

Retention Past the Onset of Adolescence. Chief among the objections to the eight-year school, and perhaps the most significant of all, was the fact that children were held in the elementary school a year or two after the onset of adolescence. The changes in interests, problems, physical development, social needs, attitudes, and so on associated with adolescence are well known. It seemed quite inappropriate to hold these youngsters in a school where the content and organization of instruction, the methods used, and the activities engaged in were predominantly for younger children. On the playground they towered over the other children, often withdrew into small cliques, and were utterly disinterested in the games that most of the children were playing. For two years they stayed on in a school that was not organized for them. They were a top minority, ahead, and out of place. New kinds of games, new organization of content, something about the vocational world, and new social activities were needed, but they were in schools where the program was set up and the teachers were trained to meet the needs of the vastly larger preadolescent group. The feeling became sharp, therefore, that something ought to be done to adjust the organization of the ladder to the needs of this group; and, above all, to meet those needs when they appeared. For most children this would be at about the beginning of the seventh grade.

Boring Repetition in the Seventh and Eighth Grades. Another objection to the eight-year school developed when repeated studies showed that the seventh and eighth grades were, for numberless children, just "more of the same." The seventh grade had essentially the same subjects as the sixth, reviewed the work of the sixth, then "went on a spell" from there. It was the same in the eighth grade. This situation presented many serious problems. For example, not only were the youngsters wasting a lot of time in school, but they might very well be developing work habits that would cause them to do a poor quality of work when they went on into high school. Furthermore, under those conditions, the educational return for the wages paid to the teachers was not what it ought to be. It seemed reasonable to a lot of people that if a good job were done in the first six grades, the repetition in the seventh and eighth grades might well be eliminated and the pupils might go on to content that was new and unfolding.

The Shock of High School. As many people viewed the eight-grade elementary school, they not only saw the seventh and eighth graders out of place and marking time, but they could see nothing taking place that would help them make a successful adjustment to high school when they finally arrived there. Here were young people who in high school would be confronted with a new type of school control, new challenges in thinking, new organization of subject matter, new methods of study and recitation, new responsibilities and freedoms, and they were getting no introduction to them. They were capable of such introduction, to be sure, but they were in a school whose structure and program were geared to preadolescent children. Hence children who should have found the transfer from elementary school to high school rather natural and easy instead found it to be a considerable shock. They were, of course, adolescents, but they had had no experience in a school that adjusted its program and activities to the needs of adolescents. Great need was felt, therefore, for converting the none-too-fruitful seventh and eighth grades into a transition school that would not only ease the shock between the elementary school and the high school but would also provide an educational program more closely geared to the needs of these early adolescents.

The Six-Year Elementary School.—The foregoing objections to the eight-year elementary school turn out to be rather good arguments for the six-year school. Again, the most important consideration is the children themselves. When this approach is made, a six-year school results, not because of any magic in this form of organization, but because secondary education ought to begin with the beginning of adolescence. Also if the fundamental job of the elementary school can be done in six years, then it is foolish to make the seventh and eighth grades just "more of the same." The contention is widespread that the basic foundations of education for good citizenship and the essential mastery of the tools to further learning can be accomplished in the six-year school if good learning conditions exist and good teachers are employed. Experience seems to show also that adjustments to the needs of the early adolescents are more difficult to make in an eight-grade school than in reorganized schools where adolescents and preadolescents are separated. In the latter case, the administration of both schools, their programs, the employment of their staffs, and their planned activities can all be directed with more singleness of purpose than if the groups are mixed. At any rate, as one views Columns (2) and (3) in Figure 6, one observes that when the eight-grade school has been reorganized, it has customarily lost the seventh and eighth grades, thus becoming a six-year school. It is even more important to observe that among the other reorganizations indicated in Figure 6, the beginning of adolescence is maintained as the beginning of secondary education. The continuous line to the right from Column (3) at about age twelve shows this. This human consideration is solid ground for reorganization.

A word of caution should be put in here about the fundamental job of the elementary school. It should not be inferred from the above discussion that by the time a youngster finishes the sixth grade he will have completed his education in the fundamentals. However, if these six years have been well employed, the fundamentals will be advanced to the point where they will no longer monopolize the pupil's time but will permit the introduction of new content and experiences in line with new interests and needs. The reader should refresh himself on the nature and sequence of objectives at all levels in the educational ladder by referring to page 53.

The Kindergarten.—The kindergarten, dealing ordinarily with children between the ages of five and six, had its origins in Germany in 1816 under Friedrich Froebel. It first appeared in this country in Watertown, Wisconsin, in 1855. The first public kindergarten in this country was opened in St. Louis in 1872. For a good while most of our kindergartens were private schools, but their value to young children was early recognized by public school leaders. State legislatures were willing enough to pass laws permitting local communities to add the kindergarten to the local tax-supported school system if they liked, but most communities found it difficult to provide for the growing enrolments, especially in the high school, let alone to add a kindergarten. Hence, its inclusion in the public school system was rather slow. However, the conditions of our national life since about 1915, involving war, depression, industrialization, unemployment, and so on, together with the demonstrated value of the kindergarten experience to young children, have served to speed up its acceptance as a part of all good elementary school systems. It no longer is in a position of having to justify itself. It can now be considered a permanent projection downward of our educational ladder, although it is not yet available to most of America's children.

The kindergarten, in its philosophy, is one of our most democratic institutions. In it the child is the center of all things. He counts as an individual. The discovery and development of his personality is earnestly sought. While this is taking place, his adjustment to other personalities is looked after. He lives in an environment that is especially prepared for him. He learns how to cooperate with others. He is not under pressure. He is not fitted into a typical first-grade mold. Froebel insisted that the children in the kindergarten ought to grow as naturally as flowers in a garden, the school providing the growth conditions that would give their personalities a chance to unfold. It is interesting to note that the Prussian government, sensing something too democratic for the Prussian system, closed the kindergartens. However, these schools had already been studied by outsiders, including Americans, and their acceptance in other countries was prompt. The philosophy and approach of the kindergarten have influenced greatly the first and second grades of the elementary school.

The Nursery School.—The nursery school is ordinarily concerned with children between the ages of two and five. However, there certainly is no uniformity of practice in this regard. The dotted lines in Columns (5) and (6) of Figure 6 are meant to indicate this variability. It may be that in a given community the nursery school children are held until they are five, thus permitting them to move directly into the kindergarten; whereas, in another community, four years may be the top age limit for nursery school children, thus producing a time gap between the nursery school and the kindergarten which is annoying to many parents. Of course, in actuality, most communities do not have nursery schools at all, or kindergartens for that matter. Kindergartens are more often attached to the public school system than nursery schools are. Both units constitute a reorganization or extension downward of the educational ladder that is quite recent.

The nursery school movement is as much a product of the social and economic conditions of our society as of the popular acceptance of the results of researches on child development. The movement began to be felt about thirty years ago. War and depression had either taken both parents away from home or had made it impossible for the parents to give the children the care and attention they ought to have. Both situations gave great impetus to nursery schools. During the great depression of the 1930's the federal government financed many nursery schools for the young children of persons on relief. When the second World War came, not only the government, but local communities, war production plants, schools, churches, and other agencies maintained child care centers. These centers varied in the nature and quality of their programs, but essentially they were nursery schools, caring for children of nursery school age. As is well known, the experience of women in employment, and the experience of employers of women, has greatly changed the status of women during the last quarter-century. Women want to work outside the home; and, in too many cases, they need to work in order to help meet family expenses. The bearing of this situation upon the maintenance of nursery schools is clear. If certain social and economic trends persist, these schools will become an established necessity.

But the educational aspects of the nursery school are important also. The philosophy of the kindergarten is reproduced here. The development of the child as an individual, together with his adjustment to other children, including the ability to cooperate with them, is most important. Effort is made to establish habits and attitudes that will promote good physical, social, intellectual, and emotional development. Special characteristics, problems, and needs of the children are discussed with the parents, and mutual plans are laid for cooperative action to benefit the children. Thus parent education forms an important part of the program of a good nursery school. Obviously the educational and developmental aspects of the nursery school are quite adequate to justify its existence, independent of the social and economic characteristics of our society.

There have been many researches and studies that have shown the effects of early environment on child development. For example, the Child Welfare Research Station at the University of Iowa made extensive studies on this and reported findings that were challenging and to some extent controversial. These studies seemed to show that if the equivalent of a good nursery school experience is present or absent in the life of the young child, the intellectual development of the child will be affected accordingly. In other words, the child's intellectual potential will be better developed if his early environment is favorable than if it is not. Furthermore, what is lost in these early years cannot of a certainty be made up by improved conditions in later years. Such researches as these, as they are repeated and verified, will establish in fact the contention of many psychologists that the cast of later life is set in the very early years. If this is demonstrated beyond doubt, then our society, in order to play fair with its future citizens, will have to see to it that conditions prevail which will make it possible for parents, schools, and communities to deal justly with the very young. Thus the nursery school becomes an important footing to our educational ladder.

The New Primary Unit.—In closing the discussion concerning the kindergarten, the statement was made that the philosophy and approach of the kindergarten had greatly influenced the first and second grades of the elementary school. In some quarters it is felt that the individualization which characterizes the kindergarten should be continued. A new primary unit that embraces the first and second grades, the kindergarten, and the frequently stranded four-year-olds has therefore been proposed. It is shown as the four-year unit above the nursery school in Column (7) of Figure 6.

Readiness. For too long, and in too many schools, first grade teachers have seemed to assume that all first grade pupils are ready on the first day of school to start the regular school subjects and move along together at a given pace. Such an assumption is incorrect. Psychological studies of readiness to learn have piled up convincing evidence to show that children are not abreast in the appearance of readiness to handle the concepts associated with reading and number work. For example: "In the typical school population, 25 to 30 per cent of the pupils entering the first grade have neither the mental maturity nor the background of common experiences necessary for a reasonable probability of success in the regular reading program." [3] Similar differences occur in relation to arithmetic readiness. Furthermore, it does not necessarily follow that readiness appears later in duller children—although late starters sometimes get the impression from the teacher that they are dull, even though they may not be. At any rate, the fact of differences in children in the appearance of readiness to learn certain kinds of materials has led some to contend that the individualization of the kindergarten could better be continued and differences in readiness better provided for if a primary unit were established in which the child, rather than the mastery of content, was the center of attention.

Flexibility. Naturally, if the primary unit concentrated attention upon the development and needs of the children, its program would have to be flexible. This would be a period of watching for and assisting in the development of new interests and capacities, of adjusting experiences and activities to the children, and of striving for the development of desirable habits and attitudes. These would be "growing-up" groups. If a youngster were not ready for the traditional subjects at the beginning of the first grade, nobody would worry; and certainly no one would create in him a sense of frustration and failure by attempting to secure from him accomplishments for which he was not yet suited. However, unusual care would be taken to seize upon readinesses as they appeared so that the child could successfully launch himself upon the systematic learnings that would be his equipment throughout life. If this were done for children up to the end of what is now the second grade, doubtless they would be better adjusted as individuals and further along in their achievement than the typical beginning third grader is now.

It is considerations such as the above that have led to the proposal of a four-year primary unit. This unit might, of course, be made to include only the kindergarten and the first and second grades, but this would leave out the four-year-olds, who, many contend, are ready for,

[3] California Test Bureau, Educational Bulletin No. 10, p. 6. Based on Ernest W. Tiegs, *The Management of Learning in the Elementary Schools* (New York: Longmans, Green & Co., 1937).

and need, the influences and adjustments that such a unit would promote. Whether or not any considerable number of school systems adopt such a unit remains to be seen. Certainly it is not widespread today. It should be noted that the four-year unit above the proposed primary unit again terminates at the end of the sixth grade, thus preserving the idea that secondary education ought to begin with the beginning of adolescence.

Such are some of the reorganizations and extensions that the traditional eight-year elementary school has undergone, or may undergo. It has lost at the top but has projected itself downward. Although this section of the ladder seems now to have its top limit pretty well established in theory at the sixth grade, just what may happen at its lower limit is not so sure. Again, a glance at Figure 6 will fix in the mind the changes referred to in this section.

4. Reorganization at the Secondary Level

Although significant things have happened at all levels of our educational ladder, it is likely that the great middle of the ladder, representing secondary education, has undergone the most significant and far-reaching changes of all. As we have said before, the traditional, and still the most prevalent, secondary school is a four-year high school above an eight-grade elementary school. But changes have occurred.

The Junior High School.—The junior high school movement, as associated with the taking-over of the seventh and eighth grades, got going around 1910. Columbus, Ohio; Berkeley, California; and Los Angeles, California, were among the first communities to change from an 8-4 to a 6-3-3 combination of grades. Column (3) in Figure 6 illustrates the change. This, of course, brought six grades instead of four under secondary school organization. As communities adopted this plan, they customarily broke up the six grades into two three-year schools. The first of these, comprising grades seven, eight, and nine, was called the junior high school.

The junior high school, as first conceived, was expected to accomplish certain things, such as the following:

1. Adapt its program and activities to early adolescence
2. Eliminate the wasteful repetition of the seventh and eighth grades in the elementary schools
3. Introduce new content in line with adolescent interests and needs

4. Reorganize subject matter on a more meaningful basis and have it taught by teachers who have specialized in certain areas
5. Offer pupils a chance to explore many types of subject matter, including vocational studies, in an effort to discover the areas in which they had special interests and aptitudes
6. Provide guidance services that would indicate the proper course for the pupil in the senior high school
7. Serve as a transition school between elementary and secondary education

The idea that the new school should be a corrective of the abuses of the eight-year elementary school is apparent in the above list. However, it should not be thought of as solely that. Here was a school for adolescents, and that was the important thing. In some regards it attempted more than it could accomplish, such as trying, through exploration and guidance, to gauge the youngsters' interests, aptitudes, and vocational plans accurately enough to determine their rightful areas of special study in the senior high school. Experience has shown that these things do not stabilize for the pupil during his junior high school years.

One of the most difficult problems of the new school was what to make of the ninth grade, which, of course, had been a part of the old four-year high school. The facts are that, generally speaking, the ninth grade did not change at all. The same work was merely offered in a different school. Any basic change in ninth grade work was discouraged by the fact that most colleges continued to admit students on the basis of four years of high school work. Colleges have been slow to release the ninth grade for free integration into the three-year junior high school by shifting from a sixteen-unit to a twelve-unit basis for admission. Junior and senior high schools alike, in spite of the fact that not more than about 20 per cent of their pupils will go on to college, still are greatly influenced by college admission requirements. It bears repeating here that the most important thing about the establishment of the junior high school was that now the organization of the ladder had been brought into line with the developmental needs of boys and girls. As time goes on, its services improve.

The Senior High School.—One does not wish to be too severe in one's comments about what the senior high school was like when it became a three-year school above the junior high school. However, as a rule, it did not change much from what it had been before. In other words, reorganization was not followed immediately by significant changes in the educational program. The senior high school grades continued essentially as they had been, and pupils moved into the tenth grade from the junior high school the same as they had moved in from the ninth grade of the old four-year school. A few years were to elapse before it became clear that the senior high school must be more than a receptacle for the pupils who had been nicely assorted in the junior high school. As the junior high school fell down in its presumed ability to finish the guidance and exploratory job with pupils, these functions were extended upward into the senior high school. The necessity for developing a program suited to the diverse needs and interests of youth became quite as urgent here as in the junior high school. The conditions of our society, too, were causing youth to enter employment later, so that vocational exploration and preparation might well be delayed until the senior high school years. Thus both the junior high school and the senior high school became engulfed in the continuous problem of adjusting the school offering, the guidance services, the activities, the work experiences, the instruction, and a hundred other items to the army of adolescents that moved on toward adulthood.

The Six-Year Secondary School.—There has developed in our country in recent years a rather strong feeling that it would be good judgment to combine the junior and senior high schools into an undivided six-year school. As some of the functions originally assigned to the junior high school have been found to continue on through the senior high school, the necessity for maintaining separate schools has been reduced accordingly. Greater effectiveness would result, too, it is argued, in such things as administration, curriculum planning, and guidance services if the schools were united. After all, the pupils have adolescence, and adolescent interests, in common. Certainly the developmental extremes found among the pupils of an eight-grade elementary school are not duplicated in a six-year secondary school. Furthermore, the states commonly prescribe the same requirements for the certification of teachers in both junior and senior high schools. A good many communities, therefore, convinced that secondary education should begin at the seventh grade, have organized their schools on a 6-6 rather than a 6-3-3 basis. Column (4) in Figure 6 shows the arrangement. A strong case can be made for the six-year secondary school. It has had a steady growth, and many people expect it to become even more widespread.

The extent of reorganization at the secondary school level is not always realized. In 1945–46 there were 23,947 public high schools in the United States. Of these, 13,625 were regular high schools and

10,322 were reorganized schools. Of the reorganized schools, 2,647 were junior high schools, 3,032 were junior-senior high schools, 3,326 were undivided five- or six-year high schools, and 1,317 were senior high schools. The reorganized schools had 61 per cent of the total public high school enrolment. It should be borne in mind also that although the reorganized schools adjusted slowly in some regards, they nevertheless have improved as time has gone on. National studies have demonstrated that education in the reorganized schools is superior to that in the traditional four-year schools. The reader knows better than to interpret this statement to mean that every reorganized school is better than every four-year school. Youth is better served when secondary education adjusts its organization and program to adolescents than when it maintains a pattern that finds its cause for continuation outside the nature and needs of youth.

The Junior College.—The junior college, ordinarily including the thirteenth and fourteenth grades, is at present one of the fastest growing units in the educational ladder. This is true both in numbers of institutions and in enrolments. We now have over 500 such institutions, and they enroll over 200,000 students. Joliet, Illinois, is generally conceded to have had the first public junior college in the country, established in 1902. Others appeared quickly. Two dozen additional institutions, both public and private, sprang up during the next two years. Private institutions outnumbered the public. This is still true, although at present there are a good many more students enrolled in public junior colleges than in private. The movement has made more headway in the West, Middle West, and South than in other sections of the country. Furthermore, in these same sections junior colleges are more often attached to the public school system than they are in other sections. Column (5) in Figure 6 shows the two-year junior college unit above the 3-3 junior and senior high school units.

How It Evolved. Junior colleges have come about as additions to local high schools, as split-offs from four-year colleges, and as independent institutions. As the high school population grew, and as youth found it more and more difficult to qualify for employment at the end of the twelfth grade, it was inevitable that a demand should arise, especially in urban centers, for continued education in the home community. This demand was felt particularly in cities in which there were no colleges. A good many such communities added the thirteenth and fourteenth grades to the public school system and met expenses from tax money. It was inevitable, too, as in the Kalamazoo

Case,[4] that someone should challenge the right of the local board of education to collect the additional taxes necessary to run the junior college. However, the courts have been consistent in maintaining the principle that it is up to the local community to decide how much education it wants to make free and available to all at public expense. Thus the practice of adding the junior college years to the local public schools has grown. Also, a good many four-year colleges have seen the necessity of using the first two years for the completion of general education and the establishment of foundations essential to later professional specialization. If they add curricula intended to prepare students to enter certain vocations at the end of the fourteenth grade, they have in fact established a junior college, although it may not be so listed on the junior college roster. Some four-year colleges have actually abandoned the junior and senior years and have turned their full attention to offering broader services to a greater variety of students on a two-year basis. Finally, of course, there are many independently organized junior colleges. These range in character from the highly vocational-technical type of school through the first-two-years-of-college type, to the fashionable finishing school.

Its Program. It is rather surprising that the junior college did not develop sooner. It is not surprising, though, that it developed rapidly after it got started. Its program meets a tremendous need in our society. A junior college with a good comprehensive program will offer vocational-terminal studies, including preparation for semiprofessional occupations. Our society needs thousands of people prepared on this level to hundreds prepared to full professional status. It will also offer general education of the sort needed for life-enrichment and citizenship purposes for the millions of young people who will go no further up the educational ladder. It will make available a freshman-sophomore program, acceptable to accredited higher institutions, which provides the foundations of general and preprofessional education considered essential. In fact, the junior college, broadly speaking, keeps the educational doors open to all youth for two additional years and provides educational experiences adapted to the needs of all kinds of people. It postpones the selections and discriminations that have ordinarily occurred at the end of the twelfth grade. It gives young people a chance to improve their prospects for useful, enriched living and for meeting the rising demands of employers. From the standpoint of society, it will fill up the gap between twelfth grade graduation and absorption into the world of work with pur-

4 See page 28.

suits that are useful and constructive. It appears more and more likely that our people will demand that junior college opportunities be extended to every youth in the land.

Its Likely Organization. As was indicated above, there are a good many cities and other communities where the secondary school population is large enough to justify the addition of the junior college years to the local public school system. There are indications that, when this is done, the 3-3-2 pattern of secondary school organization, the 6-2 pattern, and the 4-2 pattern are going to be called into question. There seems to be no convincing reason why, in such communities, the thirteenth and fourteenth grades should be administered as a separate unit.

Some people contend that the incorporation of the junior college years into the local school system should await a rise in the compulsory attendance age. This argument carries very little weight. The existing organization in most communities, topped by the twelfth grade, bears no relationship anyhow to the compulsory attendance laws in most states. The conditions in our society and the needs of youth in our time are more fundamental in shaping our educational organization and program than existing attendance laws. If these criteria are to be our guides, then the attendance laws in many states should themselves be drastically revised. If it seems wise and advantageous for youth to remain in school through the thirteenth and fourteenth grades, then the educational ladder should be organized to encourage this, whether the law requires it or not. Thus, as indicated in Columns (6) and (7) of Figure 6, a 4-4 organization of secondary education is coming forward. Under the 4-4 plan, two units of significant length, permitting better administration, programing, guidance, and use of staff would supplant three inordinately short units under the 3-3-2 plan or, under the 6-2 or 4-2 plans, two units, one of which is inordinately short.

Furthermore, the four-year junior college unit, if it offers a good program, will doubtless hold more youth in school longer than a two-year unit superimposed above the twelfth grade. Finally, if the typical compulsory attendance law continues to designate sixteen years as the permissible school-leaving age, than the 4-4 organization has the advantage of completing the first unit at about the sixteenth year. Such a parallelism between the organization of secondary education and the permissible school-leaving age has never existed in our schools. In other words, the pupils who left school when they could were ordinarily "right in the middle" and dangling, rather than at the end of a unit that might have prepared them better for school leaving.

Naturally, not every community that has a high school is going to take on the junior college years. The comments above, of course, refer to the larger communities. In the smaller communities the organization will likely be 6-3-3 or 6-6, with regional junior colleges spaced so as to be within bus-range of all pupils who desire to attend them. Some states are advancing rapidly toward the fulfilment of this goal.

The Scope of Secondary Education.—If one looks again at Figure 6 and moves to the right from the four-year high school in Column (2), he will observe immediately that secondary education in this country is being projected both downward and upward. Two years have been added both above and below the four-year school, so that an eight-year span is coming to supplant a four-year span. We should remind ourselves again, however, that it is not the span in years that is important. The really significant thing is that the secondary school must receive the young adolescent and see him through to the completion of the educational experiences our society wants to make available to all youth. It must establish the foundations for enriched living and useful work for all youth as well as provide the background essential to further studies. It is a school for adolescents, terminating on the threshold of adulthood. It is America's vast school for citizenship, and its program will reflect the educational equipment America wants its citizens to have. These considerations are apparent even in unreorganized schools. Many eight-grade elementary schools, for example, take notice of the onset of adolescence by departmentalizing the seventh and eighth grades and originating separate activities. And at the other end, in many colleges, the first two years are considered the completion of secondary education. Our reorganization, it is clear, lags far behind our acceptance of theory.

5. REORGANIZATION AT THE COLLEGE LEVEL

The colleges, no less than the secondary and elementary schools, are finding that the old patterns must change, that the nature and requirements of our society are stronger than academic traditions in shaping the forms and content of higher education.

Lower Division-Upper Division.—It has already been pointed out that the typical four-year college looks upon its first two years as the completion of secondary education. Students commonly are not permitted to enter seriously upon their fields of specialization before the junior year. This separation of function is frequently reflected in the organization of the institution into a lower division-upper division arrangement. The 2-2 division of the four-year college is indicated in Column (5) of Figure 6. Of course, the first two years are not always called the lower division; they may be designated as the general college, the university college, the junior college, or something else. The result, however, is in general the same: the student is required to round out his education, to establish nonspecialized backgrounds, before moving on to specialization in the upper division. If the lower division makes available numerous terminal curricula of a vocational as well as a general sort, then it is in fact operating as a comprehensive junior college. It is this kind of educational opportunity that America seems to want to make available to all youth. If this happens, it is indeed likely that the lower division in the typical college or university will undergo considerable change. It must either offer a junior college program that is the equal of that in the best junior colleges, or it will leave the junior college job to those institutions, thus concentrating its attention on the upper years.

General Education.—It should not be supposed that all lower divisions in colleges and universities are ambitious to become comprehensive junior colleges. Most of them have no interest at all in setting up an assortment of terminal curricula. They assume that their students will go on to complete the four-year course. Their primary interest is to implement a program of general education that is foundational for all students, without reference to their later fields of specialization or their vocational intentions. College education in this country is considered to be weak on this point. Our curricula have reflected our specialized national development and our earlier concepts of a competitive democracy, and we have been slow to change them. As pointed out in Chapter 3, in the late nineteenth and early twentieth centuries we were "cashing in" on our long struggle for national status and the fruition of our freedoms. Freedom was an individual matter. Rugged individualism, free enterprise, laissez faire, were national slogans. Privileges, rights, and opportunities were emphasized. "Go West" if you feel surrounded by too many people. Escape; don't adjust. Competition was wide open.

It is small wonder that education was affected by all this. Education was to help the individual compete successfully. Education meant money. Vocational-technical-professional curricula multiplied. Specialization, begun early and pursued late, invaded the higher insti-

tutions. The idea has held on tenaciously. However, our later interpretations of democracy are being felt. We are now all bunched up in
our living. The welfare of each is linked to the welfare of the other.
What one does affects many. A sense of social responsibility and a
willingness to cooperate and sacrifice for the good of all are quite as
important now as individual rights, privileges, and opportunities.
Escape is no longer possible. Adjustment is necessary. Above all,
cooperation is necessary. A common ground for human understanding, for fruitful living, for effective cooperation is needed. Man as a
good citizen is more important than man as a good chemist, or bac-
teriologist, or nuclear physicist. It is this common ground for intelligent, sympathetic living that is the concern of general education. It
does not deny specialization. It merely asks that early specialization
give way to broad foundations that are useful to the citizen and specialist alike. In other words, specialization must gain its time by pushing upward on the ladder rather than by pushing downward. If general education then does its job well, no specialist will ever become a
"narrowist." He will have the foundation and the understanding that
will cause him to continue as a broad-minded person and cooperative
citizen even after his specialization has been achieved.

It should be noted that the general education referred to above,
intended to equip young people for better living and thinking in these
times and in this kind of society, is not the liberal arts curriculum
brought over from Europe and perpetuated so long in American
higher institutions. Certain aspects of the traditional liberal arts will
be retained, of course; but the human concern must transcend the
purely academic concern in these institutions no less than in the elementary and secondary schools. They will not survive otherwise.
Hence, hundreds of liberal arts colleges have worked long and fruit-
fully on evolving lower-division programs of general education that
keep at their core the problems of youth in the twentieth century.

The Senior College.—Like the senior high school in its early
stages, the senior college is pretty much "what is left." Two years of
the old four-year college remain when the lower division is organized. In most cases the junior-senior requirements are not altered,
the old time-pattern for the baccalaureate degree is maintained, and
whatever additional preparation may be necessary in the area of specialization begun in the junior year will have to be secured as postgraduate work, perhaps quite disjointedly, after graduation at the end
of the traditional senior year. A good many people believe that when
the junior college years are made available to all youth at public

expense, the senior college will undergo considerable reorganization. The facts are, considerable reorganization is already in process. The discussion of "Junior Selection and Planning" below, bears directly on this.

The Master's Degree.—The master's degree program, representing one year of full-time study beyond the senior year in college, is one of the most seriously criticized units in our educational ladder. It is a kind of pick-up year that gives thousands of people the opportunity to secure the preparation society expects of them when they enter or continue in certain occupations. It is important that such an opportunity be provided, but this does not necessitate the continuation of the one-year unit. Too often the master's program is not a planned continuation of the senior college or a planned forepart of advanced graduate education. If it is to characterize the more extensive preparation that society expects of persons entering certain occupations, then it should be integrated into the work of the senior college. In this manner, also, a good many persons could continue on to the completion of the program who are now unable to do so because of time-honored limitations clustering around the degree.

Junior Selection and Planning.—There is good reason to expect that with the spread of lower-division organization, and with the general increase in education required for entrance into numerous occupations, a three-year unit above the sophomore year will develop in many higher institutions. The arrangement is indicated in Column (7), Figure 6. Certainly there can be no doubt about the trend toward increased entrance requirements into vocations that formerly accepted four-year college graduates. Engineering, teaching, and social work are illustrative. It makes good sense to many people, therefore, to establish unified three-year curricula into which such students will enter at the beginning of the junior year. Students should be selected as good potential for these fields at this time. Since a three-year stretch, short enough in itself, is known to be ahead, why cut it up needlessly into a 2-1 combination?

The suggestion that there ought to be a three-year unit above the sophomore year in college leaves the traditional baccalaureate degree dangling badly. This is very disturbing to many people who have tied the degree to a certain rung in the ladder which represents a kind of fixation in educational time-serving. Others have been bold enough to contend that the baccalaureate degree would have much more meaning if it signified the completion of general, foundational, lower-division education, and were awarded at the end of the sophomore year. Students permitted to pursue studies beyond the sophomore year would then launch themselves on a three-year program which, if completed, would represent actual mastery of a field and would result in the awarding of the master's degree. Such selection and planning, it is believed, would bring to the designation of "master" some of the attributes of purpose and integration it has lacked.

Advanced Graduate Education.—One has reached the top of our formal academic ladder in this country when he earns the so-called doctor's degree. In most graduate schools this can be done with two years of full-time study beyond the master's degree. There are certain professional fields, of course, such as medicine, which require several additional years of preparation. The degree awarded in such fields will be a professional or technical degree, and not the academic doctorate. In the academic field, graduate education beyond the master's degree ought to indicate that the student has profound abilities, is an original thinker, and is able to become a contributing scholar in his field of specialization. All of his formal studies are looked upon as furnishing the background and techniques he will need in going on to new knowledge. At this point he is prepared to be on his own; and, as it were, he leaves the educational nest to explore new regions that his researches or his curiosity have led him into.

America's great universities are now at the forefront among the universities of the world in research and graduate studies. This in spite of the fact that the development in this country is relatively young. Johns Hopkins University is credited with organizing the first graduate work in 1876. Developments have been rapid since the turn of the century. Our institutions, of course, have been spared the ravages of war which have struck twice in this century and have deterred and destroyed much significant work in foreign universities. It used to be that American scholars went abroad for most of their advanced studies. They need not go any more. In fact, the stream of students that enters our country for this purpose is much larger than the stream that leaves. Incidentally, some of our graduate schools have very interesting hold-overs in their requirements that stem from the time when so many of our graduate students studied abroad and when most of the researches were being conducted in foreign universities. The tenacious foreign language requirements, particularly French and German, are illustrative. With the growth of graduate studies in our own universities, and with the clear demonstration that some of these requirements are not uniformly useful in helping students to become contributing scholars in their fields, certain requirements are tending to become less stringent.

It is clear from the above that our organization for higher education is in a state of flux the same as is our organization for elementary and secondary education.

6. The Evolving Pattern

We can be thankful that this country permits all the fluctuations and experimentations in our educational organization which have been discussed in the previous pages. Under these circumstances we certainly shall not see in the future the development of a uniform pattern. Whatever uniformity we achieve will result from experience which proves that certain forms are better than others, rather than from government-imposed patterns. As time goes on, certain ideas and practices seem to be evolving and receiving general acceptance. Of course, conditions may arise which will change all this; but, for the moment, the shape of things to come can be discerned in part from current trends. It is these trends that have been our concern in the foregoing pages. What then, in summary, are some of the more important developments which bear upon the reorganization of the educational ladder? Let us make the enumeration concise and brief.

1. The old eight-year elementary school is losing the top two grades. Secondary education is beginning with the onset of adolescence.
2. The value of the kindergarten is accepted; this unit is rapidly being added to our public school system.
3. The value of the nursery school is also accepted, but its addition to the public school system will likely be slow.
4. The proposed new primary unit to foster the development of children between four and eight years has great merit. The establishment of such a unit will depend in good part on the extent to which local communities agree to finance the downward projection of the ladder.
5. The American secondary school is a school for adolescents. Even in the eight-year elementary schools, the program and activities of the top two grades are often set apart from the lower grades.
6. The four-year high school above the eighth grade is passing. It is being supplanted in many communities by six years of secondary education organized on a 3-3 basis, or on a six-year undivided basis.

7. Communities that add the thirteenth and fourteenth grades to the public school system are not likely to remain satisfied with them as separate two-year units.

8. The 4-4 organization of secondary education is likely to increase in communities that add the thirteenth and fourteenth grades to the public school system.

9. Secondary education is coming to be thought of as terminating at the end of the fourteenth grade. This cuts the traditional four-year college squarely in two.

10. A separate senior college unit of two years and a separate master's unit of one year are being called into question.

11. Education beyond the senior year in college is increasing for numerous occupations.

12. A three-year unit above the sophomore year in college is making headway.

13. Advanced graduate education, already strong in this country, will doubtless be greatly expanded and strengthened.

14. There is a strong feeling that the educational ladder should not be cut into too many separately administered short units (as illustrated in Column (5) of Figure 6), but that each unit should be sufficiently long to permit good administration, good curriculum planning, good guidance, good use of staff, and so on.

15. The principle is becoming established that school organization ought to respond to the nature and needs of pupils and current society. Schools are meant to adjust to the needs of people, not stubbornly to perpetuate certain forms or content.

Let the reader now contemplate the organization of the educational ladder in his own community and judge whether or not improved educational services would result if certain changes were made.

7. Factors Affecting Reorganization

Most people will likely recall communities they have known where the reorganization of the educational ladder was discussed or even desired, but certain conditions served to delay change. It should certainly be borne in mind that there are many factors which may keep a community from doing what it would like to do in this regard. In many cases, several years must elapse before it is possible to make desired changes. In other cases, of course, changes could be made if fundamental educational considerations were allowed to direct the course of action. Some of the factors affecting reorganization are noted here.

Enrolment.—It is apparent at once that the number of pupils in the local schools must be considered in deciding the organization the local ladder should take. If there aren't enough five-year-olds in the community to justify the addition of a kindergarten, then a kindergarten should not be added. If the high school enrolment is small, it would be foolish to try to add the junior college to the local system. Education is not improved when more is attempted than can be done well with existing resources, staff, and student bodies. On the other hand, if a community is teeming with five-year-olds, has a large high school population, and looks forward to further growth, it is duty-bound to consider the improvement of educational services through reorganization, if it has not already done so.

Buildings.—Sometimes the building situation in a community does not lend itself to reorganization. New buildings may be in prospect for the future. Hence, reorganization will await new construction. There can be no fundamental objection to this. The mistake comes, however, when plans for new construction are not accompanied by consideration of whether or not some reorganization should take place also. The impression should not be gained that reorganization must always involve new buildings. Often a survey of existing buildings in relation to reorganization reveals surprising possibilities, especially if some remodeling can be done.

Finance.—Certain aspects of reorganization, such as adding new grades to the system or making changes that require new buildings and new staff, are very costly. Resources may not be available to carry the financial load. This, no doubt, is one of the greatest deterrents to reorganization. Communities, of course, should finance only projects that are educationally defensible. For example, if high schools are built for too few pupils, the resulting per-pupil cost will be too high for the quality of education received. In such a case it would be better if the community could cooperate with other communities in providing at reasonable per-pupil cost an even better education.

Staff.—Ordinarily reorganization will require staff adjustments and increases. If the necessary staff members, properly trained, are not available to implement reorganization, it should not be attempted. Reorganization is not justified unless it improves educational services. Such improvement can hardly be expected if staffs are inadequate. For example, the elementary teachers in an eight-grade school may be asked to assume the load associated with the setting-up of a junior high school. If a community can have a junior high school only by asking the elementary teachers to take it on, it is doubtful if it should have one at all. The staff problem, of course, is closely associated with that of finance.

Community Familiarity with All Aspects of Reorganization.—It is easily possible for the people of a community to emphasize certain aspects of reorganization and not give due consideration to others. For example, the cost of reorganization might be emphasized, without adequate attention being given to the educational implications involved. Or, the desirability of reorganization might be understood, but a full picture of what the staff requirements would be might be lacking. In some communities reorganization should be attempted; in others it should not be. Action will be wisest if all the people of the community have become familiar with all aspects of the problem and have had time collectively to evolve a proper policy.

Alertness of Local Educational Leadership.—When communities employ school administrators and supervisors, the communities have a right to expect that they will consider how the educational services to the pupils and the people might be improved and will keep the people informed on such matters. If a community's resources are limited, it is always a temptation to a school man to let things go on as they are. Actually, however, he has not discharged his full duty if he has not acquainted the people with how the schools should be improved, even though it seems unlikely that any of his recommendations can be carried out. It is this kind of leadership that prepares the way for supplemental assistance, such as state aid. Furthermore, it is the responsibility of local leaders to achieve the all-round consideration referred to in the previous paragraph when problems of reorganization are before the people. Without good local leadership, needed changes are not likely to take place; they will at least be terribly delayed. Furthermore, without good leadership, some changes might be instituted which could not be justified.

Redistricting.—One can easily see the effect of redistricting on the organization of the ladder if he visualizes, for example, the consolidation of a half-dozen eight-grade elementary schools into one larger school. The half-dozen traditional schools might well be replaced by a K-6-3 organization which would vastly improve the educational opportunities of the pupils, but which, of course, would not have been appropriate in any one of the original districts. On the secondary level, this type of redistricting, involving the consolidation of several high school districts, is likely to be closely associated with the popularization of junior college education.

Time Requirements for Experience and Research.—The statement has been made repeatedly that reorganization is justified only if it results in the improvement of educational services. Furthermore, such improvement must be clearly and conclusively demonstrated. Mere opinion, no matter how reputable its source may be, is not enough. Research and experience must accumulate sufficiently to show the relationship between certain types of organization and their educational outcomes. This type of research takes a great deal of time. If it is to be repeated and verified, even more time is necessary. If certain patterns of organization are found to produce better educational outcomes than others, then the defensible foundations of reorganization are established. Such researches have been made, and others are in progress. They tend to establish the general educational superiority of some of the changes discussed in this chapter over the traditional 8-4-4 pattern. However, the point here is that reorganization should not be carried out until research and experience have demonstrated that a change would improve matters. In this connection, the service of the pioneering, experimental schools that are willing to adopt and appraise new practices is noteworthy.

State Laws.—There are two outstanding ways in which state laws affect the reorganization of the educational ladder. The first is the permission they give to local communities to do such things as add the kindergarten, the nursery school, and the junior college to the tax-supported school system, or to join together to form new districts in which a different educational ladder can be set up. The second is the provision they make for direct assistance by the state, such as state support for regional junior colleges and for the construction of school buildings. Again, the local public schools are parts of a state school system. The fundamental pattern must therefore first come to life in state laws.

8. Interrelationships Among the Units of the Ladder

One of the most serious problems connected with the educational ladder is that of articulation or securing good working relationships among the units of the ladder. As we know, the separate units, such as the elementary school, the junior high school, or the college, have a great deal of independence in their administration and in their educational planning. This independence can result in much disjointedness, or, on the other hand, in genuine cooperation.

Some Existing Conditions.—There are a good many evidences of disjointedness in the ladder. Three will start the reader on his way.

Overlapping in Content. A great deal of learning is lost to the student if he must spend time in school on materials that have been covered before. This does not eliminate the place of review in learning, but it does call into question the serious overlapping that is often found between units in the educational ladder. Numerous researches have demonstrated this overlapping. Perhaps an English teacher in the tenth grade of the senior high school will repeat, to the point of boredom, the materials covered in the ninth grade of the junior high school. Or the first chemistry course in college may be the high school chemistry course all over again, with a little added. History is another area in which time-wasting duplication is a serious problem. What is more, such overlapping does not occur only between separately administered units; it is a problem also within the units. One does not wish to exaggerate; but occasionally, to say the least, the eleventh grade English teacher knows all too little of what the tenth grade or the twelfth grade English teacher is doing. And on the college level, if instructors within certain departments will examine their courses for needless duplication, their findings in a good many cases are likely to be most disturbing. Worst of all, most teachers, never having gone into the matter, are not conscious of such overlapping. From the standpoint of the student, it is an example of poor articulation for which he pays in reduced learning and reduced enthusiasms.

Poor Staff Attitudes. The tendency of the staffs of various units of the ladder to work and plan independently is well known. When this is extended to the point of being critical of the work of other units, then a severe problem in articulation has arisen. It is not uncommon to find secondary school teachers, for example, who are quite critical of the work of the elementary school; and certainly college instructors can be found who can take a high school apart, even though they may not have taught in one or visited one to find out what its program and problems are. Such attitudes do not serve to bring the units of the ladder closer together; they tend to keep them apart; and, as before, the student bears the penalty.

Requirements That Are Not Defensible. The units of the ladder that fall within the education provided for all at public expense, or within the limits of compulsory attendance, do not have admission requirements in the usual sense. The elementary school does not accept certain kindergarteners and reject others; the community high school does not set certain scholarship requirements for pupils coming from the elementary schools. Students encounter such requirements, generally speaking, when they move on up from the secondary school into the colleges. Exceptions can be found, of course, in the administration of certain specialized schools on the secondary level, such as technical schools. Some of the requirements that students are forced to satisfy in order to get from one unit to another do not have the virtues so long claimed for them. For example, it has been shown repeatedly that the pattern of subjects a pupil takes in high school is not as important in determining scholastic success in college as his standing in what he did take, and, of course, his native ability. Other things being equal, an *A* in shorthand in high school should interest a college just as much as an *A* in Latin, if the probability of scholastic success in college is under consideration. Incidentally, the mental processes involved in learning shorthand are quite similar to those involved in learning Latin, so that the proponents of Latin as a college admission requirement might very well become proponents of shorthand also. The point is that some of the requirements now maintained by certain units on the ladder are actually artificial barriers which limit enrolments, and are not dependable instruments for the selection of students most likely to succeed.

The Aim.—The aim of articulation is to establish relationships among the units of the ladder that will cause the student's educational experience to be continuous and unfolding. The units must be dovetailed so that progression from one to another is not a problem of jumping barriers, but is a continuation of a related, on-going learning experience. In this way the student is permitted to progress as far up the ladder as his interests and capabilities will allow and does not have his school experience terminated by requirements that are traditionally reputable but actually meaningless. The fundamental approach ought to be that of assisting each one to progress as far as is appropriate for him, rather than to erect barriers that may actually cut him out before he ought to be cut out.

Things That Can Be Done.—There is much under way to improve articulation. The satisfactions that result when good relationships are established and the improvements that are noted in educational outcomes are certain to bring about a spread of good practices. Here again, however, we seem to act slowly on the things we know are good to do. What are a few of these good things?

Cooperative Guidance Programs. One of the most significant things that is being done to improve articulation is the setting-up of cooperative guidance programs. When this is done, the separate units on the ladder cooperate in making education most significant for students at all levels and in facilitating their successful adjustment as they move along. The elementary school seeks to discover all it can about each pupil, to use that information in making the elementary school experience most appropriate, and then to pass that information along with the child as he moves into another unit. As the pupil approaches the secondary school, the elementary school projects itself forward into the high school and the high school reaches down into the elementary school to cooperate in securing a successful transition and adjustment for the child. Similar relationships are established between secondary schools and colleges. This is cooperative guidance. Many activities and services, of course, are involved in such programs. Visiting days, festivals, published materials to be used in the schools, speakers, and, probably most important of all, well-kept cumulative record forms, are illustrative. The important thing about such programs is that each unit is not only interested in the child while it has him, but is also interested in his entire educational career and wishes to do the appropriate and wise thing for him.

Cooperative Curriculum Planning. One hears too rarely of meetings in which college, secondary school, and elementary school teachers of English, social studies, or science get together to consider what ought to be the related, unfolding experience of pupils in these fields. Curriculum planning is usually confined to separate school units. There seems to be no good reason why more cooperative curriculum planning should not be engaged in, especially within a given school system. Much of the overlapping discussed above might thus be eliminated, and attitudes among staff members improved. This kind of cooperation is on the increase.

Workshops and Conferences. Workshops and conferences on key problems related to articulation are also on the increase. To an increasing extent these are system-centered; that is to say, selected persons from an entire school system get together to work out solutions to problems that concern the entire system or to prepare materials useful throughout the system. For example, it might be felt that something ought to be done in the schools about intercultural relations. Persons throughout the system may be selected to get together, to study the problem extensively, and to produce materials and suggest activities that would be appropriate for use at various grade levels. Ordinarily such a group will have as a consultant a recognized leader in the field who may or may not be a member of the local school staff. Of course, such workshops and conferences need not be system-centered. Their value in working out usable ideas and materials has caused them to increase greatly during the last few years.

Visiting. Interrelationships among the units of the educational ladder would undoubtedly improve if more simple visiting took place. Such visiting as now occurs is usually intralevel; that is, a high school science teacher visits another science teacher in another high school, a college mathematics teacher visits another one, and so on. This is good, but it tends to delimit interests and promote a kind of "level" confinement. More college people ought to visit high schools, and more high school people ought to visit colleges. Similarly among all the units. In this way the really important thing evolves: a realization of where the pupil comes from and where he is going. Each unit will more fully appreciate the work and problems of the other. College teachers, for example, will learn that high schools have to do more than prepare pupils for college. And so the fruits of the exchange could be multiplied.

Let us repeat that the results of improved articulation are so satisfying to school personnel, and the educational outcomes are so much better for pupils, that steady progress in this regard may be expected.

9. Pupil Progress Up the Ladder

Before leave is taken of the educational ladder, it will be appropriate to mention a few items related to pupil progress up the ladder. Some of these items will be encountered again later on, but their vivid relationship to the ladder justifies brief treatment here.

Theory of the Proposed Primary Unit.—It will be remembered that sanction was given earlier to the idea of a primary unit at the bottom of the educational ladder, which would serve children from about four to eight years of age and which would remain highly flexible in its program, adjusting itself to developmental differences in young children. In such a unit, of course, the traditional grade organization would not occur, and the child would learn and do those things for which he is ready and which are desirable in terms of his full development.

Common Practice Above the Kindergarten.—Although the individualization observed in the kindergarten, and in the proposed primary unit, is on the increase further up the ladder, it is still true that when the typical American child enters the early elementary grades he encounters a set of artificial standards by which he is sometimes judged quite ruthlessly. These standards are not adjusted to him and his readiness or ability to achieve but represent a strange idea of exactly how much arithmetic should be learned in a given grade and, similarly, what the reading, writing, and spelling skills should be. These standards are often applied quite mercilessly; so much so that if a child in the first grade falls seriously short of the established goals, he is branded as a failure at the very outset of his school career and the fact is officially recorded for his contemporaries and future generations to see. All this is done without challenging the validity of the standards or ever calling into question the practice of setting one standard for all. As time goes on, however, more and more people are beginning to wonder why the individualization process cannot be continued up through the grades. This would mean that appropriate standards for each pupil would replace a common standard for all, and failures based on standards utterly out of line with individual aptitudes and capacities would be eliminated.

Standards in Relation to Abilities.—The traditional application of standards and the more recent point of view regarding them are in sharp contrast. The old idea of standards as a measured block of content set for all, left some pupils improperly challenged and others struggling beyond their depth. The newer idea is so to relate standards and abilities that each pupil will be challenged in line with his abilities and will find it possible to succeed and not fail. In this manner all will move up the ladder together, admittedly achieving at different rates and in different amounts, but each doing in kind and amount what is possible, appropriate, and fair for him.

Retardation and Skipping.—As long as uniform standards for all are employed, there is likely to be a group of pupils who cannot meet these standards and another group who can achieve far beyond them. When standards are not met, the pupil is often required to repeat a whole year and face again the requirements that were poorly adjusted to him to begin with. Thus he becomes retarded. When standards are easily met and the pupil is clearly able to go beyond them, he may develop poor work habits and underachieve or he may be skipped or double-promoted in the hope that another set of standards will somehow be a little more closely related to his abilities. Thus when school takes up in the fall, it is easily possible for pupils who had been classmates a few weeks before to be considerably apart on the ladder. This kind of management should be rigorously challenged.

The Idea of Enrichment.—The conviction is taking firm root in this country that children ought to stay together as they move up the educational ladder unless deviations among them are outstanding. Classroom teachers must learn how to take a cross section of pupils, set up minimum essentials that all are capable of achieving, and then plan additional work and activities in line with individual abilities and interests. This is enrichment. It is a ridiculous thing for a teacher to set up a common standard for all pupils and then hound the dull to reach it, while denying the bright the privilege of opening a new book until the dull have caught up. Yet it is done. It should worry no one if during a given year some pupils have learned twenty times as much as others, provided all have achieved somewhere near their capacities. This ought to be the aim of instruction: to help each to learn in terms of his ability to learn. If this happens, then pupils ought to move along together until the permissible school-leaving age is reached or until the education provided free to all in the community has been completed.

In the past our application of standards has often resulted in serious penalty to the gifted child. The concern of the teacher has more often been to help the slow child "pass" than to cause the gifted child to do all he could. The special class work, the extra time after school, and the visit to the home are more frequently devoted to the dull pupil than to the bright. No one would suggest that these services to dull pupils are not worth while or should be reduced; but the suggestion is implicit that ways should be found to enrich the education of the superior children. Incidentally, the educational returns for the amount of time and energy expended will also be greatest with this group. This enrichment, of course, should be significant and challenging. It should not be chores or busy-work like policing the corridors, dusting the erasers, or keeping the teacher's records. The full employment of pupil capacities is what is sought. Such attention to the superior child, it should be remembered, is not education for the elite. It merely asks for equal attention to individual development for children at all ability levels. Again, the idea is growing that such individualization should be achieved while the pupils move up the ladder together.

The Problem of Failure.—It is considerations such as the above which have caused some people to talk about schools in which there is no failure. The idea has merit. Too many people, however, interpret the idea as meaning that everybody will be passed whether he does any work or not or whether or not he learns anything. Their thinking stems from the old concept of standards. If, on the other hand, teachers and parents made it the responsibility of the school to discover the capabilities of children and then cause each one to use those capabilities to the full and if teachers were reasonably successful in achieving this, then there could be no cause for failure. Furthermore, children would doubtless master the traditional learnings better than under the old system and would, in addition, develop better poise, social skills, and emotional adjustments as a result of participating successfully with their own age group. The effects of failure and the fear of failure are all too well known to discerning parents and mental hygienists. To suggest that it be reduced in our schools is not to suggest that less be expected of pupils but rather that performance demands be brought into line with the ability to perform. This done, educational standards have risen, not dropped; and the sum total of learning and happiness has been greatly increased.

10. Part-Time Schools, Continuation Schools, Extension, and Home Study

What we have described in this chapter still falls short of including the entire set-up of schools in this country. The full-time student who goes from the bottom to the top of the educational ladder will ordinarily find himself in schools such as we have described. However, there are millions of people in this country, old and young, who are not pursuing education on full time but for whom educational opportunities still exist. Young people who have passed the compulsory attendance age may wish to go to work but still carry on studies on part time. Adults with a thousand interests, ranging from learning to read and write to problems of international diplomacy and covering many problems related to their vocations, may wish to attend school at night and follow up on their interests. Thousands of others may wish to pursue studies made available through extension services and summer schools. A very large number of people engage in correspondence and home-study work. It has been estimated that thirty million adults are going to sc' ool in this country, and that adult education programs "may soon include more persons over twenty-one than are enrolled in our regular schools and colleges." [5]

Thousands of short courses, conferences, and institutes dealing with special problems are attended by millions of people. Systematic studies by radio and television, in which instruction by one person can be projected to thousands of others, are expanding greatly. In other words, for just about every American who wishes to pursue studies of some sort or other, there is a school or home-study course or an institute or a radio program to serve him. Not all of these fit nicely into the educational ladder which we have discussed, but they represent nevertheless educational activities with accomplishments and possibilities too great to be exaggerated.

Thus has our educational ladder grown and changed, and thus it faces its problems of reorganization and articulation in the future. It provides the framework for the education of all of America's children. It should not be too inflexible to serve them well.

What Do YOU Say?

1

It would be a good thing for children if at about age four they could enter an ungraded primary unit which sought their full development and which skilfully related the introduction of formal studies to the onset of the child's readiness for them.

What do YOU say?

2

Teachers at any level in our school system know too little about the program and problems at other levels. All elementary, secondary, and college teachers should be encouraged to visit schools at levels other than their own until they have gained a first-hand knowledge of the problems a student encounters as he progresses up the ladder.

What do YOU say?

3

The only acceptable approach to educational standards in the schoolrooms of a democracy is to adjust learning requirements to the ability of each individual to learn. Unevenness in the amount learned by different

[5] John J. McFarland. "Potential Unlimited." *Connecticut Teacher*. XVIII, 122.

pupils should therefore be expected and sought, and no pupil should be "failed" if the amount he learns comes reasonably close to the amount he can learn.

What do YOU say?

4

What points in this chapter do you particularly support or take issue with?

Chapter 8

THE AMERICAN SCHOOL POPULATION AND RELATED PROBLEMS

That None Shall Be Denied

1. THE EDUCATIONAL LEVEL OF OUR PEOPLE

How Much Schooling Do Americans Have?—In April, 1947, the United States Bureau of the Census sampled the civilian population to ascertain the educational attainment of the people in our country who were twenty years old and over. Table 5 [1] presents part of the data reported by the Bureau. According to these data, in 1947 the typical American over nineteen years of age had had 9.5 years of schooling. This varied greatly, however, for different age groups. The oldest group, sixty-five and over, had 7.7 years of schooling, whereas the youngest group, twenty to twenty-four, had 12.1 years. About 20 per cent of the oldest group had less than five years of schooling, whereas only 3 per cent of the youngest group had less than five years. The educational background of the typical American youth leaving our schools today includes more than four years of · school beyond the eighth grade. The census report also presents data, not included in Table 5, to show that "females had a slightly higher level of educational attainment than males," 9.9 years of schooling as against 9.2 years. This was true at all age levels. For most of the age groups a greater proportion of men than women graduated from college, but the women did not drop out prior to high school graduation as often as the men, so that their average number of years in school held up. In recent years the proportion of women graduating from college has overtaken that of men. Perhaps the most encouraging aspect of the data in Table 5 is the fact that the youngest age groups had the most schooling. On the other hand, it is discouraging to find that approximately nine million people who were twenty years old and over had less than five years of schooling. Of these, close to a million were under thirty years of age. Furthermore, the number of people in our country who are functionally illiterate is still cause for genuine national embarrassment. On the matter of illiteracy, the

[1] Page 226.

TABLE 5

Years of School Completed by the Civilian Population 20 Years Old and Over, by Age, for the United States: April, 1947 [2]

Years of School Completed	Age							Total, 20 Years and Over
	20-24 Years	25-29 Years	30-34 Years	35-44 Years	45-54 Years	55-64 Years	65 and Over	
Elementary School:								
Less than 5 years *	369,000	489,000	526,000	1,280,000	1,923,000	2,099,000	2,294,000	8,980,000
5 and 6 years	554,000	539,000	582,000	1,446,000	1,754,000	1,506,000	1,463,000	7,844,000
7 and 8 years	1,661,000	1,921,000	2,481,000	6,037,000	5,947,000	4,726,000	3,906,000	26,679,000
High School:								
1 to 3 years	2,907,000	2,618,000	2,379,000	3,748,000	2,563,000	1,355,000	824,000	16,394,000
4 years	4,719,000	4,200,000	3,430,000	4,283,000	2,432,000	1,544,000	1,037,000	21,645,000
College								
1 to 3 years	1,158,000	1,057,000	851,000	1,591,000	1,031,000	628,000	375,000	6,691,000
4 or more years	292,000	641,000	737,000	1,409,000	812,000	471,000	354,000	4,716,000
School Years Not Reported	88,000	89,000	87,000	189,000	272,000	314,000	338,000	1,377,000
Total	11,748,000	11,554,000	11,073,000	19,983,000	16,734,000	12,643,000	10,591,000	94,326,000
Median Years of School Completed	12.1	12.0	11.4	9.9	8.5	8.1	7.7	9.5

* Includes persons reporting no school years completed.

[2] Adapted from U. S. Bureau of the Census, *Current Population Reports*, "Educational Attainment of the Population" (Preliminary Data), Series P-20, No. 6, p. 2 (Washington, D. C.: U. S. Government Printing Office, 1947).

Bureau of the Census pointed out in another report that in October, 1947, 2.7 per cent of our people who were fourteen years old and over could not read and write. There was 1.8 per cent of illiteracy among the whites and 11 per cent among the nonwhites. In urban areas the illiteracy rate was 2 per cent, and in rural-farm areas it was 5.3 per cent. Among all males it was 3 per cent and among females 2.3 per cent. Clearly the problem of illiteracy concentrates in the nonwhite group and in rural-farm areas.

The reader will remember other discussions, e.g., pages 178 and 179, that pointed out significant regional differences in the educational attainment of our people.

The Trend.—The trend in the years of schooling of our people is just what one would expect it to be. It is upward, as the report of the Bureau of the Census points out:

The median number of school years completed by persons in the younger age groups (20 to 29 years old) was about 12 years, representing the completion of high school. This level represents an increase of about four years of schooling over that reported by the population who completed their schooling a little more than a generation ago (those 55 to 64 years old). The general pattern among adults—of a higher educational level at successively younger ages—reflects the historic trend toward more and more schooling.[3]

This trend is certainly likely to continue. The situation with reference to compulsory attendance, the gradual addition of the thirteenth and fourteenth grades to the public school system, the availability of education to adults as well as to youth, and the rise in educational requirements for admission to many jobs and professions will doubtless cause the educational attainment of our people to rise. Now as never before, the value of a good education is appreciated, not only for vocational purposes, but for enriched living as well. Furthermore, a people like our own who have advanced in their education definitely beyond the point of ordinary literacy, and who are caught up in the events of a rapidly changing world, are desirous of keeping themselves informed about all sorts of current matters. Hence there has been a tremendous growth, especially among adults, of types of study and education that do not follow the traditional classroom lines. Institutes, study groups, forums, and the like become important agencies in this connection. Similarly, the popular press, the radio, television, and the movie take on tremendous educational significance. At any rate, as a people we tend to spend more and more years in school, and this trend seems likely to continue.

[3] *Ibid.,* p. 1.

2. Enrolments and Enrolment Trends

No useful purpose is served by presenting extended breakdowns of current school enrolments. They quickly become outdated. However, a few data of a general nature will help to reveal certain trends and to promote an appreciation of the magnitude of the educational enterprise in this country. Other considerations about the people in our schools are quite as important as their number.

In Public Elementary and Secondary Schools.—The "battle for the free schools," it will be remembered, occupied in the main the period from 1825 to 1850. Public elementary or "common" schools were established. Compulsory school-attendance laws were a logical follow-up to the establishment of tax-supported schools. In 1852 Massachusetts passed such a law, and other states and territories followed, until in 1918 Mississippi completed the list. Enrolments in elementary schools, therefore, tend to approximate the total number of children available for attendance. The same is not true for secondary schools and higher institutions. Although in the period from about 1875 to 1900 the high school became accepted as a part of free, tax-supported education, compulsory attendance laws did not require that pupils complete high school. In a very real sense, high school and college enrolments have been a gauge of the "will to learn" of our people. What do the figures show?

Table 6 presents enrolment data for public elementary and secondary schools since 1900. Again, on the whole, the elementary school enrolments, indicated in columns (4) and (5), tend to reflect the number of children available for education more than the popularization of education. Any rise or fall in the proportion of elementary school enrolment to the total population is best explained, no doubt, in terms of birth rates. Columns (6) and (7), which, combined, show enrolments in public secondary schools, tell a different story. Some of the increase in enrolments since 1900 is, of course, due to the effect of compulsory attendance laws, but more than that the increase is due to other things. The public high school, a creation of the American people, is more and more becoming their common school, without reference to attendance laws. Its growth has been phenomenal. Our total public and nonpublic secondary school enrolment increased 1,651.7 per cent between 1890 and 1948. During the same period the total number of young people fourteen to seventeen years of age increased 60 per cent. In 1890, seven out of a hundred fourteen- to seventeen-year-olds were enrolled in a secondary school. In 1948, seventy-four out of a hundred were enrolled.[5]

TABLE 6

ENROLMENTS IN PUBLIC ELEMENTARY AND SECONDARY SCHOOLS [4]

Year	Estimated Population	Enrolment				
		Total	Elementary: Kindergarten to 8th Grades		Secondary: 9 to 12 and Post-Graduate Grades	
			Boys	Girls	Boys	Girls
(1)	(2)	(3)	(4)	(5)	(6)	(7)
1951–52...						
1949–50...						
1947–48...	146,113,000	23,945,000	9,429,000	8,862,000	2,747,000	2,906,000
1945–46...	139,893,406	23,299,941	9,098,013	8,579,731	2,633,117	2,989,080
1943–44...	138,083,449	23,266,616	9,081,270	8,631,826	2,553,356	3,000,164
1941–42...	134,656,078	24,562,473	9,336,067	8,838,601	3,089,434	3,298,371
1939–40...	131,891,632	25,433,542	9,681,465	9,150,633	3,250,952	3,350,492
1929–30...	122,775,046	25,678,015	10,842,259	10,436,334	2,115,228	2,284,194
1919–20...	105,710,620	21,578,316	9,781,793	9,596,134	992,664	1,207,725
1909–10...	91,792,266	17,813,852	8,569,439	8,329,352	402,436	512,625
1899–1900.	75,602,515	15,503,110	7,600,151	7,383,708	216,207	303,044

TABLE 7

ENROLMENTS IN PRIVATE AND PAROCHIAL ELEMENTARY AND SECONDARY SCHOOLS [6]

Year	Enrolment		
	Total	Elementary	Secondary
1950–51			
1947–48	3,053,914	2,451,430	602,484
1944–45	2,724,572	2,205,796	518,776
1941–42	2,616,529	2,133,334	483,195
1939–40	2,611,047	2,153,279	457,768
1929–30	2,651,044	2,309,886	341,158
1919–20	1,699,481	1,485,561	213,920
1909–10	1,675,837	1,558,437	117,400
1899–1900	1,351,722	1,240,925	110,797

[4] Adapted from U. S. Office of Education statistical circular, Circular No. 241, May, 1948, and from *Biennial Survey of Education in the United States, 1946–48* (Washington, D. C.: U. S. Government Printing Office, 1950), chapter ii, "Statistics of State School Systems, 1947–48," p. 46.

[5] *Biennial Survey of Education in the United States, 1946–48* (Washington, D. C.: U. S. Government Printing Office, 1950), chapter i, "Statistical Summary of Education 1947–48," p. 25.   [6] *Ibid.*

In Private and Parochial Elementary and Secondary Schools.—
Table 7 gives information on enrolments in private and parochial
elementary and secondary schools since 1900.

Elementary enrolments in these schools follow very closely the
pattern found in the public schools. However, the slight decreases in
public secondary enrolments following 1940 are not paralleled by
similar decreases in the private and parochial schools. In the latter
schools the secondary enrolments, although small in relation to enrolments in the public schools, have maintained a steady increase.

In Higher Institutions.—Table 8 presents data relative to the
enrollment in full-time publicly and privately controlled higher institutions since 1900.

TABLE 8

Enrolment in Full-Time Publicly and Privately Controlled
Higher Institutions [7]

Years	Enrolment
1899–1900	237,592
1909–1910	355,215
1919–1920	597,880
1929–1930	1,100,737
1939–1940	1,494,203
1943–1944	1,155,272
1945–1946	1,676,851
1947–1948	2,616,262

Table 9, from another source, presents more recent data.

Enrolments in higher institutions are not affected, of course, by
compulsory attendance laws. Other conditions in our society determine enrolments in these schools. Some of these conditions, to be
sure, almost have the force of law, as illustrated by the educational
requirements associated with entrance into the professions. Hence
young people who wish to qualify for professional service must continue their education, sometimes at great length. Millions of others
find in higher institutions tremendous stimulation and enrichment
beyond vocational or professional preparation. Whatever the cause,
enrolments have increased steadily and at times so rapidly that great
difficulty has been experienced in providing adequate facilities for
student instruction and housing.

[7] Adapted from *Biennial Survey of Education in the United States, 1946–48*
(Washington, D. C.: U. S. Government Printing Office, 1950), chapter i, "Statistical Summary of Education 1947–48," p. 22.

TABLE 9

TOTAL FALL ENROLMENT IN HIGHER EDUCATIONAL INSTITUTIONS, BY TYPE OF
INSTITUTION, 1949 AND 1950 [8]

Type of Institution	Number of Institutions	Enrolment		Per Cent of Change
		Fall, 1949	Fall, 1950	
All institutions	1,888	2,456,000	2,295,000	—6.6
Universities	130	1,207,000	1,113,000	—7.8
Independent technical schools..	49	104,000	102,000	—2.1
Independent theological schools	122	24,000	27,000	+15.2
Other independent schools.....	146	80,000	73,000	—8.3
Liberal arts colleges...........	623	561,000	513,000	—8.6
Teachers colleges	198	184,000	182,000	—1.5
Junior colleges	512	226,000	215,000	—4.8
Negro institutions	108	70,000	70,000	0.0.

In Extended School Services.—The number of people who pursue definite studies outside the regular resident, full-time programs of our schools is seldom appreciated. Accurate and complete data are hard to assemble on how many people are enrolled in part-time and continuation schools, evening schools, adult classes, extension and home-study courses, and so on. A reasonable estimate, however, would place the number at about 35,000,000 in 1950–51. This figure represents a great increase during the last five years, particularly in extension, home study, and adult work.

The Total Enterprise.—Even a quick review of the foregoing data shows at once that there are in excess of 30,000,000 people in resident, full-time attendance at our schools. Fully as many more participate each year in other organized study. It has been estimated that almost half the total population of the country engages each year in systematic studies that involve arrangements beyond the mere decision of individuals to study. The estimate is probably conservative. The magnitude of our educational enterprise is thus apparent. America is a school-going nation. The opportunity to learn, as long as one's thirst continues, is a cherished heritage.

Effect of the Second World War on School Enrolments.—Elementary enrolments were not affected at all by the second World War, secondary enrolments were affected somewhat, and college enrolments were affected greatly. This, of course, refers to the period

[8] Robert C. Story, "1950 Fall College Enrollment," *Higher Education*, VII, 85–87.

of the war itself. Since all elementary school children were required to be in school anyhow, the war could hardly increase enrolments in these schools. Since these children were not yet old enough to carry the work of war production and war service, the war would not tend to pull them out of school and thus reduce enrolments. On the secondary level, the reduction in enrolment during the war was due less to the government's policy of induction into the armed forces than to the voluntary entry of secondary school youth into war production. Incidentally, the high school pupils who would not heed the advice of their homes, schools, and government to stay in school found that their jobs were given over after the war to veterans and that they did not have even a high school education with which to bargain in the labor market. Fortunately, this group was never very large, but in some communities, especially in the cities, it is still present with its difficult problems of adjustment. The effect of the war on college enrolments is easily seen in Table 9. The drop would not have been so drastic if the colleges had been able to count as enrollees the men and women sent to them for specialized training by the armed forces. Many an institution, for example, lost, shall we say, 500 regular students on Monday and on the next Monday received 500 uniformed soldiers for specialized training. On the whole, college facilities were used to capacity during the war, although official college enrolments dropped off greatly. Table 9 shows the effect of the Korean war on college enrolments.

Some Postwar Enrolment Trends.—Table 6 makes it clear that elementary school enrolments have risen sharply in the last few years. This reflects the marked increase in births during and after the war. The birth rate decreased somewhat between 1947 and 1950, but in 1951 the number of births actually surpassed that for 1947. There were 3,450,435 live births in this country during 1950. This was higher than for any year prior to 1947, and was 716,286 more than in 1945. If the 1945 birth rate is taken as a base, then we had 3,907,348 "extra" children born between 1945 and the end of 1950.[9] This means, of course, that for several years to come large groups of children will continue to enter the first grade. As the years go by, this will mean that all the grades will have large numbers and the total enrolment will increase accordingly. The Metropolitan Life Insurance Company has commented on this point as follows: ". . . the elementary school population as a whole—those 6 to 13 years of age

[9] Ray C. Maul, *Teacher Supply and Demand in the United States,* Report of the 1951 National Teacher Supply and Demand Study (Washington, D. C.: 1951), National Education Association, p. 35.

—will grow very considerably in the years ahead. It is expected that this group of children will increase in number annually from the present (1947) figure of about 18,200,000 to more than 23,400,000 in 1956." [10] If economic conditions in our country remain favorable, so that young people find it within their means to rear and educate families, elementary school enrolments are likely to hold up. If serious depression comes, birth rates are likely to decline and enrolments will, in due time, reflect the decline. However, the fact that the large elementary group now about to enter high school will soon begin to reproduce itself makes it most unlikely that elementary enrolments will ever again get back to prewar levels.

Since the second war did not pull out of the secondary schools any considerable number of pupils, the close of the war did not witness a great increase in secondary school enrolments. In fact, any significant increase in secondary enrolments will have to await the influx of the larger groups from the elementary schools. Hence, since increases in the elementary schools began to be felt strongly in 1946, it will be eight years later, or about 1954, before the effect of these increases will begin to be felt strongly in the ninth grade. The Metropolitan Life Insurance Company points out that the peak year in the number of six-year-olds available for first grade will be 1953. Eight years later, or in 1961, this group will enter the ninth grade, and it will be almost 50 per cent larger than the group that entered the same grade in 1945. Secondary school enrolments, therefore, just now beginning to pick up in the junior high school, will increase until about 1963, after which they will tend to reflect the birth rates earlier reflected in the elementary schools. It should be remembered, of course, that secondary school enrolments will also reflect things other than birth rates. For example, the educational requirements for entrance into jobs and the popularization of secondary education are likely to cause an increasing percentage of our youth to complete high school. This will tend to increase enrolments.

Foster and Conrad have forecasted elementary and secondary school enrolments, 1947–48 to 1959–60. The data are presented in Table 10.

The tremendous jump in postwar enrolments in higher institutions was noted in Table 8. The large exodus from the colleges caused by the war, the rapid demobilization of our forces following the war, the opportunity for subsidized education made available by the government, and the thoughtful decision of millions of youth in the armed

[10] Metropolitan Life Insurance Company, "School-Age Population to Reach New High," *Statistical Bulletin,* Vol. XXVIII.

TABLE 10

FORECAST OF ANNUAL TOTAL ENROLMENT IN PUBLIC AND NONPUBLIC SCHOOLS COMBINED, 1947-48 TO 1959-60 [11]

(All figures rounded separately to nearest hundred)

Year	Elementary Grades (Kindergarten Through Grade 8)		Secondary Grades (Grades 9-12)		Elementary and Secondary (Kindergarten Through Grade 12)	
	Total Enrolment	Change from Previous Year	Total Enrolment	Change from Previous Year	Total Enrolment	Change from Previous Year
(1)	(2)	(3)	(4)	(5)	(6)	(7)
1946-47	20,211,900	—	6,458,800	—	26,670,700	—
1947-48	20,690,900	+479,000	6,505,000	+46,200	27,195,900	+525,200
1948-49	21,736,500	+1,045,600	6,397,900	-107,100	28,134,400	+938,500
1949-50	22,759,800	+1,023,300	6,240,400	-157,500	29,000,200	+865,800
1950-51	23,686,000	+926,200	6,141,700	-98,700	29,827,700	+827,500
1951-52	24,467,600	+781,600	6,167,900	+26,200	30,635,500	+807,800
1952-53	26,064,300	+1,596,700	6,262,400	+94,500	32,326,700	+1,691,200
1953-54	27,453,000	+1,388,700	6,408,400	+146,000	33,861,400	+1,534,700
1954-55	28,651,900	+1,198,900	6,557,500	+149,100	35,209,400	+1,348,000
1955-56	29,333,700	+681,800	6,825,200	+267,700	36,158,900	+949,500
1956-57	29,497,700	+164,000	7,286,100	+460,900	36,783,800	+624,900
1957-58	29,432,800	-64,900	7,753,400	+467,300	37,186,200	+402,400
1958-59	29,004,000	-428,800	8,101,000	+347,600	37,105,000	-81,200
1959-60	28,789,200	-214,800	8,348,800	+247,800	37,138,000	+33,000
1947-60	—	+8,577,300	—	+1,890,000	—	+10,467,300

[11] E. M. Foster and H. S. Conrad, "Magnitude of the Nation's Educational Task Today and in the Years Ahead," *School Life,* XXXII, U. S. Office of Education, Washington, D. C., p. 88.

forces to continue their education led to an influx of students into the colleges which was almost more than could be handled. The problems of housing and staffing which had to be met can easily be imagined. They were met well. The number of veterans in colleges has now greatly decreased. The peak for this group, which was expected in 1950 or 1951, came a couple of years earlier than was anticipated. Furthermore, the presumed large number of high school graduates who could not go to college because of veterans' priorities turned out to be more fancy than fact. Hence, some of the earlier predictions that our college enrolments would go as high as five million students did not pan out. Postwar enrolments seem likely to level off in the neighborhood of about three million students. As pointed out before, the Korean situation has held enrolments back. One important aspect of college enrolments has to do with the number of students in junior colleges. If the thirteenth and fourteenth grades are added to the public school system, as seems increasingly likely, they are apt to be considered as the completion of secondary education, and their students will be added into secondary enrolments. If, however, these students are added to college enrolments, then college enrolments are not likely to level off at an approximate total but will steadily increase, reflecting the gradual popularization of the thirteenth and fourteenth grades.

Attention should again be called to the postwar increase in the number of people who pursue systematic studies but not on a full-time basis in our schools. Perhaps the most phenomenal increase is in the area of adult education. This is most likely to continue, particularly since the federal government itself has shown increased interest and has enlarged its support. Also, the over-all tendency of the public schools in all communities to serve people of all ages in the community will doubtless result in the pursuit by more and more people of systematic studies for improved work and enriched living.

Death Rates.[12]—Educators in the past have been greatly concerned with birth rates. This is good and proper. The statement has often been made that if birth rates could be predicted, then planning would be easier. This is true. However, it is important that our educators, and our society as a whole, give more serious attention also to death rates, and make plans for meeting a situation which is serious beyond measure, but woefully neglected.

[12] The contents of this section are based largely on an article entitled, "Ripe Old Age—It Promises U. S. a Big New Headache," which appeared in the "Controversy" section of *Science Illustrated*, Dec., 1948, p. 112.

In the time of ancient Greece and Rome the average human life span was slightly over twenty years. When the Pilgrims came to this country, it had risen to about thirty years, but close to half of the children died before they were ten years old. By 1850 life expectancy had risen to forty years, and by 1900 to fifty years. Now it is nearing seventy years, and is, in fact, already beyond seventy years for white females. These rapid increases have been brought about mainly through the advances of medical science in reducing infant mortality and in curing children's diseases. Significant advances have been made, too, in overcoming the diseases of middle life through the development of penicillin, streptomycin, and other drugs.

Very recently, an organized medical attack has been made on the diseases of older people, such as cancer and heart disease. Preliminary results indicate that startling successes may be imminent. By the year 2000, life expectancy may easily reach eighty or ninety years. In fact, some scientists insist that, if we learn how to control disease and will live healthfully, we have the physical equipment to live until we have reached about 125, or even 150 years. These data concerning life expectancy are not imaginary. They are real. Some people contend that, looking ahead, we shall be able to predict death rates with greater certainty than we can predict birth rates. And yet, in spite of what we know about future death rates, we seem to have forgotten to plan in terms of them. For example, in 1900 we had about 3,000,000 persons in our country who were aged sixty-five or older. This was about 4 per cent of our population. In 1940 we had 9,000,000 such people, or about 7 per cent of our population. By 1980 we shall have about 22,000,000 such persons, or about 11 per cent of the total population.

What will such people do? We have not tried to answer this question. In our technological age not only does the age of entry into productive labor rise, but the age of exit lowers. Hence, these older people will not be producers unless our pattern of living changes. It is estimated that before the present century is out, two-thirds of our total population will be largely economically nonproductive and will have to be supported by the labor and production of the other one-third. For the old people in this nonproductive group, life must be more than a waiting for death. Education and society have an obligation to make these years rich and full, and to realize that there can be no delay in getting about it. Problems must be anticipated. It is not entirely facetious to suggest that education for home and family living will have to consider "the care of the aged" as well as child care, and "how to get along with your great-grandmother" as well as child psychology. But basically, plans must be made for the promotion of activities that will be for the old a constructive use of time. The challenge to education seems clear.

Increase in the Holding Power of the Schools.—As has been pointed out before, our compulsory attendance laws cause the elementary schools to approximate in enrolments the total number of children available for school. Of course this varies by regions. In 1940, for the country as a whole, it was 95.5 per cent for all children seven to thirteen years of age. The highest percentage, 97.6, was in New England, and the lowest, 92.1, in the southeastern section of the country. The holding power of the elementary school, nevertheless, is in good part legal, although this does not mean that no one would attend the elementary school unless he were compelled to do so. At any rate, the compulsory nature of elementary school attendance renders pointless any consideration of the holding power of the elementary school. The same is not true, however, of secondary schools and higher institutions. The holding power of these schools does, and will, affect enrolments. Briefly, a larger and larger proportion of elementary school graduates are going on to high school, and increasing percentages are staying in high school until they finish. In 1900 about 6 per cent of all seventeen-year-olds in the country graduated from high school. The percentage is now approximately 53. Similarly in the colleges. In 1900 slightly under 2 per cent of all twenty-one-year-olds graduated from college. The percentage is now approximately 15. It is easy to see, therefore, that there are other considerations, such as holding power, which must be added to the data on birth rates if enrolments and enrolment trends are to be approximated and understood.

3. Types of Differences Within the School Population

The compulsory attendance laws in this country throw into the schools every youngster in the land, except those who, because of some atypical characteristic, may require special institutionalization. In other words, the schools, especially the elementary schools, represent a rather faithful cross section of our people. Here are assembled in an intermingling mass the citizens of the future. Here are the products of the American "melting pot," with all the differences and extremes of background and environment that that implies. It will be good to enumerate some of those differences. By so doing we shall be indicating also some of the things that our schools should take into account if they are to do the best possible job with these masses of young Americans. What are some of the differences that are found within our school population?

National Origins and Language.—Between 1820 and 1938 over thirty-eight million immigrants entered the United States. In 1924 new laws were applied which greatly restricted immigration. Even so, there are still more people entering the United States than are leaving. This is still the Promised Land for millions of people who wish to escape the conditions and restraints under which they live in other countries.

This country has had an Americanization program for immigrants for many years. After the application of the highly restrictive immigration laws in 1924 we seemed to assume that all previous immigrants had been properly Americanized and that from then on the program was not so important. However, prior to the second World War when aliens in this country were required to register, we discovered that we had close to five million such persons, that our Americanization efforts had been only partially successful, that many thousands of immigrants had neither learned our language nor sought citizenship, and that there were many "islands" in both urban and rural areas where the customs and language of the old countries were preserved and where newspapers were published in the mother tongues. The perpetuation here of the language and customs of other nations is not, of course, all bad. However, it does sharpen the point that as long as this condition exists we shall have in our schools many children whose backgrounds of country and language differ greatly.

Race.—About 90 per cent of the people in this country are classified as white. The nonwhite group is made up primarily of Negroes. Prior to 1860 only about 9 per cent of the Negroes lived outside the southern states. Now about 25 per cent live outside the South. As time goes on, the distribution of the nonwhites covers the country more and more completely. The typical American community, and the typical school room, has its assortment of racial differences.

Sex.—Of course both boys and girls are in school. Some of the presumed differences between them which were supported in the past have been proved ill founded. For example, not too long ago, in this country, girls were believed to be definitely inferior to boys in mental capacity and were either greatly restricted in their opportunities to secure an education or were limited in the kind of studies they could pursue. It is now known that mental capacity is not positively related to, or determined by, sex. However, there are certain differences of background, emotion, interests, vocational intention, and the like that ought to be understood and provided for by the school.

General Intelligence.—One of the most important types of differences found within the school population is that of general intelligence. The typical elementary school will have children ranging in intelligence quotients from 70 to the genius or near-genius classification, say 140. Even within a given classroom such extremes are often found. To adapt to these extremes is one of the most severe tests of teaching skill that can be imagined.

Aptitude.—Psychologists have long pointed out that pupils with about equal general intelligence may still differ greatly in their capacities or aptitudes. For example, of two boys with intelligence quotients of 120, one may exhibit a special aptitude or talent for things mechanical, while the other's aptitude may lie in the field of music. The problem of trying to discover and adjust to the great variety of aptitudes among pupils is prolonged and difficult.

Family Background.—Mention has already been made of family backgrounds stemming from national origins, including language differences. It is not easy for a child to attend a school during the day where English is spoken and in the evening go to a home where only a foreign language is spoken. Similarly, the ideals and practices of the typical American community regarding such things as child labor and recreation are not always in line with those held by persons from other countries. But there are other types of family backgrounds. These include such things as the economic status of parents; the occupation of parents; the standard of living in the home; and the presence or absence in the home of good reading, good music, good relationships among family members, religious influence, and a good attitude toward work. All of these, and more, are directly reflected in turn in the children who occupy our classrooms.

Personal and Social Adjustment.—The differences among pupils in personal and social adjustment have taken on increasing importance as the schools have accepted the responsibility of promoting all-round pupil development. The old emphasis on mental growth to the neglect of other aspects of personality development is weakening. As more attention is focused on personal and social adjustment, the realization grows that adjustment problems in these areas are manifold. Furthermore, many of the pupils whom we had assumed were well adjusted because they were quiet and obedient are now known to be plagued with problems that must be solved if they are ever to lead a normal and happy life. Many children from stable homes have progressed normally in the establishment of ideals and attitudes, while others less fortunate lack such decision and the security that goes with it. Similarly, many children have developed desirable skill and poise in their social relationships, while others are constantly frustrated and ill at ease, envious beyond measure of those better poised than themselves. Often the country child who leaves the rural elementary school for the urban high school has serious adjustment problems. All adolescents are faced with important new outlooks, responsibilities, decisions, and discoveries; and the manner in which they deal with these new experiences will determine their personal and social attitudes and behavior. Children and adolescents, and adults too, differ greatly in the extent to which they have adjusted well to personal and social problems. The school is beginning to take helpful notice of these differences.

Health.—Check the pupils in an ordinary American school, and great differences will be found in dental health, visual adequacy, nutritional adequacy, respiratory health, physical deficiencies, and so on. Furthermore, differences in mental and emotional health will be noted, too. The relationship of physical and mental health to school achievement has long been known. If one could have a schoolroom full of children with equal mental ability but with a wide range in their physical and mental health, a wide range in their school achievement would be apparent also. Youngsters cannot leave the state of their health at home.

Educational Achievement.—The tenth grade English teacher who receives a new class in the fall cannot assume that because all the pupils have completed ninth grade English they are equal in English achievement. The good teacher knows that the best and the poorest pupils are likely to be far apart in their achievement. The same is true for all other classes. Teachers who conduct their classes as though the accomplishments and needs of the pupils were uniform are not yet good teachers.

Vocational Intention.—Although the matter of vocational intention plays a small role in the elementary school, it takes on great significance in secondary schools and colleges. The variety of vocations in which our youth are interested is almost limitless.

Attitudes.—Check a group of pupils on their attitude toward honesty, stealing from the fruit-wagon, or protecting public property; or, for that matter, check a group of college students on what democracy requires of them as individuals—and see what you get. There will be variety enough. Such attitudes are basic to the future of our country and of the world. They are with us in the schools in all descriptions and intensities.

Physical Maturity.—Of course physical maturity differs among children of different grades and ages, but differences of this sort within a given grade or for a certain age are prominent also. For a certain age group, say the fourteen-year-olds, significant maturity differences between boys and girls will be noted, but so will they be noted among boys only or among girls only.

Let the above-mentioned differences serve to illustrate the fact that the practice of mass education in this country has brought into our schools the product of about all known human states and conditions. The utter folly of trying to make the educational experience uniform for all of these pupils, at any grade level, is obvious.

4. Differences Within a City

Although the schools in most cities are under a single city school administration, there are many conditions which make it undesirable that a uniform city-wide educational program be followed. The nature of the population varies in different sections of the city. Most cities have an "across the tracks" section and an "elite" residential area. The differences between the pupil groups in the schools serving these areas are often outstanding in many of the items discussed in the previous section. Sometimes the average intelligence of the pupils in one school in the city is definitely higher or lower than that in other schools. To expect the same accomplishment by the pupils in these schools is to be unfair and unrealistic. Yet comparisons between such schools are frequently made and the findings published. Occasionally a city will use the same final examinations in all its secondary schools. For example, all tenth graders in all schools will take the same English final, even though in one school 50 per cent of the pupils may come from homes where a foreign language is spoken, and in another school 90 per cent of the pupils may come from homes where English has always been spoken, where good home libraries exist, and where the parents have set good examples of English usage and literary taste. Fortunately, the practice of administering uniform examinations has pretty well died out. Because of the differences in occupational pursuits and interests in various sections of a city, it is often wise to vary greatly the course of instruction in the different schools, especially in the secondary schools. Other differences, too, such as the language backgrounds of pupils, will require adjustments in the educational program. Frequently cities have certain sections populated mainly by Negroes. This group presents special problems and needs. The alert city school administration will make every effort to discover significant sectional differences within the city and will vary the educational program as needed.

5. Differences Within a School

Very often the problem of differences is more severe in one school than in another. For example, prior to the second World War a school in one of our middle-sized cities, where several secondary schools were maintained, had a student body made up of twenty-two different nationalities. The largest nationality group was Italian. The Negro group was relatively large, and oddly enough it divided itself into "northern" and "southern" Negroes. Serious clashes took place between these groups. More than a third of all the relief cases in the city were concentrated in the area served by this school. Many children were special problem cases. Juvenile delinquency was high. A large proportion of the pupils quit school when they reached the permissible school-leaving age, thus making very severe the problems of guidance and curriculum adjustment. The range in ability levels among the pupils was, as in most schools, great; but this school had more than its share of pupils at the lower levels. The problem of attitudes and of developing seriousness of purpose among the pupils was always present. The presence in the school of so many pupils who were looking forward to the day when they could leave did not have a stabilizing effect upon the student body as a whole. In all of this assortment there were, of course, some pupils with high ability, good background, good judgment, and clear-cut ambitions.

In another secondary school in the same city the principal and staff were dealing with another kind of student body. Most of the pupils came from home-owning families. Relief was practically unknown. The community had good recreational facilities. A very high percentage of the pupils went on to college. Problems of guidance and curriculum adjustment were, therefore, less severe. On the whole, the school had purpose and continuity; the pupils were there to complete an educational program and then move on to other schools. Some, of course, neither desired nor were able to go on; but they were not the ones who determined the atmosphere or set the pattern of the school.

Such differences within schools as those described above sharpen the necessity of having in each school leaders who know how to discover and deal with such differences. These leaders will not be too concerned about what goes on in other schools, except as certain practices in other schools may hold suggestion for the better adjustment of education in their own. It goes without saying, also, that superintendents of schools will attempt to find principals who can do this kind of job in individual schools and, having found them, will support them in their task of making education more serviceable and more democratic.

6. Differences Within the Classroom

It is only necessary here to remind ourselves that the conglomerate of American youngsters that we have been talking about ultimately finds its way into individual classrooms. Here the dull boy and the bright boy, perhaps sitting side by side, face the teacher together. Here the healthy and the sick, the happy and the confused, the white and the nonwhite, the bully and the bullied, the well-dressed and the poorly dressed, the well-nourished and the undernourished, the introvert and the extrovert, the athlete and the cripple, the interested and the negligent, the nervous and the poised spend hours and days and months together. The classroom teacher who thinks that the basic responsibility for dealing with differences rests with the superintendent or the principal or somebody else has not yet alerted himself to the most important aspect of his calling. If individual worth is fundamental in our concept of democracy, then every one of democracy's schools, and every teacher in every school, must accept the obligation to adjust education to individual differences rather than to require that all individuals attempt some imaginary standard for all. The ability to move individuals along toward the goals of education in terms of their own abilities and characteristics is the essence of good teaching today. Every difference carries its special need. To be interested in differences, to discover them and to adjust to them, is to serve the children well. It also represents a long step in the direction of making the school the vital agency it ought to be in helping people to make their best contribution to society.

7. Adjusting Education to the School Population

Many practices are in effect in our schools that are a direct outgrowth of efforts to meet the varying needs of the school population.

Some schools are far ahead of others in making use of recognized good practices. Some of the adjustments discussed in this section will be dealt with at greater length in subsequent chapters. However, they ought to be mentioned here as a means of getting a more definite idea of some of the more basic things that are done to make the school experience more suitable for all pupils. How can we adjust education to the school population?

Establishment of Different Types of Schools.—Many schools in this country find their reason for existence in the needs of a certain group of people. They are not intended to meet the needs of all but rather to serve a special need in our society. For example, on the elementary level, there may be enough handicapped children in a community or city to justify the establishment of a separate school which will work with this group only. In some such cases, even the buildings are constructed with the needs of this group in mind. Occasionally schools are established, usually under private auspices, to take care of certain kinds of problem children. Such schools may have highly trained staff members who are skilled in the study of human personality and in fostering desirable personality adjustments. There are a good many children whose sight and hearing are so deficient that they cannot benefit by the ordinary classroom work. Special methods for their instruction are required. Schools to serve these groups are well known.

On the secondary level it is not uncommon to find specialized high schools within a city, such as a commercial high school, a technical high school, and an academic high school. In some sections of the country also, agricultural schools at the secondary level are common. Among junior colleges, of course, separate schools frequently concentrate on terminal-vocational work; on academic, first-two-years-of-college work; or on the niceties of a "finishing" school.

The higher one goes up the educational ladder, the more specialization he encounters. Hence, as would be expected, there are more specialized schools among higher institutions than among either secondary or elementary schools. Below the college level, education tends to be more the common heritage of all in which adjustments to meet the needs of groups are more within the schools than among the schools. Of course adjustments within higher institutions are common, too, but at this level there is a great range in types of institutions, extending from the traditional liberal-cultural college to institutions for the training of labor organizers. In between are all the independent schools of law, medicine, pharmacy, technology, music, agriculture, education, business, mining, nursing, physical culture, social work, divinity, forestry, dentistry, chiropractic, osteopathy, veterinary medicine, architecture, journalism, and so on.

Many special schools also exist to serve the needs of adults who are not in the regular school program at all, or in regular attendance.

We have, therefore, many different types of schools that have been organized to meet varying needs within our school population. Such schools have been developed under both public and private auspices.

Curriculum Arrangements Within Schools.—It is characteristic of the schools of a democracy to meet individual and group needs more through curriculum adjustments within schools than through the establishment of separate specialized schools. Somehow we feel that, since we should all live together harmoniously as citizens following our school experience, it is desirable that we all stay together in school. Consequently, it is far more common for a city with three high schools, for example, to make them all comprehensive high schools rather than to have, let us say, a commercial high school, a technical high school, and an academic high school. Each of the schools will take its cross section of young people and arrange its curriculum to meet their needs.

One of the most outstanding curriculum adjustments in our schools during the present century has been the multiplication of subjects taught. This applies at all levels—elementary, secondary, and higher. Although many additions have been desirable, in some schools the process has continued to the point where the fundamental purposes of the school have been diluted or lost sight of. Furthermore, the willingness to add subjects or activities has not always been accompanied by a willingness to eliminate subjects or activities considered less worth while. Hence we have seen in some cases a simple piling-up, without the evaluation and coordination necessary to a good program.

Formal curriculum adjustments are much more common within secondary schools and colleges than in elementary schools. This, again, reflects the move toward specialization which accompanies the climb up the ladder. However, elementary schools are more and more adjusting instruction to individual differences, even though many pupils may be studying the same subjects. Take reading, for example. The good reading teacher, although she may have thirty children in second grade reading, will in effect teach several levels of reading because she knows that in such a group significant differences in reading readiness and accomplishment will ordinarily be found. So it will be in other learning areas.

In secondary schools and colleges more formal curriculum arrangements appear, based on the interests and needs of various pupil groups. In high school there is a group that intends to go on to college, so a college-preparatory curriculum is set up. Such a curriculum usually contains several prescribed subjects, some of which are maintained more by the force of tradition than by the force of reason. Other pupils seem to be interested in farming and homemaking, so a pattern of subjects is set up, constituting curricula in those fields. Thus it will go for trade and technical work, for commercial or business work, and so on. For pupils who are unable to specify any certain interest or after-school intention, the so-called "general" or "citizenship" curriculum is maintained. In general, the separate curricula in the secondary schools do not go excessively far in the direction of specialization. Recent years have tended more to strengthen general foundational education than to increase specialization.

In higher institutions, where specialization really occurs, curriculum arrangements are many. Although the emphasis on general education at the college level is increasing, the requirements for specialization in the various areas are not decreasing; hence college curricula are tending to become longer. Here we find curriculum requirements for the first two years and the second two years; for the bachelor of arts and the bachelor of science; for law and business and teaching; for majors in mathematics and French and animal husbandry; for electrical engineering and civil engineering and aeronautical engineering; for nursing and philosophy and dairy manufacturing; for graduate work in all areas; and on and on.

Attention should be called to the fact that existing curriculum arrangements are not necessarily good or even the best possible. For example, in view of the tremendous variety in admission requirements among colleges and in view of the tremendous variety of curricula within colleges, it simply does not make sense to have all pupils who plan to go to college take the same subjects in high school. There is no reason why high school curricula, beyond the foundational work that all pupils should have, cannot be planned in terms of individuals rather than in terms of groups. This principle ought to apply at all educational levels. It cannot be carried out, however, without an excellent philosophy of adjusted education and excellent counseling services and school offerings to make the implementation effective. The regard our schools have shown, therefore, for the needs of various groups of students is likely further to refine itself by giving greater attention to individuals within those groups.

Grouping.—In many American schools, and for a long time, grouping has been employed as a means of providing for individual differences. Grouping is the school's effort to improve instruction by setting up learning groups whose members show considerable similarity in their characteristics. Grouping eliminates the extremes from any one group and forms those extremes into other separate groups. Differences within groups are thereby reduced, although differences among groups will still be great. For example, if a school has a hundred pupils in ninth grade algebra, it will doubtless find a great range among them in their general intelligence, in their ability to learn mathematics, and in their mathematical achievement. The top 25 per cent on these counts is likely to be far removed from the bottom 25 per cent. Some schools feel that the top group, the bottom group, and the great middle group will all benefit if they are taught separately. Thus they are set up separately, and the nature and amount of content are varied as seems best. Teachers may even be employed in terms of their ability to work with pupils in certain of those groups. Similar groups may be established widely throughout the school.

Grouping, of course, is practicable only in the larger schools. If the ninth grade algebra class has twenty-five pupils instead of a hundred, as mentioned above, it can hardly be broken down further into three separate instructional groups. Also, as many bases as possible should be used in setting up the groups. One would hardly group the algebra pupils on the basis of general intelligence only and disregard mathematics aptitude, mathematics achievement, and other factors. In fact, some of these other factors, involving physical, psychological, and social needs, have taken on so much importance recently that some of the more academic bases have had to give ground. This has been based on the proposition that the total personality development of the individual is more important than his achievement in any given subject. It is also recognized that problems of total personality development are present in every classroom and cannot be set aside, shall we say, while we are taking care of the pupil's instruction in algebra. Furthermore, the supposed gains in subject-matter learning resulting from grouping are not always supported by research. Although the findings of researchers vary, the general conclusion seems to be that the low group benefits by segregation; the middle group benefits little, if any; and the high group benefits little, if any. Some investigators contend that, if all factors are considered, the groups, particularly the high group, are actually harmed by segregation. Hence, although grouping is widely practiced, it has not yet been clearly established as an effective means of providing for individual differences when the sum total of personality development is held in the fore. Finally, it should be pointed out that grouping need not take the form of an administrative set-up, in which separate groups, as within the algebra class, are established and perhaps taught by different teachers. A great deal of grouping is now being practiced within classes. Mention was made earlier of the reading teacher who, because of differences in reading readiness and achievement among her pupils, actually taught several levels of reading. This is often done by forming groups within the class for whom materials and instruction are varied in terms of need. The children thus are able to receive the educational benefits of grouping without losing the developmental benefits of mutual association.

Special Classes.—Some schools, although they do not practice grouping in the strict sense of the word, still set up special classes. For example, a special class may be established in physical education for a group of crippled children or for another group of children with weak hearts. Classes for children with serious eye defects are sometimes formed, and similarly for children with deficient hearing. Perhaps the most common special classes are for pupils having certain scholastic difficulties. Classes are frequently maintained where pupils have the opportunity, beyond their regular classes, to receive help if they need it. Pupils are not necessarily permanent members of such classes but will join them or not in terms of the acceptability of their work in their regular classes.

Classroom Methods.—So far as organization for instruction is concerned, it appears likely that in the future individual differences will be provided for less through separately organized groups than through adjustments in teaching methods within the classroom. Instead of attempting to give a teacher a rather homogeneous group for which method and content can be uniform, effort is being made to have teachers vary their instruction so that differences within a random sampling of pupils can be accommodated. The development of the unit plan of instruction has resulted from this emphasis. Under this plan the teacher is more concerned with the major concepts and understandings that pupils get out of their studies than with the number of problems or pages they cover. For example, the American history teacher will determine, preferably with the cooperation of the pupils, the major ideas associated with the development of our country which all pupils should understand. They will then plan their activities and select their materials so that they will develop and clarify those ideas. The teacher knows that some pupils in the group are capable of doing much more work than others. Consequently, the units are set up with a minimum of activities for the slow learners, but always with sufficient additional materials, activities, projects, researches, and so on to challenge even the most brilliant pupil in the class. In this way the concepts important to all pupils are adhered to, but the abler pupils will have broader understandings than the less able because they will have sampled more widely the materials and experiences underlying those understandings. Always under this plan activities involving the entire group are included, so that the benefits involved in the give and take of all are not lost.

Other variations in classroom procedures in recognition of differences among pupils include such things as the careful selection of pupils who will work together as committees on certain projects, the division of class time so as to provide for supervised study, the indulgence of individual pupil interests and experiences as they apply and contribute to the studies in hand, and the careful assignment of routine or leadership duties within the classroom.

School Activities.—The so-called extraclass activities are assuming an increasingly important place in the modern school. They offer a fine opportunity for the school to share, as it cannot without them, in aspects of pupil development beyond the intellectual or scholastic. Many pupils have problems of a physical, social, emotional, vocational, or ethical nature which can be reached more effectively through these activities than through classroom studies. Hence it is apparent that these activities loom large as a means of providing for individual differences. Schools that view extraclass activities in this light make every effort to see to it that pupils with certain needs engage in helpful activities. It is probably more important that the shy adolescent participate in social dancing in the gymnasium during the noon hour than that he belong to the creative writing club. This is not to say that he cannot also do other things which may be more in line with his interests and inclinations; but if the school is to render its best service, it will at least make the effort to parallel certain needs with appropriate activities. It is this concept that has led some schools to make the guidance director the director of pupil activities also. Care should be taken, not only to get pupils into appropriate activities, but also not to exclude them from activities that would be extremely helpful to them. Sometimes schools exclude pupils from such activities if they do not have a certain scholarship rating. This reflects the obsolescent idea that schools exist for the mind only, or for scholarship, or that all aspects of human development have been rated and scholarship has somehow been placed at the top of the heap. Such schools know full well that some of their pupils, under the most perfect conditions, could never come up to high scholarship requirements and that, for them, physical, manipulative, or other activities would be more useful than some of the academic work they are held to. At any rate, much can be done through school activities to provide for individual differences among pupils.

Counseling.—One of the outstanding movements in American education during recent years is the counseling movement. It was fairly forced upon us by the conscience of democracy. We found, as multiplied millions flocked into our schools, that we could not be consistent with our doctrine of individual worth if we did not develop in our schools a service intended to adjust education to individual needs. The extreme variety in our school population, the diversity of pupil needs and capabilities, and the complexity of the society into which pupils went simply outlawed all doctrines of educational uniformity. However, educational adjustments in terms of individual needs cannot be based on snap judgments. Systematic studies of individuals and of communities and continuous revisions of our educational offerings in terms of apparent needs are necessary. The skilful service of bringing individuals to make wise decisions on their own, using the information and assistance of the counseling services, is also fundamental. Counseling is exceedingly important as a means of adjusting education to the school population. A more complete discussion of it comprises the whole of Chapter 10.

Evaluation.—There is considerable weight to the contention that if we build educational programs and teach in terms of individuals, then we ought also to evaluate in the same way. Tests should reflect educational objectives and be based on materials covered. If, therefore, individual capacities, interests, and needs have been provided for by the teacher and if learning materials have varied accordingly, then, if the teacher is consistent, he can hardly administer the same test to all pupils. Actually, very little progress has been made in adjusting education to the school population through evaluation. However, if as we have said the tendency in our country is to adjust educational standards to each individual, even though the general objectives remain the same, then something will have to happen to our habits of uniform evaluation. The reader can think of a host of problems related to this. For example, what about marking? If a dull pupil in an arithmetic class measures up to standards well suited to him, what mark will he get? How are such factors as working up to capacity and actual achievement to be accounted for? Or, will the rising emphasis on adjusted education necessitate a complete overhauling of our marking system? Worse things could happen. One thing seems sure: We shall have to move toward individualization in evaluation the same as we have moved toward it in curriculum planning, counseling, methods, and other matters.

8. Education Appropriate to All

When one reviews the means at our disposal for adjusting education to the school population, the feeling arises that some of our delays in achieving this goal are inexcusable. Our interpretations of democracy as applied to education are clear, and ways of putting those interpretations into practices are known. Why, then, have we faltered and delayed? One should not judge too speedily.

The growth in the school population in this country was recounted at the beginning of this chapter. If those figures were projected back to about 1850, the phenomenal growth in our school enrolments during a hundred years would be seen at once. During that time we have tried to keep up with the task of making education available to all. We are still trying to get buildings and classrooms and desks and buses for the increasing millions who have flocked to school. Our insistence that education should be available to all has brought such numbers into our schools that attention and resources have had to be turned in good part to problems of adequate housing and staffing.

During the years of great growth in school population, we have known that whereas we were making education available to all, it was by no means appropriate to all. We need now to do the things that will make the school experience really appropriate to those who learn. For example, it may be that some schools are much too large for maximum effectiveness or much too small. If this can be shown, then proper reorganization should follow. It may be, too, that we have been getting along with too few teachers. Some classes are too large. Others, of course, are too small. If it can be shown that classes above and below certain approximate numbers diminish in effectiveness, then reorganization and restaffing should be carried out as needed. If the setting-up of counseling services in the schools results in the better adjustment of youth to school and afterschool life, then those services should be established. If the studies and experiences in some schools are not extensive enough to meet the needs of all the pupils, then they should be expanded. Also, if some things now done are inappropriate and useless, they should be abandoned and others substituted. If it can be shown that learning improves when better-qualified and better-trained teachers are employed, then there should be no hesitancy in raising certification requirements and in paying salaries that will attract excellent people to the schools. In a democracy the educational job is only half done when facilities are provided for all who wish to learn; the other half, which is just as significant, calls for a thousand arrangements whereby the school experience of every pupil is made appropriate and profitable for him.

9. There Is Still a Common Ground

Even as one dwells on the manifold differences found within the school population, he should never lose sight of the fact that, in spite of such differences, all are citizens of a common country. Of course, differences among individuals should be understood and provided for, but this is not enough. All should have the masteries and understandings basic to conducting their own affairs, communicating with others, and discharging constructively their duties as citizens. All should be able to think straight on problems of great and small concern. The desire to cooperate with others, and skill in carrying on such relationships for the common good, should be the possession of all. All should feel a keen sense of social responsibility. The school is as concerned with these things, with the common ground of democratic living, as it is with educating in terms of individual differences. The commanding idea bobs up again: we are staking our future on the proposition that education for individual development and for social responsibility are compatible and that the two can and must coexist in the schools of the land.

10. How Subsequent Topics Stem from This One

The topics dealt with in the next four chapters have their roots in the great diversity of the school population. If children were uniform, the educational offering could be the same for all, the need for counseling services would disappear, teaching procedures could become standardized, and the teeming problems of educational evaluation and improvement would be greatly simplified. But children are not uniform, as we have seen. There are very urgent human problems associated with school offerings, counseling services, learning-teaching relationships, and educational improvement and evaluation. These topics command our attention now.

What Do YOU Say?

1

The conditions of our society make it appear almost certain that the school population will continue to increase for a long time and that the permissible school-leaving age will rise.

What do YOU say?

2

Our democracy will be served best if all our high schools are cosmopolitan, each school having a full cross section of pupils and a variety of offerings to meet their needs. Furthermore, it is better within our classrooms to have a cross section of all pupils and to ask teachers to adapt instruction to pupil differences, than to set up high, medium, and low groups in a given subject.

What do YOU say?

3

With the increase in life expectancy in our country, new types of employment for persons over 65 will have to be devised. Our public schools ought to provide an appropriate educational program for this group.

What do YOU say?

4

The greatest educational and social loss in our schools is not with the people who "fail" or "flunk out," but with the people who get by and do not do all they can.

What do YOU say?

5

What points in this chapter do you particularly support or take issue with?

Chapter 9

THE EDUCATIONAL OFFERING

The Right Thing for All

For purposes of discussion in this chapter, the educational offering and the program of studies in the schools are considered as synonymous. Some readers may feel that the first term is broader than the second; that the offering includes the "studies" and more. Differences in meaning can be argued, of course, but since our purpose is general in nature, let us avoid needless involvements, attempting at the same time not to do violence to good usage.

1. A Restricted Concept of the Educational Offering

Throughout most of the history of education in this country, the educational offering has been thought of as the collection of subjects taught in the school. Only formal, respectable, systematized studies like mathematics, history, foreign languages, and English were included. Credit, direction by a teacher, examinations to test achievement, and definite time-scheduling were involved. If the offering were expanded, it meant that additional subjects, regularly taught, were added. Other activities which might be tolerated were a kind of necessary evil associated with the interests and development of pupils, but they were not a part of the educational offering. They were not "solid" enough.

The attitude that the school exists to teach subjects, and respectable, "solid" subjects at that, accounts for the slowness with which music, physical education, vocational subjects, and the like were accepted as a part of the educational offering. College admission requirements still reflect this attitude. A good many parents and school people, too, insist that schools exist to provide an intellectual experience for pupils, and any slackening of requirements in subjects that have provided mental exercise for pupils for generations on end is viewed with alarm. The offering, in other words, is thought of as consisting of formal subjects organized to be taught for their intellectual and informational values. Activities beyond these are not "educational"; they are "extras."

2. A Broader Concept of the Educational Offering

Within recent years there has been a definite tendency to interpret the educational offering much more broadly than previously. To be sure, restricted interpretations such as that described above still exist, but the modern school stands on broader foundations. Anything that is supervised by the school as a means of realizing its educational objectives is a part of the educational offering. Thus if the school believes that it should contribute to the physical development of the child as well as to his intellectual development, then the school health services, the work of the doctors and nurses, the hot lunches, and the physical activities become just as important as the study of spelling or algebra and are just as truly a part of the educational offering. If the school believes that it has an obligation to adjust education to the nature and needs of pupils and of society, then a good counseling service is just as important as a good English department, and is just as surely a part of the educational offering. So it will go in many areas. Whatever the school does to obtain its objectives constitutes its program or offering. It will be noted immediately, of course, that the school which subscribes to modern educational objectives will introduce activities and experiences that go far beyond formal studies. Such experiences are important because they implement important objectives; and they are as much a part of the offering as the traditional subjects.

3. Considerations Underlying the Broader Concept

Educational Philosophy and Aims.—Our schools and communities today are faced with a task of ordinary honesty: the putting into practice of objectives to which they have given lip-service since about 1918. We have said that we are a democracy and that the schools ought to promote growth in democratic action; but we have too often conducted our schools as though democracy were somehow to be found within the pages of a book, that knowledge is the primary thing. Knowledge is important, of course; but democracy is not knowledge. It is a way of life. The study of American history is not enough. An effective student council can be as useful in learning the ways of democracy as a chronological course in American history. Experiences that represent growth in democratic understandings and actions must therefore be added to the traditional knowledges. It is this kind of thinking that has given support to the expanded activities of the modern school. If the aims of education are to function, the school will have to become the place where they are practiced, not just studied about. The school that is interested in promoting ethical character will not depend upon books or instruction in religion as the sole means; but it will bring the pupils to set up and observe their own standards of courtesy in the school, of sportsmanship on the field of play, of honesty in the classroom, of respect for the rights and opinions of others, of sharing responsibility, and of cooperating with others. The school will not simply tell the pupil that he should make good use of his leisure time. It will attempt to establish good leisure-time habits by promoting many constructive leisure-time activities in which the pupil can participate, can experience the satisfactions of participation, and can carry over his interest and participation into after-school years. Thus, schools today are realizing that education requires living as well as study. Their sincere desire to make the philosophy and aims of education come to life has caused them greatly to expand their ideas as to what the educational offering actually is.

Full Development of the Individual.—Another consideration which has caused schools to enlarge their programs is the realization that human personality is unified and that no part of it can properly be isolated and developed to the exclusion of other parts. The school is slack, therefore, in its full educational responsibility if it limits itself to the intellectual development of the individual. Even if it wished to do this, it could not do it well unless it concerned itself with other aspects of development also. However, the really alert school maintains its broad program, not simply as a means of stimulating intellectual growth, but because it believes that good physical, social, emotional, and ethical development are as important as intellectual development and deserve an equal place in the plan and program of the school. The expansion in school activities that will accompany this point of view can easily be imagined; and all activities contributing to such full development will hold equal significance in the total offering.

Education Appropriate to All.—It is conceivable, of course, that a school might agree that the full development of the individual is important and then proceed to build a program of studies and experiences, the same for all, to accomplish that end. The discussion in Chapter 9 made clear the folly of such an approach. Individual differences are so pronounced and numerous that any doctrine of uniformity is out of the question. Clearly, the school that seriously attempts to make the educational experience appropriate to all will maintain an offering broadly conceived and practiced.

Social Responsibility and Needs.—The point has been made repeatedly that individual development is not the only concern of the school. The society into which individuals go is also important. The good school will adjust its offering to the needs of society. It will also bring pupils into contact with the problems of society and foster participation in social activities. Its efforts in the direction of individual development will be paralleled by an attempt to develop a sense of social responsibility and skill in cooperating with others. If this is done, the studies and activities of the school will leap out of the ruts of the past.

Flexibility.—For a good many years our schools have been moving slowly toward acceptance of the doctrine of flexibility. First the elementary schools, then the secondary schools, and lastly the higher institutions made the break. The perpetuation of a traditional offering has gradually given way to an offering adapted to social and individual needs. The principle has become clear that, in this kind of country, the school that adjusts its program to meet such needs survives. Schools that will not adjust but seek to perpetuate a rarefied academic tradition will perish. The history of education is full of verifications of this principle. Hence, the modern school seeks to understand people and the kind of communities and world they live in. It responds to new discoveries concerning people, their biological nature, how they learn, their needs in a complex society, and so on. It also responds to changes in our social order. The air age is here; so is the atomic age, and the idea of "one world." Intercultural problems plague us. Our machines shorten our work days and years, while we live to be older and older. If these and other considerations loom so large that they crowd less vital matters out of the school program, so let it be. At any rate, it is this doctrine of flexibility that has taken hold. Our people and our present world are important—much more important in determining the educational offering than any tradition.

Thus the foundation underlying the broader concept of the educational offering has developed. To meet its responsibility, the school will maintain a broad pattern of studies, of course; but it will also sponsor many activities and experiences that have not been formalized in the traditional sense of the word. All activities that promote educational objectives are equally important; and together they constitute the educational offering of the modern school.

TABLE 11

GROWTH IN THE EDUCATIONAL OFFERING

Level	18th Century	19th Century	20th Century
Elementary	Reading Writing Spelling Bible Arithmetic	Bookkeeping Grammar Geography U. S. history Elementary science Drawing Music Physical exercises	Sewing Cooking Manual training Literature Oral language Nature study Vocational subjects Expansion of kindergarten work
Secondary	Greek Latin English Some mathematics	Algebra Botany Chemistry General history U. S. history English literature Surveying	Modern languages General science Home economics Industrial arts Agriculture Business subjects Problems of democracy Music Physical education Art
Higher	Hebrew Greek Latin Mathematics Ethics Philosophy Chronological history Rhetoric Logic Oratory Some natural science	Professional education: Medicine, law, dentistry, pharmacy, education, journalism, etc. Engineering and technical subjects Mining and forestry Fine arts Liberal arts New sciences	Modification of "liberal" education toward "general" education New studies in old fields (aeronautical engineering, nuclear physics, diplomacy, etc.) Expansions in social sciences, biological and physical sciences, psychology, etc. Adaptations in English (radio, theater, motion pictures), economics (labor-management, international trade, government, social welfare), political science (civics, government service and research), etc. Outstanding research developments in all areas

4. Examples of Growth in the Offering

Table 11 illustrates the manner in which the subjects taught in the school have reflected the growth in our idea of what the schools should do. The information is by no means complete, but it shows the general nature of changes as they came along. For the most part the changes were additions, so that today's offering is an accumulation of all that has gone before. Some things have lost ground, of course, and not all schools will offer all the subjects listed; but all the subjects listed, and many more, are offered today. The most important thing to observe is the increase in the schools' responsibilities with the passage of time. These demands reflect the growth of a nation and the demands of its people. This is particularly noticeable for the secondary and higher levels, although, on closer observation, it is equally true for the elementary level. It will be remembered from previous discussions that thousands of schools have died in this country because they would not consent to make the kinds of adjustments indicated in general in Table 11. An eighteenth century offering is of little use to the twentieth century. Let us hope that the present disposition to place modern man and his many relationships at the heart of educational planning continues to guide the school through the years ahead.

In view of the broadened concept of the educational offering we now have, we should not fail to add to the formal subject expansion indicated in Table 11 the host of additional activities and experiences that accompanied this expansion. These have done much to bring to life the real objectives that lie back of the formal subjects.

5. Types of Program Organization

Separate Subjects.—For many years the instructional content of our schools has been organized into separate subjects. These subjects, as it were, are "packages" of content within certain fields of learning, and each is kept highly independent of other subjects. In some cases subjects seem almost to be the personal property of the teacher, and any questions or suggestions concerning them which may be raised by others are looked upon as positive intrusions. Furthermore, it often happens, especially in colleges and universities, that separate courses are built up around the special interest or research activity of a staff member. As time has gone on, separate courses have tended to multiply. Departments within schools and colleges, such as English, mathematics, the sciences, the social sciences, business, agriculture, and home economics have added many new subjects, and have frequently broken themselves down into new departments. Certain subjects themselves have become subdivided. And along with it all has gone a strong emphasis on separation. Sometimes the English I teacher does not know very much about what goes on in English II, and the economics teacher looks askance at the idea that some of his content might properly be blended with content from other subjects to form other meaningful studies. Only in recent years has there been any appreciable reversal in the tendency to multiply separate subjects. Certain combinations and regroupings of content have been made at all levels in our educational ladder. The prevailing pattern, however, is separate "bundles," securely tied, which, no matter how they may be piled with other bundles, remain distinct and never blend.

Correlation.—Correlation, in the strict sense of the word, does not represent a type of program organization. It is important, though, because it indicates some modification of the extreme separateness of subject organization described above. Under correlation, separate subjects are retained, but points of similarity and common ground are recognized and used. If the history teacher and the literature teacher have pupils in common and if each deals with the Colonial period, there is every reason why they should correlate their instruction, including a paralleling in time, so that the pupils will see relationships and meanings they would not otherwise see. The mathematics teacher and the business teacher, the science teacher and the agriculture teacher, music and physics, dramatics and shop, homemaking and art, and all the rest can find many points of contact. In some schools the English teachers are willing to accept for English the papers prepared in other subjects. This practice is supported by the strong argument that it leads to a school-wide application on the part of the pupil of the things he learns in the English classes. Correlation does not eliminate the fences, but it results in a lot of over-the-fence talking and planning.

Broad Fields.—The idea of program organization in terms of relationships and meanings has gained considerable headway. If there are certain areas or fields in which the separate subjects bear close relationship, then it seems wise to break down subject barriers and organize "broad field" studies, particularly when basic understandings and nonspecialized knowledges are sought. Take the social studies for example. The close relationship between history, government, sociology, and economics is known. It is better, in terms of general usefulness and as foundation for later specialization in any one of these fields, to see them in a "broad field" relationship .han to approach them initially as divided, departmentalized studies. Actually, no one of them can be well understood without the others. It is a service, therefore, if the school will integrate them rather than expect the pupil to do so by sampling each separately or, what is worse, permit him to remain deficient in the broad field by studying only part of them. Such field studies, aimed at broad understandings and useful, nonspecialized knowledge, are increasing in secondary schools and colleges. General science, general social studies, general language, general mathematics in high school, and the survey and interdepartmental courses in college are illustrative. The movement is so strong in secondary schools that state certification requirements are beginning to specify broad-field preparation in college as a prerequisite to high school teaching. Similarly, the movement is strong enough in colleges to cause graduate schools to approve general curricula on the doctoral level intended to prepare instructors for general education in undergraduate colleges.

Integration.—For all practical purposes the integrated, fused, and unified types of program organization are the same type. Integration seeks to break down almost entirely the old subject-matter barriers and to relate learning to meaningful projects or problems. Thus, in the early grades of the elementary school, classroom activities might center around a village store project. In order to participate successfully in such a project, the children will have to master and use learnings of many sorts, including, of course, the usual reading, writing, arithmetic, and spelling. The importance of selecting projects or problems that will call for and motivate the kinds of masteries the children should have is recognized at once. One of the arguments in favor of this kind of organization is that it tends to be a true reflection of experience. In the ordinary course of events people do not encounter mathematics problems separately, then problems in history, then science, then reading. Experience is not exclusive in this manner; it is associative and highly interrelated. It is, shall we say, integrated. Perhaps, so say some, the learning experiences in the school should be integrated in the same manner.

The integrated program is more easily conducted and probably more defensible in the lower grades where the common learnings are dealt with than in the upper grades where the areas of knowledge begin to multiply. Thus such programs are almost always found in the lower grades of the elementary school. However, it should be pointed out clearly that the basic idea of the plan, that of organizing learning around problem or experience situations, is applicable in any kind of program organization and on any level and ought to be used a lot more than it is. Even in the strictest kind of separate subject organization, it is possible for teachers to relate learning to such meaningful problems or projects. In the broad-field arrangement this approach is most fruitful. Such a topic as "The Development of the Middle West," for example, will tie together in a meaningful manner tremendous amounts of history, geography, government, sociology, economics, and other content as well.

Major Curricula.—In the elementary school all pupils are concerned basically with common learnings that should be the possession of all citizens. Individual differences are recognized, but they are not recognized through the setting-up of separate studies for different groups of pupils. Generally speaking, all pupils study the same things. In the secondary schools and colleges, it is different. Effort is made in both to adjust the offering to the varied interests and varied futures of the students. Hence, selected subjects are grouped together to form curricula intended to serve students having certain interests and vocational intentions. Some high schools maintain several curricula, such as college-preparatory, general, homemaking, agriculture, technical, and business. Each curriculum includes selected school subjects, and when a pupil chooses a curriculum he contracts for the subjects it contains. Within each curriculum there are usually both prescribed subjects and elective subjects. Some small high schools, usually in rural areas, can have only one curriculum, with perhaps a few special subjects. When this is the case, the usual single curriculum is college-preparatory. In colleges and universities, of course, there are many curricula because there are many areas of specialization. In each case the student must satisfy the curriculum requirements as to the subjects to be included.

This grouping of separate subjects to form major curricula, in both secondary schools and colleges, is very common. Furthermore, each curriculum is administered for large groups of students. The suggestion has already been made in another chapter that there are great differences among students within these groups and that major curricula should tend more and more to become individual curricula, allowing desirable deviations by separate students without sacrificing adequate preparation in the field of major interest.

The Core Concept.—The core concept in curriculum-building actually stems from our ideas about democracy and living together.

It emphasizes that on any level of education there is a common body of knowledge and experience that all students should have, without reference to special interests or specialized curricula. On the elementary level, of course, most of the program is concerned with the things we all need in order properly to conduct our own affairs and discharge our responsibilities as citizens. In the secondary school, as we have seen, numerous major curricula are maintained to meet the special needs of certain groups of pupils. However, there is much at the high school level that all pupils should learn and experience in common, no matter what curriculum they are in. This will constitute the core. It is this type of reasoning also that supports the general education movement at the college level. Even the graduate schools are emphasizing more and more the importance of relatedness in learning, of common foundations that give specialization a broader and more useful frame of reference. At no level in our school system should education lose its solid center. The core, broadly conceived, is this unifying center from which all specializations stem, find their relatedness, and draw their larger significance.

When the core was first set up in schools having various major curricula, the common practice was to designate certain subjects that had to be taken by all pupils in all curricula. English, for example, was commonly prescribed. United States history, some mathematics, and perhaps some science might also be prescribed. More recently, certain content in vocational areas and in the arts has been considered essential for all. But in the early stages things didn't work out so well. The mere taking of certain subjects or the learning of selected content did not secure the effective personal and social living that all should display in a democracy. Learning the facts of American history did not insure good citizenship. It was soon learned that the practice of citizenship in the school must supplement the study of our nation's history. The common ground, after all, was not merely factual; it included experiences in democratic living as well. Thus the core has tended more and more to add common experiences to common content. It has to do this because, in this country, people and their behavior are considered more important than the accumulation of knowledge. Knowledge is important; but it is important only as it affects the lives and conduct of people, not as an end in itself. The trend in the core, therefore, is to supplement the emphasis on content with emphasis on experiences in democratic living. In a school that does this, participation in appropriate pupil activities, such as student government, will take on equal importance with the study of English. In such a school also, the teachers of the core subjects and all other teachers as well will employ methods that simultaneously promote habits of good living and the mastery of content.

The Strand Idea.—When the educational ladder was considered in Chapter 7, it was pointed out that when the ladder is divided up into too many independent administrative units there is danger that desirable continuity in the learning of pupils may be interrupted. The strand idea seeks to establish such continuity in the basic areas of learning. Some people contend that, in such fields as language, social studies, science, and perhaps mathematics, there ought to be a continuous, expanding learning experience for all pupils from the time they start to school until they graduate from high school. As it is, there is a great deal of skipping around, of having a subject for awhile and then missing a year or two or three. The strand corrects this. If, however, there is to be a strand at all, cooperative program planning among the units of the ladder will have to be practiced.

The Classroom Teaching Unit as an Adaptation of Content.— Much has been done within subjects themselves to secure better organization of the educational offering. One of the outstanding developments in this connection is the subject-matter unit. When units are used, the daily assignment, page-by-page procedure is abandoned, and the work of the semester or the year is organized into large units of study, each of which will ordinarily cover several weeks. Each unit has a major idea or concept as its focal point around which all assignments and activities cluster. A great variety of materials may be used in clarifying the concept or in solving the problem it poses. Hence, this kind of organization forsakes the single-textbook idea and utilizes helpful materials wherever they can be found. Actually the unit idea is at the heart of such well-known methods as the problem method, the project method, the contract plan, the laboratory plan, and others. Its dual strength is in its adaptability to differences in learning ability among pupils and the manner in which learning is made to support meaningful concepts.

Extending Learning Experiences Under Guidance.—As time goes on, it becomes more and more evident that some of the rigidities in the organization and administration of the educational program are not really defensible. The strict organization by separate subjects, the core that has no functional accompanying experiences, and the extensive subject prescription in the major curricula, especially in high school, are cases in point. Take the college-preparatory curriculum, for example. A few years ago the Progressive Education

Association, in its well-known eight-year study, demonstrated beyond question that, other things being equal, it isn't the subjects a youngster takes in high school that determine his success in college, but how much native ability he has, how well he did in the high school subjects he took, where he ranked among his classmates, and so on. In fact, this study showed that college entrants who came from high schools which disregarded college entrance subject prescriptions as such and built individual programs in terms of pupil needs did better in college than entrants who stuck strictly to the high school subjects prescribed for college admission. It is becoming quite clear that, even in terms of success in college, the secondary school will serve its college preparatory group best if it will build programs of studies and experiences that make the pupil and his development primary rather than college admission requirements. Stated differently, the secondary school can no longer stand behind college admission requirements in defense of its highly restricted college-preparatory curriculum. The evidence does not support such a practice. This simply means that the sharp lines of the separate curricula in the secondary schools must gradually break down, and the school must desist from herding large groups into separate curricula; it must, on the other hand, make more and more of its total offerings available to all pupils. Through effective guidance and planning, each pupil's program will then be suited specifically to him. It should be emphasized again that before such curriculum changes can be made, the school's guidance services must be well established and well equipped for their great responsibilities. One of the results of such changes would be to cause each subject and each teacher not to depend upon prescription for status and enrolment, but upon useful and meaningful materials, skilfully handled. An even more important result would be the extension to pupils, of additional learning experiences, selected under guidance to meet their needs.

Reorganization in Terms of Objectives.—The customary organization of the school program into subject-matter departments is being called into question in some quarters. Our people are increasingly serious as they ask the question: What should our schools accomplish anyhow? The answer goes far beyond the mere mastery of content, although it includes that. Some people feel that as long as our organization is so predominantly in terms of content, and as long as our requirements emphasize content so completely, it will be hard for patrons or teachers or pupils not to be dominated too much by the content idea, possibly to the near-exclusion of other things that the school should accomplish. It is a tremendous shift in educational thinking when schools become as much interested in what people are as in what they know. That shift is gaining headway. As it gains support, the question is asked more and more if it might not be possible to reorganize the schools so that more emphasis is put on the objectives of education, which, after all, are the real reasons why the people are willing to support the schools to begin with. Objectives, it will be remembered, are expressed in terms of people, not subjects. Yet, generally speaking, our schools are organized in terms of subjects, not people. The demand seems to be increasing that we exalt and implement the goals of education through reorganization rather than hope that the goals will come about automatically as a result of content learning. The implications are great. For example, to what extent could the school be organized and pupils counseled in terms of the seven cardinal principles discussed in Chapter 3: physical and mental health, vocational preparation, citizenship, worthy home membership, worthy use of leisure time, command of the fundamental processes, and ethical character? Could requirements be administered for objectives as well as for subjects, units, years, and all the rest? The State Department of Education in Connecticut has given the matter of the reorganization of the secondary school in terms of such objectives a great deal of thought, and has produced a bulletin entitled *The Redirection, Reorganization, and Retooling of Secondary Education* which suggests steps in program reorganization that secondary schools might well consider. This document is only one among many which have been or will be produced dealing with the general problem of making our school organization more directly support our educational program.

6. Approach to Program Development and Revision

As one views the extent of the school offering in this country, he is likely to wonder just what principles or approaches were followed in developing the program. On what bases have more courses and content been justified? What have been the guides to schools as they developed and revised their offerings? A great deal has been written about this. A few approaches stand out.

Objectives, Materials, Grade Placement.—One very comprehensive approach to program development emphasizes that the offering should be based squarely upon educational objectives. In setting up or revising an over-all school program, or, for that matter, when dealing with a single subject, the first job, and it is fundamental, is to clarify the objectives to be achieved. When that is done, many materials, activities, experiences, and aids of all sorts related to the objectives will be assembled. The job is not done, however, until the materials have been properly scaled to pupils at various grade levels. The importance of these three steps is apparent at once; but the execution of the steps is not as simple as it may appear. Certainly every school and every teacher should have a clear idea of what is aimed at, but unfortunately such clarity does not always exist. Similarly, not all teachers are resourceful in discovering and utilizing the hosts of materials available to vitalize teaching and bring the objectives to life.

The textbook in some cases just about sets the limits. Furthermore, grade placement of materials will determine in good part whether or not the whole process will actually improve pupil learning. There is not much point in presenting to a junior high school social studies class the materials developed in the social studies seminar in college. But it has been done. If a pupil gets American history in both the eighth and eleventh grades, how should the work differ? What types of activity and study is he ready for in the eleventh grade that he wasn't ready for in the eighth? Some specialists in certain content areas such as mathematics and science are spending their lives trying to determine the difficulty rating of materials, the kind of thinking involved in their understanding and mastery, the time of development in pupils of the capacity to do certain types of thinking, and the skilful paralleling of content with the individual's ability to handle it.

Common Practice.—A good bit of program development in the past has been based on common practice. If a kindergarten needed to be started or a home economics curriculum added to the high school offering or a teacher education program set up in a college, a survey of common practices provided the "safe" pattern to follow. It is good, of course, to know what common practice is; but, basically, it is the lazy way out. In the first place, if one happens to be unfortunate in the schools or people he contacts, he may come out with a survey of common bad practice rather than of common good practice. Also, and more important, such a procedure fails to call into play the resources of the local staff and community in thinking about education and taking steps in terms of their own convictions. Common practice serves a better purpose if it is used only as a springboard for local follow-up rather than as a pattern to be followed.

Nature of the Community.—The idea that the school ought to serve the community in which it is located has influenced program development a great deal and has given many schools genuine individuality. Some school leaders have studied carefully the communities in which they work and have adjusted the school program to community needs. If inquiry shows, for example, that a good share of the boys graduating from high school go into factory work or farming, then the local high school will see to it that technical and agricultural studies are offered. It will be the same for other areas such as homemaking and business. But the response to community needs will not stop there. Schools are attempting more and more to serve persons of all ages in the community. If there is a group of foreign-born people in the community that needs help with English, the school will provide that help. Similarly, the services of the home-making department, the agriculture department, and all the rest are available to community groups. The program of the school is thus extended in terms of the nature of the community.

Job and Activity Analysis.—If a school decides that it ought to offer work, shall we say, in the fields of business and agriculture, it should not, many insist, follow the traditional patterns in these fields, or borrow what some other school is doing; it ought, on the other hand, to study direct the nature of jobs in these fields and the activities actually engaged in by successful practitioners. The agriculture people should find out what the agricultural pursuits of the region are. Is the region devoted primarily to wheat, poultry, cotton, dairy cattle, beef cattle, fruit, tobacco, or potatoes? If it is wheat and beef cattle or cherries and chickens, the program in agriculture will be planned accordingly, and it will be further determined by a careful study of the activities of successful people in these jobs. So it will be with business. The types of jobs present in the community will be discovered, and the activities required for successful participation will be determined. This approach to program development is particularly applicable, of course, to vocational fields.

Pupil Interests, Abilities, Usage, Errors.—Here the emphasis in program development changes from mainly outward considerations so far as the pupil is concerned to inward considerations. Pupil interests ought to be observed in program development. The basic interests of twelve-year-olds are quite different from those of sixteen-year-olds. Problems of vocational choice and preparation, social adjustment, homemaking, physical maturity, citizenship responsibilities, and educational planning loom much larger to the sixteen-year-old than to the twelve-year-old. The well-adjusted educational program will act on such interests for the sixteen-year-olds and will not press such interests or decisions on the twelve-year-olds. Similarly, within certain subjects the differences in interests based upon sex, age, background, vocational or educational intention, and the like are utilized by the good teacher in determining learning content and activities. The need to adjust the program to ability differences has been discussed in other places [1] and is apparent to all. Although the principle of such adjustment is clearly recognized, its effective application is most imperfect. Pupil usage is also emphasized as a determiner of the program. What kind of mathematical problems do pupils at different ages use most? These, so it is insisted, should be mastered first. What words do people at various age levels use most? These are the ones that ought certainly to get into the language and spelling work at these levels. Errors, too, can be used as an approach. What words do third graders or tenth graders misspell most frequently in all of their free writing? What are the most common mistakes in English usage? These should get into the program for special attention. It stands to reason that if a good job is done under the common-usage approach, the common-errors approach will practically disappear.

Psychology of Learning.—One of the most important guides in program development is the psychology of learning. If, as we have seen, learning takes place only when the learner is motivated and active and is challenged by problems that are meaningful and significant to him, then the school program should emphasize participation more than memorization and should organize materials as a pursuit and a challenge for the pupils rather than as information to be accepted and learned. The so-called "activity curriculum" and "experience curriculum" make great stock of what we know about how people learn.

Relationship to Life.—The school program must be demonstrably good in terms of improved and enriched living. In Chapter 4 reference was made to a statement by the philosopher, A. N. Whitehead, which began: "There is only one subject matter for education, and that is life in all its ramifications." J. Paul Leonard, in the following statement, gets down to specifics:

Rockets, jet planes, Bikini, Paris; fascism, communism, democracy; Jew, Negro, Indian; production, profits, employment, price control; log-rolling,

---

[1] See pages 220–222.

pork barrel, seniority, pressure groups; conservatism, reaction, liberalism; evolution, fundamentalism, pragmatism; capital, labor, management; bureaucrats, demagogues, special interests; delinquency, crime, peace or war. Such are the issues of society, of life. Each word is flooded with excitement, with the uncertainty of living, with the cry for an original solution. The problems they represent enlist the greatest minds—the inventors, the moral philosophers, the creative artists, the social, political, and economic architects.

Love, social acceptance, that strange feeling, sex; reputation, conscience, bad habits; etiquette, customs, tradition, mistakes, rules; home, family, school, independence; necking, dating, romancing, boy friend, girl friend; dancing, smoking, drinking, sin; a job, a career, right preparation, right college; finances, popularity, carelessness, criticisms, jealousy; headache, stomachache, heartache, underweight, overweight, the blues; religion, heaven and hell, lonesome, "wishing I were dead." Such are the concerns of youth, the dominating and haunting drives to study, thought, and action. These we leave largely to youthful ingenuity, to play friends, parents, and church leaders against one another for answers.

Grammar, algebra, history, language; gerunds, square root, Punic Wars, figures of speech; bells, schedule, recess, recitations, tests, neat rows of seats; Miss Jones, Mr. Brown, Dean Barrett, Principal Showers; 8:55, 10:02, lunch; 1:18, 3:47, go home; report cards, college-entrance requirements, grades. Such is the conventional school; each day the same, a continuous round of exactness and duplication; studying what is known, learning what others have done, avoiding the uncertain, the future, the issues of life. Thus the common conventional school through average teachers, ministers to conventional and average children, filling the brighter pupils with restlessness and wandering, to be saved only by the dribble of God-given creative teachers.

The issues of life; the concerns of youth; the routine of the school. Uncertainty, doubt, worry and fear; certainty and exactness—the world, the child, the school, still a long way apart.[2]

It is not fair of the school to consume the time of the pupil with content that may be well ordered and of long standing but does not help the pupil to understand and deal with the problems of his times. Judge, for example, the effectiveness of the typical secondary school in relation to the following list of topics given by the older youth of one state [3] as items on which they wanted help and information. For most of these young people, school had ended with graduation from high school. The high school had the last chance to help them meet life as they would live it, but it had not given them the understandings and guides to thought and action they desired on such things as:

[2] J. Paul Leonard, from "Our Readers Say," *Educational Leadership,* Nov., 1946, p. 131.

[3] Connecticut. Part of a list assembled under the leadership of Warren E. Schmidt, Assistant State Club Leader, Older Youth, 1947.

1. Legal papers and wills
2. Life insurance
3. Automobile insurance
4. Simple business law
5. Simple common law
6. Taxes, their uses and abuses
7. Labor unions
8. The role of money and the borrowing of money
9. Why prices rise and fall
10. Helps for amateur acting and play-producing
11. Suggestions for effective speaking
12. Good letter-writing
13. What is the world made of?
14. Natural resources, minerals, and precious stones
15. What makes weather?
16. Local flora and fauna
17. Local, county, state, and national government
18. United Nations
19. International relations and the American foreign policy
20. Democracy versus totalitarianism
21. How laws are made
22. Law-enforcement
23. The responsibilities of voting
24. Current public problems
25. Ways in which the individual citizen can make his influence felt
26. Compulsory military training
27. Historical backgrounds to present problems
28. Music appreciation
29. Simple song-leading
30. Modern morals
31. Religion and life
32. Sex and courtship
33. Life values
34. Simple atomic theory
35. Getting along with people
36. Ways of working together successfully
37. What goes to make up personality and leadership?
38. Living with our emotions—worry, jealousy, anger, fear
39. Escapes we use and their effects
40. Qualities to look for in a mate
41. Making daily routines meaningful
42. What is human nature?
43. Facts about heredity and environment
44. Selecting a life partner
45. How much money does it take to get married?
46. Success in marriage
47. Family relations
48. Race and prejudice
49. Minority groups and intolerance
50. You and cancer, tuberculosis, heart trouble, social diseases, diet, etc.
51. Improving health and personal appearance
52. Developing good taste in clothes, music, reading, movies, television, etc.
53. Hospitalization and health insurance
54. Group health programs
55. Vocational guidance
56. What about strikes?
57. Audio-visual materials and equipment for the home
58. Photography, gardening, practical electricity
59. Methods and activities suitable for use by youth groups
60. Parliamentary procedure
61. Good manners

It is not suggested here that every one of the above topics should be incorporated into the high school offering or that there are not other types of content important for secondary school youth; but it is suggested that unless the school can justify everything that it does by the criterion of significant relationship to "life in all its ramifications," it is falling short in rendering the service it ought to render.

The Principle of Relative Values.—It can be said, of course, that all facts and events and experiences are related to "life in all its ramifications" in some way. The principle of relative values holds that since there is not time enough to learn everything, the best possible use should be made of the time available. The school should elevate those things that are of great use and significance in the lives of pupils and reduce or eliminate those things that are of little significance. This principle is sometimes hard to apply because it frequently requires that "dead wood" be eliminated, the very content which may be of longest standing in the school. Furthermore, this principle is not limited to whole subjects in its application, but applies to content within subjects as well. Of course, problems of democracy as a course may be more useful than ancient history, if there isn't time for both, and science more important than Greek; but also within the science course, simple atomic theory may need to replace the study of the work of the alchemists of old. With our fast-moving civilization and rapid advances in all fields of learning, the principle of relative values in the building of the school program takes on increasing importance.

Experimentation and Eclecticism.—Much emphasis is placed today on the great need for experimentation in program development and revision. It is not enough to decide to adopt or change something; it should be carefully studied and evaluated to see whether or not the ends sought are actually achieved. Furthermore, good practice requires that many proposals with reference to the offering be tried out during an experimental period before being widely accepted and applied. The eclectic approach, too, is stressed. Certainly no educational leader or group responsible for program development or revision would attempt to use as a guide one of the approaches in this section to the exclusion of all others. Guides and suggestions of all sorts will be accepted and used. Some approaches may be more acceptable in certain areas than in others. For example, job and activity analysis will have more to offer in vocational agriculture than in music appreciation. The good planner will attempt to make his program and every subdivision of it qualify by as many legitimate criteria as possible.

7. Who Should Share in Program Development?

One need not go very far back in the history of our schools to find that program development was the work of a very few people. The "armchair" era saw the top school authorities closet themselves for the purpose of deciding on the subjects to be taught and the content to be included. All eyes were on the board of education or the superintendent of schools to see what would come out. Often also the authorities in the county superintendent's office or in the state department of education made most of the decisions, developed the courses of study, decided on the texts to be used, and so on.

But things are changing now. Of course, as before, the basic responsibility for program planning and revision rests squarely upon the school and the school leaders. However, such responsibility does not mean that these people must make all the decisions. Real leadership requires that in the process of making their decisions these people ask for the cooperation of many others who are competent to think constructively about such matters and give valuable suggestions.

Within the School.—In building and improving the school offering, the real school leader will of course place much responsibility on units in his school organized for instructional purposes. These are most commonly the subject-matter departments. The heads of these departments will not, however, have the last word. Teacher committees will be formed to make systematic studies out of which recommendations will come. Such committees will be school-wide or not, depending upon the scope of the project in hand. Individual teachers will also be consulted. These are the people who deal most intimately with the program at the point where it meets the learner. Other special functionaries such as the school physician, the school nurse, the director of counseling, and the visiting teacher frequently have suggestions to give that are invaluable. Who in the school, for example, has a better chance to view the program in its total operation than the director of counseling? The pupils, too, should share in program development. When this happens, not only has the way been opened to receive real help from the students, but an important step has been taken in improving the attitude of pupils toward their school work. There are many persons within the school, therefore, who ought to share in the study and revision of the offering. Certainly people beyond the immediate subject or field being dealt with will be included. This will improve correlation and understanding in the over-all program and is likely to add to the broad serviceableness of all parts of the offering.

Community Participation.—Much help can be secured from the community in developing the school offering. Again, it should be stressed that the school is not giving over to the community the responsibility for making decisions; it is, on the other hand, attempting to secure help and suggestions wherever they can be found. For example, it stands to reason that if the business curriculum in the local high school is being revised, the manager of a successful business or an outstanding supervisor of an office staff would be able to give some real help. The same for other fields. In fact, it is probably not too much to say that there should be community representation ôn all such studies in the school. No area of study should be excepted. We have had too little of such school-community cooperation and too little understanding by the community of the real purposes and program of the school.

Consultants.—There are some people who have made the educational offering their special life study. They may even give special attention to certain subject areas such as vocational and technical studies, social studies, homemaking, and science. They have visited scores of schools and worked with many committees and faculties on problems of program development. Their up-to-dateness and grasp with reference to all that is involved in tackling a problem of program improvement places them in a position to render a great service to local schools and save local people a great deal of time. These people may be attached to state departments of education or college or university staffs, or they may themselves be members of local schools. Wherever they are, they are valuable people to secure as consultants, not to do the work for the local schools, but to cooperate with local groups in getting started right, deciding on proper procedures, assembling the right information, making decisions, and instituting practices.

Workshops as a Sharing Technique.—The workshop is being used more and more as a sharing technique in program development. Its possibilities are extremely varied, but a typical situation will illustrate its usefulness. A university may assemble a staff of consultants as described in the previous paragraph and announce that a workshop in English and social studies for junior high school teachers will be held for a period of weeks. The number of teachers allowed to participate is limited. Activities are carefully scheduled and planned.

The job is to develop an interrelated program in English and social studies for junior high school pupils. A class of junior high school pupils is assembled and held in regular session throughout the workshop. All the teachers share in building the program, expert teachers teach the pupils in the presence of all the participants, and opportunity is given for suggestion, change, debate, and criticism, until out of it all comes a type of offering that seems effective, has evolved under the combined scrutiny of all participants, and has been subjected to tryout on the pupils themselves. In all of this each teacher has contributed in terms of his experience and study and the consultants have worked along with the teachers, giving aid as they could. The result, ideally, is not a blueprint to be taken home and used as such, but a pattern that can be tried out as desired, adapted to local situations, and used by local teachers to improve their classroom instruction. In any event, the experience of having had such an exchange and sharing with other teachers and of having observed the handling of selected materials and activities by expert teachers can hardly be lost on the participants.

Interlevel Work Conferences.—It has already been emphasized that the learning experience of pupils should be as meaningful and connected as possible as they progress from grade to grade. This was seen to be the heart of the articulation problem in our educational ladder, and it also underlies the strand idea in curriculum development. If such continuity in the program is to be achieved, it is clear that there needs to be a great deal of intergrade and interlevel cooperation. Persons dealing with pupils in a given grade and in a given field of study need to know what has gone before and what comes after. Hence, interlevel work conferences are an important means of improving program development.

8. THE EXTRACURRICULUM

Its Growth and Development.—The term "extracurriculum" had its origins when it was insisted that the school's separate and dignified job was to teach formal subjects and be concerned with the intellectual development of pupils. Activities beyond these "solid" or "academic" studies were "extra" and "nonacademic." Actual hostility existed in many schools to these activities. They were ridiculed in numerous writings. However, these activities have had an interesting development since they were so considered. Hostility and ridicule changed to toleration when it began to appear 'that the school's job might extend beyond the academic and the intellectual. As the broad task of the school in these times took on design and clarity, toleration in turn became acceptance, and acceptance took on definite planning and supervision. Actual interest developed to use these activities for educational purposes as surely as the traditional studies were used. They were not long in demonstrating that, properly handled, they were an exceedingly helpful means of enriching school experience and of promoting individual development. Their possibilities have not been realized yet by any means. There is much to be done in making them really measure up to educational standards, in better integrating them into the total school program, and in giving them the support and leadership they deserve. Briefly, therefore, the extracurriculum has had a varied past, enjoys a respectable present, and has a future of high potentiality. Strangely enough, as extracurriculum activities were accepted and used and as the idea that they were "extra" disappeared, there was no satisfactory new term created to describe them. Hence, the term "extracurriculum activities" continues in use, but no longer carries the connotation of "outside the pale" which used to accompany it.

The Nature of Extracurriculum Activities.—Very likely the earliest type of extracurriculum activity was oratory or argumentation. In their earliest stages, these activities were serious studies in themselves. Gradually they took on the nature of an extraclass activity and expanded into other forms of "literary" activities. From these beginnings have evolved the extensive array of activities today. Every reader knows what they are. Some of the more common ones can be listed under major headings:

1. Music—glee clubs, orchestras, bands, choirs, etc.
2. Forensics and dramatics—plays, contests, etc.
3. Athletics—interscholastic and intramural
4. Publications—school paper, yearbook, literary journals, handbooks, etc.
5. Clubs—subject matter, social, hobby and special interest, etc.
6. Assemblies—planned and conducted by students
7. Student government
8. Class activities—fourth grade, eighth grade, eleventh grade, etc.
9. Homeroom activities
10. Guidance activities—career days, college club, etc.

The fact that it is very common for a school to have activities under all the above headings serves to illustrate the relative importance of the extracurriculum in the total program of the modern school.

Problems Related to the Extracurriculum.—As the extracurriculum has taken on scope and status, many problems have arisen.

Finance. As a general rule, extracurriculum activities have had to make their own way financially. They have not had access to the regular funds which support the school. Frequently also the activities with little money-making possibilities have had to be supported by others which have greater appeal to the public. Football and basketball, for example, have been the great money-earners. However, the security and continuity of the other activities should not have to depend upon such uncertain financial backing. A losing season in a money-making sport may very well mean disaster to a lot of other activities. There is a rather urgent and rather successful movement of late to change this situation. As local school leaders make it clear in their communities that these activities function in the school program and in the development of pupils just as surely as other things for which money is spent, the point of view grows that they have a legitimate claim on the regular school budget. It is as defensible educationally to spend public money for music for the school orchestra as for magazines for the school library. Most writers on this subject do not contend that all admissions to all activities should be free; but they do contend that no activity should have to depend upon another for its full support and that all activities which are educationally defensible should be underwritten so that, in spite of a losing season or a low public gate, their continuity will be assured.

There are other aspects to the problem of financing the extracurriculum. For example, should each activity operate independently in the management of its funds? To what extent should pupils share in managing the financial aspects of an activity and in handling the money? Should the financing of all extracurriculum activities in a school be centralized and under the supervision of the principal or a responsible faculty member? How can the managing and financing of the extracurriculum be made an experience in responsible living for pupils?

Participation. Some schools maintain as many as three or four dozen regularly organized extracurriculum activities. Others, of course, have far too few. Enough ought to be maintained to permit all pupils to participate in activities appropriate to their interests and needs. In any school the problem of pupil participation is sure to arise. How many activities should a pupil be permitted to engage in? How many must he engage in? Both overparticipation and underparticipation are to be guarded against. What account should be taken of office-holding as over against ordinary membership? Suffice it to say here that increasing numbers of schools are requiring that all pupils participate in these activities. Again, underlying such a requirement is the conviction that participation plays an important part in the pupil's well-rounded development.

Credit. Should schools give credit for participation in extracurriculum activities? It was pointed out above that increasing numbers of schools are requiring participation. Many schools go further and establish a system of point values for participation in the activities and then require a certain number of points for graduation. Membership in a club may be worth one point, whereas being its president may be worth two. In this sense, of course, credit is given for participation. However, these points are required in addition to the usual academic requirements for graduation. There is also a growing tendency for schools to recognize and encourage certain activities that pupils may engage in in the community. This includes such things as music lessons, Boy Scout activities, 4-H Club activities, and the like.

Time. One of the most serious problems associated with the extracurriculum is that of time. The remainder of the school program so often takes up the whole day. These activities are, therefore, "afterschool" activities in fact. And yet, as they have taken on added significance, it is not entirely fair that they must still be treated as "extras" so far as schooltime is concerned. And if they are important, should they not come under the regular supervision of the school? Sincere effort is being made in many schools to organize these activities into the regular school day, and give them time allotments and adequate supervision along with the regular studies. In order to do this, some schools have actually lengthened the school day. Sometimes these activities are concentrated largely within the last period. In other cases, periods staggered throughout the school week are given over to them. All in all, their time requirements tend to be recognized and more and more adequately met.

Sponsorship. Pupils frequently generate more interest in extracurriculum activities than in their regular studies. This is not surprising, and it should not be held against the pupils. The natural interest that pupils have in activities and the eager response they give to them when they are well planned and conducted should hold a suggestion and challenge to the regular classroom teacher. This enthusiasm of pupils for interesting activities, and their willingness to spend time and shed blood for them places tremendous responsibility and opportunity in the hands of the leaders. Parents have frequently said that they are more concerned about who is in charge of their children on the football field than in the English classroom. They know how youngsters are inclined to swear by the coach and how they respond to leadership in activities that offer release, excitement, real action, and visible achievement. All well-directed activities present much the same picture. And yet, sponsorship and leadership have often been an extra burden on the teacher, sponsorship assignments have frequently been given to persons not qualified to take over, and the extracurriculum has had to go without the leadership it so much needs and deserves. The time must come when the ability to direct extracurriculum activities will be considered in the selection of teachers just as seriously as the ability to teach a subject. Furthermore, in schools where the extracurriculum is considered a regular part of the educational program and is so organized, responsibility for these activities will be considered as part of the regular teaching load. If proper supervision is to be secured, proper provisions for it will have to be made.

Evaluation. As the idea of what should be accomplished through extracurriculum activities becomes clearer, there is better ground on which to judge them. They should not be permitted to multiply or continue indiscriminately. Activities that cannot be shown to promote specific educational objectives should be eliminated. For example, if junior high school football as conducted in a given school is more harmful than helpful to pupil health, then it should be conducted so as to promote health or else thrown out. Each activity should have specific objectives associated with it; and these objectives should control the thinking and planning of all who lead and participate. They should also provide a basis for evaluating the activity as worthy of retention or not as well as a basis for growth and improvement. It is very likely that in some schools a good many of the activities, as at present conducted, would have to go by the board if they were subjected to careful educational scrutiny. They do not have the facilities, support, leadership, or program they ought to have to justify their existence. And yet, it is imperative that just such evaluation be made. In these activities it is very easy to sacrifice the educational for the spectacular, to permit the tail to wag the dog. This will not occur if they are associated with very definite objectives to begin with and are examined from time to time to make sure that those objectives are really being served.

Democratic Sharing. Extracurriculum activities afford a fine opportunity for the practice of democracy. Even in their origins they should stem from pupil interests and needs that have become articulate among the pupils themselves. They should not come into being as a result of administrative decision and pronouncement. Neither should they be dominated by faculty members who are acting as advisers or sponsors. Pupils should have much to do in planning and conducting activities, making decisions, and carrying them out. Student leaders should be chosen. Here they can experience what it means to plan for the good of all and enlist the help of all. Here they learn that the good leader is actually one who knows how to get the best out of others and properly organizes and coordinates their activities. He does not make the decisions and expect others to follow. In fact, extracurriculum activities can do much to break down the too greatly emphasized leader-follower idea, and substitute for it the idea of equality, of team play, of cooperation, and of the importance of the contribution of each person. Followership is thereby raised to a position of equal sharing, of being out front with all the others in thinking and contributing, rather than of getting behind the decisions of a few leaders and pushing. Much has been said in previous pages about the concern in these times that education shall become an experience in living as well as an experience in learning. The extracurriculum, rightly planned and conducted, can bring to life and into practice many of the goals of education so generally subscribed to.

9. Some Topics Related to the Offering

Controversial Issues.—The idea that controversial issues should be kept out of the school offering is so contrary to the ideal of education for democratic living that it seems almost ridiculous that it should be a problem at all. But it is. Controversial issues are often, of course, of a local nature; and in many communities there are local groups whose every desire is to keep these issues submerged. Even school authorities oppose them sometimes. A few months ago a national magazine told of a local radio station that suggested a Junior Town Meeting of the Air for students. The board of education opposed the idea on the ground that controversial issues might be discussed. It is not surprising that special interest groups should sometimes oppose the introduction of controversial issues into the school program, but it is hard to understand how boards of education, administrators, and even teachers who appreciate the job of the school in preparing pupils for citizenship in a democracy can be against it. Fundamentally there is only one reason for public support of schools in this country; namely, that we shall have coming out of our public schools young people who understand our society and know how to make it better. Schools that refuse to introduce pupils to controversial issues and give them some experience in grappling with them are, as it were, graduating cowboys who have never roped a calf or been on a bucking bronco. Such people are likely to get hurt when they begin the job of a cowhand. So are youth likely to get hurt when they assume the duties of citizenship if they have been shielded from the problems of citizenship and have no idea of how to attack such problems and think for themselves concerning them. If they are weak in this kind of experience, they cannot function constructively themselves and may become an easy prey to others who pose as having solutions to problems that are bothersome.

When schools and communities become realistic in exposing youth to issues and problems of all sorts and in giving them a chance to do something about them, the results are often surprising. In more than one community tremendous improvements in health services, housing, recreational facilities, intercultural relations, and government services have emanated straight from the school, more frequently from the secondary school. In an evolving society the chief responsibility of the citizen is to be able to understand his society and think intelligently about proposals for changing it. The school must do its share in producing this kind of citizen.

The manner of handling controversial issues in the classroom varies greatly. Some teachers insist that all such matters must be left open, that no summations or conclusions shall even be considered. Others say that the teacher should take special care not to let his opinion be known, although he may say that students have a right to their opinions. Surely it seems a little odd to say that the pupils have a right to their opinions on such items but the teacher does not. It seems more proper to say that the pupils are entitled to a demonstration of complete thought on the part of the teacher in such matters, if the evidence at hand is adequate to a conclusion. Of course there will be many times when no conclusion is justified, when the main thing for all is to keep an open mind. Teachers may postpone the expression of their viewpoints so as not to color too much the thinking of the pupils while issues are being discussed, but they most certainly should take a position before the issue is closed or, if the evidence is insufficient, they should urge the necessity of not forcing a conclusion until additional evidence is in. Anything less than this is falling short of the real opportunity and responsibility the teacher has in dealing with these issues. Teachers sometimes viciously violate the democratic process when, having stated their own points of view, they require that all pupils accept these as their own. The outcomes of dealing with controversial issues ought to be open-mindedness, careful study using good procedures, and defensible conclusions that will guide intelligent action, not the domination of one judgment over another.

Academic Freedom.—The essence of academic freedom is the right of the learner to have access to all facts and points of view, no matter what is being studied. Academic freedom has too often been associated only with teachers. It certainly applies to teachers, but teachers are actually the open doors of truth to pupils, and they have no right to interpret academic freedom as the right to defend a bias or wilfully to fail to present all the evidence. The right to defend a point of view is not at stake in academic freedom, but in defending his point of view the teacher must expose it to all kinds of evidence, thus inviting the possibility that others will interpret the evidence differently from himself. It seems right also to say that in a country like this, where we hold that the school must be free in its search for truth, it is not right to use that freedom to promote doctrines and practices that would in turn destroy freedom. Academic freedom does not, of course, release one from his regular responsibilities in the school. If one is employed to teach mathematics, he is hardly justified in giving over his class time to problems of religion and politics, no matter how fervent he may be in private life with reference to such matters. On the other hand, academic freedom does defend the right of a teacher to hold such points of view as he pleases on such matters and to discuss and promote them openly as a free citizen. Again, let us say that in its essence the problem of academic freedom lies with the freedom of the learner to learn, and, perhaps also, with preserving free education so that it does not itself destroy the freedom it defends.

Legislating the School Offering.—In a good many states laws have been passed requiring that certain subjects be taught in the schools, such as physical education or American history. Most people are agreed, no doubt, that these subjects should be taught, but they are not agreed that laws should be passed requiring them. In an improving democracy, individual citizens in their local communities are called on more and more to make decisions concerning the community and to direct its institutions. The problem with reference to the school offering, therefore, is not one of securing state legislation but of getting local communities interested in what their schools should do for their young people. When this is done, the essential freedom of the school is maintained and it is spared the influences and fixations in law which can so easily turn it away from its primary purposes. It should be remembered that local public schools are in fact state schools and the state is within its legal rights to legislate the curriculum; however, a state that understands the position of the public schools in a democracy is not likely to wish to control the school offering but will instead wish to promote general education among all the people and delegate to them the responsibility for local school policy and program.

The Cosmopolitan School.—In connection with the discussion concerning the diversity within our school population, it was pointed out that a good many different types of schools, primarily above the elementary level, had been established to meet the needs of different groups of students. Although the Industrial Revolution and the demand for specialization accompanying the two world wars created a continuing pull toward such institutional specialization, it is also true that there has been a counterpull toward the cosmopolitan school. The cosmopolitan school maintains a widely diversified offering and brings together under one roof general cross sections of our pupil population. It is noncaste. It promotes the type of mingling that fosters harmony and understanding among pupils, which, in turn, will increase harmony and understanding among adults. Specialization in line with vocational and educational needs is, of course, necessary; but to a very large degree this will be achieved within the larger group, which is the cosmopolitan school. Ordinarily this idea has been most closely associated with secondary schools. However, it is also the strength of our great universities. It is good for a law school, medical school, arts school, and all the rest to be parts of an integrated institution. It is also good if each will make appropriate instruction and services available to the whole institution. There is good reason why, on all levels of our school system, students should maintain the contacts and cross references essential to breadth and graciousness in living.

Cooperative Plans.—The cooperative plan in the school program is essentially an effort to bridge some of the gaps that exist between the work of the school and the work of the world. In an organized sense, it represents an arrangement between the school and other agencies in society whereby the students can supplement their instruction in the school with applications of that instruction in society. For example, an engineering school may arrange with industrial concerns for the absorption of students on the job for a period of weeks, after which they will return to school, then return to the job, and so on. Ordinarily it will take such students longer than is common to complete their engineering education, but they will have had a background of experience and understanding that will greatly enrich their preparation. On the secondary level the regular high school will sometimes combine with a local technical or trade school to permit a pupil to count certain trade school work toward meeting high school graduation requirements. Again the bridge is between the academic and the practical. It needs to be added that there is much such bridging that does not take the form of organized arrangements. Individual teachers do it in such fields as business, government, and agriculture.

Curriculum "Lag."—For those who believe that the school ought to be alert to our changing society and serve it in appropriate ways, it is genuinely irksome when the school lags behind the times, perpetuating an academic tradition and failing to serve in ways clearly desirable. For example, take safety and health education. Accidents are the fourth most important cause of death in this country. In 1946 approximately 99,000 persons lost their lives in accidents. This was an increase of 3 per cent over 1945. Over 10,000,000 people were injured by accidents in 1946. Eleven persons were killed by accident every hour, and an additional 1,190 were injured.[4] Slightly more than a third of the accidental deaths were caused by motor vehicles. Four persons every hour died from this cause. The traffic death rate for the fifteen-to-twenty-four-year age group was higher than for any other age group with the exception of persons sixty-five years old and over.[5] Most youngsters reach the legal age for driving an automobile while they are in high school. Some high schools, realizing this, have set up programs of driver education. The effect of these programs on the number of deaths by automobile accidents among high school pupils is indeed impressive. In some metropolitan areas where the program has been extensive and records have been well kept, such deaths have been reduced approximately 50 per cent. And yet, driver education in the high schools of the nation is still greatly retarded. This is curriculum "lag." The same for health education. The need is certainly apparent. Two world wars have

[4] National Safety Council, *Accident Facts* (1947 ed.; Chicago: The Council, 1947).
[5] *Ibid.*, p. 53.

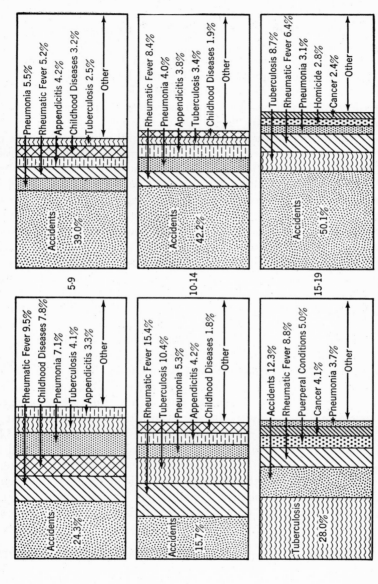

Figure 7. Leading Causes of Death Among School-Age Children as Per Cent of All Deaths [6]

[6] *Health Bulletin for Teachers*, XIX, No. 1, Oct., 1947. Published by Metropolitan Life Insurance Company.

embarrassed us by revealing a surprisingly high percentage of young people unfit for military service because of health deficiencies. Furthermore, the evidence occurs over and over concerning the health needs of school-age children themselves. The data presented in Figure 7 are typical. Note the rise in tuberculosis as a cause of death among school-age children, especially among girls. Cancer, too, rears its head ominously. Data concerning death by accidents for this group are startling. But the typical school health program is not based on such facts. In fact, in some communities any mention in the school of grave health problems such as cancer and social diseases is taboo. This is curriculum "lag." Other examples, of course, could be given, such as sex education and intercultural education. Some of the gravest problems faced by youth, problems on which the school could be of tremendous help, are precisely those that the school has been slowest to touch. But a word should be added. The school is not separate from the community in this regard. As long as our schools are subject to the public will, progress in these matters must involve real community participation in considering the kinds of services the school can properly render.

Curriculum "lag" is not confined to new services the school may appropriately render. It is an equally important problem within the existing school program. It is easy to get into a rut in the classroom, using the same content, the same materials, and the same examinations and illustrations year after year. It took a war to change some of our illustrations in mathematics and physics. It would be a good thing if teachers placed upon themselves the obligation constantly to make their teaching meaningful and pertinent in the lives of pupils. Frequently also the findings of useful research are slow of application in the classroom. School curricula, too, such as the college-preparatory curriculum, are slow to change, even after studies show that in their present form they are not defensible. The philosophy of "let good enough alone," "things as they are are all right," is hard to break down, once it is established in a school system. Such a system, though, can never know the challenge, the satisfaction, and the excitement that result when the central philosophy becomes one of adjustment and service rather than one of maintaining a smooth-running status quo.

The Offering as Determiner of School Plants and Budgets.—The time was when school building committees in our communities used to be concerned primarily with getting simple buildings with as much floor space as possible for the money spent. In a very real sense, the committee presented the school authorities with a nice new building, and the authorities took over from there. After that, a process of "this can go here, and that can go there" was begun, and the educational program was thus fitted into the plant. But this has changed. Today, in the modern community, when a school building is being planned the school leaders, the board of education, and the people of the community think long and hard about the type of program they want the building to accommodate. This will include not only the areas of instruction but also the broad program of school and community activities. Facilities in line with good methods of instruction will also be sought, such as audio-visual facilities. The school services desired, such as health and medical services and a cafeteria, will be decided upon. All this, and more too, will be clarified locally, oftentimes before the services of an architect are sought. The architect, in turn, must be able to plan a building to house such a program. In this way the offering is not fitted into the new plant but determines it.

Similarly with the school budget. Now such questions are asked as "What kind of educational program do we want in our community?" and "How can we best allocate our funds for its achievement?" Thus, the budget, instead of determining the offering, is determined by it. These are aspects of school administration which, when properly handled, reveal educational leadership at its best.

Democracy Through School Experiences.—It may become dreary in the telling, but let it be said again that the program of the school must give an experience in democratic living as well as a mastery of content judged to be important. The implications of this for the citizen, the school administrator, the teacher, and the pupil are very far-reaching. This is the chief challenge of education in our time. The programs we have built with the demands of various vocational pursuits in mind must now be supplemented with experiences that will produce the effective citizen in a democracy. Knowledge is important, and we will cling to it; but ways of living, and the development of a real capacity to direct knowledge into useful channels, **are** the present-day frontier in program-building.

What Do YOU Say?

1

The determination of the school curriculum and the content of the courses taught is not a job for school people only; the community as a whole and selected people in the community should help.

What do YOU say?

2

It is just as suitable and workable in a school to set up departments in terms of the objectives of the school as to set them up in terms of the subjects the school teaches.

What do YOU say?

3

If the needs of youth in relation to their times are accepted as a guiding criterion in curriculum-building, then such matters as driver training, sex education, narcotics and alcohol, intercultural relations, and mental hygiene are just as acceptable as mathematics and English for classroom study.

What do YOU say?

4

What points in this chapter do you particularly support or take issue with?

Chapter 10

COUNSELING IN THE SCHOOL

Helping People Help Themselves

1. THE COUNSELING CONCEPT

The development of counseling activities in the schools of our country is one of the most important things that have been done to bring education into line with our national ideals. In view of the basic character of counseling, it is rather surprising that it did not develop sooner. It is still in its infancy as an organized, well-planned, adequately supported program, but the fundamental need for it is becoming convincingly clear. Counseling, which does so much to relate educational experiences to developmental needs, is catching on. What are some of the basic ingredients of the counseling concept?

Individual Responsibility for Decision-making.—The whole doctrine of freedom and of responsibility for citizenship in our country emphasizes the self-directive character of the individual. One must make his own decisions. The school seeks to give back to society generation after generation of young people who are able to discharge this responsibility wisely. The counseling service within the school seeks to give young people experience in meeting their problems squarely, studying them systematically, and developing a course of action concerning them. Self-thinking, self-direction, and the habit of making use of all available information and counsel are sought. The counseling service does not assemble information about a student, call him in, and tell him what to do next. Such a procedure would nullify completely the school's opportunity and responsibility to give students vital experience in formulating their own judgments and planning courses of action.

Utilizing the Study and Experience of Others.—The idea that counseling services seek to develop self-thinking, self-directing individuals does not mean that young people are to be left unassisted and completely on their own when problems arise. By its very nature, counseling assumes that persons of experience and, above all, persons of experience who are trained as counselors, can be of help when problems arise and decisions are to be made. The important thing is that the study and experience of the elder shall not dominate the younger in the problem-solving situation. Adults who are interested in youth problems can supply much information that should be considered when courses of action are planned. Such information might be completely overlooked by youth if they kept their own counsels. The idea is that, from whatever source, all the pertinent information and aid that can possibly be assembled should be on hand when decisions are to be made and courses of action planned. In other words, counseling recognizes the assistance that qualified and interested persons can give at times of choice, crisis, decision-making, or problem-solving—without dominating the situation.

Taking Counsel Together.—The twofold idea that individuals in our society are expected to think and act for themselves and can gain much help from others sets the stage perfectly for the sharing that is involved in counseling. For counseling is sharing; and in the sharing of experience, all hands benefit. As an ancient biblical proverb puts it, "Where no counsel is the people fall: but in the multitude of counselors there is safety." [1] The idea of taking counsel *together* is paramount in the counseling work of the modern school. Above all, the student whose problem is at hand will be one of the principal participants. In this way he is his own counselor, and it will be his own counsel that he will in the end take. Thus, counseling, through a cooperative approach to problems, does not abandon youth to trial and error. On the other hand, it attempts to surround a problem with all possible pertinent information and gives youth opportunity to make choices intelligently.

Putting the Cards on the Table.—If counseling is to be an experience in sharing from which skill in decision-making will develop, then there is no point to an earlier practice of withholding vital information when a problem is to be solved. Time was, for example, when students were not permitted to know their standing on tests they had taken. Fear was expressed that harm might be done if the truth were known. However, it is doubtless true that more harm is done when the facts are obscured than when they are faced squarely. In this regard we have certainly underestimated the capacity of youth to face facts. We do an injustice to a high school boy who dreams about becoming an engineer if we withhold from him the fact that his mental ability is too low, his aptitude and achievement in mathematics deficient, and his health too unstable to become a successful engineer,

[1] Prov. 11:14.

if indeed he is deficient in these regards. He will be grateful and he will be better adjusted and happier if he is encouraged to share in a frank evaluation of his potentialities in relation to the requirements of the engineering profession. It is possible, of course, to handle certain types of information unwisely, but if the principle is accepted that there can be no real sharing in solving problems without a full presentation of the facts, then the practice of tactfully "putting all the cards on the table" will certainly be followed.

People Involved in Effective Counseling.—The task of counseling would be relatively simple if the only relationships involved were those between the counselor and the pupil in the school. But father, mother, uncle, preacher, doctor, teacher, coach, and many other persons must be involved if the job is to be well done. Real self-reliance cannot be developed in a young person unless all hands cooperate to that end. Certainly, self-reliance that may be encouraged at home can easily be encountered by domination at school, and vice versa. Taking counsel together will involve all who have a stake in a problem or a contribution to make to its solution. And when the cards are put on the table, it is as necessary that parents and teachers face the facts squarely as that the youngster himself do so. One of the common shortcomings of school counselors is that they confine their work too largely to the pupils in the school and do not reach out to all others who must be involved if counseling is to be really effective.

Counseling Without Directing.—The modern school is not interested in setting up a service that will make youth's decisions for them, tell them what to do, and direct their planning. On the other hand, a service that will use the cooperative, sharing, nondirective approach is needed greatly. Growth in the capacity to make one's own decisions with increasing wisdom is the end that is sought. This can be achieved by encouraging youth to face their problems, marshal the facts, counsel with all who can help, and then determine a course of action. This type of responsibility will face each citizen of this country as long as he lives. The school should do its share in starting him on his responsible way.

2. Counseling in Relation to Our Educational Goals

There is a close relationship between the counseling movement and the goals of present-day education.

Adjusting Education to the Individual and His World.—In Chapter 3 the point was made that the central position of the individual in a democracy makes it mandatory on democracy's schools that they study carefully the characteristics of each school member in order that school experience can be brought better into line with individual needs. Furthermore, the society into which these people go should also be studied, and all possible steps taken to make school life dovetail into responsible community living. In the accomplishment of this task, the school will go far beyond the usual activities of the classroom teacher. Much information must be assembled about pupils, jobs, homes, curricula, schools, and so on. When the school sets about really to understand those whom it serves and to secure a favorable adjustment between them and their school and community environment, then it has accepted the counseling philosophy, the human approach. It will immediately find that there are new jobs that have to be done. Somebody must know which facts are most pertinent to assemble, what methods are most reliable in securing information, and how information is to be interpreted and used in securing the right change and direction in the individual, the school, and the community. This is the counseling approach; it is the conscious effort of the school to understand and adjust to the individual and his world and to bring about a better adjustment of the individual to his total environment. No educational goal could be more important.

The Fully Developed Person.—It will be remembered also from Chapter 3 that the present-day school accepts responsibilities for aiding in individual developments beyond the intellectual or scholastic. Clearly, if physical, emotional, social, and ethical developments are sought, then the school will promote many types of activities and services beyond those ordinarily found in the classroom. This, again, is the counseling, human approach; and the program of a good counseling service will contribute greatly to over-all personality development.

Eliminating Barriers.—As the counseling concept has taken hold in our schools, human concerns have been placed above some time-honored practices which now seem incompatible with the counseling concept. For example, the purposes and means of discipline have changed from the old retribution-example idea to the insight-self-discipline idea. Curricula, too, are losing some of their subjects-assorted-and-grouped characteristics and are being built more and more in line with what each pupil ought to have. Teaching methods are being adjusted more and more to the abilities, backgrounds, and needs of each child in the classroom. It is the counseling concept that is at the heart of these and many more changes. When the democratic doctrine of individual worth permeates the schools, then flexibility will supplant rigidity and the traditional barriers to adjusted education will disappear.

Again the point is made that the counseling movement is, shall we say, an invention born of the necessity of bringing our school practices into line with our educational objectives. It brings into tangible existence for the pupil the humanization of education which goes beyond the restricted education of long ago. Incidentally, it has been clearly shown that on the important matter of subject-matter mastery the pupils in the humanized schools of the present are superior to their counterparts in the drill-ridden schools of the past. The humanization of education does not penalize the pupil in his content learning.

3. Conditions Giving Rise to the Development of Counseling Programs

Numerous things have set the stage for the counseling movement and have rendered its development a near-necessity. Most of these things are characteristic of the twentieth century.

Increased Size and Diversity of Our School Population.—It is only relatively recently (1912) that the last of our states enacted a compulsory school attendance law. The projection upward of the permissible school-leaving age is also recent. Both of these have served to increase greatly our school population. The popularization of secondary and higher education has had its main growth in the last three or four decades. Prior to that time the secondary school and college groups were rather highly selected. Since that time, these groups have become greatly diversified and the secondary school group in particular has tended more and more to approach a cross section of our general population. Individual differences have become much more pronounced. Recognition of these differences and the knowledge that the occupational destinies of these young people will blanket the work of the nation have forced the issue of adjusting education to our nonselected school population. Long ago, in the seventeenth century, John Locke spoke wisely concerning this matter:

He therefore, that is about children, should well study their nature and aptitudes, and see, by often trials, what turn they easily take, and what becomes them; observe what their native stock is, how it may be improved, and what it is fit for: he should consider what they want; whether they be capable of having it wrought into them by industry, and incorporated there by practice; and whether it be worth while to endeavor it. For in many cases, all that we can do, or should aim at, is to make the best of what nature has given; to prevent the vices and faults to which such a constitution is most inclined, and give it all the advantages it is capable of. Everyone's natural genius should be carried as far as it could, but to attempt the putting another upon him, will be but labour in vain; and what is so plastered on, will at best fit but untowardly, and have always hanging to it the ungracefulness of constraint and affectation.[2]

We have too often been guilty, as we all know, of attempting to "plaster on" to certain children types of learning for which they are not suited and which fit them most "untowardly." Counseling programs, on the other hand, have been developed to assist in studying "their nature and aptitudes," "to make the best of what nature has given," and to carry their natural genius "as far as it could." To do this for every person in our schools is the measure of our educational responsibility.

Development of Instruments of Measurement and Evaluation.— Counseling services have been expedited also by the development of ways and means of securing vital and dependable information about people and their environment. Achievement tests, for example, by which a pupil's progress in the various fields of learning can be measured, are rather highly developed. Mental ability tests which are intended to indicate the strength or weakness of a pupil's intellectual endowment are improving all the time. Considerable progress has been made in constructing tests that will help in determining what special aptitude or capacity a pupil may have, such as musical, mechanical, or mathematical aptitude. Interest inventories are more and more common and their uses more and more understood. Personal and social adjustment tests are receiving much attention. Measures of physical growth and development are being perfected. Studies intended to improve our evaluation of growth and change in such things as personality and attitudes are continuously in progress. It is evident, therefore, that we have at hand ways and means of securing information about people that go far beyond merely what they have learned in the classroom. Other sources of valuable information, such as the physician, the psychiatrist, and the social worker, are always on hand also.

Similarly, great improvement has been made in the way we gather information about the communities in which we live. The survey technique has been greatly improved. Systematic approaches to the

---

[2] R. H. Quick, *Locke on Education* (rev. ed.; London: Cambridge University Press, 1884), p. 40.

study of such things as job conditions, social problems and institutions, and economic status and trends have been well developed. Even the details of good interviewing techniques have been studied. Vocational analyses, in which the characteristics, requirements, hazards, and rewards of vocations are determined, are well worked out.

Schools are lax in their responsibility if they do not use all the means at their disposal to understand better the persons and communities they serve. The development of better and better instruments of measurement and evaluation makes such improved services possible, adding great strength and point, of course, to the counseling movement.

Expansion of Educational Opportunities.—One of the outstanding characteristics of education in this country, particularly during the present century, is the rapid expansion of educational opportunities. A great number of different types of schools is available to the person who is pursuing his education, particularly as he gets into secondary and higher education. Furthermore, within many schools special fields of study have increased also. The very existence of this diversity in types of schools and patterns of study calls for earnest counseling with youth so that they may choose schools and programs that are most appropriate for them.

Expansion of Work Opportunities.—The relatively simple life of our Colonial forebears began to be more complicated as the Industrial Revolution got under way. With the advent of great inventions and of developments on industrial and commercial fronts, there arose a need for large numbers of workers in new jobs. The youth of today are, of course, witnessing changes that are more rapid and more sweeping than any seen previously. Airplanes fill the air, radio and television are commonplace, miracle medicines appear, and atomic stockpiles begin to be harnessed for uses that may affect deeply our basic manner of living. All of this affects jobs. New jobs arise; old jobs disappear. Social service jobs increase greatly; the blacksmith vanishes. Technical jobs multiply; the old way of farming dies. It is no simple problem to a young person to get his bearings in the world of work. There are over 40,000 job titles from which he can choose his life work. It is doubtful if there is anything done by the school that is more appreciated by youth today than serious, skilful vocational counseling.

Increasing Complexity of Society.—Man's inventions have always tended to extend the horizons of his living. The automobile, train, and airplane have gotten him out of his small neighborhood. The telephone, radio, photograph, newspaper, and television have brought the world to his door. He now clashes with all kinds of problems in a large number of places. His neighbors now are not only across the fence but across the street and across the ocean. He is subjected to all kinds of influences by many persons and groups. Fears born of his own inventive genius stalk him. He wonders about his family, his faith, his future. He may even entertain the distressing thought that freedom and security cannot exist side by side. Life is pretty complicated these days. Young people are squarely in the middle of it. The very nature of our society brings young people into contact with many problems earlier than used to be the case. The press, radio, and modern transportation have helped to bring this about. A great deal of skilful advertising and propaganda is aimed directly at youth. The pressures of special interest groups that clamor for allegiance and loyalty call for straight thinking if bias, intolerance, and a narrow-gauge sense of responsibility are to be avoided. In such an environment as this the school should do everything it can to help young people think critically and remain fearless and free.

Such are some of the conditions that have given rise to the development of counseling programs in our schools.

4. Nature of the Early Programs

As may be supposed, early counseling programs fell far short of the comprehensive programs that can be found in schools today. Naturally enough, they gave primary attention to the vocational problems of pupils, primarily placement. The problem a pupil faces when he is about to leave school is immediate and tangible. All through his school experience he has been confronted with "What are you going to do when you leave school?" Leaving school means going to work; but work at what? Assistance in the area of vocational preparation and placement was perhaps the first well-developed aspect of school counseling. Furthermore, in a way, it is the easiest area in which to work. A school can gather a good bit of information about jobs in the community and can actually make direct contacts with concerns that may employ pupils when they leave school. In addition, the concreteness of this kind of service appeals not only to pupils but to parents as well. The problem of determining carefully the vocational aptitudes of pupils, training them for appropriate work, and skilfully matching the pupils to jobs was not, of course, too clearly understood at first, and certainly not adequately met. For that matter, this problem is not solved today, although services along these lines are far superior to what they used to be. At any rate, the services of the earliest counseling programs clustered around the vocational problems of pupils.

5. Types of Counseling Problems

It is a far cry from the relatively narrow nature of the early counseling programs to the comprehensive programs today. Emphasis has been broadened to include many types of problems beyond those of a vocational nature. What are some of the problem areas that counseling services attend to? In other words, what kinds of problems can pupils find help with in schools with good counseling programs?

Vocation.—As mentioned above, one of the most universal problems that people encounter is that of choosing a vocation, preparing for it, and getting started in it. Until quite recently the school did relatively little in meeting this problem. Now, however, effort is made to help young people make wise vocational choices. They may take advantage of extensive testing services, may explore various types of work first hand, may read as widely as they care to among published materials about vocations, and so on. Furthermore, the school is not through when a vocational decision is made. It follows up to adjust the educational program so that adequate vocational preparation is secured, and it cooperates in securing appropriate work when the preparation is complete.

Education.—In former days when we did not have so many types of schools, when people spent fewer years in school, and when everyone in school did about the same thing, the problem of educational counseling was simple. Now, with our great variety of schools, of differing programs within schools, and especially our insistence that the educational experience of each child should be built to fit his needs, it is not so simple. Pupils are constantly facing such questions as: Shall I, or shall I not, take the college-preparatory course? Should I try to carry typewriting as an extra subject? Should I drop advanced algebra in order to have more time for French? Is it wise to study Latin if I plan to go into business? Which college should I go to? What are the entrance requirements and the tuition charges of the college up the river? Just what does one have to do to become a pharmacist or secretary or mechanic? How can I do better in the things I am studying? Should I please Dad and study dentistry or

take up aviation like I want to? All I want to do is farm; why go on
to high school anyhow? So it goes on endlessly. These are counseling problems of an educational nature. The sensitive school gives
serious ear to them all and tries diligently to work with pupils so that
when such problems arise their import will be made clear and the
right decision made.

Social Adjustment.—Today, problems of social adjustment in
pupils are attended to as earnestly as any other problems. And there
are many such problems. In fact, there are relatively few people who
are well adjusted and poised in all their social relationships. In many
cases, if proper care had been taken in younger years to develop social
poise and effectiveness, the tensions and insecurities of later years
would have been greatly reduced. It is the intention of the good
school to use the younger years to secure such adjustments. Hence,
the parties, the dances, the school plays, the organization of the classes
for much pupil participation, and many other activities take on a new
significance. If they are well supervised they can mean for many
pupils the development of satisfying types of social behavior that will
bring continuing happiness throughout life. Problems of social adjustment constitute one of the newer but no less important responsibilities of the counseling program.

Family Relationships.—Schools that have good counseling set-ups
and sympathetic counseling personnel find that inevitably they must
deal with problems involving the family relationships of pupils. In
fact, any counselor will say that there are hundreds of pupils who are
involved in unhappy or difficult family relationships and are in des-
perate need of an opportunity to air their problems before some sympathetic person. Many such pupils have no one outside the home with
whom they can talk confidentially, and they welcome the help and
stability of a good school counselor. In the strictest sense it may not
be the responsibility of the school to deal with these matters, and the
school has never sought to take over responsibility for them. It is
only a case of not turning away the troubled youngsters who are
plagued with such problems and who so frequently, with the helpful
assistance of counselors, establish goals and secure a perspective that
will see them through the uncertain years.

Activities.—School activities ought to contribute to the development of pupils and the enrichment of their lives. If this is to be
accomplished, they must be as carefully selected as the subjects of
regular study. Which activities are most likely to give Henry the

social development he needs? Should he choose dramatics or the radio club? In which activities can he do well enough to experience a feeling of equality in comparison with others? How many activities can he engage in without having his scholarship affected unduly? How can his activities be scheduled so that he can continue with the after-school job he must keep in order to buy the clothes his parents cannot afford to buy? Again, as the school attempts to make activities contribute to larger educational objectives, it will make systematic efforts to bring pupils into activities that are most appropriate and helpful to them. This is a type of counseling service that is relatively new; nevertheless, some schools have moved in this direction by placing the general oversight of school activities within the organization for counseling.

Attitudes.—It is quite common to find pupils in school who may have plenty of ability to succeed but whose attitudes toward school work and school citizenship are not good. Frequently such pupils are dealt with immediately as disciplinary cases and a long period of mutual endurance and unhappiness may ensue. Experience shows, however, that if some interested and responsible school person takes the trouble to seek out the reasons for existing attitudes, plans how better attitudes may be developed, and follows through with the plans, many, if not most, of these pupils become cooperative and entirely acceptable citizens in the school. Furthermore, it is usually found that not all the blame rests with the pupil. A home situation may be involved, cliques and gangs may be at fault, and even the classroom teachers may be a major reason for the bad attitude of the pupil. When such is the case, it is positively unfair immediately to turn the case into a disciplinary problem. Thus problems of attitudes and school citizenship are common fodder for the counseling mill.

Other types of counseling problems could be dealt with at length. Prominent among them would be problems of personality development, health problems, and personal problems involving courtship, morals, religion, and so on. It should be said again that the school does not seek to pre-empt any field so far as counseling is concerned. It just so happens that many young people, finding no other service within their reach, use the school's service extensively and appreciatively. School counselors frequently remark on the clear evidence that there are many pupils who have no source of help to which they may turn. It is not surprising, therefore, that they bring their endless variety of problems into the school.

6. Counseling as a Unified Activity

When counseling first became an organized program in the school, there was a tendency to look upon its services as separate and specialized. Vocational counseling, which was the main feature of the early programs, was a distinct type of service. Persons would specialize in vocational counseling. As other types of services developed, they too were quite distinct and were looked upon as additional specialized areas.

If some exaggeration can be pardoned, it was as though a pupil who needed a lot of help stopped at Room 22 for his vocational counseling, went on to Room 23 for his educational counseling, then to Room 24 for counseling concerning his activities, and finally to Room 25 for help on a social adjustment problem. Clearly, this kind of breakdown was no good. Fortunately, a strong reaction against it quickly sprang up, and the unity of the counseling problem began to be recognized.

It does not take a great deal of discernment to see how interrelated the aspects of a problem are or how unified human experience is. Good counseling procedures, therefore, hold the personal problem at the center of things. Suppose John has failed to make a vocational decision by the end of his sophomore year in college. Whoever counsels with him will find that making a vocational decision involves a hundred things that cannot be separated. His studies in school are involved. So are his intellectual ability, his finances, the attitude of his family, his health, and, who knows, maybe his height. Information on all such matters must be focused; it cannot be farmed out, as it were, with John passing himself around interminably until he despairs of ever finding himself. Furthermore, when John has made his decision, many parts must now fall into their rightful places. Proper educational plans must be made. Appropriate courses must be taken; perhaps a transfer to another institution will be necessary; and maybe a year or two of additional schooling will have to be arranged. Also it may be well for John now to get some useful experience through one of the school activities, like the school paper or debating. Dramatics might help, or swimming. Today's counseling, clearly, seeks not to become disintegrated nor to dangle; on the other hand, it seeks the same cohesion and interrelatedness as are always found in the problems that are dealt with and in the individual himself.

7. The Comprehensive Counseling Program

If one were asked to set up a comprehensive counseling program in, let us say, a secondary school, he would need to have a pretty good idea of what constitutes such a program. Or if a parent wished to know whether the counseling service in the local school were complete, he too would need to know what to look for. The following four items indicate in a general way just what is encompassed in the counseling services.

Facts First.—One of the sharpest responsibilities that a counseling service has is to assemble the information that will be used as the factual foundation of problem-solving. Many types of information should be on hand for all pupils. Their mental ability should be known, as should their pattern of studies at a given time and how well they are doing in those studies. Their home backgrounds should be known, at least in general, as well as the status of their health. Something of each pupil's interests and ambitions is important, also the manner in which he spends his spare time. Of course, much additional information can be gathered for all pupils if time and facilities are available. The school should stand ready to gather whatever additional facts seem to be needed in individual cases. It will be seen at once that a great deal of the testing in the modern school is part of an effort to have on hand information about individuals that will be useful in counseling.

Other types of information that do not deal with the individual are also necessary. Take jobs, for example. Facts about a great array of jobs should be available to pupils through the counseling service. What kind of preparation is required to enter specific vocations? What about wages? What are the hazards to health in certain jobs, and what opportunities for advancement exist? What kinds of jobs are there in the immediate community, and how many people are employed? Which are on the increase, and which are on the decrease? The counseling service needs to assemble much information about jobs.

The same holds for schools. About 25 per cent of high school graduates in this country go on to some other kind of school. In many individual high schools the percentage is much higher. The counseling service should make available extensive information about all the schools the graduates are likely to attend. If, again, it does not **have** such information on hand for a given school when a pupil makes inquiry, it should secure it at once.

Thus the fact-finding responsibility of a counseling service looms large. Every effort should be made to anticipate counseling problems and assemble as much information as possible ahead of time. Facts are foundational; they are step number one in counseling.

The facts to be used in counseling should not only be adequate; they should also be up to date. Dream College may have revised its entrance requirements recently, and it is no favor to a pupil planning to go there if the school counselor uses a two-year-old catalog as he plans a high school program with the pupil. Wages, too, change rapidly sometimes. So may the demand for employees in certain jobs. Facts need to be as current as possible.

In-School Counseling.—In-school counseling includes the whole array of problems and crises that pupils encounter while in school and in connection with which the facts referred to above will be used. Here is the school's extended effort to make available to pupils information and counsel that will be helpful. Significant problems growing out of such work with pupils immediately arise. Under what conditions is counseling most effective? What is a proper office arrangement for counseling? Who should counsel? What is the best procedure to follow during an interview with a pupil? When should assistance from parents, psychiatrists, social workers, or other professional people be called for? How can the pupil be led to face his problem, to use the facts wisely, and to make constructive plans? How can teachers, school officials, parents, and others be induced to alter school and home practices and requirements when it is clear that the pupil's welfare calls for it? What techniques may be employed to gain the confidence of pupils so that the opportunity for counseling may develop? What sorts of aids may be given to pupils, such as guides for effective study, information to freshmen, and exploratory testing that will help them to avoid certain problems in the first place? The second major aspect of a comprehensive counseling program, then, is the skilful handling of problems as they arise. This involves not only the cooperation of all who can help and the working-out of a favorable solution, but it must involve, above all, earnest sharing by the pupil in thinking straight about his own problems. Skill in human relationships must be manifested here. Nothing is routine.

It may seem rather strange to point out that in the counseling program the first function discussed above should precede the second. The assembling of information should precede counseling. This would not need to be emphasized so much if it were not violated so often. It is amazing how frequently a counselor is able to blueprint a young life in twenty minutes with only such information at hand as the pupil cares to supply. Such a practice violates again the principle that counseling is sharing, is weighing facts together, and is not making somebody's decisions for him. In-school counseling at its best proceeds only after the facts are in.

Placement.—There are still a few school people today who feel that the responsibility of the school to the pupil does not extend beyond graduation. Placement, they say, is the pupil's own lookout. However, a more common point of view holds that it is not fair either to the pupil or to society to drop a pupil as soon as he graduates. The school's long acquaintance with him should come to some use in securing appropriate placement after graduation. Hence, it is generally conceded that a counseling program is incomplete if it does not render the service of placement.

If the placement service is undertaken, it will necessitate a good and full listing for each graduate of such things as his special field of study, his vocational experience to date, his scholastic standing, the activities he has engaged in, the kind of employment he desires, and special items bearing on the work he can do, such as his physical condition, state of health, and the like. Such records should be completed prior to graduation so that placement may precede graduation and work can begin as soon after graduation as is desired.

Placement services also require an active and continuous contact with concerns that may employ graduates. Every effort is made to discover employment possibilities and to interest employers in considering the school's graduates as potential employees. Records such as those referred to above are supplied. Personal interviews between pupils and prospective employers are arranged.

Placement services will also be available to the nongraduate. Oftentimes pupils quit school prior to graduation and need to go to work. Sometimes also the pupils in a certain curriculum, such as the commercial or agricultural curriculum, can profit by working in an office or on a farm to give greater point and practicability to their training. The placement service can function here. Furthermore, some schools are now seeking work experience for all pupils prior to graduation. When this is undertaken, the sheer task of making arrangements can be appreciated. Here, too, the placement service can be used, but in this case a careful check should be made to see to it that the educational values sought in such arrangements are realized. Placement, therefore, the third function of a comprehensive counseling program, turns out to have rather broad dimensions itself.

Postschool Follow-up.—There are two outstanding benefits that result from postschool follow-up; the first accrues to those who have left the school, and the second accrues to the school itself.

If a school has a policy of following up on those who have graduated or dropped out, and if the follow-up is done by persons who are genuinely interested and wish to be helpful, then there will be many times when help can be given. Naturally, not all placements are perfectly made, and a worker's adjustment to his first job is not always favorable. The checkup by the school is ordinarily a most welcome thing, and on many occasions the school's representative can make suggestions to the worker or the employer that will lead to better adjustment all around. It should be borne in mind that such follow-up work as this must be done with the full knowledge and invitation of the employer. In no sense will the school supervise the worker on the job. The air is completely one of interest and helpfulness. Follow-up work, in addition, is an excellent way for the placement service to get a line on persons who are especially competent on the job and who can be recommended when more advanced jobs of greater responsibility come along. Finally, follow-up should be made on those who have gone on to school as well as on those who have gone to work. More than one student who has gone on to school has been encouraged to continue his studies by a simple interested inquiry from a former teacher, counselor, or principal at a time when the going was a little rough or the goals a little clouded. Follow-up, therefore, becomes something more than a mere check to determine the percentages of graduates who succeed or fail. It is, again, a campaign of helpfulness to all who have left the school.

The school also benefits from follow-up. If a business teacher follows up on the secretaries he has trained, he cannot help but observe the work they are called upon to do, the types of machines they must use, and the problems in human relationships they encounter. As the requirements of the job are viewed at first hand, the training program in the school is certain to be brought into review, and the stage for improvement is thus effectively set. So it will be in many areas, including also the schools that the graduates attend. Follow-up studies of students who have gone on to school have sometimes revealed certain common scholastic difficulties that stem from a weakness in the local school. These weaknesses might go on uncorrected, the preparatory programs in many areas might become seriously outdated, and pupils might go on indefinitely under a lagging curriculum if follow-up activities were not engaged in. Such activities can be the means of improved education, of bridging the gap between the school and the larger community of which it is a part.

A comprehensive counseling program is a project of major dimensions. Many of its activities are such as are not performed by classroom teachers. Its numerous services call for an organization which, to be sure, will use classroom teachers but which will also require specially trained people who know how to marshal the facts, will perform skilfully in the counseling situation, can carry on effective placement activities, and will follow up tactfully and helpfully on all who leave the school. In the entire process never once is sight lost of the fact that the whole thing is a cooperative matter, not a directive one.

8. Organization for Counseling

As indicated above, if counseling services are to be carried out properly, definite responsibility and organization must be provided. If a school contends that "of course we do all of these things" and then leaves them to the principal and teachers to accomplish "as the need arises," it is quite likely that the services are only incidental.

A complicated organization for counseling in a school is not necessary. Experience has demonstrated that a few things, however, are essential. In the first place, there needs to be an office in which counseling services are headed up. This office will be responsible for determining the over-all pattern, launching and coordinating the activities, and organizing the personnel. All personnel should cooperate continuously for the better understanding and operation of the services. It is considered wise for the responsible head to have an advisory committee, not too large, composed not only of school people but some community people as well.

Provision should be made also for certain kinds of pupil activities that can be carried on in groups. There is much that can be done in the way of studying vocations, testing, excursions, and so on that would require exorbitant time if carried on individually. The school administrator must be willing to schedule special classes if it seems desirable, arrange for many special group meetings, and permit groups to leave the school building when it is clear that this will be most helpful. Sometimes the homerooms in the schools are used for group counseling. In fact, in numerous cases the homerooms were established in the first place primarily as organizations for counseling. Some are used very effectively for this purpose, while others are not.

They are most effective when all homeroom teachers are part of an all-staff organization for counseling which gives concerted attention to the problem of how to make homerooms really function as centers of group counseling. After all, when a school provides responsible leadership for counseling, it should also be willing to make the adjustments necessary for effective group counseling.

The same can be said for individual counseling. There will be many pupils who will need help beyond that which can be given through group work. Special tests will need to be administered, contacts with homes and community agencies will need to be made, and special interviews with the pupils will need to be conducted. Here again, a definite understanding and provision needs to exist in the school for proper individual follow-up. If it is clear that a pupil needs special testing or counseling, then it should be possible to withdraw him from class if the need arises. Furthermore, and this is extremely important, counseling should be so arranged that pupils with special problems will have the cooperation and help of qualified people who can devote whatever time is necessary to see their problems through. Group counseling is an important service to render, but the school falls far short of its real job if it does not have the follow-through involved in individual cases.

Finally in the set-up for counseling, provision needs to be made for a good many activities of a specialized sort. These include such things as career days, visits to colleges and other schools, work with doctors, parents, psychologists, juvenile court officers, and others, and cooperation with all sorts of employers for purposes of work experience and placement. In other words, whatever can be done in school or out of school to bring pupils into contact with experiences or information that will help them solve problems that are common to all or specialized to some should be done with real purpose and system.

One does not have to be reminded that if a good counseling program is to be had, some extra money will have to be available. There will be added personnel costs, but these do not have to be great, as will be seen in the next section. Records will cost more because they will be better kept and more complete. Tests will be more widely used, and these will be an added expense. Some of the special activities will involve additional costs. Expenses of visiting speakers may have to be met, buses may have to be hired, and so on. Schools should be willing to invest in counseling. To say this, however, does not mean that schools should delay taking any action with reference to counseling until extra money is available. There is a great deal of counseling that can be done without entailing any added expenditures at all. The point is, if a good job is to be done, it will require a basic understanding of purposes, a good organization of services, good staffing, and adequate support. The resulting benefit to pupils is inestimable.

9. COUNSELING PERSONNEL

There has been a considerable shift with reference to the problem of personnel in counseling.

Earlier Practice.—It was the general practice in the earlier programs to restrict all counseling activities to specialized personnel. As we have seen before, there was a great deal of specialization for counseling in various fields, so that the regular teachers looked upon these services as beyond them and certainly not a part of their responsibility. In fact, it was sometimes made very clear to teachers that they were not to engage in any counseling activities. Pupils were to be referred to members of the counseling staff. This led, of course, to some ridiculous situations. Staffs that were too small were presuming to meet counseling needs by meeting pupils ten minutes a semester or under some such schedule. Furthermore, the tremendous overload of such short conferences meant that other services, including much-needed follow-up on individual cases, were neglected.

Later Practice.—As time went on and it became clearer that counseling programs were only one aspect of the larger job of adjusting education to the needs of everybody in school, it was realized that everyone had a stake in it. Certainly all teachers and all other school officials should understand the larger job and, as a consequence, should be willing to help. This idea took hold so well that counseling and education became fairly synonymous. This had a telling effect on ideas as to who was responsible for counseling. Specialized personnel no longer did it all. The entire school staff should share. The specialist, therefore, became the leader and coordinator of the whole group, making it possible for pupils who were moving along normally through school to receive their basic counseling from teachers who were interested in counseling and took their duties seriously. Thus the specialist, done with monopolizing counseling activities, became a leader and consultant to the larger group. He also realized that, whereas the teachers could counsel satisfactorily with most of the pupils, they could not be expected to handle the problem cases. He would himself take over such cases and follow through as was appropriate, using techniques and specialized services not familiar to teachers. Thus, all school personnel are becoming counseling personnel; and specialized personnel are becoming coordinators and consultants to whom a wide variety of special problems can be referred. Thus the number of specialized personnel that needs to be employed by a school is relatively small, and the resulting additional cost for this purpose is also small.

Incidentally, the nature of counseling is such that it is ordinarily not considered good practice to have the director of counseling responsible for the administration of the school. More specifically, it is probably not good for the high school principal to head up the counseling program. Common reference is made to the fact that the rapport that should obtain between pupils and counselors is not likely to obtain between pupils and one who holds final authority over them, particularly as pertains to discipline. By the same token, school officials should not ask counselors to assume disciplinary responsibilities. This does not mean that pupils who are disciplinary problems will not be referred to the counselors. They may be; and in many cases should be. But they will be referred for study, counsel, and help, not for the administration of justice.

Using All Who Can Contribute.—It is worth repeating that the counseling personnel should include all who have a contribution to make in the solution of a counseling problem. This, in many cases, will go beyond the regular school staff. Such persons as doctors, nurses, social workers, parents, ministers, psychiatrists, police, specialized testers, and others may be able to help immeasurably if they are consulted. They will not necessarily play the role of counselor, although they may; but they are often sources of information which no careful counselor will pass by.

Preparation of Counselors.—The number of persons who are trained as counselors and are employed in the schools is on the increase. In addition, the standards these persons are expected to meet are rising steadily. Actually, certification requirements in this area reflect the conviction that only highly qualified people should work at a job where problems of such great human consequence are dealt with so intimately. Persons of high ability, good insight and common sense, and real maturity are necessary. Their interest in this type of work should be genuinely deep-seated. They should see it as of great consequence to the individuals they serve, to the success or failure of democracy, and to the world.

A great deal of vocational experience is needed as a background for counseling. This experience might well include work in several different types of jobs. Teaching experience is also necessary. The supposition is that such experience has made the teacher familiar with the nature of pupils and their problems, has given him a chance to prove to himself that he is interested in such problems, and has also demonstrated that pupils will approach him for help. Frequently, and with considerable justification, a principal or superintendent in a school that wishes to set up counseling services will look about to see which teacher the pupils seem to respect and confide in most and will then suggest that this teacher take time off to get the specialized training necessary to organize and carry on the program. Such specialized training, of course, increases in extensity as time goes by. This, in turn, reflects the importance attached to the job. Fair familiarity with the world of work, a good groundwork in psychology with considerable attention to the nature of personality, a great deal in the field of testing and evaluation, clear concepts as to a good organization for counseling, and good counseling techniques are a few of the essentials in the specialized training. The personality development of the counselor himself is also exceedingly important, as is his emotional stability. He should be able to generate confidence in others and maintain poise, good nature, dignity, and clear purposes in his manifold dealings with all sorts of people.

Young people who are looking forward to a career in counseling should not be in a hurry. The rich satisfactions that will come as a result of having secured a good background of training and experience will more than repay for the added time involved. Neither should persons enter the counseling field who have not demonstrated to themselves and to others that they have the necessary human qualities, including a sincere willingness to break all the routines of a job, including its hours, when problems of human concern arise.

10. COUNSELING RECORDS

The point was made earlier that facts are foundational in counseling, and that counseling should proceed only after the facts are in. If such information is to be available when it is needed, then a good system of records will have to be maintained.

Types of Records Kept.—Records should be kept of all types of information useful in counseling. This includes the information that will be gathered for all pupils, such as their program of studies at a given time, their scholastic standing in all fields, their mental ability, their interests and aptitudes, their health status, something of their home background, the activities they engage in, and so on. There will be information also about certain pupils that has come to light in connection with special problems or incidents. Perhaps a pupil has held a certain leadership post, has accomplished something outstanding and been honored for it, has been involved in a school fracas, has been rated on tests individually administered, or has revealed marked personal characteristics or attitudes on certain occasions. These things should not be lost. If they are properly recorded and interpreted, their accumulation is likely in time to form the factual basis for some most vital subsequent counseling. The anecdotal record is intended to preserve this type of information. Under this system a separate folder is maintained for each pupil, and teachers and others who observe pupils closely are urged to drop into the folder short descriptive accounts of behavior they consider significant. Furthermore, a good record system will include reports of all the conferences held with pupils, including problems that were up for discussion, the outcomes of the conferences, plans of action that may have been laid, and the pupil's attitude throughout.

Records adequate to the placement and follow-up services of the counseling program should also be kept. In this connection, records relating to employment opportunities and to educational opportunities must be matched skilfully against records relating to the individual.

Almost everyone knows that in the past the typical school fell far short of the adequate records suggested in the previous paragraphs. However, as time goes on records are being expanded to tell, not only the story of the pupil's scholastic development, but of other aspects of his development as well.

The Cumulative Record.—One of the outstanding developments during the last few years, so far as records are concerned, is the cumulative record. This type of record is designed to carry the reports on a pupil for a number of years and not just for one semester or one year. Furthermore, the cumulative record is intended to follow the pupil as long as he is in school. If he transfers from one school to another or if he goes to another town to high school or college, his record goes with him. The comprehensiveness of the record is also important. It contains much more than the usual records that are kept on pupils. In addition to the pupil's name, sex, birth date, school, grade, mental age, chronological age, and so on, considerable information about the pupil's parents is given. The language spoken in the pupil's home before and after he was ten years of age and the types of communities he has lived in are indicated. His adviser, his attendance record, and his discipline record, if any, are given. Of course, his subjects, marks, and credits are shown, as are his scores and percentiles on achievement tests. Incidentally, on some such records the marks awarded by teachers and the scores on achievement tests do not always tally closely. Opportunity is given on the record to show the pupil's relative standing in various subject areas and to connect these standings to produce a curve over a number of years. In this manner a glance will tell the story of high standing, low standing, consistency, or fluctuation in any study that was continued for any length of time. Space is also provided for reporting on home influences and cooperation, mental and emotional characteristics, physical and athletic record, extracurricular activities and interests, notable accomplishments and experiences, and educational plans. Personality ratings by principals, counselors, or others qualified to judge may be entered also. It is evident, therefore, that the record is more complete than the usual record, and it is this very completeness that makes it such a valuable instrument for counseling. As the record becomes cumulative for several years, it becomes even more significant. Its use, as might be expected, is becoming more and more widespread. Some colleges, for example, are indicating that if the secondary schools will do a good job of keeping the cumulative record, they, the colleges, will use the record as the basis for admission. In the minds of many, it would be a good thing if the colleges would consider a few things contained in this record beyond scholastic standings in determining admissions.

Actually, the development and use of the cumulative record reflects our insistence that in our schools every individual must be accounted for. This record portrays an individual. It holds him, as it were, on a single card where a good look can be taken at him over a period of years, involving pretty much his entire personality. If one remembers the mass and variety of pupils that are found in our schools today, the magnitude of the task of keeping good cumulative records becomes apparent. However, the humanity and personal interest which the record typifies make its keeping a welcomed responsibility.

Availability of Records.—Records are kept to be used. Whatever information there is in them that will be helpful to anybody in connection with any problem should be available. This applies to pupils as well as to professional personnel. It does not mean that all records will be available at all times to all people. It does mean, however, that in general the school will proceed on the supposition that school personnel will use records wisely and that more good than harm will be done if availability is kept at a maximum. In line with this principle, many schools have actually centralized the records in the counselor's office rather than in the principal's office. If a school has a really good counseling service, the need for the records will concentrate in the counselor's office. They should first be as complete, accurate, and up-to-date as possible and should then be available for maximum use.

11. MAKING COUNSELING CONTINUOUS

Counseling is one way of putting into operation our idea that in the conduct of our schools people are more important than anything else. If we hold this view, then the school must be continuously interested in all pupils and always willing to help them. The pupil will not find himself the temporary charge of one teacher or one school, then passed on, with a kind of washing of hands, to another, with only a record of passing or failure in a few subjects to remain. The idea of continuous counseling changes all that. At every step as he progresses up the educational ladder, his achievement and development are noted. Whenever problems arise, help is at hand. His successful adjustment all along the line is sought. If he goes to another school, effort is made to have enough information go with him to secure his favorable adjustment there. Continuous counseling, therefore, involves the pupil in all his relationships, his passage from year to year and activity to activity in the school system, his continuation to further schooling, and his successful entrance upon a vocation. The well-adjusted, progressing individual is the goal.

What Do YOU Say?

1

It is not the responsibility of the schools in a democracy to educate children in line with the preconceptions of any faculty or institution but to encourage and assist them in the fine art of wise self-direction and searching self-evaluation.

What do YOU say?

2

Almost without exception young people in schools and colleges want good counseling services, and they appreciate them greatly when they get them. At present such services are so inadequate in the home and the church that the school must do its best to take up the slack.

What do YOU say?

3

What points in this chapter do you particularly support or take issue with?

Chapter 11

THE LEARNING-TEACHING RELATIONSHIP

The Kingdom Is Within

A great deal is known about learning and teaching. Much experimentation has taken place, and many books have been written. Much of the writing is technical and detailed, albeit significant and useful. Furthermore, learning and teaching are often discussed separately. It will be the purpose of this chapter to garner some of the more basic and useful concepts concerning both and to hold them in relationship as the discussion progresses.

1. BREADTH OF THE PROBLEM

Not Limited to Schools.—When learning and teaching are referred to, one is immediately inclined to associate them with schools. A good many parents whose children go off to school every day do not realize that their effectiveness with their children would be greatly increased if they knew and practiced a few basic concepts about learning and teaching. Similarly, in a thousand other situations, things would be better if good learning-teaching practices were observed. This does not mean that the school's practices in this regard are always good. They are not. The school itself stands in urgent need of putting into practice basic principles that are already known. The point is, learning-teaching problems are not confined to the school. Life all about us is filled with them. Consequently, whatever useful principles we may be able to clarify can be broadly applied.

Some Areas of Application.—If we should try to enumerate all the situations in which one person seeks to learn and another seeks to assist him in his learning, we would never get through. Start out for yourself.

1. Parent-child and numerous other home relationships
2. The whole program of religious education in churches
3. Labor-management relationships
4. Foreman-worker relationships

5. The education of workers in labor unions
6. Politics and political campaigns
7. Boy Scouts, summer camps, 4-H Clubs
8. Community councils and parent-teacher groups
9. Service club activities
10. Salesmanship and advertising
11. Armed forces recruiting and training
12. Press, radio, stage, and screen
13. International relations

We are all constantly involved in learning-teaching situations. What are some of the more basic principles that can be put to work to improve our whole living?

2. Earlier Ideas Concerning Learning

Nature of the Earlier Concepts.—At one time the mind was thought to be entirely dissociated from the body. It was very much akin to the spiritual, largely out of reach, and improvable pretty much in the same way that man sought to improve his soul. It was a kind of entity set apart that waited to be attended to. After the idea of the separation of mind and body broke down and the unity of the two was accepted, the mind was still thought of pretty much as a wax tablet on which impressions could be made by an outside influence. Sometimes it was referred to as a piece of white paper waiting to be written upon. It was also likened to a cistern; and pupils were admonished to attend carefully to their instruction so that "not one drop that fell from the lips of the teacher" would be lost. The sponge idea also had its day. The mind could "soak up" and hold learning. Such a concept, although it may not be held by many teachers today, nevertheless seems rather closely in line with examinations or "squeezing" procedures used by so many. Examinations that are properly constructed and wisely used are excellent learning experiences, but when they are used merely as a means of getting back what has previously been "poured in" and presumably "soaked up," they are indeed a magnificent "squeeze," and students can be excused when they come out of them as a sponge does—white from pressure and whistling for air. Finally, the mind was sometimes likened to a post office with many pigeonholes into which items of information could be appropriately placed.

Reference to the mind as a kind of post office suggests at once a psychological concept that was only recently dispelled. This was the so-called faculty psychology. Under this concept the mind was made up of various faculties, such as memory and reason, which could be separately trained and developed and, once developed, would function efficiently in all situations. The present doctrine of the unity of the personality and of the totality of the organism in all its reactions has, of course, displaced the faculty idea.

It is important to observe in the earlier concepts outlined above that learning was largely passive. Learning was receiving; a kind of waiting to be impressed or filled up or cultivated. The conditions of learning pertained to improving reception, to the discipline of acceptance, and to drill in line with assignments.

Implications for Teaching.—The idea that learning is receiving certainly has its implications for teaching. Under this idea the teacher, the parent, or the foreman takes on the role of the informant. Conditions favorable to the informant are insisted upon. Order must be maintained; everyone must pay attention. The informant sets the tasks for the learner, and the learner does his best to conform. The teacher "pours it in," and the pupil is expected to remember. The constant harangue in school and out of school is: "Listen to what I am telling you," "Can't you remember what I told you last month?" and "Just do as I say and ask no questions." Adults shake their fingers in the faces of youngsters and say, "I want to impress this upon you," just as though learning were directly related to the amount of outside pressure exerted. The learner seems to be there to "take it," the teacher to "dish it out." The lecture method reflects this point of view. Too many classroom lecturers have insisted that: "My job is to give it to 'em; whether they get it or not is no concern of mine." When learning is thought of as a passive, receptive sort of thing, teaching takes on the role of supplying the information, setting the task, and exerting the pressure.

3. Present Concept of Learning

The Principle of Self-Activity.—Today's idea concerning learning is almost the opposite of the earlier concepts. Learning is directly tied in with our behavior. It is activity. Learning will not take place unless the organism reacts and is motivated to solve its own problems. The drive for learning issues from the inside, not the outside. There is no learning unless the learner himself is active, is challenged, and sees good reason for what he is doing. Self-motivation, therefore, is one of the essential conditions of learning.

Learning Imbedded in the Nervous System.—We now know that one's capacity to learn is not determined by whether or not he was lucky in having a good "mind" pent up in his body when he was born. The capacity to learn is an aspect of our physical equipment. This physical equipment includes a nervous system that is sensitive, complex, and modifiable. Certain wants, drives, and purposes are present. If all these are highly developed, the learning potential is high; if they are deficient, the potential is low. Low learning ability does not indicate that the wrath of the gods is responsible any more than high ability indicates the favor of the gods. They both indicate a certain set of physical conditions, and wise people will respect such conditions for what they are and will expect no more or less than is justified.

It is each individual, then, with his particular learning equipment, who is the starting point in learning. It is important, too, to visualize this individual as confronted with a multitude of problems and challenges as the days and years go by. If he meets a problem and has a desire to solve it, the stage for learning is set—and it is not set until such a desire is present. If he actively attacks the problem and finds the solution and is able to reach the solution more quickly each time the problem recurs, then he has learned. Learning, then, is solving problems through action and practice. It is the change in the organism which occurs as it adjusts to problem situations.

It is most necessary to realize that learning involves an active organism rather than a passive one; it is the organism reaching out to solve more and more problems in its environment. This attitude of self-generated attack is most fundamental. It is not a matter of waiting, of submitting, of being a cistern. Organisms of this sort are not adaptable and are overcome by their environment. It is a matter of going to meet the problem, of finding, testing, and fixing solutions. Learning broadens the organism's experiences and intensifies its sense of well-being through solving its problems. Such successful experiences in adaptation give us great satisfaction. These satisfactions, in turn, cause us to welcome more challenges. And so it goes: challenge, action, solution, adjustment, and satisfaction. When this stops, learning and growth have stopped, and so has the joy of living. It all adds up to a motivated organism finding solutions to problems it has accepted as its own. It is moving out to get the answers rather than sitting back and waiting to be told. And, again, the capacity to adapt in this manner is embodied in a physical structure that is modifiable, one that can be studied, and one in which the changes and processes involved can be observed and measured. Learning is as tangible as that.

Learning, or Problem-Solving Diagramed.—Figure 8 below was first presented by a well-known psychologist, Dr. John Frederick Dashiell, to illustrate what takes place in a problem or learning situation. Examine the figure; then let us suppose that someone you know

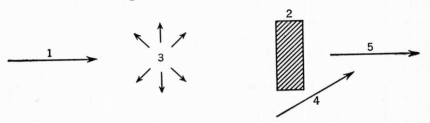

Figure 8. Problem-Solving [1]

(1) The motivated organism. (2) The problem, obstacle, or difficulty. (3) Excess and varied activity. (4) One of the ways of acting proves successful. (5) the goal is reached, the problem is solved, the obstacle is overcome.

confronts you with a puzzle of twisted nails or wire that you have never seen before (No. 2 in the diagram) and bets you that you cannot take it apart. You immediately accept the challenge (No. 1) and start out. You twist, turn, and pull at the pieces (No. 3); having no previous experience to guide you, and with no particular plan of approach, you waste a lot of motions and wonder if maybe you are stuck. Your motivation continues, however, and you work away. Finally, and perhaps very much to your surprise, a certain twist you give permits the pieces to come apart (No. 4). You hold up the pieces and say, "I told you I could!" (No. 5), and you probably experience considerable satisfaction from your feat. But wait. Your friend retrieves the pieces, holds them behind his back, puts them together again and then says, "Do it again." If you fiddle and fuss (No. 3) the same amount the second time as you did the first, you have not learned. Learning has not taken place unless when the problem arises again it can be solved with less time and effort. This reduction in time and effort continues with practice to the point of habit or fixed response, and the only limitation to further reduction is in the nature of the neuromuscular system itself. It actually means that all the arrows in No. 3 are eliminated except the right arrow, which is No. 4. Immediately when the problem presents itself anew the solution is known. There is no random or wasted activity. Thus the proper twist to the puzzle is immediate, the answer to two plus two is automatic, and the note on the musical score is immediately translated into the proper motor response.

[1] From *Fundamentals of Objective Psychology* by J. F. Dashiell. Copyright, 1928, by Houghton Mifflin Co. and used with their permission.

The pattern of learning illustrated in Figure 8 applies to all the problems we encounter, no matter how simple or complex they may be. No. 2 in the diagram may be learning to walk, working a puzzle, spelling a word, throwing a curve, solving a mathematics problem, getting elected to office, disciplining children, preventing strikes, or any one of a thousand other things. In all these situations there is a response or behavior that will solve the problem more acceptably than other responses and will yield more satisfaction because it results in better adaptation and adjustment.

It must be remembered that the whole process of meeting and solving our problems through selective behavior is made possible because of our physical make-up, which in turn retains the effects of behavior and will be modified further as experience accumulates. It is this extreme complexity, sensitivity, and modifiability of the human organism that renders man so educable.

Developing the "Laws" of Learning.—Most of the controlled experimentation relating to learning has been carried on during the last forty or fifty years. These studies have contributed information that is basic and fundamental. The primary concern during the first part of this period was to determine what goes on in the nervous system when learning takes place. If this were known, then the conditions most favorable to learning could be discovered. The well-known "laws of learning" resulted from this kind of inquiry. The work of E. L. Thorndike is outstanding in this regard. Thorndike's laws of exercise, effect, and readiness, based squarely on the nature of the nervous system, have had a tremendous influence. The law of exercise states that the more an act is repeated the more the resistance in the nervous system that accompanied the initial performance of the act is reduced and the act tends to become habitual. Conversely, if a learned response is not used, resistance in the nervous system tends to be restored and the response becomes less automatic or less habitual. Clearly, this law of learning is closely connected with the problem of drill. At first glance it might appear as though drill, drill, and constant repetition were the primary condition of learning. But it is quite as possible to impede learning through drill as to expedite it. The law of exercise has numerous corollaries dealing with such related matters. The law of effect states that the organism tends to repeat the actions which give it satisfaction and to avoid those that are annoying. The people who believe that tasks should be made as distasteful as possible are on the wrong track if they are interested in having people learn or wish to have them continue in what they are doing. Care should be taken here to make sure that "giving satisfaction" is not interpreted to mean "being easy." If difficulty is superimposed for its own sake, then learning is likely to be reduced; but the most difficult task can be the most satisfying if the learner has been motivated to attack it with interest and challenge instead of being driven to it. The law of readiness states that if an organism is ready to act and is prevented from acting, the result will be annoyance. On the other hand, if an organism is ready to act and is permitted to act, the result will be satisfaction. It is apparent from this that learning is not aided when the learner is dominated, subdued, hounded, threatened, and forced to work against his will. More constructively, that time is well spent which is used to set the stage for learning, to bring learners to see the nature and significance of the task to be done, to accept the problem as their own, and, above all, to generate real curiosity, challenge, and enthusiasm for it.

Discussion could go on almost indefinitely about the developments that have been made as experimentation concerning learning has progressed. Certainly not all the answers are in; and the passing years bring new information and changing emphases.

Present-Day Emphases on Motivation.—If there is one thing emphasized above all others today in the field of learning it is the matter of motivation. Here again, attention is turned to the self-activity referred to in an earlier section. There can be no learning unless there is activity on the part of the learner. The stage for learning is not set until the organism moves to attack its problems. Such attack will not come unless impelled by firm motivation. The laws of learning defined rather well the nature and conditions of learning, but they did not emphasize the self-drive that must be present if learning is to progress. And yet, the relationship of motivation to the laws seems almost a matter of ordinary common sense. Keeping in mind the laws of exercise, effect, and readiness, it makes good sense to say that meaning, interest, and purpose must be back of drill or it will be a dusty humdrum; we must see to it that our children and workers and pupils get real satisfaction out of what they are doing if we are to expect them to wish to continue and improve in their work and studies; and it is stupid to try to force learning upon a person when there is no readiness in his system. Undergirding all these laws, then, is the primary necessity for motivation. An organism doesn't even start to learn until it is motivated to act. It's like a steam engine. That beautiful piece of machinery whose workings we may understand isn't going to get very far down the track unless enough pressure to drive the pistons has been built up on the inside. One doesn't make an engine go by shouting at it; he builds a fire in it. Neither does one make children learn by shouting at them; rather, he builds up the fires of motivation within them. These motivations will induce them to do their own learning.

Implications for Teaching.—On page 316 some brief comments were made concerning the implications for teaching of the earlier concepts of learning. What are the implications of our present concept?

Certainly today the teacher cannot be viewed as one who wields the stylus, as the "filler-upper," or as the one who makes decisions as to what others will do and then constitutes himself as a policeman to see that they do it. The skilful teacher is one who sets up an environment favorable to learning. He stimulates self-drive in others. He seeks to establish the attack attitude toward problems that are understood and accepted. But he does more than that. The good teacher sees to it that the learner has within his reach the resources for a successful solution to his problem. If the learner succeeds in his task, he will experience satisfaction and will come back for more. If he is stymied and cannot find a solution, he will experience annoyance and a feeling of futility, and the motivation for further activity in this direction will tend to disappear. Good teaching requires the adaptation of tasks to the capacity of learners to meet them. Success is the essence of learning, and teachers or others who, in the name of "standards," blindly set tasks that are beyond the capacity of the learner to perform are actually violating the individual and should not be teaching at all. Good teachers always accept and work with the learning equipment they find in those they teach. In learning, the organism moves out to meet its problems. In good teaching, the teacher cooperates in this moving-out process, to develop its power and work for its success.

Let us return for a moment to Figure 8, page 318, in which learning, or problem-solving, was diagramed. One point concerning good teaching deserves emphasis. Teachers bear a heavy responsibility to see to it that as learners face new problems the right solutions are initially arrived at. This is No. 4 in the diagram. In the case of the wire puzzle, only one solution was possible, and it was the right one. However, in many problems more than one solution is possible. Not all the solutions are equally acceptable, and one may pick unacceptable solutions and fix them through practice. For example, it may be that when I was a child and found it necessary to write the word "government," I solved the problem by putting down the letters

G-O-V-E-R-M-E-N-T. Nobody checked me; so I did it the same way again and again until that particular solution became my habitual response whenever I was confronted with the necessity of spelling the word. So it can go in numberless situations. Unacceptable responses can become fixed. The responsibility of the teacher in cooperating with the learner to get the right solution to start with is great indeed. How do you feel when your history teacher is not well informed and may even give incorrect answers to your questions? How about the foreign-language teacher who could not pronounce correctly the words of the language he taught, or the piano teacher who taught you a fingering technique that had to be laboriously changed later on? And just how do you feel toward the elementary school teacher who let you get away with "murder" in your reading, writing, and arithmetic? This failure to establish the right solutions to begin with becomes particularly serious when one realizes that it is harder to change a response that has once been learned than it is to establish the response to begin with. In other words, it is easier to learn to spell "government" correctly when the need first arises than it is to change from G-O-V-E-R-M-E-N-T to G-O-V-E-R-N-M-E-N-T after the first pattern has become habitual. The importance of selecting and fixing the right solution to the problems we face is apparent; and teachers, parents, and others have an urgent responsibility in this connection.

The prominent place of motivation in learning holds great significance for teaching. One has not even begun to be a teacher until he has accepted the necessity of setting up the conditions that will motivate the learner to learn. The problem is not one of requiring youngsters to sit still and listen; rather, it is one of getting them going on things they see good reason for doing. Teacher activity should be aimed at securing pupil activity. The good teacher's concern is not "What can I talk about today?" or "Do I have notes enough to carry me through the period?" It centers on "What are the worth-while activities we can engage in today?", "What can I do to get the youngsters to take hold?", and "What are the resources I should make available to them as they go to work?" Unless the learner generates some drive of his own, is motivated to tackle his own problems, precious little learning will result. It is this motivation or drive that constitutes the morale of an army. It is the thing the coach tries to secure through his pep talk between halves. It is the pride of the good workman and the thing that causes children to cooperate because they want to rather than because they have to. It is the thing sought for in workers when incentive pay arrangements are set up. In all this, the teacher or parent or leader cooperates rather than dominates. He first helps the learner to generate real drive from within and then aids him as he moves along.

The present-day concept of learning, then, requires that we view the learner not as a passive cistern waiting to be filled up but as an organism that learns only if it acts. Good teaching seeks to secure self-activity on the part of the learner, cooperating with him as he moves to the solution of his own problems.

4. THE SIGNIFICANCE OF MEANING IN LEARNING

Learning is expedited if it is accompanied by meaning. Try memorizing the following:

> Er ek zid res bekquizessic otciction,
> Rerecputma laz bo ect sakmecask snare.

Now try this:

> Her blushes rose so faintly;
> She was much enthralled;
> But then he tipped his hat—
> And his head was bald!

In the first example you struggle in vain for recognition, for something to get hold of, for something that makes sense. The very last word offers hope enough to drive you back to try again for a connection, but in spite of your efforts you can't build the syllables into a meaningful whole. In the second example there is something to get hold of; ideas come to light; the effort to find the meaning is successful, and the result is real satisfaction. So you go back and repeat; the ideas fall into a pattern, and learning becomes easier—much easier than in the first example. This is why it is important when learning prose or poetry to first read for the ideas in the whole selection, or in significant portions of it. To repeat a line a hundred times without seeing it in context and then to take another line and do the same is time wasted. To find the meaning is to provide the objective; the problem is located, and the stage for learning is set.

It will be seen immediately that discovering meanings is an aspect of motivation. Take the first example above. The futile hunt for meanings is like an army fighting an enemy that it cannot find. One cannot generate much enthusiasm for this. However, once the enemy, or the idea, is located, then the situation has focus and the attack is on. There is something to drive at. Things have sharpened up.

Implications for Teaching.—The practical aspects of the importance of meaning in learning are manifold. Suppose you are a teacher or a parent and you make a new assignment in the classroom or ask a child in the home to perform a task. Do not be disturbed if the youngsters begin to ask questions immediately about why or how, or what it involves for them. Actually, what they are seeking for is meaning, clarity, something around which they can marshal a little enthusiasm. To be impatient with a reasonable array of these questions and to fail to come forward with good answers is to deny to the youngsters the understanding and motivation that will cause them to go to work under their own drive. Most adults will complain bitterly if they must work in the dark or see no sense to what they are doing. Children, under similar circumstances, may not be permitted to complain like adults, but they suffer the same mental anguish nevertheless.

Consider the place of the meaning or significance of work to persons in industry or business. Workers who have it produce more and improve on the job. Those who don't have it waste more time, are absent more, change jobs oftener, and may never improve. The story is told of a group of workers during the war who worked in a small factory and made nothing but one small part of an airplane motor. The work was tedious, and the sameness and simplicity of the single part were distracting. Someone had the wise idea of loading the workers into buses and taking them to an airport where powerful planes took off for foreign ports and others came down out of the far sky and landed. They were permitted to examine the motors in these planes, and they saw the very part that had come from their own benches. According to the story, these workers, with a brand-new sense of the meaning of their work and a clear idea of its importance, increased their production sharply, improved in their skills, and had a lot more fun doing it. To be sure, learning is aided if it is accompanied by meaning. In all teaching-learning relationships, the teacher should dispel as much darkness as possible, assist in making the goals clear, making the pursuit of learning worth while.

5. LEARNING, IF POSSIBLE, SHOULD BE CARRIED ON IN THE "USE" SITUATION

Learning Must Go On to Application or Expression.—Since, as we have seen, learning is action, it follows that learning which involves application or expression is incomplete until such application or expression is made. Learning should be pursued to the point of application. Pupils who can work the problems in board feet in the arithmetic book but who stand helpless in the school yard when asked to compute the requirements of a proposed board walk have not completed their learning because they cannot apply it. And have you ever been in the presence of a person who, when trying to explain something to you, will say, "I know, but I can't tell it"? Or he may say, "You know what I mean" and give up on the whole matter. It's annoying. The facts are that he does not know what he cannot give expression to.

Implications for Teaching.—The idea that learning must go on to the point of application or expression has far-flung implications. It actually lies back of the present demand in our country that education draw nearer to the realities of life. The old idea of education as "culture," in which diligent effort was actually made to stay away from life "as it is known in the midst of the living of it" is being replaced by a firm demand that the school come down to earth and contribute directly to improved and enriched living. Let's be specific. Science instruction is not only for scientists. It ought to be adapted to the needs of every citizen so that each can live more successfully in a scientific age. Health instruction in the schools is useless if it involves only textbook learning. Health instruction must be linked to actual health practices. Instruction in government and citizenship too often results in knowledge "about" things rather than in the ability to "do" things. Sharp challenge has been given to more than one college instructor to show that he can apply his instruction in a practical situation. The challenge is a good one because his students are earnestly seeking assistance in doing just that. The field projects and the cooperative plans between schools and industries are a direct result of the effort to relate learning more closely to the "use" situation. The hospital experience of nurses in training, the field work of the social worker, and the student theater follow the same line.

Industry and business have been far ahead of the school in placing their instruction on an application basis. But even they have done far too much telling and not enough actual doing. The foreman who will first make a few basic things clear to the worker and will then start him carefully on the job and supervise him during the early stages of his work is on the right track. The churches have gotten the idea too. It is no longer sufficient just to learn the scriptures and pray. The social gospel seems to insist that religion be translated into better conduct, better business relations, more kindness and helpfulness. "By their works ye shall know them" and not by the creed they repeat. Life in the home presents numberless opportunities for relating learning to realities. The Boy Scouts, the 4-H Clubs, and camping groups owe much of their strength to the tangibleness of the things they learn. Even the gap between the so-called pure and applied sciences is being reduced because of the realization that science has not made its complete contribution until its discoveries have taken on significance for living. The discovery of atomic fission and fusion is no more "pure" than putting these to work in a transoceanic liner. Learning in the "use" situation, therefore, has implications that project strongly into many aspects of our living. The reader will go on for himself.

Use Should Follow Close upon Learning.—We sometimes show very poor judgment in the things we expect and require others to learn. People should learn those things that have meaning and application now. It is foolish and actually unfair to say to a child, "Now learn this because you will need it after you have grown up." Use should follow close upon learning; in fact, if learning has no significance or use at the moment for the learner, it should be postponed. Considerations of this sort should bear heavily upon parents, teachers, and others. They are, of course, exceedingly important to all who are concerned with the building of the school curriculum. Ideally, learning should accumulate during the years to give the organism the best possible continuing adjustment to the problems in its environment. To get away from that environment at any stage is wasteful.

6. Individual Differences in Learning Ability

The Fact of Differences.—The fact of individual differences in learning ability does not need to be argued. The inmates of our feeble-minded institutions and the geniuses in our society point up the range of abilities. In the American public elementary school, where compulsory attendance laws require the attendance of almost a complete cross section of our people, intelligence quotients ranging from 70 to 140 are common. Intelligence quotients as low as 40 have been reported, and, of course, others above 140 have been reported also. On the whole, persons having intelligence quotients of about 140 and above constitute the genius group; and those below 70 are feeble-minded. Every teacher, parent, religious worker, or manager is continuously confronted with the problem of how to adjust to these marked differences in the ability to learn. The fact of differences is known and never questioned; adjusting to the differences is another matter.

For a good many years a controversy has raged as to whether differences in mental ability are only general or unitary in nature or whether they may be specialized also. Some people contend that two persons with the same general mental ability may have markedly different specialized abilities or capacities. In other words, people may have not only a general ability to learn but within that general ability there may be areas of special or primary abilities also. One investigator, L. L. Thurstone, announced around 1935 that he had identified nine primary abilities. Other investigators have contended that seeming differences in aptitude are not due to specialized factors in intelligence but to environmental factors such as childhood influences, training, motivation, interest, and so on. This group cites numerous cases in which persons of apparent genius in one field showed similar ability in other fields when the circumstances called for it; that is, when the environmental circumstances called forth the capacity which was presumed not to be there at all. Clearly, though, people differ in their ability to learn; and whatever refinements can be made in discovering and describing these differences will be valuable.

Implications for Teaching.—If one believes that intelligence is unitary and that the presumed special abilities of people are not actually primary factors in intelligence, he stands in danger of committing a fundamental educational error. He may say to himself that since the differences in special abilities among children of the same general ability are not fundamental in nature, the school experiences can be identical for all, just so long as they are pitched to the general ability level of the group. Such a practice, although it might seem to be in line with the theory, would fail to take note of one of the most important principles in all education, namely, that the starting point in teaching is not only how people learn, but, as well, what they are as a result of their previous experiences. Good teaching adapts to environmental differences as well as to inherent ability differences.

The old idea of standards can hardly stand up if one takes the matter of differences in learning ability seriously. The practice of setting up a standard for all in a group and giving passing or failing grades to individuals in terms of the standard becomes rather silly. This is particularly true for the typical public school with its complete sampling of the children in the community. Furthermore, the teacher who constantly nags at a slow pupil in the room and chides him because he does not do the same kind of work as the brightest pupil shows an ignorance that is not only deep but abusive. Parents sometimes make the same mistake by urging one of their children to be like another; but in the next breath they will tell you they "wouldn't have believed that two children in the same family could be so different." The fact of differences is causing us to set up standards for each individual in place of a single standard for all.

When one talks about adjusting standards to individual differences, he greatly complicates the teaching situation, but he is moving toward an educational potential we have yet to realize. The losses caused by hopeless failure and lack of challenge involved in the single standard are replaced by the gains that result from suiting the learning challenge to the learning capacity. In this way everyone learns as he is able to learn instead of being deprived of the privilege of learning because he is not able to do a given uniform job or is not challenged by it. It is clear, then, that breaking away from the old uniform standard for all and substituting individual standards is, in fact, raising standards and not lowering them. Certainly, anything that results in more learning is a rise in standards even though fewer failures in the old sense may be reported. The point is, learning capacity ought to be used, whether it be high, low, or in the middle; and it will be best used if it is attended to individually.

"Getting by" is an aspect of adjusting standards to differences. Frequently teachers, parents, and others are satisfied with a certain minimum accomplishment in things they have asked others to do. When this is known, children, and adults too, are likely quickly to determine what the minimum is and to do that much and no more. This certainly is not making use of learning capacity, and it is likely to result in attitudes and habits that will never permit the individual to become what he ought to become. On the other hand, if individuals are encouraged to work up to their capacity and if they will do so under their own drive, then society is not going to be deprived of their best contribution. Again the importance of motivation becomes apparent. People will not work and learn up to their capacity unless they have plenty of self-drive. The mere knowledge by the teacher or the foreman that the pupil or the worker can do better work, plus the external pressure that he must do better, will not get results. Motivation or purpose must be there. If they are present, "getting by" ceases to be a problem. Teaching, then, is more a matter of arousing internals than of applying externals.

Some of the implications associated with differences in the ability to learn and perform strike deep into our society. What about workers? Is it right for labor unions to establish a uniform work prescription for, let us say, all bricklayers when, as we know, bricklayers differ in their performance abilities? Does something devastating happen to the pride, conscience, and inner drive of the skilled and competent workman when he is required not to do his best? Can any benefit ever result when policies are adopted which deny to individuals the prideful experience of doing their best at all times? On the other hand, is management justified in expecting all workers to work up to their various productive capacities and then pay them all a uniform and perhaps a minimum wage? Is there a way to promote honest and prideful work on the part of all and to tie wages to production rates and profit take? Is not the moral obligation to develop and use the abilities that we have basic in any economic, political, or social order? Is it not right and reasonable to apply in everyday life the same observance of working up to capacity that we insist on in the schools? It may be that, as time goes on, some of the things we know about the conditions under which man learns and lives best will find far-reaching application throughout all our living.

7. INDIVIDUAL AND GROUP LEARNING

Group Learning a Misnomer.—Of course, strictly speaking, there is no such thing as group learning. All learning is done by individuals. However, group situations can easily motivate individual learning. A group is actually an external which can be used or abused, can be an asset or a hindrance, in promoting learning by individuals. Frequently individuals who have found no particular motivation to follow through on learning activities have found much motivation in favorable group situations. The teacher or leader who can hold the group situation in this perspective and will not permit group objectives to overshadow or obliterate individual objectives is acting wisely. The real issue remains that of releasing individuals to learning activities that are appropriate to them and to which they attend personally. Individual learning is the goal; group situations may become a technique.

Cooperative Techniques Are Important.—It should not be drawn from the above that there are no situations involving more than individual interests. There are. As has been said before, the very technique of how individuals can work together effectively has received too little attention in our schools. So-called group projects involving cooperative action are excellent. But such projects cannot succeed unless each individual sees the point of the whole thing and willingly does his share. This, in fact, is a primary characteristc of democracy.

The recent movement in "group dynamics" does not contend that groups in some way have a kind of separate existence; its real essence, rather, is to make individuals dynamic as they interact and cooperate among themselves.

Implications for Teaching.—People who make use of group situations to stimulate individual learning need to be careful lest they fall into an easy error. It is easy to let the group goal predominate. For example, the spelling class may be divided into the reds and the blues, and immediately everyone wonders if the reds or the blues will win. The teacher may join in; and while he promotes the contest, the real spelling difficulties of a lot of children may be woefully neglected. Norms on standardized tests present something of the same difficulty. Schools or classes within schools may constantly wonder how they compare with the norms. To teach with this kind of group standard in mind is, of course, baseless. Let the teacher get back to the task of helping each youngster do the best he can. This will involve competition and standards, but it will be competition against his own record and a standard based on his own abilities. Some of the best teaching in the land is done by teachers who are helping low-ability pupils learn up to capacity. These pupils will always rank low by any national norm, but there is little educational waste. On the other hand, some of the worst teaching is done by teachers whose high-ability groups are up to the national norm, permitting a kind of false academic security on the part of the teacher but, in terms of working up to capacity, representing unpardonable educational waste.

Caution should be taken again to make sure that no one gets the idea that individuals should always be isolated to do their own learning. They must learn for themselves, but isolation is not always the best motivator. Group situations that are known to result in more and better learning by individuals should be used. Furthermore, learning the techniques of cooperative study and action is as important to people as spelling, history, or calculus. These cooperative techniques are precisely the group situations which are almost certain to result in a better attitude toward learning to begin with and more effective learning in the end. They become a means by which the learner contacts the ideas of his mates, and they present the further problem of learning how to resolve these ideas into agreements which can be the basis of cooperative action. These are the kinds of group experiences that keep individuals awake. They discover and stimulate rather than obliterate the special abilities and contributions of individuals. This is the kind of group or cooperative activity which ought to replace a lot of the commonplace rivalry between the reds and the blues.

If individuals must learn for themselves, then group situations are merely aids to individual learning. The group goal is secondary to the individual goal; and so-called group techniques are actually techniques for securing more effective performance by individuals in all their interactions. Hence we may say that organizations or clubs or unions or churches or governments or homes or schools are not ends in themselves. They are not to become patterns to which individuals conform. Their essential purpose, on the other hand, is to help individuals to become their best selves, to discover and develop their talents, and to lead them in the end to turn their constructive attention back upon the groups that set their powers free. What we know about individual activity in learning conforms ever so closely with individual responsibility in a democracy and with working out "one's own salvation" in religion. So run the implications if one lets himself go.

8. Adult Learning

Growth in Adult Learning.—Persons who worked with large numbers of adults some yeas ago pointed out that many of them were afflicted with one or both of two unfortunate ideas; that is, that they already knew enough or that it was useless to try to learn more. Today, however, millions of adults feel the need for improvement in their jobs, have experienced the satisfactions of pursuing special interests, and know that they will be able to continue to learn as long as they are alive and well. The tremendous growth in all kinds of adult education in this country during the last few years is comparable to the growth of the secondary school from about 1890 to about 1940. We have witnessed and are still witnessing a kind of educational emancipation of the adult. The program and funds that will be necessary to serve these people in the future are little appreciated today.

Adult Ability to Learn.—Studies in recent years have proved to everyone's satisfaction that adults can learn. The amount that a person can learn in a given unit of time, such as an hour, seems to increase from early childhood until about the age of twenty-five. A slight decline begins around age thirty, but it is slow, and at age sixty-five one can still learn about half as much in an hour's time as he could at twenty-five. The rate of decline in the ability to learn increases very little between the ages of forty-five and seventy, and at any time between these ages one learns fully as well as he could when he was in the third or fourth grade. There is no point, therefore, to adults looking back longingly to their early school days and saying, "If only I could learn now like I could then!" They can.

Types of Learning in Relation to Age.—There are certain types of learning that seem not to decline after other types have begun to wane. One may notice that his ability to remember names has begun to slip. His speed on the uptake isn't what it used to be. His mind doesn't quickly survey the elements of a situation and leap to a conclusion as it used to. The eager grasp on new information and experiences seems to decline. The "going out after it" attitude tapers off. But there are compensations. Nature seems to have ruled that for each of us there ought to come a time when the accumulated experiences of our lives will be thrown into relationships and meanings. So the judgment, reflective, and evaluative power aspect of our learning continues strong after the accumulative aspects begin to decline. Our store of information is not lost. Our vocabulary remains. But the keen edge we had for multiplying the items of experience gives way to the profounder assignment of reflection, evaluation, and the discovery of meanings. This change in the type of thing we can do best may hold a suggestion for the art of living. If adults, realizing the change, would dwell more on overviews and meanings and less on their inability to keep up with the young in their rapid-fire experiencing, fewer frustrations and more happiness might result, and adults would be in a better position to play their rightful role in the balance of drive and judgment which is so desirable in our society.

Implications.—In the whole field of adult learning, two things stand out from which important consequences follow. First, the establishment of the fact that the ability to learn continues on to the end of our days; and second, beyond a certain general age there is a shift in the type of thing we can do best. The first fact gives firm foundation to the whole adult education movement. Incidentally, the tremendous increase in the number of adults in the older age brackets relative to our total population is an educational challenge of the first order. The second fact should give some direction to the nature of adult education itself. Of course, not all adults should suddenly begin the study of philosophy; but it is quite likely that the program that has in it elements which promote the broader integrations of experience will not only be more helpful but will be better received also.

9. Methods of Teaching in Relation to Learning

Principles of Learning as Bases for Methods.—It is a truism to say that methods of teaching ought to stand firmly on the principles of learning. Methods which do this provide environmental conditions which will motivate the learner. They will assist him in clarifying his problems, will place within his reach the materials he will need to solve his problems successfully, and, above all, will seek a maximum amount of self-activity on his part. Methods, then, are the techniques by which problems are introduced and solved, care being taken that the learner has accepted the problem as his own. The goal of method is to assist others in doing their own learning better. In this process the activity of the teacher is effective and justified only in so far as it results in appropriate learning activity by the pupil.

Sometimes method is thought of as the orderly routine to be followed in attempting to secure learning on the part of others. Furthermore, it is a pattern which applies to an entire group. It is planned in advance, and deviations from the plan will not be allowed. This, as we know, is poor business. Our knowledge of individual differences in learning ability will fix the necessity of flexibility in methods and, actually, the adjustment of methods to each person in the group.

Let us enumerate a few well-known methods and relate them briefly to some of the principles presented in this chapter.

Some Methods Considered.—To what extent do certain methods seem to reflect or reject our present concept of learning? To what extent do they view the learner as a receiver or a doer; as one to "take it" or one to be launched on his own learning?

The lecture method was the stand-by of the older thinking concerning learning. The lecturer's job was to inform people who waited to be taught; it was not to stimulate them to learn for themselves. It should not be supposed that this method can have no virtues; that people do not learn from a good lecturer. They do. The thing that is fervently objected to, however, is a lecturer who disclaims any responsibility for bringing his people along with him, for being concerned about their attitude toward the work at hand, or for giving cause and clarity to the topics he pursues. A lecture can motivate listeners to further study and action on their own, or it can be one more gallon poured into the waiting cistern. If its goal and outcome are the former, it is in line with present-day emphasis in learning; if it is the latter, it is still reflecting the old idea that learning is passive in character.

The textbook-recitation method may fall short in the same manner. Here the process is largely one of memorizing facts and handing them back on request. There is very little setting-up and pursuing of problems by pupils. They are constantly finding out what someone else thinks are problems and what someone else thinks are the answers, but they seldom evolve problems of their own on which they work with real purpose. What goes on is more of a filling process than a thinking process. The word is, "I want you to know what is in Chapter 10 tomorrow. I'll ask you questions on it." This process, endlessly, is one of acceptance rather than of challenge so far as the learner is concerned. It does not strike for the self-drive and motivation considered so essential to learning.

The project and problem methods are something different. They have evolved since the new ideas concerning learning came in, and they make direct use of these ideas. The project method, emphasizing activity on the part of the pupil, developed first in vocational fields such as agriculture and homemaking. It emphasized four important steps, namely, purposing, planning, doing, and judging. If a boy had an acre of land for a season as his project, he ordinarily would go through all the above steps. The wholehearted acceptance of the idea that having the acre under his complete control for a year would be a good thing is essential. Then he plans its use, works his plan, and evaluates the outcomes and the procedures he has used. The same way with the girl who decides she wants to make a dress for herself. She goes through the same steps. In all such cases it is essential to note that the youngster himself must purpose, plan, do, and judge. At first it seemed that the activities called for in the project method might be applicable only to the more tangible vocational fields. However, it soon became apparent that a similar approach could be made to problems in the social studies, in science, or in other fields. One can go after an understanding of a problem in health, history, reducing accidents, or producing a historical play, just as systematically as he goes after his acre. For some reason the project method has continued to carry with it a connotation of tangibleness, whereas the problem method has dealt with the more academic or intangible. However, both methods place great stock in self-motivation and in pupil self-activity, insisting that the stage for learning is really set only when the youngster has made a problem his own and that learning is not complete until he has worked his problem through all the way to the point of evaluating its outcomes.

The socialized recitation, by its very name, reveals the effort to secure more pupil activity in the classroom as over against the dominating teacher activity of the lecture method. A great deal of skill is required if this is to work well. Interchanges, of course, should not be only between teacher and pupils, but between pupils and pupils as well. If real problems are being discovered, if pupil contributions are based on real thought and study, and if all share in the activity, much learning can take place. Furthermore, the conditions of the socialized recitation will be duplicated many times throughout life.

The growth of supervised study in recent years has also drawn much of its support from the self-activity movement. Class periods have been lengthened; but instead of using all the time in customary recitation procedures, perhaps half of the time is devoted to supervised study. Here each pupil, having received his assignment and being still with his teacher, starts to work. If he has trouble understanding his jobs or encounters difficulty as he attempts to go ahead, the teacher is at hand to help him get on the right track. Hence he can be more independent as he pursues his studies outside the classroom, and learning becomes the self-propelled experience that it ought to be.

The more recent development of the unit and the unit assignment is another good example of basing methods on the nature of learning. When a teacher builds a unit, he starts out with a concept, an idea, or an important generalization which all of the pupils need to understand. It is stated as a question or problem or challenge, and the pupils themselves may share in the clarification of the problem they want the answer to.

The activities of the pupils will center around all the textbooks, references, materials, records, movies, maps, visits to museums, interviews, and the like that will be useful in solving the problem and arriving at the concept stated in the unit. There would be no slavish bondage to a single textbook whose contents were to be memorized. Rather, learning activities would concentrate on problems and ideas that are meaningful. Under such circumstances the attitude of attack that is so helpful in learning is more likely to be present.

Methods vary greatly in the extent to which they make use of the basic principle of self-activity in learning. They will yield far better results if they motivate youngsters to get going under their own steam than if they require them to sit still while we tell them what we want them to know.

What Do YOU Say?

1

In spite of what we know about the nature and conditions of learning, we are still far from solving the problem of translating that knowledge into better teaching, better teacher education, better home relationships, better work, and better community living.

What do YOU say?

2

It is utterly inconsistent and damaging to character to insist that all future bricklayers learn and perform to the limit of their abilities while they are in school, and then insist that their performance become uniform when they get on the job.

What do YOU say?

3

What we know about learning confirms the democratic way of life and rejects the authoritarian.

What do YOU say?

4

What points in this chapter do you particularly support or take issue with?

Chapter 12

THE IMPROVEMENT OF EDUCATION AND THE EVALUATION OF ITS OUTCOMES

We Can Do Better

---

1. THE IMPROVEMENT OF EDUCATION

In any free society the schools are free. As such, they are not only in a position freely to examine and report on the society that supports them, but they are also subject to the influences of a free-thinking people. The school's nature and program are not determined and kept inviolate by some high authority; rather, the free school is very close to the free people, and the people view and react to its services from day to day. This fact presents a great opportunity for our people to examine the quality of our education and keep it abreast of the times, and it also fixes the finger of responsibility if the schools fall behind. Our schools will always be as good as our people want them to be. The will of the whole people must lie in back of enduring improvements. We should say, then, that educational improvements cannot be left solely to the school staff in the community. Further than that, any school staff that attempts to bring about school improvements without community cooperation is less than half-clear in its vision. The improvement of free education must involve us all, and if all of us will become really interested in the project, the results will command the thanks of all men everywhere.

It will be useful to identify some of the areas in education which should always be studied with the idea of effecting improvements. They will be recognized at once as areas that concern not only school pupils and school personnel but also the parents of pupils and the community at large.

Areas of Improvement.—The effectiveness or ineffectiveness of a school in a community is tied in with many things. On some counts the school may be excellent; on other counts, poor. No school is ever uniformly good on all counts. There is always room for improvement. Pick a school you know and judge whether or not it is uni-

337

formly good or could stand improvement in the following respects, which, as we know, bear directly on the quality of education a school provides.

School Plant. School buildings, grounds, and equipment are always subject to deterioration, wearing-out, becoming inadequate or too small, and becoming outmoded. Since the school plant places definite limitations on the educational program that can be made available, it will in turn reflect the kind of education the community wants for its people. In countless communities the school plant falls far short of being able to house the kind of educational program the people want the pupils to have. Here, indeed, is a fruitful area of improvement.

School Personnel. The people who are employed to manage the schools of the community, carry out policies, and teach the pupils in the classroom ought to be persons of high ability, sympathetic and skilful in all human relations, and genuinely interested in the schools as an agency through which important service to society can be rendered. To be negligent in the attempt to secure the best personnel and to provide conditions under which they can be retained is to lay a heavy penalty on the children. The most vital attribute of good education is good personnel. If this is absent, other areas of improvement are largely negated; if it is present, much improvement will result even though other areas may be weak. If good personnel is complemented by strength in other areas, then education can perform its rightful service.

Educational Program. The educational program includes all the learning experiences provided by the school. If a high school should add Spanish to its offerings, then it has expanded its educational program just that much, and the same for driver training or debating. But the adequacy of the educational program is not determined merely by its scope. What actually goes on within the classroom, the kinds of activities and materials that are included, and the extent to which the work of the school ties in with the life of the community are illustrative of other important considerations. Since curriculum patterns, once established, are so hard to change, the educational program, as a consequence, is an area ever in need of much study and improvement.

School Activities. Many activities outside the classroom, but still supervised by the school, can be made to contribute greatly to the attainment of educational objectives. Since these activities are vital in the over-all development of pupils, they constitute a whole area of improvement in themselves.

School Services. Some schools have gone far in making non-instructional services available to pupils, such as medical and dental services, counseling services, and food services in the cafeteria. The relationship of these services to satisfactory educational progress by pupils is well known. They should, therefore, be made and kept as good as possible.

Teaching Methods. Some teachers who know their subject matter well are ineffective in teaching it. They have not mastered the technique of putting together the principles of learning, the abilities and interests of pupils, the nature of the learning materials, and the manner of presenting learning projects so that pupil participation will be at a maximum. Need for improvement will always be present here, and it immediately involves not only the schools and communities themselves but also other agencies such as teacher education institutions.

Financial Support. Adequate financial support is prerequisite to many of the improvements sought in our schools. If ways and means can be found of securing adequate funds, and if wisdom and efficiency are applied in their expenditure, then we shall have eliminated one of our greatest weaknesses. Let us say again that if local resources are not sufficient to buy the kind of education that the children are entitled to, then it is the obligation of the local board of education to stand by its children and seek funds from outside sources. It is on these grounds that state and federal aid are justified, and it is for this cause that state and federal funds should be willingly contributed.

Methods of Evaluating Outcomes. As the purposes of education enlarge and as the educational enterprise in the community expands, it is necessary to check at every turn to make sure that desired outcomes are being secured. There is room for much improvement in the area of evaluation. For example, if we say that the school ought to be as much concerned about the attitudes of a pupil as about his achievement in arithmetic, then we must devise ways and means of discovering his attitudes to begin with, of measuring attitude changes, and of teaching for the establishment of desirable attitudes. This is an aspect of being interested in what people become as well as in what they learn. Similarly, improved approaches to determining the effectiveness of the school plant, school personnel, teaching methods, and the like are constantly in order.

School-Community Relations. One of the areas related to educational improvement that has been greatly emphasized of late is that of school-community relations. Unless this relationship is open, two-way, and continuous, the school cannot become what it should or render the services it should. The present move to make our public schools into real community schools ought to be supported by every school and lay person.

The above list of areas of improvement is not, of course, complete. Other areas will occur to the reader. For example, mention might have been made of school morale. Things are not always right with the work tone, the mood, the atmosphere of the school. The spirit of cooperation, of mutual respect and friendliness between pupils and staff members, is not always present. Under such circumstances tremendous losses are suffered in achievement, in spirit, and in the desire to continue learning; and something should be done about it. Let the reader go on from here, adding other areas in education which ought to be made the subject of study and improvement.

Importance of Clarifying Goals as a Basis of Improvement.— One can always get plenty of advice about how to improve our schools. The trouble is, such advice is more often than not mere private opinion. What is needed is a pooling of private opinions, a real community approach to the problem of clarifying what we want our schools to accomplish anyhow. We may think we know this, but we do not. Actually, many of the teachers in our schools have not given it careful thought. But before improvements come, the ends they will serve should be known. Ordinarily in the past we have felt that the people associated with the schools should understand the goals of education, and so they should; but so should all the people of the community. If people know what they are aiming at, the mood is good and the movement is forward; if all they can see is certain glaring weaknesses in the school system, then the mood is bad, and objections, criticisms, investigations, and "housecleanings" are the order of the day. Let us take a look at an actual occurrence.

The board of education in a rather small community was plagued with complaints about the high school. Some things, it was alleged, were bad. One of the teachers drew particular fire. The board, although it had considerable sympathy with the complaints, felt that it did not have evidence enough to take action. A subcommittee was appointed to seek the services of certain staff members in a higher institution who would survey the school in very short order and make a report to the board. It was felt that then sufficient evidence would be on hand to support the complaints and the action already contemplated could be taken. When the subcommittee visited the higher institution it was taken somewhat aback. No interest was shown in the quick survey, but willingness was expressed to cooperate with the board and the people in a long-term approach to educational improvement. Naturally the board could not indicate disinterest in long-term improvement, and plans got under way. From the start it was insisted that basic agreements concerning the purposes of public education in the community must be arrived at. Discussions at first limited to board members were expanded to include school staffs, then parents and representatives of the community at large. Direct contact with patrons was made, giving them opportunity to express themselves as to the purposes of public education. In this process the original intent of meeting criticism by "getting" certain staff members was lost and constructive planning replaced it. As the goals became clear, the steps needed to reach the goals became clear also, and some of the complaints became meaningless and far-fetched. The whole affair was an excellent example of what happens when goals are cooperatively arrived at. Clarity replaces obscurity, forward movement replaces confusion and stagnation, and good morale replaces bad feeling.

The form used to contact patrons in the above-mentioned community concerning the purposes of public education may be of some interest and may contain suggestions for other communities. It is presented here in greatly abbreviated form, but its structure is given and the nature of the items is indicated.

An Analysis of the Purposes of Our Public Schools

Directions: On the following pages are statements about the purposes of public education. Read each statement carefully. At the right of each statement are two columns. You are to mark in each column.

In the first column, circle "yes" if you believe that this should be one of the purposes of the public schools of our community. Circle "no" if you think it should not be.

In the second column, circle "l" if you think our schools now do this *little*; circle "s" if you think our schools now do this *some*; circle "m" if you think our schools now do this *much*.

---

[1] Adapted from an unpublished form developed by education staff members at the University of Connecticut.

Purposes	Should We?		Do We?		
A. To help pupils become skilful in understanding the thinking of others and in expressing their own ideas	Yes	No	1	s	m
1. To use the fundamentals of mathematics in solving everyday problems	Yes	No	1	s	m
2. To read, spell, and write well	Yes	No	1	s	m
3. To speak clearly and forcefully, using good oral English	Yes	No	1	s	m
4. To talk interestingly with other people........	Yes	No	1	s	m
5. To discuss issues with others	Yes	No	1	s	m
6. To develop a good vocabulary	Yes	No	1	s	m
B. To help pupils develop a keen desire to learn......	Yes	No	1	s	m
1. To study only what they can understand	Yes	No	1	s	m
2. To learn independently in areas of special interest to them	Yes	No	1	s	m
3. To know clearly their own progress toward goals suited to them	Yes	No	1	s	m
C. To help pupils become healthy..................	Yes	No	1	s	m
1. To learn and use good personal and community health practices	Yes	No	1	s	m
2. To have regular medical examinations and remedial work if needed	Yes	No	1	s	m
D. To help pupils use intelligence in solving problems.	Yes	No	1	s	m
1. To get the facts needed in solving their problems	Yes	No	1	s	m
2. To be able to tell the difference between fact and fiction, propaganda and truth............	Yes	No	1	s	m
E. To help pupils become effective citizens in a democracy	Yes	No	1	s	m
1. To have many experiences in governing themselves	Yes	No	1	s	m
2. To study ways of solving problems in town, state, and nation	Yes	No	1	s	m
F. To help pupils use their leisure time well.........	Yes	No	1	s	m
1. To develop appropriate hobbies	Yes	No	1	s	m
2. To know and use library, recreational, and other community resources	Yes	No	1	s	m
G. To help pupils become intelligent consumers......	Yes	No	1	s	m
1. To know how to judge the value of goods and services sold	Yes	No	1	s	m
2. To know the facts about instalment buying, taxes, insurance, etc.	Yes	No	1	s	m
H. To help pupils appreciate beauty	Yes	No	1	s	m
1. To recognize beauty in common things........	Yes	No	1	s	m
2. To discover the joy of original work..........	Yes	No	1	s	m

Purposes	Should We?		Do We?		
I. To help pupils become effective members of the home	Yes	No	1	s	m
1. To accept responsibility in a cooperative project	Yes	No	1	s	m
2. To learn the skills and procedures associated with good homemaking	Yes	No	1	s	m
J. To help pupils plan, work, and play together......	Yes	No	1	s	m
1. To respect the worth and judgments of each fellow-pupil and cooperate with him..........	Yes	No	1	s	m
2. To set up their own organizations to improve the school, choosing their own leaders.........	Yes	No	1	s	m
K. To help pupils conserve resources...............	Yes	No	1	s	m
1. To learn basic facts about the use of natural resources	Yes	No	1	s	m
2. To consider the effects of war, poverty, and disease on human resources	Yes	No	1	s	m

L. Please add other purposes and make comments as you like:
....

Whatever time is necessary to get the community together on its purposes for the public schools is time well spent. Actually it will save time, for what is done on the basis of these understandings will be lasting and permanent; and what is more, it will be supported. The above form may serve as a starter for groups that want to develop in the community the basic understandings that ought to underlie school improvement.

What we demand of the community as a whole with reference to the clarification of goals we should demand also of smaller groups and of ourselves as individuals. Most readers already realize that some boards of education, even though they constitute the primary policy-making group in the community, have given very little systematic attention to the real purposes of the schools they direct. Problems are met singly as they arise and pretty much without the general direction that a clarification of goals could give. In other instances the board of education has developed a written statement of goals, an educational code, or other document. Here all action is purposeful, and it promotes goals that are understood and desired. School faculties too, in cooperation with their supervisors, should freely discuss and write down the real purposes their schools ought to serve as they see them. So it will be with each individual on the staff. Believe it or not, there are plenty of persons teaching school who have never pinned themselves down to the simple intellectual task of stating what they really wish to achieve in their mathematics classes or in English or in interscholastic athletics. Some of us have seen the statements of such people when they have been asked to declare their purposes, and it is rather pitiful to see how frequently the mathematics teacher, for example, is unable to go further in his objectives than to teach pupils mathematics, the history teacher a knowledge of history, and the Latin teacher Latin. Certainly if the goals of these people are thus limited to the specifics of a content area, we cannot be surprised at the slowness with which we move toward the achievement of our major educational objectives. Let us say, then, that the beginning point in the improvement of education at whatever level, and involving whatever number of people, is to make clear the ends we seek; and since we are forgetful people and new knowledge and circumstances always arise to affect our goals, it follows that our study and clarification of goals ought to be continuous. If our goals are kept in mind we will be restless to achieve them; this is the real basis of educational improvement.

Closing the Gap Between Goals and Practices.—Educational improvements may be thought of as closing the gap between current school practices and accepted goals. Sometimes it is a sizable gap that needs to be closed. Mention has already been made in Chapter 3 of our general willingness sincerely to accept certain goals in theory but to act with discouraging slowness in translating those goals into changed school organization, curricula, and procedures. Illustrations of distance between goals and practices are many. Only one must suffice. In the evaluative criteria of the Cooperative Study of Secondary School Standards used for the evaluation of secondary schools, forms are provided for use by the secondary school in stating its own philosophy of education. Anyone who has read a number of these statements and then has gone on to help evaluate the schools in terms of their stated philosophies will appreciate how frequently practices fall far short of goals. This is not meant as a criticism of the schools. On the contrary, it is very much to the good that a school staff will thus state its goals; and ordinarily these staff members are the first to recognize the shortcomings of their own school. The stage for improvement is in this manner set, and steps to close the gap between goals and practices can be taken with purpose and clarity.

Means of Improving Education.—There is a very simple pattern which, if remembered and followed, would not permit programs of educational improvement to go very far astray. It emphasizes three things : find out, try out, and round out. These items, plus two or three that will be discussed, will provide a general approach within which any school or community can carry on extensive activities.

Find Out. If, as is called for above, educational goals are understood and desired, then it is only natural to want to find out how they can be achieved. What information is needed in order to move forward wisely? What are the facts with reference to existing conditions? There is much to find out.

In the first place, a great deal of dependable information about pupils needs to be assembled. For them the schools exist; and we have too frequently built buildings, set up curricula, and hired teachers without having the welfare of pupils uppermost in our minds. We need accurate information for each pupil concerning health needs, native ability, special aptitudes, social and emotional development, achievement in his fields of study, vocational interests, attitudes, and the like. Much of this information can be secured if the school can have a comprehensive testing program, a good counseling service, and school health and medical services. The necessity of having this information about pupils will be seen immediately when one reviews the areas of school improvement listed at the beginning of this chapter. We cannot claim to be proceeding soundly if we do without it.

We need also to find out about the community that is served by the school and that, in turn, reacts upon the school. What occupational groups are served by the school? To what extent do graduates of the school take up jobs in the community? What economic and social advantages or disadvantages does the community hold? What is there in the community that could be used as educational source material for pupils? What recreational and cultural opportunities are there, and how might they be improved or expanded? What is the financial capacity of the community to support public services, including education? So grows the list of things we need to know about our communities. The most widely used means of getting answers to questions like these is the community survey. Good techniques have been developed for assembling and evaluating primary data on the community. The people in more than one community have viewed with urgent interest the clear presentation of survey data which they could not possibly question. It is, of course, understood that in our efforts to improve education we shall seek to promote also the interests of the larger society of which our community is a part. Our pupils, we know, will be citizens of the state, the nation, and the world, and our basic studies must include these if our schools are to serve their larger social purposes.

Lastly, studies should always be in progress to find out just what the situation is with reference to the areas of improvement already discussed. These are: school plant, school personnel, educational program, school activities, school services, teaching methods, financial support, methods of evaluating outcomes, and school-community relations. Responsibility for studies dealing with these areas will rest with different groups or persons, but they must be made if the information essential to improvement is to be on hand. Again, much has been done that can be helpful to those who are making these studies locally. For example, scales have been developed for the evaluation of school buildings, equipment, and grounds; rating schemes to evaluate the work and services of school personnel are used in some places, although great care must be used in their application if they are to be worth while; and excellent procedures for the study and revision of the educational program have been worked out.

If our people get their goals straight and if in their efforts to achieve those goals they take care to get their facts straight, the judgments they will then make as to next steps can be depended upon.

Try Out. But, even so, judgments should not be too summarily made or action too summarily taken. On many matters of educational improvement, answers are not obtained by merely adding up figures. It is necessary to "try out." Contemplated steps should not become permanent until their wisdom has been demonstrated. Take the areas of improvement again. Certainly there are many things about the educational program, school services, and school activities which ought to be tried out and proved feasible before the equipment and staff necessary for their permanent retention are secured. So it will be with teaching methods, school-community relations, and methods of evaluating outcomes. The point may seem less obvious with school personnel. However, the policy of requiring a satisfactory probationary period before permanent tenure can be gained is almost universally accepted. There may even be some aspects of school support which could well be tried out with a view to making them permanent if they proved sound. In larger school systems, certain types of school construction or equipment in a given building can be carefully judged with the idea of using them in other buildings if they are good. Glass brick, construction of windows, heating and ventilating systems, and types of interior decorating are illustrative. Even small school systems with only one building can benefit greatly if they will check the tryouts that other school systems have made. To go "all out" in any area of improvement without first finding out what a tryout reveals is to flirt with waste and error.

Perhaps the most exacting procedure having to do with tryouts is the controlled experiment. When this procedure is followed, a specific problem is isolated, systematic and carefully controlled steps are taken to study the problem, data are collected and analyzed, and conclusions supported by verifiable evidence are drawn. This type of study is not used enough in education. Suppose a school wants to know whether pupils learn more history in a class where they read a textbook and are lectured to or in a class where they help decide what they will study, organize themselves into groups to follow up on definite things, discuss historical problems freely, and evaluate their own progress. There is only one way really to get at the answer to this question, and that is to equalize all elements in the two situations as nearly as possible and allow only the methods of teaching to vary. Thus pupils in both groups will need to be equal with reference to such things as general intelligence, background, achievement in history, motivation to learn, and skill of their teachers. If things are properly set up and controlled, and if the teaching and evaluating are well done, then a dependable judgment can be drawn as to the merits of the two methods for the learning of history. If more such experiments were engaged in, there would be less guesswork in our schools, less argument, and more good reason in back of the things we do. Furthermore, this procedure can be used widely in educational problems. It goes without saying that only qualified people should use it. It takes time; but it pays off in the long run.

Another practice with reference to tryout is the "pilot" school. Let us describe what is meant. Today, for example, there is great interest among secondary education people in the country in what is called "life adjustment" education. Meeting the needs of every adolescent, no matter what his abilities, background, or future intentions may be, is emphasized as the obligation of every high school. To accomplish this would mean drastic changes in the point of view, educational offering, teaching procedures, organization, and activities of most high schools now in existence. Hence most of these schools view life adjustment education as a fine thing, but impossible for them. But advocates of the program say, "Let's pick out a few pilot schools where the program can be started and ways of meeting problems can be discovered and made known to other schools so that these other schools will be spared much of the trial and error of the pilot schools." Thus the pilot idea operates. A good many of the laboratory schools on college and university campuses are of the same nature, and occasionally a school in a city system serves the same purpose. The pilot school is important in discovering things that are good and may be adapted for the broad improvement of education.

Round Out. The meaning of "round out" is now apparent. When the goals are clear and the facts are in, and when good practices have been demonstrated through tryout, then follows the obligation to round out the system by adopting the improvements indicated. If, as is urged above, there is continuous attention to goals, fact-finding, and tryout, then there will doubtless be continuous progress also in providing broader and better education to all we seek to serve.

One might summarize the suggestions to this point as : work out the goals, find out the facts, try out new practices, round out the system.

Using Available Services. No school in the land is so isolated or poor that it cannot obtain a great deal of help in improving itself if it so desires. There are available many types of services that can be of significant help and that, for the most part, are free. In most states there is a very active state department of education that is staffed with people who are qualified and available to give advice and service to local schools. These services touch upon practically all aspects of education. Much assistance can be obtained also from the federal government. This help is mainly in the form of published materials. The publicly supported higher institutions in the states feel a very close relationship to the public schools, and many of them are quite willing to furnish staff members who will become consultants in the study of local school problems. These people also are highly trained and can be of much help on such matters as curriculum studies, adult education programs, audio-visual aids, testing programs, and the like. Private institutions frequently offer the same kinds of services. In many communities public libraries, museums, historical societies, and service clubs would cooperate gladly with the schools if they were approached. Transportation companies often go to surprising lengths in making field trips and other activities possible. Doctors, dentists, social workers, police, psychiatrists, and others can and do cooperate. Farmers, bankers, mechanics, religious workers, and others are glad to do what they can to acquaint pupils with the nature of their work. Manufacturers and publishers make available to schools a great deal of free material that is frequently extremely good. Such materials need to be carefully scrutinized so that propaganda and advertising are avoided. More often than not, newspapers and radio stations will give schools a great advantage in providing an opportunity to tell their story. All these, and more, are avenues of educational improvement which not only could be used but which actually wait to be used in most cases. A careful appraisal by any school of the services available will certainly show that there is much help to be had for the mere asking.

Determining Fundamentals. A great deal of real discernment is necessary if superficiality is to be avoided in improving education. One frequently hears it said, "This year we painted the building, built a sidewalk, and approved a new kind of report card." Or, "We are very proud of our new bus and the new type of desks that have been installed." Maybe someone will say, "We lost a couple of good teachers, and there's no money for the library, but the folks are certainly going to like those new football bleachers." Now all of these things are related to improved education, but it is quite possible to have them without improving education at all. The real test is whether or not the things that are done result in improved human beings. To suppose that the mere presence of the externals will save the day is error; to attend well to things that assure human development, such as good teachers, good libraries, good courses of study, and good school and community morale, is wisdom. A school or community that is really fundamental in its approach to improving education will not be satisfied to buy demonstration materials in mathematics; it will make sure that it has mathematics teachers who use those materials for the improved learning of pupils. Comment has already been made in another chapter on the tendency of supervisors to urge teachers to buy new materials, keep new records, use audio-visual aids, make this excursion or that, without ever checking on the actual effectiveness of the teachers in the classroom or seeing if the use of these things actually results in better learning on the part of the pupils. Improvement, then, involves the externals, but it must also always involve the human fundamentals. When the personnel and program are right, then the externals become important means to human ends. It is rather shallow and not a little wasteful to point pridefully to the externals when the real job of improvement remains yet to be done.

2. EVALUATING THE OUTCOMES OF EDUCATION

The modern testing movement in education, characterized by the introduction of new types of tests known as "objective" tests, got under way roughly at the beginning of the twentieth century. To be sure, before 1900 there had been plenty of testing in schools, but by that time the conviction had become strong that more systematic and dependable means of measuring the outcomes of education should be developed. The unreliability of previous examination marks had been demonstrated. The last half-century has witnessed great progress in the development and use of tests, and significant changes in basic concepts regarding testing have taken place.

Scope of the Modern Movement.—The new kinds of tests that began to be developed about a half-century ago caught on quickly in the schools. They were first developed for the more exacting studies such as arithmetic and spelling but were soon expanded to include other fields. Scales for handwriting, composition, and language came along early. By 1925 about 1,000 different tests and scales had been developed and catalogued for sale. Since 1925 there has been no letup in either the development and revision of tests in the earlier fields or in the new fields entered. This rapid expansion actually reflected the eagerness of the schools to use the new tests and scales. In fact, once these measures became available in certain fields, teachers in other fields created such a demand for similar instruments that no field was left untouched by the new movement. Furthermore, the movement did not stop with the development of measures in teaching fields; it reached out to include measures of many aspects of human nature and development beyond the mere acquisition of knowledge. Today the alert school uses tests widely and takes great care in selecting the tests that are used. Numerous school systems have employed specially trained persons who are coordinators and consultants in the entire system on matters pertaining to research and testing. The counseling programs, too, have greatly increased the use of tests of all types. In recent years the amount of money set aside in the school budget to meet expenses connected with testing has steadily increased.

But the testing movement has by no means been limited to the schools. In fact, the acceptance and use of tests in certain other segments of our society, once they gained a foothold, have outstripped their use in the schools. One has only to refer to the armed forces with their highly developed systems of tests all up and down the line or to the civil service and merit systems throughout the country. Business and industry, too, have greatly altered their personnel practices to include a wide use of tests. The admission of persons to practice in their chosen professions, such as law, medicine, and psychiatry, and the selection of policemen and firemen are examples of other areas in which tests are used extensively. The modern testing movement, then, although it was begun in the schools, has permeated our whole society.

The Expanding Concept.—As time has gone on, ideas directing the new testing movement have been greatly modified and expanded. The rather narrow concepts at the beginning have given place to much broader concepts. For purposes of clarity and brevity, let us say that we have moved from testing to measurement to evaluation.

The primary purpose of the first tests and scales was to get a score or a rating. The amount or degree of accomplishment, determined by tests made up of items easily checked for exactness of answers, was sought. The immediate goal was to find out "how much" of this or that was known. Tests of the factual sort multiplied rapidly. The prevailing questions were, "What is his score?" and "How does he rank?" The careful construction of the tests to make sure that they were good to begin with had not yet become a science. However, the many problems associated with the proper construction and use of the new tests, as well as the old tests, came to the fore rapidly.

This set the stage for the measurement period. How to select good items for the new tests, how to make the tests really measure what they were supposed to measure, how to administer the tests to the best advantage, how to interpret and use test results, and other like questions required broad knowledge, great skill, and extensive research. The dimensions of this task increased as tests were developed that dealt with aspects of human nature and development beyond the learning of factual materials. Effort was also made to make more reliable the essay test which had been used so extensively before the development of the new tests. Measurement, then, greatly extended the testing movement, and made test-construction a thoroughly scientific undertaking.

Evaluation broadened the base still more. Here a clear understanding of the objectives of education became primary, and the kinds of measures that were used to determine whether or not the objectives were being achieved varied in terms of the nature of the objectives themselves. For example, if we say that citizenship is an educational objective, we will recognize at once that we cannot measure its attainment merely by administering informational tests in American history. We shall have to observe and record things that are extremely important in citizenship but do not lend themselves to customary testing procedures. Changes in attitudes toward teachers and schoolmates are important. Precise descriptions of behavior patterns in the classroom, on the playground, and in the community must be recorded. Willingness to assume responsibilities, to give the other fellow his say, to express one's own opinions calmly and pointedly, and to cooperate with others in common projects must be carefully observed. Consequently, as progress toward the larger goals is evaluated, a larger variety of information and evidence will be sought. These will constitute an over-all picture that extends far beyond ordinary test scores. There will be anecdotal records, reports on observations, reports on interviews, and the like. Clearly, evaluation carries connotations that are broader than those for measurement or testing. The nature and development of the individual and the basic objectives of education are the essential points of reference rather than the measurement of accumulated knowledge in any field. It is understood, of course, that testing, measurement, and evaluation are not discrete and separate. On the contrary, they are related and inseparable. The movement has been cumulative, so that evaluation today actually encompasses all that has gone before. It will be useful in the next section briefly to indicate how the expanded concepts have produced new emphases and have affected general practices.

New Trends and Emphases in the School.—In line with the growth in the purpose and nature of evaluation, changes have occurred in the schools. We have moved from attempting merely to test for facts and information to an effort to discover whether or not pupils are gaining broad understandings and are able to apply the things they learn. For example, as stated before, good citizenship now begins to overshadow in importance the ability to make high scores on American history tests. The two, of course, are not incompatible; but the latter is good only as it contributes to the former, and present-day evaluation is turning its attention vigorously to the task of determining the degree to which the larger goals are achieved. Similarly, the schools are administering their testing programs more and more as means of improving their counseling services to pupils and less and less as merely means of determining the marks that will be awarded to pupils. Present-day evaluation insists also that procedures and standards must be related directly to the individual pupil. This individualized evaluation should be continuous. It is more important to secure a picture of a pupil's progress over an extended period of time than to compare him with a hundred others at a given time. This emphasis on the continuous measurement of individual progress has necessitated the development of comparable forms of tests. One can hardly give the same test over and over to the same pupil, even though a common base is necessary if progress is to be noted accurately. Hence, comparable forms of the same test have had to be developed. This means that any of the forms of a test, although different from the other forms, could be given and the outcomes would be the same as for the other forms. It is no small task to develop test forms that are really comparable, and yet it is imperative that it be done if continuous measurement of individual progress is to be well carried out. In line with the emphasis on relating evaluation to individual progress, a great deal of attention is being given to self-appraisal. If competition of pupils against other pupils is to be lessened and if pupils are to compete more against their own previous records, then self-appraisal can play a great part in the establishment of good learning attitudes. When standards are set in terms of individual pupils and are accepted by them, evaluation procedures based on those standards are valid and become motivations to progress and not merely measures of progress. It is apparent that new trends and emphases in the school are resulting from our expanding concepts of evaluation.

Tests in Education.—As has been said before, many kinds of tests have been developed. At first the primary interest was to develop tests that would measure the amount of learning that had taken place. From this beginning it was only natural that interest should also turn to tests that would reveal the nature of the learner himself. These two basic purposes give significance to the two major classifications of tests, namely, psychological and educational. Psychological tests include tests of intelligence, aptitude, attitudes, personality, interests, and so on. Here the objective is not to measure learning but to determine the individual's equipment, background, and conditions for learning. Educational tests, on the other hand, are concerned with learning, with achievement, accomplishment, or performance. The main purpose is to find out what and how much learning has taken place and, more recently, to determine the extent to which growth has occurred in the ability to apply what has been learned.

Essay or Old-Type Tests. Actually, the modern testing movement arose as a kind of protest against the inadequacies and inequities of essay examinations. Scores of studies have shown that these tests do not give pupils a fair chance to demonstrate what they know within the body of subject matter ordinarily covered by a test. The questions are usually too few and too generalized. For example, a definite injustice is done to pupils when a teacher picks a couple of items from the whole body of eligible material and asks the pupils to "tell all you know about" one and "discuss fully" the other. Actually it is quite possible that, for some very good pupils, the two items selected may be the only ones on which they are weak. Thus too much depends on too little. Sampling should be better than that.

Furthermore, the score on the essay test is terribly subject to such things as how sleepy the marker is when he marks the paper, his like or dislike of the pupil, or whether the fruit bought yesterday in the grocery store of the pupil's father turned out to be overripe. Teachers have frequently admitted that more than once they have been half-way through a pile of essay examinations, suddenly felt that they were getting too many very high or very low papers, and at midway have drastically changed their standards of marking so as to have a better distribution of papers. Such subjective factors make the score on the test a reflection of many things beside the achievement of the pupil.

However, essay tests are still widely used and for good reason. They have very definite advantages as well as weaknesses. The essay question is one of the best means we have of determining the pupil's ability to organize his thinking, express himself clearly, and marshal facts and ideas in support of a conclusion. Pupils need more and not less practice in this kind of thinking. It is very likely a mistake, though, for a teacher to use essay tests exclusively. If occasionally this is justified, it is probably because of the nature of the learning involved and the uncommon skill of the teacher in constructing and evaluating this type of test. Essay tests, then, should continue in use, although the construction of the items and the evaluation of the answers should be improved. Such improvement is in fact developing rapidly, and the essay item, in skilled hands, is in a good way to eliminating much of the criticism formerly leveled against it.

Objective or New-Type Tests. One of the correctives of the essay examination was a new, objective type of test. The other main corrective, as indicated above, was a sincere move to improve the construction and evaluation of the essay test itself. However, for a time, as so often happens when something new comes in, one energetic group of people contended that the new-type tests were the answer to all our problems in testing. Another group, just as energetic, defended the old-type test, refusing even to examine the "newfangled" instruments. More recently, of course, each group realizes that both types are needed, and all hands are interested in the use and improvement of both.

Objective tests are intended to eliminate subjectivity in scoring. Test items are constructed so that only one correct answer can be given. Scoring the test, therefore, does not require the judgment of a scorer. A scoring key replaces the scorer. Objective tests are now scored in countless thousands by machines. On a test that is purely objective, the score will be the same no matter how many different people score it. The key of right answers becomes the arbiter, and the scorer merely administers the key. The importance of preparing good items for objective tests becomes apparent at once. They must be unambiguous and uncontroversial. They must mean the same to all. They must call for an answer that is exact and unmistakable.

Several different types of objective test items have been developed, all of which call for the exactitude indicated above. One type is the alternate-response item. Here the truth or falsity of a statement is called for or the rightness or wrongness of a given spelling, problem solution, or the like:

> In 1950 the population of the United States was smaller than it was in 1940.
>
> If the base of an isosceles triangle is 6 feet and its altitude is 4 feet, its area is 24 square feet.

In answering this type of item, a simple mark is all that is necessary. To the left of the item the letters T and F may appear, T to be circled if the statement is true and F to be circled if the statement is false; or the letters R and W may be used: R for right and W for wrong. Sometimes the symbols are plus and minus: plus for true and minus for false. Frequently these symbols do not appear at all, but instructions are given as to what symbols to use in answering the items. Occasionally an O is used to indicate a false statement, although many teachers prefer to retain this for their own use in designating an omitted item when scoring the tests.

Another type of objective test item is the multiple-response item. Here the response is not limited to the alternative of right or wrong, but several responses are indicated, preferably four or five, among which is included the correct response. The pupil is expected to choose and check the correct response:

> When General Douglas MacArthur was relieved of his post in the Far East, he was replaced by:

1. George Marshall
2. J. Lawton Collins
3. Omar Bradley
4. Matthew B. Ridgway
5. James A. Van Fleet

Actually, the responses to this type of item may also be all correct but one, in which case the pupil will choose and check the incorrect response; or responses with varying degrees of correctness may be given, none of which is entirely correct, in which case the pupil will choose and check the best answer. The greatest care must be exercised in constructing items where degrees of correctness are indicated, for clearly unless a best answer can be discovered, the objectivity of the item is lost.

Matching items are also frequently included in objective tests. Here, ordinarily, two column of items are presented in parallel, and proper matching of the items is called for. The subject matter within the items of a matching group should be homogeneous. If more than six or seven items are included in a group, the pupil, each time he seeks to match two items, will waste too much time in running over the long list of possible answers to find the answer he wants to use. If the groups are kept relatively short, the response column, to a good degree, can be remembered and the problem of correctly matching the items can be attended to without delay. If the correct matching of authors and book titles is sought, the columns might be set up somewhat as follows:

_____ *This I Remember*	1. Leo Tolstoy
_____ *The Grand Alliance*	2. Eleanor Roosevelt
_____ *Peace Can Be Won*	3. Abraham Lincoln
_____ *Kon-Tiki*	4. Paul Hoffman
_____ *Their Finest Hour*	5. Thor Heyerdahl
_____ *Out of the Night*	6. Winston Churchill
_____ *Modern Arms and Free Men*	7. Margaret Mitchell
	8. Jean Valtin
	9. Vannevar Bush

In the spaces at the left of the items in the stimulus column are to be placed the numbers of the correct matching items in the response column. Hence, the number "2" would be placed in the space at the left of the title *This I Remember,* since Eleanor Roosevelt is the book's author. It is good practice to have more response items than stimulus items so that some answers cannot be arrived at by mere elimination. Also, it is quite permissible to have a single response item matched with more than one stimulus item. In the case above, number 6 in the response column applies to both the second and fifth titles in the stimulus column. When this is contemplated, instructions preceding the items should make it clear to the pupil that it is a possibility.

The free-response item is a fourth kind of item used in objective tests. Here the pupil does not simply react to items listed in the test; he must supply some material himself. Perhaps a direct question is asked and space is provided for the answer:

What is the area of an isosceles triangle if its base is 6 feet and its altitude is 4 feet? _____

Sometimes a statement is left incomplete at the end and the pupil is expected to complete it correctly.

The process by which green plants, under the influence of light, form carbohydrates from the carbon dioxide and water of the air is called _____

Diagrams and maps on which points are indicated for identification are also a form of the free-response item. A tooth may be diagramed with certain parts labeled for identification, or the location of selected cities on a map of the United States may be shown and the pupil asked to identify the cities. At any rate, in the free-response item the pupil originates the answer and does not simply choose among possible answers provided for him. The number of possible responses now becomes infinite or "free." The pupil is expected to eliminate all the wild and irrelevant possibilities and supply the right answer.

The last type of objective test item to be mentioned here is the completion item. In this type of item key words are removed from one or more sentences, leaving blank spaces. The pupil, after studying the general idea, is expected to enter the proper words in the blank spaces.

If the _____ dies during his term of office, he will be succeeded by the _____. The _____ is next in line of succession; and, if all three of these should die during the same term, the Speaker of the House of Representatives would assume the office.

Here the general idea or theme (succession in office) is given, and important details related to the theme supply the answers for the blanks. This kind of item, if carefully used, can call for a great deal of real thinking as opposed to memorization. This is why it is urged that completion items shall not be sentences copied from a textbook with key words removed. Such a practice encourages the memorizing of the book, which, of course, is not the outcome this kind of item seeks to promote.

Short-Answer Tests. Much use is being made lately of the short-answer test item. To a considerable extent, this type of item, if well handled, combines a good many of the advantages of both essay and objective tests. Here a topic is indicated and the pupil is required to clarify it.

Make a brief, clarifying statement about each of the following:

1. The Tenth Amendment
2. UNESCO
3. "Gerrymandering"

When tests are mimeographed, a half-dozen spaces can be left after each topic for the pupil's answer, thus limiting the amount of writing that can be done and requiring the pupil to organize a brief statement, hit the nail on the head, and have done with it. Although no key can be developed for this kind of test item, objectivity is nevertheless closely approached because in a direct, brief statement the pupil will most certainly reveal whether or not he knows the answer. Furthermore, this type of question calls for clear thinking and an organization of that thinking into precise expression. This is one of the prime virtues of the essay examination. Of course the topics on the short-answer test must be capable of pointed responses. One would hardly include such topics as "The Near East" or "Communist Diplomacy" or "The Pros and Cons of Wage and Price Controls."

Performance Tests. For certain types of learning the performance test is most appropriate. If a boy is studying auto mechanics, he will not only want to know about engines as described in books but also how to repair them. Hence his tests in auto mechanics will include more problem situations involving real engines than paper-and-pencil tests of the academic sort. In the chemistry laboratory, also, it may be more important that the student be able to conduct a successful experiment than that he be able to indicate on paper what will happen if two chemicals are combined. In fact, the idea of the performance test has permeated other fields, such as the social studies. Even in the written tests in these fields, so-called problem situations are set up and the student is asked to indicate what ought to be done under these circumstances. The next step, if the "performance" situation is actually to exist, of course, is to place him under these circumstances and see what he does.

Oral Tests. Oral tests are used much less than written tests. This is due in good part to the fact that oral testing must be individualized, whereas a single written test can be administered to large groups at once. Furthermore, oral testing is not easy. It can readily degenerate into a rather meaningless conversation with lots of time wasted and without any real evaluation taking place. However, studies have shown that the oral test, if properly prepared and conducted, can be just as effective as written tests. It ought to be used more for the simple reason that in the life of the ordinary citizen the problem situations requiring oral responses will far outnumber the situations requiring written responses. It would be well if the school could give the citizen some basic experience in hearing problems presented orally, thinking on his feet, and making guarded, coherent responses.

Standardized Tests. A standardized test is an objective test the items of which have been statistically analyzed to make sure that they really discriminate and for which norms have been established. Most standardized tests had many more items when they were first assembled than when they came from the publisher. The preliminary test was given to many people, and each item was analyzed for its discriminating power. Clearly, an item that everyone gets right or that everyone gets wrong has no such discriminatory power and must be thrown out. The items remaining in the published test have been shown to have such power. Norms have also been worked out for standardized tests and are available to the purchaser. A norm indicates the average performance on the standardized test of a significantly large number of people for whom the test is intended. For example, a standardized English test that has been developed for the seventh, eighth, and ninth grades will be administered to several hundred pupils selected at random in each of the three grades, and norms for each grade will be computed. These norms furnish a basis for comparison when the tests are given to other individuals or groups throughout the country. Norms, of course, may be computed on a national, regional, or local basis, and they may be restricted to selected groups. Actually, norms can be reduced to an individual basis, in which case an individual's past performance becomes the norm by which subsequent performance is judged.

Importance of Good Teacher-made Tests. For a good many years after standardized tests became available, teachers were inclined to use them heavily in their classrooms. The publication and sale of such tests became a flourishing business. Many local schools budgeted funds for the purchase of tests. However, it soon became apparent that these tests, even though they were excellent in their construction, were limited in their uses. If a test is to be really valid, and if its use is to be really justified, it must be developed in line with the materials and experiences actually dealt with in the classroom. As we have seen before, the teacher in today's school is expected to adapt his instruction to the group he is dealing with. These groups often differ widely among schools or within schools. Sometimes within a city system significant differences between two schools located in different sections of the city are noted. Furthermore, many schools practice homogeneous grouping in which the pupils in a building are separated into groups and their instruction is adapted to such things as their ability, background, and achievement. Obviously, no seventh grade English test that is developed by a publishing company is going to be adapted to the needs and to the varied instructional backgrounds of all the seventh graders in all of these situations. Thus tremendous emphasis has been placed lately on the importance of good teacher-made tests. As a matter of good education and of fairness to pupils, classroom teachers should know what is involved in good testing and be able to construct good tests in line with the goals and content of their teaching. This will not, of course, eliminate the usefulness of the published standardized tests, but it will fill a gap that the published test cannot possibly fill. It ought to be added that in the development of their own tests teachers should approach the excellence of the published tests, assuming, of course, that the published tests are carefully derived. Good education for our children requires such competence.

The School's Use of Test Results.—The common attitude of pupils toward the tests they take in school is one of dislike and fearfulness. Some pupils experience extreme anxiety or even horror as the hour of a heralded test draws near. Recently the writer collected some of the quips that had been written by college students on crude tables in a room where large group tests were administered. They are quite revealing.

> Lord God of Hosts, be with us yet,
> Lest we forget.
> Doomed am I.
> Another funeral this day.
> Here endeth my college career.
> Where is my wandering mind today?
> Into the valley of death.
> I wish I had wings of an angel;
> Away from this Ex. I would fly.
> Here I sit all scared and blue;
> Here comes the exam . . .
> I don't know what to do.
> The funeral march.
> Oh brain, fail me not!
> Here's where I am annihilated.

It is genuinely refreshing when one finds within the whole weird lot a simple, courageous

> Charge, cerebellum!

No matter that it isn't the cerebellum at all that is involved in the higher thinking processes—give the student credit for breaking a terrible spell! Orchids, too, to the student who, reacting to the pressures of our examination system, said:

> Breathes there a scholar
> With soul so dead
> Who never to himself hath said
> To hell with exams—
> I'm going to bed.

But tests are not disagreeable in themselves. Witness the many quiz programs on the radio and the thousands of dollars that are spent for parlor games that in many cases are of the precise nature and content of school tests. Thousands of people look forward to the current events tests published periodically by *Time* and take the tests regularly without thinking of peeking at the answers in the back pages. It is the uses to which tests are put that determine our attitude toward them. In school, tests have been used overwhelmingly for the purpose of determining a mark for a pupil. Always a life-or-death, pass-or-fail situation exists; and the test is the sinister vehicle. As long as this limited use of tests continues in schools, we cannot hope for any significant change in attitude toward them.

But there are numerous uses for test results other than to determine marks, promotions, awards, recommendations, and the like. Let use enumerate a few:

a) To stimulate learning. If tests results are examined by the pupil and he accepts them as the record against which he will compete in the future, then they have become a motivation for further learning.

b) To evaluate instruction. Conscientious teachers view test results not only as a measure of how well pupils have progressed but also of how well they themselves have taught. On a larger scale, school administrators and supervisors can evaluate the work of instructors through carefully controlled testing programs.

c) To determine the content of instruction. Test results should be analyzed to determine what material has been poorly mastered and in what areas remedial instruction is necessary. Sometimes at the beginning of a course a comprehensive pretest is given so that materials will not be included which are already generally understood. The results of the pretest are most helpful also in adapting content to the individuals in the group.

d) To group pupils. In schools where grouping is practiced, test results are used widely in determining into which group pupils will be placed. In this connection it is important that the testing be adequate, so that placement will not depend upon the results of a single test.

e) To predict likely scholastic success. Tests intended to predict likely scholastic success are usually known as prognostic tests. They range all the way from reading or number readiness tests at the preschool level to tests intended to show the likelihood of success in graduate studies. Scholastic aptitude tests given to large numbers of college freshmen are of this sort.

f) To compare groups. As was pointed out above, standardized tests with their norms are widely used in making comparisons among groups. When a group wishes to compare its present achievement in a field with its own previous achievement, an equivalent form of the test previously used will be required, since obviously the same test should not be given over again.

g) To provide information useful in counseling. There are many kinds of information useful in counseling which can be obtained from tests and which should have no relationship at all to the pupil's standing in the school.

It is clear from the above that there is a variety of uses to which test results can be put. If tests were used more frequently in a variety of roles, the anxiety associated with their use as measuring devices would be greatly reduced.

Combining Test Results for the Individual.—Separate test scores standing alone are not very meaningful. If a youngster takes a test along with ninety-nine others and gets a certain score, not much has been found out except that he got that particular score on that particular good or bad test and that the other youngsters got certain scores also. It is important that test results be combined for the individual to show relationships that are important for him.

The Ages. In order to show relationships for the individual, the basic information involved in those relationships must be known. Some of this information has been described as the "ages" of the individual—chronological age, mental age, and educational age. The chronological age, of course, is the age of the individual in years and months. No tests are involved in deriving this knowledge. However, in deriving mental and educational ages, tests are necessary. For example, if the mental age of a twelve-year-old child is desired, one must assume the existence of a good mental ability test that has been given to thousands of persons at various chronological age levels. Norms will have been computed for all the chronological age groups for which the test is intended. This certain twelve-year-old will then take the test, and his score on it will be matched against the norms that have been established for the various chronological age groups. If his·score matches the norm for the fourteen-year-old group, he will then be said to have a mental age of fourteen, even though his chronological age is only twelve. The same procedure is followed in determining the educational age, except that the tests involved are achievement or educational tests rather than mental ability tests. Norms on achievement tests will again be established for the various chronological age groups. Our twelve-year-old will then take the tests and his scores will be matched against the norms. If his achievement falls at the level of that for ten-year-olds, he will be said to have an educational age of ten, even though his chronological age is twelve. Thus the basic "ages" of the individual can vary, being twelve, fourteen, and ten in our hypothetical case; and the relationships among these results take on a significance not attached to isolated test scores.

The Quotients. The quotients express the relationships among the ages indicated above. Three quotients are most common: intelligence quotient (I.Q.), educational quotient (E.Q.), and accomplishment quotient (A.Q.). The intelligence quotient is computed by dividing the mental age by the chronological age, and multiplying by one hundred: $I.Q. = \dfrac{M.A.}{C.A.} \times 100$. Here the individual's mental age is related to the mental age average for his own chronological age group. Since his own chronological age is the same as the average mental age for his chronological age group, it is used in the equation as an accurate substitute for the latter. Hence the I.Q. of our case above would be $\dfrac{14}{12} \times 100 = 116$. Relatively, then, the mental ability of our twelve-year-old is higher than the average mental ability of his own chronological age group. If he were at the level of his chronological age group, his I.Q. would be 100.

The educational quotient is computed by dividing the educational age by the chronological age, and multiplying by one hundred: $E.Q. = \dfrac{E.A.}{C.A.} \times 100$. Here the educational age of the individual is related to the average educational age for his own chronological age group. The educational age of our twelve-year-old was assumed to be ten, hence his E.Q. would be $\dfrac{10}{12} \times 100 = 83$. Relative to others in his chronological age group, his educational age or achievement is low.

The accomplishment quotient eliminates all reference to the chronological age and establishes the relationship between the individual's educational age and his own mental age: $\text{A.Q.} = \dfrac{\text{E.A.}}{\text{M.A.}} \times 100$. Thus, for our case above, the A.Q. will be $\dfrac{10}{14} \times 100 = 71$. His educational achievement, in terms of his ability to achieve, is much too low.

Clearly, test results take on added significance when relationships such as the above are considered. Yet the use of the quotients has come rather slowly. They are subject, of course, to abuse and misunderstanding; and their maximum usefulness will come only after the general public as well as teachers themselves know what they mean. The I.Q. has very likely been more widely used than either the E.Q. or the A.Q.; and the A.Q. least of the three. However, the importance of the A.Q. is being recognized. Whereas in the I.Q. and the E.Q. the ability and achievement of the individual are compared with that of others, in the A.Q. the individual's achievement is matched with his own ability to achieve. This gets the problem back to where it belongs; and, more importantly, to where constructive things can be done about it.

Suppose, for example, a bright boy in a class of twenty pupils manages without much trouble to lead his class in achievement. The typical teacher or parent is inclined to pat such a youngster on the back, say he is the best in the bunch, and let it go at that. However, if the boy's ability to achieve is determined, it might well be shown that his achievement is not nearly up to where it should be and that what he needs is not a pat on the back but a prod in the ribs and some real cooperation and motivation from teachers and parents to get achievement up to where it belongs. Anyhow, the relationship of test results involved in the A.Q. commands more and more interest and is being computed for more and more pupils.

Composite Rather Than Single Results. The movement to combine test results in the quotients to show significant relationships is part of a larger tendency to place less emphasis on the results of single tests and more on composite results. For example, many teacher-education institutions now administer definite admissions criteria for students seeking to begin preparation for the profession. Specific minimum standards are set for such criteria as mental ability, scholastic achievement, health, teaching aptitude, and personality. It is generally agreed that it is better to look for a favorable composite rating on these criteria, allowing outstanding strength on some items to offset slight weaknesses on others, than to permit the least deficiency on a single item to disqualify the student. The total picture thus becomes more important than any one of its parts. This, indeed, is an outstanding characteristic of the whole testing movement. Test results help to paint the larger picture; and they are really properly at work when they are held in clear relationship to educational goals and human development. They are abused when an individual result becomes an end in itself and is not given its rightful interpretation in a larger setting.

Reporting Pupil Progress.—The foregoing discussion may explain some of the changes that have taken place in reporting pupil progress to parents. The old-fashioned report card is having a hard time of it. For generations past and to a large extent today, the only report of pupil progress that went home to parents was a small card on which the subjects taken by the pupil were indicated, together with a per-centage mark for each subject. "Deportment" was also included and it, too, received a percentage mark. All the parents knew from this report was that this month Mary got 78 in arithmetic and last month she got 79. They also knew that Janet, across the street and in the same grade as Mary, got 79 in arithmetic, and the implications were unthinkable. On the basis of the one-point difference they might go to work on the teacher, the neighbors, or, worst of all, on Mary. Such hairline differences were troublesome; and considerable relief was felt when a system whereby pupils could be lumped into more general groups was introduced. Instead of a 78 or a 79, the report card could now carry *A, B, C, D, F* or I, II, III, IV, *F*, meaning something akin to excellent, good, fair, poor, and failure. It would now be easier to put Mary and Janet together in one of these groups and thus avoid the hairline situation. Of course, hairline decisions concerning which group a pupil should go into still had to be made, but they were made privately by the teacher, and the closeness of the decision was not indicated on the report card.

But such reporting carries very little meaning. It certainly does not deal with the relationships dealt with in the quotients and does not reflect the child in his over-all reaction to the school or in his total development. Hence the demand for more meaningful reporting. What is the result?

The result in some school systems is a progress report that reflects the school's desire to promote the full development of the pupil and not only his scholastic development. Hence, in addition to the studies taken, items having to do with health, personal and social develop-ment, school citizenship, and the like are included in the report. Also space is provided to report such things as performance in relation to ability, work habits, and special interests or problems revealed through the school work. It is, of course, obvious that when such matters are included in the report they cannot be tied down to a 78 or a 79. Consequently, a good many reports are tending to be descriptive or explanatory in nature rather than numerical. Instead of carrying a 75 in reading, the report may carry a short paragraph stating that, whereas Bertha recognizes words readily and can read rapidly, she is weak in reading comprehension, losing ideas in the rapid pronunciation of words. This report, if it has been substantiated by tests given in the school, is certainly worth more to the parents and the pupil than a mere numerical report. Furthermore, it can and often does carry suggestions as to how the home can cooperate with the school in promoting improvement.

In a few instances schools have eliminated written reports altogether and have replaced them by conferences with parents. Instead of the regular report being sent home, the parent now makes regular calls at the school to discuss the child's progress. In this way parents meet personally the people who have direct charge of their children, and together they can come to understandings that bear directly upon the children's welfare. The conference method of reporting progress has worked out well, and more than one group of parents has voted overwhelmingly for its continuance.

In reporting pogress, therefore, the emphasis is on the over-all situation in all its relationships, on the full development of the individual, and on the broader goals of education rather than on the isolated item. Thus it takes on the broader aspects of evaluation rather than the narrower aspects of measurement.

3. Techniques Are Still Subordinate to the Larger Goals

In all considerations bearing upon the improvement of education and the evaluation of its outcomes, the primary purposes must be kept clear. No new building or bus or set of tests is an end in itself. The ultimate goal is improved human beings; unless all other factors are made to contribute to this end, the endeavor falls short. No amount of equipment, skill, or money can guarantee good education. All must cluster around and be driven by the human motive. It is quite possible, of course, to lose the human touch and place too much faith in things and techniques. The people, the board, the superintendent, and the teachers may think they have the best schools because they have the best equipment. The counselor may think he does the best job of counseling because he gives the most tests. It does not necessarily follow. If the goals are clear and all these other things are kept in proper relationship to the goals, then all that is done becomes important and significant; otherwise, much time and energy are wasted. Of course, too much cannot be done in providing the best possible educational opportunities for all our people. This fundamental concern for human betterment explains the tremendous interest and investment that Americans have in their schools, and it gives substance to their willingness constantly to evaluate and improve them.

What Do YOU Say?

1

The surest way of securing educational improvements in a community is to put the whole community to work on determining the kind of education it wants for its people.

What do YOU say?

2

On the whole, school principals and supervisors have too little interest in, and know too little about, conducting fundamental studies to determine whether or not the materials and methods used by their teachers really result in good pupil learning.

What do YOU say?

3

Evaluation in education needs to move closer to the measurement of the growth and development of the whole person and be less confined to measuring the amount of information learned.

What do YOU say?

4

Most students would object to classes in which no testing or evaluating were done. They would rather be tested too much than too little.

What do YOU say?

5

What points in this chapter do you particularly support or take issue with?

Chapter 13

SCHOOL AND COMMUNITY INTERRELATIONSHIPS
Everybody's Business

Most people are genuinely interested in youngsters; certainly most parents are interested in their own children. In the typical American community the people have a deep interest in the school because it concerns their own children. Furthermore, most Americans want to be proud of the communities in which they live, and they know full well that the quality of their communities is determined in good part by the quality of their schools. Find out for yourself. Contact a hundred families with children that have moved within the last five years, and check the number in which the schools were an important factor in the selection of a new location. Families seek out communities with good schools; they avoid those with poor ones. Good schools are a practical necessity to a good community, and Americans demand both as the birthright of their children.

But this fundamental demand for good schools has not always been accompanied by close working relationships between the school and the community. In too many cases, the school, while it has expected the community to support it, has been inclined to go it alone. As a result, the people of the community have felt pretty much like outsiders, wondering about the schools and basically interested in them but not quite sure of what is going on or how to find out about it. On the other hand, communities, expecting their schools to be good, have sometimes been inclined to take them for granted. They seem to suppose that the school is possessed of some kind of magic by which it can do a quality job without money and moral support. As a result, the school, conscious of its task of equipping boys and girls for the real business of citizenship, may also feel abandoned and may wonder if staff and equipment will hold out until needs are recognized and community interest and support are revived. Now the common element in these situations is an interest in good schools. The thing that is absent is a real cooperative approach to community education. Here lies one of our most crucial problems today. Public education, involving the destinies of all the people, must not be caught in the maelstrom of a divided people or of people who in their communities have not learned to cooperate in behalf of their fundamental institutions. The problem, far-reaching in its nature, is not mysterious and removed in its solution. This chapter is concerned with simple, sometimes obvious things that can be done to secure the kind of working relationship between school and community that all desire.

1. COMMUNITY LIVING CONSTITUTES EDUCATION

The child's complete living in his community constitutes his education. What he experiences at the schoolhouse is an important part, but only a part, of his learning. This fact becomes more and more important as one reflects on it, and it is equally applicable at all levels of education. Even when a student leaves his local community and goes away to college, his college education will involve the college community and out-of-class experiences to a very great degree. Study in a foreign institution is valued for its contacts with another society as well as for its classroom work. Education, then, involves the wider environment, the whole community. This realization immediately sets the stage and creates the necessity for a community approach to education.

Take a local community. Think, too, of our educational objectives. Any thought that the health, citizenship, vocational preparation, use of leisure time, home membership, and ethical character of the pupils in the schools are determined solely by the schools is farfetched indeed. These are specific educational objectives, but they require the cooperative attention of the entire community if they are to be realized. When a youngster attends a school in which some effort is made to help him find and develop leisure activities that will enrich his whole life, he should find in the same community good libraries, recreation facilities, music organizations, clubs, theaters, and the like that will supplement his school experience. The same for health, citizenship, and the rest. Unless conscious attention is given to these areas of cooperative concern and to ways of working together on them, schools and their communities will continue to offer poorer education than children deserve. If the approach is united, the prospect is different.

2. AREAS OF MUTUAL UNDERSTANDING AND ACTION

The people in charge of the schools and the people who constitute our communities should be together on many things. This does not mean merely keeping one another informed or one accepting the decisions of the other. It means working together from the beginning, using intelligence in developing understandings and agreements, and cooperating in laying and working plans. What are some of the areas in which the school and the community thus share mutual responsibility?

Clarifying the Purposes of Education.—In the previous chapter considerable attention was given to community participation in clarifying the purposes of its schools as a first step in improving education. An abbreviated inquiry form was presented which could be used in getting the community together on this project. The reader is urged to review that discussion. It is sufficient to point out here that the whole community ought to know and understand the real purposes of education and share in restating those purposes for the local schools. This is a task for all, not merely for the professional school people. School administrators know that unless this kind of understanding undergirds the educational program in the community, the program will remain forever on shaky legs. Agreement on purposes, mutually evolved, is basic.

Determining Broad Outlines of the Educational Program.—In America our educational history presents a running story of our people reacting to the program of the schools. Actually, our whole public school system is a result of such reaction. Public high schools and public colleges arose because our people did not like the then narrow and too inflexible programs of the academies and the private colleges. It is to be expected and desired that much community reaction to the adequacy of the educational program will continue. The people of a rural community in which only 8 per cent of the high school graduates go on to college ought to be heard from if the local high school offers only the college-preparatory course. The people of an industrial community in which two-thirds of the high school graduates go to work in factories and offices should be heard from if the local high school has no work in industrial or business education. The people of all communities need to know whether or not their children are getting good grounding in the fundamentals, good health training, and appropriate enrichment in music and art activities. In other words, communities ought to share in evaluating the over-all educational program that is found in the schools they support.

Whereas all the people are involved in determining the broad outlines of the educational program, they do not determine the details within the separate areas. The whole people may support a policy of adding homemaking to the school's program, but the whole people will not hire the teacher, decide on the equipment to be bought, and choose the units of instruction to be taught. If all the people in a community decide to have a police department and a fire department, they will not subsequently decide on all the details involved in their operation. Thus the area of mutual understanding with reference to the educational program remains at the general level, leaving the specifics for people hired especially to take care of them. This principle applies generally in all public education as, in fact, it does in all public services.

Providing Adequately for School Personnel.—The school leaders and the community as a whole need to agree completely on needs with reference to school personnel. This should not be difficult if the people have shared properly in evolving the purposes and program of the school. The whole community should agree not only on the number of staff members needed but also on certain other standards having to do with working conditions. School patrons are fully capable of understanding the relationship between a teacher's load, salary, and instructional equipment and his effectiveness in the classroom. They will understand it more fully if they share in examining some of the problems related to it. In more than one community, citizen's groups studying such things as school buildings and grounds, teachers' salaries in relation to living costs in the community, and the adequacy of instructional materials have come up with recommendations that the school people themselves would scarcely dare to suggest. On such matters as this, favorable action will be forthcoming much sooner if the full community is really informed.

Looking Ahead on Building Needs.—As one patron put it to a member of a school building committee, "How do you know we are going to have that much increase in our school enrolments during the next five years? I think you are hoodwinking the taxpayers." The perfect response to this kind of patron is to put him on a committee to count all the little noses between one and five that are already in the community and are headed straight for school. Sometimes it is surprising how oblivious people are to facts that ought to be common knowledge. The fault is not always their own. Their daily work and routine may not bring them into contact with the facts or present any need for them. Nevertheless, as patrons of the school they ought to be part of an active body that keeps itself informed on pertinent matters. So it will be with building needs, not only for new buildings but for remodelings, additions, renovations, new equipment, improved and enlarged grounds, and so on. Patrons give excellent service as members of groups to look into such things, and they will often gain entree to sources of useful information not always easily accessible to school officials. They will often come up with facts about population trends, real estate developments, legal and political angles, materials, and costs that are invaluable.

It goes without saying that building needs should be anticipated as early as possible. Procrastination may result in an emergency, with all the haste and waste that goes with it. Thus the building problem becomes a continuing community problem.

Meeting the Costs.—This certainly is an item for the cooperative study and action of the school and the community. Here again, if the entire community understands and believes in the total educational enterprise, it will make a reasonable effort to support it. If it does not, such support as is forthcoming is apt to be grudgingly given. Let the people in charge of school finances keep the problem constantly before the people. Too frequently the financial blow falls all at once in a single public meeting, the budget-makers hopeful that no questions will be asked and the people scarcely informed enough to ask intelligent questions. Why, for example, should the need for providing audio-visual equipment in all the schools and for adding driver training in the high schools first appear at such a meeting? There is much information related to both which fully justify them, and the people should not be expected to approve them without this knowledge. Sufficient time should be taken prior to their being presented in the budget to make this knowledge public. It should be remembered that school finances strike closer home with the people than a good many other items pertaining to education. It is, of course, their money; and mutual understanding with reference to its expenditure is essential.

Clarifying Responsibility.—Many misunderstandings and bad moments will be avoided in a community if everyone is familiar with the responsibilities of the many people involved in the operation of the schools. For example, school patrons sometimes act as though the board of education had no responsibility to anyone but themselves. They forget that the local school has many legal connections beyond the local community that must be observed. On the other hand, the legal status of the board in presiding over a part of a state school system does not reduce the responsibility of the board to the local community. A clear understanding in the community of the dual role played by the board of education will help in the promotion of over-all unity. Also, the community at large should have a good appreciation of the work done by administrators, supervisors, teachers, special committees, special survey groups, and other school personnel. Above all, patrons should include themselves among groups having direct responsibilities for the improvement of their schools, and they should know what those responsibilities are.

We have, then, noted a half-dozen broad areas in which the school and the community should work cooperatively. None of these areas is so specialized that mutual participation is not desirable. All the people need to discuss the purposes of education, to react to the broad outlines of the school program, to know staff needs, to keep alert to building and equipment needs in relation to changing conditions, to know school expenses and how they must be met, and to appreciate the duties of all persons, including themselves, who share in the great project of community education.

Are There Some Limitations?—Let us enter here the reminder that in schools, as in any other highly organized undertaking, there are many matters which must be taken care of by people who are trained to do them and who make these duties their lifework. In other words, there is a host of things associated with running a school system which the people will leave entirely to those in charge of the schools. It is, roughly, the difference between planning and operating, policy and practice, legislative and executive; the community as a whole will work at the planning, policy, or legislative level, leaving the specialized operational jobs to those prepared to do them. Although operational responsibilities fall directly and quite completely on the school people, this does not mean that the people of the community will not be interested in the effective running of the school. They will be. However, if the school is run poorly, the corrective is not for the people to take over the details and run it; the corrective, frankly, is to let some ineffective school people go and employ others who can run the school as it ought to be run. Give us more communities in which there is over-all interest and cooperation in school matters; but deliver us from communities in which every citizen feels a personal responsibility for choosing a principal or for deciding whether or not the methods used by the first grade teacher in teaching beginning reading are satisfactory. There is a nice division of responsibility between the general and the special groups; its detection and observance is a thing of art and a primary characteristic of good community schools.

3. Desirable Activities on the School's Part

Any school that wishes to promote community understanding and cooperation with reference to education will think of many things it can do. The following items are only a starter. The secret really lies in the ingenuity of school leaders in evolving plans locally and in doing what ought to be done under the circumstances.

Informing the Community.—There are many ways of keeping a community informed about its schools. Publications are probably most common. Newspaper space is sometimes given over to the schools for reporting school news. Some schools now issue periodicals of their own. The annual school reports have, in many cases, undergone almost miraculous changes. Instead of the older formal reports, dealing primarily with statistical matters, some are now beautifully prepared, presenting excellent graphs, replete with meaningful pictures, and containing much descriptive matter that gives an inside view of the schools at work. Special bulletins devoted to certain phases of the school's program or to current problems are frequently prepared and distributed to parents and to the community at large Some schools have made a practice of distributing rather widely their handbooks, the yearly calendar of school activities, selected materials prepared for pupil counseling, and the like.

The radio is a good means of bringing certain types of information to the people. Incidentally, such radio time should not be monopolized by the school's leaders. It is quite likely that more people listen to good programs put on by the pupils themselves than to a series of speeches by the superintendent of schools. Radio interviews with selected students, staff members, and others, if they are well planned and presented, are excellent.

Exhibits and displays of school work are a good thing. Such exhibits ought to show what is going on in the classrooms where the children of the community are spending their time. Special programs in which demonstrations are given of such activities as music, health, physical education, and dramatics are useful. An occasional school now is filming its activities throughout a school year and then showing the film to community groups. This seems to be an effective way of attracting larger crowds to such gatherings and offers a fine opportunity for the interpolator to call attention to an excellent library or a hazardous stairway.

Open house is also held in many schools. When this is done the regular work of the school should continue. Parents and others should be able during open house to visit classes where regular work is in progress. Unfortunately, many parents are unable to attend open house during the day and many children cannot return to school at night. Nevertheless, the practice of throwing the working school open to observation by the community is commendable.

The school is always able to hold special meetings as a means of informing the community on certain matters. The half-dozen things discussed in the previous section are of the type which might well be discussed in such meetings. At any rate, the school has a basic obligation to present to the community such information as will give a true picture of its activities and problems. If this is well done, an important step in the establishment of close working relationships has been taken.

Initiating Cooperative Activities.—But the job is not merely one of informing the community about the school's activities and needs or of selling it on a program of school support. Ways of actually working together must be discovered and used. Joint committees should be set up in which school and community people work side by side. Persons from the community should be brought in on many committees and advisory councils that have ordinarily been limited to school people. Committees having to do with planning, curriculum-building, and population studies are illustrative. Advisory groups to the counseling services, the library, the cafeteria, and the like should have patrons on them. The school can also actively promote cooperation with such groups as the parent-teacher association, the community council, the chamber of commerce, and the YMCA. Frequently specific projects can be suggested on which these organizations, in cooperation with the school, can work. More than one chamber of commerce has helped to solve the problem of band uniforms, and more than one PTA has promoted the kind of child study that is basic to good education. In some communities other types of joint activities are sponsored. Occasionally a school-community music group is organized, and parents and pupils alike find a new thrill in playing or singing together. Schools that have worked with their communities on father-son and mother-daughter banquets have often found that the way is cleared for better working relationships. The point is that the initiation of cooperative action causes the old feelings of separateness to give way to new feelings of oneness in a common cause.

Choosing Good Teachers.—Without doubt the most important single thing that responsible school officers can do to unite a community behind its schools is to employ good teachers. Rare is the community that will admit that it is willing to get along with poor teachers in order to save money. Good teachers are desired; and the recognition that good teachers are actually in the classrooms is a source of real satisfaction and pride. Incidentally, no amount of joining of community organizations by a poor teacher will offset the dissatisfaction engendered by his weakness in the classroom.

Making Teaching Effective.—Communities are pleased with their schools if they see that proper attention is given to the improvement of instruction in the classroom. Increasingly boards of education are helping teachers in service to bear the expense of continued study, visitation to other school systems, and research intended to improve the effectiveness of the schools. Teachers ought to improve in their effectiveness as the years go by. Good supervision also is essential in helping to stave off incipient stagnation. The result, of course, is happy, progressing children, who are the best possible agents of school and community cooperation.

Promoting Professional Unity.—Sometimes the people of the community get in a real quandary over school problems because there seems to be no unity among the school people themselves. The board of education and the school administrators may disagree on policies; the superintendent and the teachers may not be together on curriculum matters; and the teachers themselves may be at odds over salary recommendations. Now no one expects that complete agreement on all matters will ever be forthcoming, but as a matter of ordinary common sense the people in the profession ought to realize that unity within the profession on educational problems will promote unity in the community and lack of unity will promote uncertainty and hesitation. School people should give themselves sufficient time and opportunity to get together on points of view, if they can, before issues are thrown out for public discussion. They are certain to be questioned by the citizens at large on these issues; and if their own thinking is enlightened and coherent, the thinking of the whole community is more likely to be the same.

Assuming Responsibility for Leadership.—The recent realization that the public school in this country is public not only for purposes of support but also for purposes of understanding and participation has placed a new responsibility on school leaders. The school administrator is no longer merely a public employee assigned to the routines of a certain job; he must now know how to point up issues, organize the people and the resources of the community to meet those issues, and stimulate many, many people to contribute their special abilities and services. This does not mean that the school leader gives over to others the responsibility for making decisions that he is employed to make; it does mean that in making decisions that involve the welfare of the community's schools he will tap the community's best counsel on problems that are in fact their own and in so doing will arouse the kind of interest and understanding that ought to undergird the schools anyhow. Communities are expecting more and more of this kind of leadership. If they get it, the school is secure and the children will be better served.

There are, of course, many other things resourceful schools will find to do as working members of school-community teams. In all cases the primary emphasis will be on activities that actually pay off in terms of better education for the community. If this result can be demonstrated, the school's role is in proper focus.

4. Desirable Activities on the Part of the Community

If cooperative teamwork in school-community relations is the goal, then it must be clear that the community, as well as the school, has certain responsibilities to discharge. Again these responsibilities are quite obvious. They are such as can be practiced by every citizen, but they frequently fall far short of actual fulfilment.

Reading and Listening.—What good is it to have fine reports from the school, good coverage in the newspaper, and carefully prepared radio programs if only a few people pay any heed? Citizens, knowing that the schools affect them and their community now and forever, ought to make school matters a part of their assigned reading and listening.

Knowing and Inquiring.—If the citizen does not get information enough to satisfy him through the school's regular channels, he should set himself the task of inquiring at the proper sources for the information he wants. For example, it may be that the people of the community are talking about a proposed new route for a school bus or a proposed site for a new school building; before formulating a judgment on these proposals, patrons should examine spot maps showing where the pupils live and data on residential developments in the community. This information should be freely asked for. Too often judgments are formed on the basis of some remark dropped by a friend or of mere emotion. Inquiry will reveal the facts. Also parents sometimes hesitate to ask questions that bear directly upon the work of their children in the school. This feeling should not exist. Inquiry reflects interest. A school that is in fact a community school welcomes it.

Going to School Events.—It would be a good thing if more citizens worked school events into their calendars as they do the theater, the church, or the golf links. School plays, exhibits, games, PTA meetings, commencement exercises, conferences on school problems, and musicals with homemade costumes are not only worthy, they are interesting. Furthermore, the lift experienced by the pupils and the school people when their activities are well attended is genuine, to say nothing of the good feeling that patrons themselves have as they become a part of a going, human concern.

Accepting Responsibility.—It is easy to insist that our schools must be good. Of course we want the best for our children. It is not as easy, however, to accept the chairmanship of the school lunch committee, to plan the mother-daughter banquet, to work with a school committee that is studying the homemaking curriculum, to head the school building committee, to provide an extra car to get youngsters to the regional music festival, or to accept a post on the board of education. But these jobs and a hundred more like them must be done if we are to be able to point with pride to our schools. Furthermore, they are jobs for the citizen, not the school people. It is one of the primary inconsistencies of many adults in our communities that they want the best for themselves and their children but hesitate to assume their fair share of responsibility for bringing about the conditions they desire. If, on the other hand, responsibility is assumed, the load can be distributed so that none is overburdened.

Relating Support to Significance.—Citizens have need to consider the many things to which they may give moral and financial support and to support them in relation to their importance. The school certainly does not ask for support to which it is not entitled; and it realizes that there are other things that must be cared for. However, sometimes a good perspective is lost in the glare of pressures that are immediate and often spectacular. For example, a community chest drive in deft hands will often draw from the community surprising amounts of money for agencies whose loads would be lightened if the schools were more adequately supported. Clinics and penal and mental institutions that handle spectacular cases often find their support more easily forthcoming than do schools, whose costs are lower and who, again, could lighten the costlier load if they were better supported. Sometimes the people of a community are quite willing to entertain city youngsters for two weeks during the summer but are quite unwilling to provide their own children with recreational facilities and supervised summer activity programs. It seems much easier to rally round the deviates than to stand by the normal, even though a careful second thought will certainly show that to stand by the normal will eliminate the deviates in good part. Citizens must establish in their minds the things that come first in their communities, the fundamental things of continuing consequence to which adequate and continuing support should be given.

Using Proper Channels.—The schools of a typical American community are pretty well set up to deal with educational problems. Not only is a responsible board of education elected, but professional people are employed to carry out school policies and handle the operation of the program. Sometimes patrons forget to use these established channels in following up on problems they are concerned with. Rather, they may seek by their own means to bring about action. This is unwise on three immediate counts: first, it negates the kind of school-community cooperation we are talking about; second, it is quite likely that less will be accomplished this way than if the regular channels are used; and third, such cases ought to be used to determine whether or not the local school leaders have the skill and the caliber necessary to deal with such problems successfully.

Avoiding Pressure Groups.—Since the public schools are an enterprise of all the people and since we wish to maintain them free and untrammeled, it follows that no segment of the people should wish to use the schools in its own behalf. If the people of a community are really thinking straight, they will see themselves more as a proper subject of study by the schools than as persons free to exert pressures on the schools. Furthermore, if any group succeeds in having its special interest promoted by the school, there is no reason on earth why any other group should be denied the same privilege. Groups are acting democratically when they insist on relieving the school of such pressures and seek to conduct their affairs in the community so that the school, observing them, will see their devotion to the general welfare and to schools that are in fact free. Sometimes religious groups, business groups, patriotic organizations, parent-teacher organizations, and others slide into the role of pressure groups almost without knowing it. The line between genuine interest and active participation in school affairs and pressure activities is rather finely drawn; yet it must be discovered and observed. The key test to the

individual citizen is this: Am I interested in this matter because it
meets a general need or because it promotes the interest of a special
group?

Thus the responsibilities of the citizen in the community parallel
those of the people in the school if we are to have real strength in the
total project.

5. THE COMMUNITY AS A RESOURCE FOR EDUCATION

The close relationship between the school and the community goes
beyond the activities involved in the cooperation of citizens and school
people. The community is itself a remarkable resource for education.

A Resource for Content.—There is scarcely an area of study in
the school, from the kindergarten through the graduate school, for
which there is not to be found in the community a rich store of content
for learning. Take science. From the simplest nature study of young
children to the chemistry and physics offered in the typical high
school, the fields and farms and homes and factories of the community
are replete with plants, animals, weather, foods, machinery, soils,
health problems, and a thousand other things waiting to become meat
on the dry bones of ordinary textbook teaching. It is still literally true
that in many biology classrooms the pupils pore over classifications
to be memorized from the textbooks while within easy walking distance of the school is a world of things that would change rote learning
into learning with some interesting and useful connections. Take the
social studies. Think of the local history that would come to life for
youngsters if they examined the old records, interviewed elderly resi-
dents, dug into the local library, or visited historical sites and museums
in the region. Pupils ought also to get a first-hand look at how local
government is run and what some of its problems are. It is a good
thing when local authorities are willing to "turn over the reins" of
government for a day to pupils from the school. Such an experience
can be invaluable if it is preceded and followed by careful preparation
and evaluation. In some communities pupils are actually being appointed to groups that are set up to study housing, health, recreational
facilities, and the like. For English, geography, arithmetic, foreign
language, agriculture, homemaking, business subjects, and all the rest,
the opportunity to use the community as a resource for content is ever
present. Furthermore, the interest the pupil generates in his own
community when it is used as a resource for content and the working
relationship he sees between the school and the community will affect
greatly his own actions when he becomes an adult.

A Resource for the Application of Learning.—In recent years there has been much emphasis in education on carrying learning through to the point of application. "Ivory tower" education, where students are removed from the warp and woof of living and cloistered behind walls of green ivy, has become an object of considerable derision. "Learning by doing" has become a kind of catch phrase to indicate that, as far as possible, learning should be direct as well as vicarious, that one ought to study engines as well as about engines, and that the school should give the pupils an opportunity to apply the things they learn. In fact, as was pointed out in Chapter 12, learning that is capable of practical applications is not complete until those applications have been made. The homemaking teacher who seeks to have the things learned in school actually applied in the homes of the pupils is on the right track, and the same holds for the agriculture teacher and the shop and business teachers. It may seem less obvious in some other learning areas, but manifold applications can be made in science, English, civics, and so on. In some high schools the pupils, usually seniors, who take the work in problems of democracy have studied economic, social, and political problems in the community and have seen their projects transform housing conditions, parks and playgrounds, health conditions, and political practices. So the list would continue. Teachers and parents alike should view with alarm any school to which pupils go from year to year that does not promote projects involving the application of the things the children learn. The opportunities in the community for such applications are too numerous to justify such inertness.

Work Experience.—A good many young people leaving our schools today have never had any real work experience. This is not always their own fault. In many homes, particularly in the cities, there simply is no work to be assigned to children; and the labor laws in many states, together with the tendency in business and industry to raise the minimum age of employees, deny to high-school-age youth the opportunity to work. And yet, there are many people, including the parents of these youngsters, who feel that no one should be graduated from high school who does not know what real work is and who has not developed a sense of responsibility for work well done. Hence, some high schools are attempting to provide work experience for all pupils. This, of course, requires the fullest cooperation of the community; and happily most communities cooperate remarkably well. When such a program really gets under way, it will be necssary for a school of any size at all to employ a person whose full job it will be to coordinate it. Naturally, the school will want to make sure that the conditions under which pupils work are satisfactory. Hence, in addition to making initial contacts with stores, offices, farms, factories, and so on, the coordinator will need to check on these conditions. Furthermore, checking with the families of pupils, determining the type of work that is suitable to different pupils, keeping adequate records, and making follow-up studies will leave no time for leisure.

The length of time involved in work experience is not ordinarily great for a pupil. However, it ought to be long enough for him to learn the job, get the experience of adapting to it, and become skilful enough to do his work well and be proud of it. He should be paid a reasonable sum, but this is not the real objective. Neither is it intended that work experience by high school pupils should affect the jobs of regular workers in the community. But it is important that the school and the community cooperate to fill the serious gap left in the education of our youth when they get out of school with no real feel for responsible work.

The Community School.—The feeling of closeness between the school and the community in some places has actually resulted in a new concept of educational services and a new name—the "community school." Here the regular education of the children is continued, of course, but beyond that, the school is made to serve broadly the diverse needs of the community. Adult groups look just as freely to the community school for help as do the children of school age. The school plant becomes the center of many community activities beyond the school activities. School leaders are just as eager to secure facilities for broader community needs as for regular school needs. Faculty members find tremendous stimulation in working with adult groups in addition to their usual classes. The community school, serving all the people all the time, is actually the culmination of the school-community idea. It finds its richness within itself. The problems and interests and needs of the people are so interwoven and so challenging that, once discovered, they seem to provide an educational program for years to come. Certainly in cases like this the community has become a resource for education in the broadest terms.

6. School Personnel as Members of the Community

As we know, our people today are viewing their schools as places where all-round development takes place and where attention is not limited to mere book learning. We know also that such development cannot take place unless all-round teachers are in the classroom. Communities are becoming less and less interested in teachers who show up daily for classes, teach certain subjects to pupils, and then go into seclusion every evening and over week ends. Obviously, if we are to have community schools, we must have teachers with community interest. This means that teachers, by choice, will wish to be not only members of the school staff but members of the community as well. On the other hand, communities must permit teachers to be normal people and lead normal lives. In some cases very strange requirements and restrictions are placed upon teachers, so that instead of their becoming normal, participating citizens, they are set up as an object of special check and restraint. In the well-integrated community there exists the mutual responsibility of teachers to live all-round lives as members of the school and the community and of the community to accept teachers as citizens who are as free to manage their own affairs as anybody else.

Types of Teacher Participation in Community Life.—When it comes right down to it, few groups contribute more to community activities than school people. They are all over the place. They are active in religious affairs, not only as attendants at church services but also as leaders and responsible workers. They accept assignments in special drives such as the community chest, Red Cross, and March of Dimes. They help in the observance of special holidays and fairs. They participate in community plays, musicals, and sporting events and many times assume responsibility for organizing and leading these activities. They are members and office-holders in civic groups, service organizations, fraternal orders, women's organizations, cultural groups, and so on. During times of war they have gone right along with the community in getting its special jobs done such as rationing, bond drives, and Red Cross. In fact, the American teacher has done so much in the typical community that there has been danger at times that his extra activities and services would be taken for granted. Basically, of course, he has been employed to teach school; and that is a full-time job in any case. He will, however, as a result of his interest in people and his ideas of responsible citizenship, engage in many extra activities; but he should not be asked to conduct the census, as almost happened in 1950, or assume duties that will weaken him in his primary job.

Some Limitations to Community Participation.—The rightness and urgency of certain community projects are sometimes the near-downfall of teachers. Perhaps there is a drive on to improve the recreational facilities for young people. Maybe the PTA has launched a campaign for better libraries. The annual push is on for the boys' club, the Boy Scouts, or the "Y." Funds for the March of Dimes must not fall below the mark set last year. Now these are good causes affecting school-age youngsters, a fact which frequently leads the people of the community to expect and request a lot of help from school people. Of course they will help; but if too much of this sort of thing is done, the teachers' overload will become excessive and their effectiveness in school will be lessened. Good work in the thing they are employed to do comes first. Sure enough, participation in community affairs will help them to do that fundamental job better; but if it is carried to excess, nothing is gained.

Finally, communities should not expect public school teachers to align themselves with pressure groups. Teachers should be citizens and think and vote as freely as anyone else; but as members of an institution devoted to free inquiry and the general welfare, they will not wish to be committed to any special-interest group.

7. COMMUNITY BALANCE: PULLING ABREAST IS THE GOAL

What we seek, then, is a community with institutions and organizations adequate to its needs; and, above all, with citizens who give these their proper place in the total scene. If a community neglects any of its basic institutions, or if it magnifies unduly its less basic affairs, it will be out of balance. All community projects, including public education, are a part of, and indeed determine the quality of, the living that will go on. They should, therefore, be seen as interrelated, each worthy of support as it contributes to the general good. Thus the citizens maintaining their personal freedom within the community will realize that a community has unity and goals the same as individuals do; and they will, in the free exercise of their intelligence, get behind the things that make for good community living. Fortunate are the children who live in communities where such clarity of purpose and unity of action exist.

Within this array of community projects and activities, public and private, stands the public school, bearing a direct relationship to every organization and individual. It must involve all of our people all of the time, not only as taxpayers but also as thinking participants. It will receive the active support of everyone because it represents a service that is fundamental to all, a common ground for community improvement, and a means of eliminating barriers that tend to disunite us.

What Do YOU Say?

1

It is a good thing for a community to have a cooperative, nongovernmental community council that encourages and coordinates the activities of many community organizations, so that all will promote common goals of community living and none will run counter to these goals. School leaders might well take the initiative in forming such a council.

What do YOU say?

2

There is some danger that, as increased community participation in school affairs comes about, the delicate dividing line between such participation and the operation of the schools by professionally trained people will be violated. This fact does not lessen the desirability of securing greater participation, and it makes even more urgent the necessity of having the dividing line discovered, understood, and observed in the community.

What do YOU say?

3

What points in this chapter do you particularly support or take issue with?

Chapter 14

THE PROFESSION OF EDUCATION

Joining Hands with the Future

The conduct of our schools in America engages the full-time services of over a million people. These people cannot be picked up on the street from ordinary good folks if they are expected to perform satisfactorily in the classroom or in an administrative post. We have come to recognize that special preparation is required for persons entering the profession. Neither can the people in education be borrowed from other professions. There is a definite body of knowledge, skills, and attitudes necessary to success in this field. There have been times when persons in other fields, finding the going rough, have, as a last resort, sought to enter teaching. Fortunately, certification regulations tend more and more to prevent this. Throughout the country, and much too slowly, effort is being made to guarantee that the people who guide the lives and learning of those in our classrooms will do so with skill and understanding. Furthermore, education is a service vocation; and anyone not sincerely interested in human beings and not willing to sacrifice for them has no business in it. Let us look further at the profession of education.

1. ITS GENERAL IMPORTANCE

Those who work in the schools of our country are dealing in the future. They are influencing the thought life of those who will determine the nature of our society, direct its economy, and control its politics. Education affects the happiness and effectiveness of all—mechanics, doctors, homemakers, lawyers, farmers, writers, statesmen, bakers, and all the rest. A single teacher constantly deals with this kind of cross section. In this country our teachers seek always to release these people, whatever their calling, to full and useful living, to self-reliance, to responsible living in the community, and to the constructive uses of freedom. Education can, of course, develop narrowness, intolerance, and selfishness. It can lead whole peoples into delusions of grandeur or hate. It can distort truth. But if its proper nature and function are clear and if it is in hands that are skilled and true, then breadth will replace narrowness, cooperation will replace selfishness and intolerance, and open-mindedness will replace the distortions to which we seem so subject. It is considerations such as these that give the profession of education its real color and significance. How greatly this transcends the careless idea that the core of the school is reading, writing, and arithmetic and that the job of the teacher is to "maintain order" and check on the spelling.

The essence of what is being discussed here is pointed up in a portion of a letter written by a veteran of the second World War:

Dear sir,

During my stay overseas, I became intensely interested in the alarming short-sightedness of my fellow-Americans. Men regarded as intelligent looked upon world political and economic developments with a narrowness, a stupidity, and a prejudicial outlook that, to me, was appalling. It seemed to me that a continuance of such blindness would result, one day, in a great tragedy to our nation and the world.

With that in mind, I've since been driven to seek a profession wherein I might have a part in improving the outlook and attitudes of future generations of Americans. Thus I decided on the teaching profession. . . .

Theodore Roosevelt once said, "If the teachers of America did not do their work well, this Republic would not outlast the span of a generation." Clearly, then, those who work in education are at the heart of our democracy. They are concerned not only with the information people accumulate, but with how they approach problems, how they think and act, and what their attitudes are. Success in this field is no less demanding, complicated, or important than success in any other field.

2. Its Requirements in Terms of Numbers and Types of Jobs

Few people appreciate how many persons are employed to carry on the educational project in this country or how diversified the jobs within the profession are. Let us look at a few facts.

Number of Persons Employed 1947–48.—The data in Table 12 give an accurate picture of the number of people who were at work in the education profession in 1947–48. The fact that an overwhelming majority of school people is employed in public rather than private schools will be noted at once.

TABLE 12

NUMBER OF TEACHERS IN SCHOOLS AND COLLEGES, BY TYPE OF SCHOOL, AND BY SEX, 1947–48 [1]

Level of School, by Type	No. of Teachers, 1947–48		
	Men	Women	Total
Kindergartens and elementary schools:			
Public	39,655	515,284	554,939
Nonpublic	3,753	63,677	67,430
Secondary schools:			
Public	122,258	183,481	305,739
Nonpublic	15,578	25,990	41,568
Noncollegiate departments of colleges.........	2,618	2,493	5,111
Higher education:			
Full-time equivalent normal schools and teachers colleges:			
Publicly controlled	5,794	5,208	11,002
Privately controlled	359	543	902
Universities, colleges, and professional schools...	124,545	37,755	162,300
Residential schools for exceptional children.......	1,148	4,771	5,919
Federal schools for Indians and Alaskans.........	555	1,118	1,673
Private commercial and business schools..........	3,537	4,338	7,875
Total	319,800	844,658	1,164,458

Types of Teaching Jobs.—When a person decides to make teaching his career, he is faced with the task of selecting the type of job he will prepare for. One just doesn't "prepare to teach." The jobs are so diverse, and the preparation essential to entering them is so different, that a choice has to be made.

Level of Instruction. One classification of teaching jobs has to do with levels of instruction. The range is something like this: preschool, kindergarten, primary, intermediate, upper elementary grades, junior high school, senior high school, junior college, collegiate undergraduate, and collegiate graduate. To this should be added the whole field of adult education, in which the problems and approaches are distinct and for which special preparation is necessary. It is obvious that beyond selecting teaching as a profession, one must also decide

[1] Adapted from *Biennial Survey of Education in the United States, 1946–48* (Washington, D. C.: U. S. Government Printing Office, 1950), chap. 1, "Statistical Summary of Education, 1947–48," p. 38.

whether he will teach at the kindergarten, junior college, or some other level. His subsequent preparation will be affected accordingly.

Subjects Taught. Another classification of teaching jobs is based on subjects taught. One person cannot teach everything. He must choose a teaching field. This kind of classification is applicable primarily at the high school and collegiate levels. In the lower schools the teachers are not as free to specialize in certain subject fields, although in some schools certain teachers are assigned to the regular elementary subjects, while others handle the special subjects such as music and art. When teaching jobs are classified on the basis of subjects taught, it is customary further to group the subjects into regular academic subjects and special subjects. The regular subjects include English, social science, mathematics, foreign languages, and natural science. Even within these subject areas further selections must be made. For example, one may choose biology within the natural sciences, economics in the social sciences, or Spanish among the foreign languages. Special subjects are quite diversified. One group includes the near-academic, less vocational subjects, such as music, art, health, and physical education. Another group includes vocational subjects found more particularly in secondary schools, such as agriculture, homemaking, trades and industries, and commerial and secretarial subjects. A third group centers mainly at the collegiate level and has to do with professional and semiprofessional subjects associated with law, medicine, pharmacy, engineering-technical, education, and the like. Of course, profesional programs at the collegiate level are available in the vocational areas found in the high schools. The range of subjects offered in the schools of our country creates at once a whole category of teaching jobs.

Kind of School. Decision on the kind of school in which teaching will be done is a third approach to teaching jobs. Someone who has decided to teach English may choose to do so in a private school or a public school. If a private school is chosen, he may further choose between a school supported by a certain religious group or an independent school. Perhaps he will wish to teach English in a vocational or technical school, in a liberal arts college or a teachers college, or in a federally controlled school such as West Point or a school on an Indian reservation. Other specialized schools such as music schools, schools for boys or girls and men or women, labor colleges, and a large number of other schools focusing on certain vocations and professions would be added to the long list of types of schools in which English instruction is called for.

Kind of Pupil. Teaching jobs are also related to the kinds of pupils to be taught. Of course, the majority of teachers deal with the more-or-less normal cross section of pupils found in the ordinary classroom. However, certain groups of pupils require teachers with special preparation. Teaching the blind or partially sighted is a specialty in itself, and similarly for the deaf, the physically handicapped, and the dull. The brilliant also need special attention. One may choose to work with Indians, Mexicans, or Eskimos. Adults, too, are a special group. Their instruction may range from beginning reading to law, but the fact that they are adults requires many adaptations not called for in the regular school.

Types of Nonteaching Jobs.—If one reviews in his mind the setup of our schools and the services we try to render to pupils, he realizes at once that many people beyond classroom teachers have to be employed. Here is a partial list.

> President or superintendent
> Deans of schools and colleges in universities
> Assistant superintendents and supervisors
> Principals of elementary and secondary schools
> Deans of boys or girls
> Counselors
> Librarians
> Research and testing directors
> Curriculum directors
> Directors of audio-visual aids
> School social workers
> School doctors, nurses, and dentists
> Business officers
> Recorders, stenographers, and clerks
> Plant engineers and custodial workers
> Cafeteria workers
> Bus drivers

Some of our larger school systems and highly organized universities have employees in all of these categories.

Numbers Will Increase.—A substantial increase in the number of teachers in this country may be expected and, in fact, is now apparent. At present there is a serious shortage of elementary teachers due to the rapid increase of enrolments following the second World War. What is more, an additional increase of about 7,000,000 pupils will occur between 1951 and 1957. This increase will soon reach the secondary schools, thus requiring increased numbers of teachers there. Approximately a million new teachers will be needed in our elementary and secondary schools during the next ten years. This number will be needed not only to meet enrolment increases but also to replace teachers who will retire, to relieve overcrowding, to add educational services, and to replace teachers who are unqualified. Incidentally, whereas the demand in September, 1951, was for 80,000 qualified elementary school teachers to replace retired teachers, accommodate the expanding enrolment, and relieve overcrowding, 45,943 students who could be certified for this work were graduated from training institutions in 1951.[2] The supply of high school teachers, on the other hand, was greater than the demand. About 50,000 new high school teachers will be needed annually until 1956; thereafter the demand will increase steadily for several years.

Increased numbers of nonteaching personnel will also be needed. Many schools would now add counselors, librarians, curriculum directors, psychologists, directors of audio-visual aids, and others if the supply of trained people were adequate.

As long as the number to be educated increases, as long as we require by law that our children attend school, and as long as we cling to the belief that we should make our education serve the needs of all, we can do no less than supply the trained workers necessary to carry on the program.

3. Its Requirements in Terms of Attitudes

Unless a person's attitudes are right, he has little chance of either succeeding in the educational profession or of being happy in it. It is most unfortunate for both teachers and pupils when teachers work away miserably, dreading the beginning of each school day, and longing for the romantic life of an actress or a seaman. There are certain attitudes that people who go into educational work ought to have. The following are fairly beyond question:

a) Deliberate choice of the profession; a strong feeling that "this is the kind of work I want to do"

b) Genuine love of children (people); a desire to promote, and enrich their development and learning

c) Realization of the importance of education to society

[2] Ray C. Maul, *Teacher Supply and Demand in the United States*, Report of the 1951 National Teacher Supply and Demand Study (Washington, D. C.: National Education Association, 1951).

d) Real desire to act on the opportunity the profession affords to promote and practice democratic living

e) Preference for diversified work with people, rather than for a single skill or activity that is carried on with few such contacts

f) Willingness to work hard, to study and improve, and, if need be, to sacrifice in order that educational opportunities will be denied to none

g) Respect for and faith in human personality; a sincere and studied desire to bring out the best in everyone, and to foster understanding and cooperation among all men

4. Its Requirements in Terms of Qualities

In addition to desirable attitudes, there are also desirable qualities that the educational worker should have. Some of these are hereditary in nature, while others can be in good part developed. It is meaningless to say that "teachers are born and not made," or, for that matter, that "teachers are made and not born"; good native abilities coupled with a constant effort to develop traits essential in good teaching are called for. The following qualities are representative of those desirable for educational workers:

a) Good intellectual ability; initiative in planning activities and attacking problems

b) Good physical health, to the extent that the ordinary duties of teaching can be discharged; no handicap or ailment should be present which will jeopardize the teacher's own health or the health of those who work with him in the school

c) Emotional stability, nurturing security rather than anxiety in others

d) Social poise and effectiveness

e) High standards of conduct, in line with the responsibilities attached to being a leader

f) Originality and resourcefulness, so that deadening sameness can be avoided

g) Keen observation, with ability to adjust and adapt accordingly

h) Good humor, a relaxed air, with the grace to take a joke as well as make one

i) Patience; not only in matters pertaining to the conduct of pupils, but also in the willingness to wait for an awakening of interest or a change in attitude

j) Dramatic ability; enough to be considered alive one's self and to give living interpretations to materials being learned by others

5. Its Requirements in Terms of Preparation

In connection with preparation for the profession, let us consider two simple categories : teaching personnel and nonteaching personnel.

The Over-all Preparation of the Teacher.—Certainly in recent years our people have expected more and more of their schoolteachers. This is a consequence of their expecting more and more of their schools. Not only are better people sought for teaching, but also better-prepared people. Furthermore, teachers who are merely masters of content in their teaching fields are no longer acceptable. This is necessary, of course ; but the teacher must extend his horizons far beyond such confines and must know and practice the important things the biological and social sciences are revealing about people.

More specifically, all teachers should have a good background of general education at the college level. This is the common ground of knowledge and understanding that all college-educated people should possess, no matter what their vocational intentions are. It establishes general foundations, without specialization, in such fields as the social sciences, the natural sciences, mathematics, the humanities, and the arts. Such a background is considered necessary for the elementary teacher, as well as for the high school or college teacher, and for the music teacher as well as for the teacher of history. Beyond this, there will be parts of the general education studies which students will pursue further as their fields of specialization. For example, having completed the general education foundations, a student may now decide to go on into a specialized study of mathematics and make it his teaching field. Or, if one is planning to teach in the elementary school, he will consider the adaptations of mathematics, English, music and the like to elementary school children. Thus beyond general education there will be further dealing with content, specializing in it and adapting it to the requirements of those who will be taught. Finally, the preparation of the teacher must include professional studies ; studies dealing with such things as the techniques of instruction in the classroom, the suitable organization and placement of teaching materials, the nature and purposes of education in a society like ours, and the characteristics of those who flock into our schools— how they learn and how to adjust to the great differences among them. The day is gone when teachers flaunt their own knowledge in a teaching field and give passing or failing grades to pupils as by a rule. The new demand is for a sympathetic understanding of human differences and a skilful adaptation of learning experiences to those differences. This does not come casually; it requires deep study and careful practice. Thus professional studies must include direct contact with children in schools, with homes and communities, and with many other things that will lead to a better understanding of those in our classrooms. Actual practice in teaching, under good supervision, should be included for all students, so that some of the mistakes of the neophyte can be eliminated before the full responsibilities of teaching are assumed. The moot court of the future lawyer, the internship of the doctor, and the field work of the social worker are to the same point. Anyone, then, who wishes to prepare for teaching will wish to do an adequate job in the backgrounds of general education, in a chosen teaching field, and in professional studies.

A longer period of time than is now customary will be necessary to permit the student really to get ready to teach. It is impossible to telescope the preparations outlined above into a short period, to say nothing of the lack of maturity of a person who has only a year or two of study beyond high school. Actually, in some states it is still possible to be certified to teach in the elementary schools with only two years of college preparation. In some states no practice teaching is required for certification, and occasionally a state permits a college graduate to teach almost any subject that is offered in the high school. Under these circumstances we will have to admit that the pupils are to a great extent guinea-pigs, standing by while the new teacher finds out whether or not he likes teaching to begin with and gets the "feel" of the job, informs himself in the subjects he is expected to teach, and develops classroom techniques through trial and error that are costly beyond measure in learning. There is a clear disposition in this country to prevent this kind of waste. States are rapidly going to the requirement that no one may teach in the public schools who does not have at least four years of preparation beyond the high school. In some states, five years are required, particularly for secondary teachers. A six-year requirement has been suggested. There is considerable sentiment in favor of keeping the requirements the same for elementary and secondary teachers on the grounds that the time is necessary for adequate preparation in either case and that differences in preparation tend to create differences in salary and professional status and to beget false notions concerning the importance of work on the two levels. Some people like to insist that, if additional time is to be taken in preparation for teaching, it be spent on the job in some form of internship. The internship is a good idea, but it can never eliminate the ethical necessity of bringing to the pupils in the classroom only such people, including interns, as have shown real professional promise, have prepared adequately, and have demonstrated proficiency in teaching. It is a conspicuous fact that the period of preservice preparation in other professions such as law, medicine, and dentistry has been lengthened greatly in recent years. If an internship has been involved, it has not prevented the preinternship period from lengthening. So it will be in education; but only on the ground that the lengthened preparation will result in better instruction in the classrooms of the nation. The profession will hardly perform its rightful service or command its proper respect if it accepts for its teachers a preparation no greater than that for dental hygienists or beauty specialists.

Preparation for Nonteaching Jobs.—A partial list of nonteaching jobs in education was presented on page 390. Presidents, principals, curriculum directors, school doctors, business officers, and plant engineers are representative of that list. If the list is examined again and the general nature of each job is reviewed, a few ideas concerning desirable preparation are likely to stand out. For example, for many of the jobs the most fundamental preparation that can be obtained is teaching experience itself. Take a college president. It seems superfluous to say that such a person ought to have been a teacher. The primary function of a college is to teach, and its head should have that background of experience. The basic job of the president is educational, not legal or financial. To be sure, as everyone knows, there have been outstanding presidents who have never taught, just as there have been outstanding coaches who have never played the games they coach; but it is a matter of common good judgment to say that if a man is at the head of an institution devoted to teaching, he ought to have taught. This goes for schools at all levels; and so far as the public schools are concerned, it is a requirement for elementary and secondary administrators and supervisors. It is common also for deans of boys and girls, counselors, curriculum directors, directors of audio-visual aids, and school social workers. It ought to apply to school librarians and research and testing directors. Even business officers might well have had teaching experience. Business management in schools is supposed to promote the educational objectives, and unless those objectives have been understood and lived, management is in danger of becoming inflexible and cold. Teaching experience cannot be required of school medical workers, clerical workers, custodians, cafeteria workers, or bus drivers. Their duties do not bear directly enough on the instructional program of the school to justify it. Let us say in principle that nonteaching personnel in the school should be required to have teaching experience if their jobs bear directly on the instructional program.

Each of the nonteaching jobs will, of course, have specialized training appropriate to itself. If teaching experience is involved, it will be apparent that this alone is not enough. Teaching does not make a librarian, a principal, a research director, or a school social worker. Additional preparation is necessary. Obviously, whatever the job, adequate preparation should be required before hiring takes place. This applies to custodians, cafeteria workers, and bus drivers as well as to doctors, deans, and superintendents. These people should know very definite things and possess very definite skills. At all events, no job in the entire school roster should be occupied by a poorly qualified person.

The Education of School Board Members.—School board members, to an overwhelming extent, are elected by the people. They are not certified, they do not receive salaries, and no teaching is associated with their position. No professional standards are set up and administered for them. However, they occupy one of the most influential positions in the whole school system. They are constantly dealing with over-all policies, determining budgets, and approving or rejecting personnel.

The decisions of board members should be based on an adequate understanding of the school and its problems. This understanding, naturally, is not always adequate when a board member is elected to his post. He should be eager, therefore, to get himself informed. Most of this information will result from his own study. His local school administrator will be glad to give him materials to read that describe the work of a school board member. His experienced associates on the board and the administrator too will be more than glad to spend a great deal of time conferring on any and all matters that will give him a working knowledge of conditions. The departments of education in the states and the federal Office of Education will be glad to send him bulletins on request. Even movies that depict problems of board members and ways of meeting those problems are now available. In some states, the commissioners of education actually hold classes for school board members in various sections of the state. This affords an excellent chance for board members to raise a multitude of questions and get answers from the most authoritative source of all. Thus school board members, too, need definite preparation in line with the responsibilities they carry. It would be a little absurd if high standards were adhered to for all the people who carry out the policies of the board, while the policy-making board itself remained sluggish and uninformed. The amount of voluntary action being taken by board members to improve themselves is praiseworthy. In some states they have organized themselves into associations, hold regular meetings, and set up committees to study certain problems and report back to the whole group. This kind of self-initiated action for improvement among the lay leaders of public education bodes well for the future.

6. Its Requirements on the Job

The preservice preparation of professional workers is merely to get them started. It should insure a reasonably good start, without undue penalty to themselves or others; but it cannot bring them up to their best possible performance. Growth on the job must follow. The term of service of a real professional has certain outstanding characteristics. Attention to three or four of these will start the reader on his way.

Devotion to Duty.—Anyone who ponders on the nature of the educational job will see at once that it requires the best a worker has to offer. Ordinary production of goods is not involved. One does not work for a single employer seeking profits; he works for the children, for a kind of country, and a way of life. Negligence or inefficiency or walking off the job does harm to the children and society itself. Excellence on the job, in turn, promotes human development, modes of thought, and the welfare of all. One does not take this responsibility lightly. To work half-heartedly, to fail to prepare each day's activities carefully, or to view the job merely as a way to earn a living is actually to let the future down. As long as one remains in the profession and accepts its pay, his devotion to duty should be complete and sincere.

Continuous Study and Improvement.—There are many ways through which people in education have sought to improve themselves while in service. The following are representative:

a) Personal research on problems encountered on the job
b) Working on committees that study more general problems such as curriculum changes, personnel policies, the nature of the community, and pupil characteristics and needs
c) Continued studies in colleges and universities through extension courses and summer sessions
d) Workshops cooperatively organized that pool local and outside resources and limit themselves to specific school problems

e) Reading groups, in which staff members with similar interests unite to share the benefits of reading in their field

f) Teacher exchange, in which teachers from different schools change jobs for a semester or a year

g) Visits to other schools to observe how things are done

h) Self-evaluation, in which local schools select approved educational criteria and judge their own work and program by those criteria

i) Travel, particularly in the summer, that is planned in terms of its local uses

j) Professional writing

The administration and the board of education have definite responsibilities for in-service improvement as well as the staff members themselves. The employment of good supervisors whose duty it is to cooperate with the staff in motivating and coordinating improvement activities is important. Large school systems will have several such people. One neglected area in this regard is the supervision of beginning teachers. Much confusion and heartache could be avoided and better work assured if beginners were not so often left to their own uncertain fortunes. Also there has been a growing tendency in recent years for boards of education to help staff members bear the expense of in-service improvement programs. Sometimes the fees for extension or summer study are paid in whole or in part. The board may bear the expense of subscriptions to professional publications or of a lecture series and may hire substitutes for teachers who are observing in other schools without loss of pay. Certainly a board of education must know that a small investment here pays off many-fold in better schools. Furthermore, such a policy is clear proof that the board not only expects improvement but will assist in it, and it results in a rapport that can hardly be achieved in any other way.

Activity in Professional Organizations.—Much benefit comes to the educational worker who not only belongs to his professional organizations but is active in them. It is probably reasonable to suggest that one should belong to the local, state, and national educational associations and to the organization in his own special field. There are, of course, organizations for teachers of mathematics, school secretaries, rural teachers, secondary school principals, music supervisors, and so on. Most of these organizations have very good publications which ought to be subscribed to and read. Furthermore, whenever possible, one ought to attend the conferences and conventions held by these organizations. He should participate and accept responsible assignments. The good that comes from working with others in the profession cannot be overestimated. Sometimes school people say they are not interested in one of their organizations because it is weak, has poor policies, or has leaders who are not acceptable. Such people need to be reminded that professional organizations have a real service to perform, that the way to make them what they ought to be is to get in and help, and that extreme satisfaction comes from working in an organization whose members are actively supporting a good program.

Beyond the School.—As was emphasized in Chapter 13, the educational worker today has a community job to do as well as a school job. This is a responsibility that has loomed large in recent years and now constitutes one of the more urgent requirements of school people. To succeed on the job requires diligent work beyond the school. Reference to Chapter 13 will re-establish some of the specifics involved in getting this done.

7. Its Salaries

A few years ago a magazine carried a cartoon showing a hoodlum with turned-up collar holding up a frightened gentleman in spectacles behind a board fence in a dark alley. The frightened gentleman, noting the concealed revolver in the hoodlum's coat pocket, throws up his hands and exclaims, "You're wasting your time, Mac, I'm a schoolteacher!"

Teachers' salaries have, indeed, been woefully low, so low that in thousands of cases teachers have had to do additional work in order to meet expenses. There have been salary increases during the last few years, but they have been more than absorbed by increased living costs and taxes. Table 13 presents average teachers' salaries by states for 1944–45, 1946–47, and 1948–49, with an estimated national average for 1950–51.

The data show a steady increase in average salaries since 1945. There is no exception among the states. Clearly, though, the states are far apart in the salaries they pay and in the rate of increase since 1945. The Research Division of the National Education Association estimated the average salary for the forty-eight states at $3,080 in 1950–51. Actually, though, the higher salaries in 1950–51 would

TABLE 13

Average Teachers' Salaries by States, 1944–45, 1946–47, and 1948–49

State	Average Salary			
	1944–45 [3]	1946–47 [4]	1948–49 [5]	1950–51
Alabama	$1,050	$1,443	$2,036	
Arizona	2,085	2,368	3,640	
Arkansas	918	1,255	1,626	
California	2,749	3,304	4,178	
Colorado	1,730	2,170	2,643	
Connecticut	2,085	2,790	3,538	
Delaware	1,975	2,416	2,849	
Florida	1,621	1,939	2,840	
Georgia	1,077	1,618	1,732	
Idaho	1,517	2,117	2,297	
Illinois	2,139	2,681	3,452	
Indiana	2,017	2,433	3,243	
Iowa	1,357	1,922	2,479	
Kansas	1,501	1,904	2,452	
Kentucky	1,226	1,481	1,865	
Louisiana	1,515	1,959	2,771	
Maine	1,367	1,586	1,942	
Maryland	2,080	2,443	3,506	
Massachusetts	2,386	2,852	3,159	
Michigan	2,147	2,635	3,289	
Minnesota	1,757	2,050	2,750	
Mississippi	842	984	1,356	
Missouri	1,442	1,871	2,304	
Montana	1,456	1,838	2,898	
Nebraska	1,379	1,696	2,162	
Nevada	1,953	2,175	3,110	
New Hampshire	1,467	1,981	2,571	
New Jersey	2,467	2,837	3,712	
New Mexico	1,725	2,307	3,069	
New York	2,783	3,302	4,129	
North Carolina	1,382	1,810	2,438	
North Dakota	1,314	1,486	1,810	
Ohio	2,122	2,350	3,029	
Oklahoma	1,543	1,920	2,288	
Oregon	2,026	2,461	3,187	
Pennsylvania	2,008	2,304	3,053	
Rhode Island	2,117	2,414	3,352	
South Carolina	1,064	1,298	1,769	
South Dakota	1,307	1,711	2,136	
Tennessee	1,324	1,480	1,845	
Texas	1,524	1,915	2,517	
Utah	1,868	2,269	3,106	
Vermont	1,508	1,672	2,513	
Virginia	1,376	1,845	2,236	
Washington	2,304	2,628	3,374	
West Virginia	1,526	1,711	2,402	
Wisconsin	1,844	2,259	2,803	
Wyoming	1,586	1,810	2,563	
All States	1,846	2,254	2,847	$3,080 (est.)

[3] *National Education Association Journal*, XXXVI, 172.
[4] *N.E.A. Journal*, March, 1949, p. 172.   [5] *N.E.A. Journal*, March, 1951, p. 172.

buy less than the salaries in 1944–45; hence, the increases were nominal. In a good many school systems the increases have been labeled as "cost of living" increases and are not accepted as permanent additions to basic salaries. This is not good. It is most urgent that salaries in the profession rise to a point where reasonable standards of living can be maintained. If this is not done, the profession will not only be seeking constantly for any personnel at all, but it will also have to do without the caliber of people it ought to employ.

During recent years real interest has been shown in stabilizing the teaching profession by passing minimum salary laws. Thirty-one states had such a law in 1950. The California law, for example, provides that no teacher in the public schools of that state shall receive a salary under $2,400. This applies to all teachers, no matter what their preparation. Other states set minima according to levels of preparation, including bachelor's, master's, and doctor's degrees. There has been some fear that the minimum thus established by law might become the starting salary in communities able to pay more and, for that matter, might become maximum in communities that have no interest in salary schedules for teachers whereby they receive increases from year to year. Hence interest is developing in state legislation that establishes minimum salary schedules in addition to minimum salaries. Fifteen states had such a law in 1950. Delaware, for example, requires "that teachers (a) with no degree, (b) with bachelor's degree, (c) with master's degree, and (d) with doctor's degree, be paid minimum salaries, respectively, of $2,000, $2,400, $2,600, and $3,000. In addition, ten annual increments of $160 each are specified leading to required salaries of from $3,600 to $4,600.[6] One of the outstanding problems connected with such legislation is how to motivate the school districts able to exceed the minimum to do so.

In local communities and cities where salary schedules for teachers are in effect, there has been a definite tendency to raise the maximum that can be earned by classroom teachers. Many schedules now go up to $4,000, some to $5,000, and a few to $6,000.

On the whole, there is a healthy indication in the country that communities wish to do their very best for teachers and that teachers' salaries will soon support a standard of living expected of school people. This will be good news to competent young people who would like to make their contribution to society through the teaching profession.

[6] National Education Association of the United States, "Teachers in the Public Schools," *Research Bulletin,* XXVII, p. 142.

8. Some of Its Problems

All professions have their problems. In a free society where the professions to a large extent are left to evolve their own policies and practices, it is important that they point up their problems and attack them openly. What are some of the problems of the educational profession? A half-dozen will do.

Concern for First Principles.—In a time of world tension, economic instability, startling scientific discoveries, and shifts in social and political living, it is essential that the school people in our democracy keep their lights burning and their purposes clear. The profession is faced with the problem of reviewing first principles, of establishing its real objectives. The clear mission of the school among us, the sacred worth of individual personality, the equal right of all to a good education, and the moral obligation to do one's best must hang as a halo above the routines of each worker. This is the profession's primary problem.

Unity.—The unity which the profession most needs is that which would come if its first principles were remembered and used by school people in specific situations. Some of the divisions which occur between teachers and administrators, boards and staffs, local and state groups, and the like could not possibly occur if the real goals were actually sought. Responsibility for this unity does not rest with some over-all body at the national level. It rests with leaders at all levels to secure the participation of the whole profession in continuously evolving the principles around which it will rally.

Relations with the Public.—The problem in this area is not limited to the kind of desirable interrelationships between school and community that were discussed in Chapter 12. It includes also the question of how to meet the attacks on the public schools which in some cases have become organized on the grand scale. Something must be wrong with public relations if, as has happened in certain communities, such groups are able completely to upset the normal conduct of the schools. The profession must find ways and means of eliminating the distance between itself and its supporting public.

The Role of Certification.—The principle that the states ought to certify all professional workers in their public schools seems to be pretty well accepted in this country. The profession itself can help in evolving the standards, but the legal authority and the administration of standards should rest with the states. But other questions arise.

Should there be a permanent or a life certificate? Would it be better if teachers' certificates were reviewed at given intervals, renewals to be based on satisfactory study and growth on the job? Should there be reciprocity among states in certifying teachers? How general or how specific should requirements be? How can requirements be couched so that they do not determine the curriculum or make experimentation impossible in teacher-education institutions? The implications of questions like these are far-flung, and they deserve careful study.

Automatic Salary Increments.—Is it better to have salary increases in public schools based on improvement on the job or an automatic increments set down in a salary schedule? Can it be assumed that merely putting in time on the job will result in improved service? Would the profession be better off if it emphasized the careful selection and preparation of its personnel and the adoption of a beginning wage that is in line with this, and then left increases to merit? Is it to be assumed that proper salary increases will not occur unless they are provided for in an operating salary schedule? Does experience show that the salary schedule may result in mediocrity in the staff because the superior work of some is lost in the satisfying thought that "everybody's getting a raise anyhow"? Is it possible to set up a plan which combines the good features of automatic increments and merit? Are there any aspects of professional services which are incompatible with the idea of automatic salary increments? In more than one instance public school staffs have voted not to recommend that they be placed under an automatic increment plan. The issue, of course, is not that of adequate salaries in the profession. It is, rather, whether or not mere continuance on the job should result in increased salaries.

Strikes.—Should public school teachers strike? The issue has been brought sharply to the American people during the last decade. There have been some crippling school strikes. The problem has received much attention in the general press, in professional magazines, and in public and private discussions. One exchange of opinion on the question by two professional people was recorded recently in a magazine concerned with teacher education: [7] the present writer supported the point of view that public school teachers should not strike. That brief article is reproduced here with the urgent insistence that the reader secure the magazine and read in full the able presentation of the other side.

[7] James A. Wheeler, "Should Teachers Strike? Yes," Connecticut State Department of Education, *Teacher Education Quarterly* (Hartford, Conn.), VII, 150–56; P. Roy Brammell, "Should Teachers Strike? No," *ibid.*, pp. 157–59.

For purposes of brief presentation here, let us take the position that public school teachers should not strike; that the integrity of free education is enhanced if it is known that they will not strike; and that strikes are incompatible with the basic character of public education.

Strikes, in the public school situation, may be thought of as deliberate and concerted absence from normal duties agreed to in contract. With this in mind, the following considerations should be noted.

First, free public education is foundational to our democracy. The strike jeopardizes free public education. The right of public school teachers to strike must carry with it the logic of the strike; that is, the possibility of a complete and indefinite suspension of public education because disagreeing groups cannot get together. Such an impasse would not be so bad if only teachers and their employers were involved. What happens to children, their attitudes, and the notions they get during a strike about how to settle disputes in a democracy is the important thing. It certainly is better for young citizens to see problems solved through the use of reason and cooperation than through division and strife. It may not be too much to say that those who are willing to see public education jeopardized are willing to see democratic government and the democratic way of life endangered and shaken, if not destroyed.

Second, public education emphasizes the common, unifying elements of our society, of living together successfully and harmoniously. Public schools justify their existence when they are institutions of amalgamation and cohesion. Public funds are used to pay teachers for this kind of citizenship training. The right of public school teachers to strike is in turn the right to weaken this unity.

Third, those who receive public funds for public services should not strike against the public interest. We are not willing to see public services discontinued while public employees, duly contracted, stand by. Any service considered by the public so important to the general welfare that it digs down and taxes itself for the whole bill, should not be struck. The taxpayer of the community should not be expected to support a fire department that stands by while the city burns, or a police force that stands by while crime runs riot, or public school teachers who stand by, perhaps indefinitely, while the children wait. If public servants, duly contracted and paid for out of public funds, strike, then we are pretty close to the strange dilemma of the public financing the instability of services it considers foundational to the general welfare.

Fourth, the right to strike is usually accompanied by the desire to make the strike weapon effective, which in turn gives birth to organizations so rigid that freedom of speech and action on the part of individuals within and without the organizations is frequently curtailed. Certainly public school teachers are not an appropriate group to share in the curtailment of such rights. It is not in line with the kind of responsible citizenship they teach in their classrooms. Citizenship in this country carries with it the moral obligation to be a good citizen personally and to think and act and be heard in line with individual conscience. It is no more appropriate to require that all teachers in a group think and act alike than to require that all the scientists investigating a problem adjust their data so that all will come to the same conclusion.

Fifth, it is quite likely that if public school teachers strike, as organized labor strikes, they will tend to affiliate with organized labor groups in order to marshal the power of those groups behind them. Such affiliation may in turn result in the profession's throwing away its opportunity fully to operate under its own leadership, to speak for itself, and to establish its own set of values. Affiliation by public school teachers with social and economic groups that support strikes by public employees against public services is not in line with the need in the public schools for teachers who are themselves students of society, able to help young people analyze society intelligently, and eager to train future citizens in the art and the necessity of intergroup coopera-tion.

Sixth, failure by teachers to renew contracts, even leaving the profession if necessary, is as effective as the strike in awakening the public to the need for improved conditions within the profession. In this way one does not walk out on the children, and he honorably exercises his privilege without the stigma of breaking the terms of a contract he freely subscribed to.

Seventh, experience is accumulating to show that community cooperation under good leadership is a better way to improve community education than the strike. Furthermore, the cooperative approach establishes conditions for continued improvements. Strikes set up a victor-and-vanquished situation, a winner and a loser—hardly the kind of community unity that needs forever to be in back of public education. We are on firm ground in public education if we make community understanding and agreement the basis of progress. We are on weak ground if we rely on the strike. It makes good sense for education to use education, rather than the strike, in its own behalf.

Finally, there are some things involved in public education greater than the right of the teachers to strike, and which the teacher who is a real pro-fessional will not violate. These are the service commitments, the things that stand above personal desire or convenience. Some of these are (a) the right of the child not to be abandoned, (b) the right of our communities to receive the democratic education they have contracted for in good faith, (c) the right of our government not to have to risk its solidarity through a conceivable strike of the total profession which could not be resolved or arbitrated, and (d) the right, and moral obligation, of each teacher to exer-cise the kind of responsible, cooperative citizenship he teaches in his class-room.

Public school teachers will be better off if they will outlaw strikes as such and in cooperation with the whole community seek through press, platform, radio, and other means to establish the idea that the fortunes of our com-munities and our country are very directly linked to the quality of our public schools. Teachers do not need to strike to improve school conditions; neither do they need to leave the jobs they are trained to do. They need to develop and use the cooperative techniques that our democracy has grown up to and which it must use if it is to survive.

As the reader well knows, there are many other problems confronting the education profession. The manner in which they are faced and solved will affect the mood and character of the profession for many years to come.

9. ITS ETHICS

The teaching profession, like other professions, has a high sense of ethical responsibility. The following code of ethics drawn up by the National Education Association will indicate the kind of conduct that is expected of educational workers.

CODE OF ETHICS FOR THE TEACHING PROFESSION [8]

Believing: That true democracy can best be achieved by a process of free public education made available to all the children of all the people;

That the teachers in the United States have a large and inescapable responsibility in fashioning the ideals of children and youth;

That such responsibility requires the services of men and women of high ideals, broad education, and profound human understanding; and, in order that the aims of democratic education may be realized more fully, that the welfare of the teaching profession may be promoted; and,

That teachers may observe proper standards of conduct in their professional relations, the National Education Association of the United States proposes this code of ethics for its members.

The term "teacher" as used in this code shall include all persons directly engaged in educational work, whether in a teaching, an administrative, or a supervisory capacity.

Article I. Relations to Pupils and Home

SECTION 1. It is the duty of the teacher to be just, courteous, and professional in all his relations with pupils. He should consider their individual differences, needs, interests, temperaments, aptitudes, and environments.

SECTION 2. He should refrain from tutoring pupils of his classes for pay and from referring such pupils to any member of his immediate family for tutoring.

SECTION 3. The professional relations of a teacher with his pupils demand the same scrupulous care that is required in the confidential relations of one teacher with another. A teacher, therefore, should not disclose any information obtained confidentially from his pupils, unless it is for the best interest of the child and the public.

[8] National Education Association of the United States, *N.E.A. Handbook, 1950–51* (Washington, D. C.: The Association, 1951), pp. 343–5.

Section 4. A teacher should seek to establish friendly and intelligent co-operation between home and school, ever keeping in mind the dignity of his profession and the welfare of the pupils. He should do or say nothing that would undermine the confidence and respect of his pupils for their parents. He should inform the pupils and parents regarding the importance, purposes, accomplishments, and needs of the schools.

Article II. Relations to Civic Affairs

Section 1. It is the obligation of every teacher to inculcate in his pupils an appreciation of the principles of democracy. He should direct full and free discussion of appropriate controversial issues with the expectation that comparisons, contrasts, and interpretations will lead to an understanding, appreciation, acceptance, and practice of the principles of democracy. A teacher should refrain from using his classroom privileges and prestige to promote partisan politics, sectarian religious views, or selfish propaganda of any kind.

Section 2. A teacher should recognize and perform all the duties of citizenship. He should subordinate his personal desires to the best interests of the public good. He should be loyal to the school system, the state, and the nation but should exercise his right to give constructive criticisms.

Section 3. A teacher's life should show that education makes people better citizens and better neighbors. His personal conduct should not need-lessly offend the accepted pattern of behavior of the community in which he serves.

Article III. Relations to the Profession

Section 1. Each member of the teaching profession should dignify his calling on all occasions and should uphold the importance of his services to society. On the other hand, he should not indulge in personal exploitation.

Section 2. A teacher should encourage able and sincere individuals to enter the teaching profession and discourage those who plan to use this profession merely as a steppingstone to some other vocation.

Section 3. It is the duty of the teacher to maintain his own efficiency by study, by travel, and by other means which keep him abreast of the trends in education and the world in which he lives.

Section 4. Every teacher should have membership in his local, state, and national professional organizations and should participate actively and unselfishly in them. Professional growth and personality development are the natural product of such professional activity. Teachers should avoid the promotion of organization rivalry and divisive competition which weaken the cause of education.

Section 5. While not limiting their services by reason of small salary, teachers should insist upon a salary scale commensurate with the social de-mands laid upon them by society. They should not knowingly underbid a rival or agree to accept a salary lower than that provided by a recognized schedule. They should not apply for positions for the sole purpose of forcing an increase in salary in their present position; correspondingly, school officials should not refuse to give deserved salary increases to efficient employees until offers from other school authorities have forced them to do so.

SECTION 6. A teacher should not apply for a specific position currently held by another teacher. Unless the rules of the school system otherwise prescribe, he should file his application with the chief executive officer.

SECTION 7. Since qualification should be the sole determining factor in appointment and promotion, the use of pressure on school officials to secure a position or to obtain other favors is unethical.

SECTION 8. Testimonials regarding teachers should be truthful and confidential and should be treated as confidential information by the school authorities receiving them.

SECTION 9. A contract, once signed, should be faithfully adhered to until it is dissolved by mutual consent. Ample notification should be given both by school officials and teachers in case a change in position is to be made.

SECTION 10. Democratic procedures should be practiced by members of the teaching profession. Cooperation should be predicated upon the recognition of the worth and the dignity of individual personality. All teachers should observe the professional courtesy of transacting official business with the properly designated authority.

SECTION 11. School officials should encourage and nurture the professional growth of all teachers by promotion or by other appropriate methods of recognition. School officials who fail to recommend a worthy teacher for a better position outside their school system because they do not desire to lose his services are acting unethically.

SECTION 12. A teacher should avoid unfavorable criticism of other teachers except that formally presented to a school official for the welfare of the school. It is unethical to fail to report to the duly constituted authority any matters which are detrimental to the welfare of the school.

SECTION 13. Except when called upon for counsel or other assistance, a teacher should not interfere in any matter between another teacher and a pupil.

SECTION 14. A teacher should not act as an agent or accept a commission, royalty, or other compensation for endorsing books or other school materials in the selection or purchase of which he can exert influence or concerning which he can exercise the right of decision; nor should he accept a commission or other compensation for helping another to secure a position.

10. ITS DRAWBACKS

There are some things about the profession of education, particularly the teaching end of it, which cause some people to avoid choosing it as a lifework and others already in it to want to get out. It is well, of course, to consider these things before getting in. Certainly the profession will be better off, and, above all, the children will be happier and more successful if the people who are in it still prefer it in spite of its drawbacks. Naturally, specific drawbacks will not be equally serious to everyone, but there are some things that ought to be considered by anyone who may be weighing the possibility of entering the field. Consider the following

1. The period of preparation necessary to enter the profession is lengthening; consequently the cost of getting ready to start is increasing.
2. Salaries are too low; they are not in line with the high cost of preparation, the standard of living expected, the responsibilities carried, and the services rendered.
3. Actually, competition is very keen; one meets it when he seeks admission to the preservice program, at the time of employment, and on the job. No one can get his job and then rest on his laurels. Life certificates are going out; improvement on the job is necessary for continuance.
4. Adjustment to immature minds and to all variations in abilities and backgrounds is necessary; the teacher cannot remain always with his own profound thoughts; he must spend much time patiently thinking simply with others.
5. The mental and nervous strain is great; the desire to do well, the apparent failure of some pupils to learn, disciplinary problems, and the keen edge of comment by displeased pupils all take their toll. Working with human beings is the most strenuous thing on earth; what the mechanic feels as he faces a damaged car is less enervating than what the teacher feels as he faces a damaged pupil.
6. Sometimes teachers or other school workers must take unwarranted abuse; they may be blamed by irate parents for the failure or poor attitudes of pupils they have in fact tried to help. In some communities teachers are "watched"; they are the center of critical eyes that look for deviations from the model of goodness they are supposed to be. Occasionally their ideas are suspect also, and a chance remark about socialized medicine, world government, or better local government will lead to difficulties.

11. ITS REWARDS

The rewards that come from a job well done in education are no less real than the drawbacks. Millions of people have given all their active years to the profession, never for a moment supposing that any other work could have brought them equal satisfactions. Most of these satisfactions are very deep-seated, and are of the sort that keep the teacher on the job although he knows good and well his financial status can never be too good. This is striking testimony to the magnetism of the educational task once it is understood and experienced. Incidentally, most school people have the ability and the training to obtain other jobs or to set up businesses of their own which would lead to greater financial returns. On the whole, they have more that is salable in our society than many other specialized workers. Yet their loyalty to the profession is marked, and as time goes on it increases. No list of rewards could ever cover the experience of all who have worked in this field; only a sampling can be offered as a guide to those who may be considering the field vocationally or who, as members of the community, wish to understand what it is that gives drive, purpose, and stability to staff members in their schools. The rewards are varied:

a) Satisfactions which come from the feeling that what is being done is humanly important: working in an institution that is basic to a successful democracy and to good world citizenship; witnessing and sharing in the development of human personalities mentally, physically, socially, emotionally, aesthetically, ethically; equipping youth with the learning necessary for successful and enriched living in vocations and avocations; assisting in the task of improving and uniting the communities in which children grow up; aiding youth in their adjustment to their times.

b) Security that is based on dependable pay, steady work, and improving tenure and retirement conditions; school taxes make the payment of salaries almost certain, the school year is established in law, laws establishing tenure are common, and retirement plans are making retirement incomes more certain and more adequate;

c) Security that results from the knowledge that the social status of the teacher has risen impressively during recent years. If participation in community affairs, membership in community organizations, selection to head community projects, and, for that matter, marriageability are any indication of social acceptance, then the social status of the educational worker is secure. The typical superintendent, athletic coach, music teacher, kindergarten teacher, dramatics coach, or school principal are not only admired and respected, but the citizens love to have them walk and work among them.

d) Living in the environment of learning and research. There is real satisfaction in helping others to learn, keeping up in one's field, conducting research studies, and keeping close company with millions of others, past and present, whose lives support our free education project.

e) Vacations that are long enough to permit continued study, travel, experience in other jobs, and recreational activities that will mean better work when the new school year begins.

The profession of education, big, independent, and at times disunited, is nevertheless establishing its goals, finding its unity, and acting on its responsibilities. It is demanding quality, integrity, and hard work on the part of its personnel; and it now asks for public support in line with its public service. It has its problems and its disadvantages, but it gives opportunity to the honest worker to deal in human qualities that are from everlasting to everlasting.

What Do YOU Say?

1

When one considers the qualities a teacher ought to have, the nature of his work, and the preparation he needs to do his work well, it is apparent that teachers' salaries, on the whole, are too low. By the same token, five or six years of preparation beyond the high school should be required before a teacher begins to teach, so that his pupils will not be retarded in their learning while he catches up in his field and "finds himself" in the classroom.

What do YOU say?

2

Our democracy will be strengthened if all public school teachers will adopt and observe a no-strike policy; it will be weakened at its foundations if the use of the strike spreads.

What do YOU say?

3

We have had many very good and a few very bad teachers in our classrooms. The grouch, the dictator, the unrefined, and the emotional deviate no longer belong.

What do YOU say?

4

What points in this chapter do you particularly support or take issue with?

Chapter 15

THE EDUCATIONAL FRONT

Our Tasks Become Clear

The educational front should not be thought of as synonymous with the educational frontier. The frontier is out on the far horizon, where new ground is being broken, where new problems arise. The front, on the other hand, is in our own backyard. We are in the trenches. Some of the problems we face are as common as the back fence. We need not gaze into the distance or ponder vaguely on the future. The front is here.

Where, then, do the battle lines form in education? What objectives do we seek to gain, and what do we seek to defend? Where do the issues lie, and at what points do we take up the fight? Certainly every real American wants to devote all his strength and intelligence to the preservation of his free schools. Let him consider the following challenges, take his stand, and go to work.

CHALLENGE TO AMERICANS

1. Will we, as Americans, clarify and renew the clear purposes that lie back of our free institutions, re-establish our goals, and resist encroachments on our essential freedoms?

2. Will our people act on their belief that public education is the cornerstone of democracy? Will they support it to the extent it deserves as a means of making democracy work? Will they instruct governmental agencies at all levels to share in this support, to secure for every child in America a fitting educational opportunity?

3. As the general education of all the people rises, and as education itself becomes more and more an experience in democratic living, will state and federal governments display added confidence in our people to control wisely their own local affairs and institutions?

4. Will school administrators and classroom teachers go to the trouble first to ponder on the principles and practices basic to democracy and then carry them out in all the interrelationships of school administration and in the conduct of education in the classroom?

412

5. Will we be honest enough with the youth in our schools, and courageous enough with ourselves, to study intercultural and international conditions in the light of democratic principles and seek consciously through education to bring about a fuller practice of these principles within this nation and among all nations?

6. Will we act on the proposition that the public school must magnify the common ground of intelligent, harmonious, and ethical living, and as such may not be used for the magnification or perpetuation of doctrines or dogmas which could divide or dominate us?

7. Will we direct that public funds shall be used only for public schools?

8. Will we be wise enough to insist that the public schools make their "ethical character" objective really effective rather than to insist on the introduction into the public schools of instruction by organized religious groups?

9. Will we repudiate the institutionalism of the school, in which pupils are made to conform to imaginary standards, and require instead that the school adapt its program to those who learn? Will we be willing impartially to evaluate our education in these terms?

10. Will we see to it that the program of education stems from the needs of youth in their times, adjusts to the changing conditions in society, and deals with content and experience recognized by youth as significant to them?

11. Will our public schools organize the educational experiences of young people so that, as they take over in our society, they will be mindful of their social responsibility and will run its economy and institutions to promote the general welfare? Will we seek in turn to avoid a situation in which large numbers of citizens become employees of the government, a condition that at length can scarcely help but jeopardize both the stability of the government and the freedom of the people?

12. Will we enlist the power of the school for world welfare and peace and so balance our education that those who leave our schools will maintain a balanced world order in which social and scientific developments will move abreast? Will the United Nations, accordingly, vastly increase its support of UNESCO?

13. Will we be willing in fact to make the school a community school, extending to the people the opportunity to share as consultants in its direction, to join in its activities, and to have its services available to children and adults alike, all day, all year?

14. Will we be willing to alter the organization of our schools when such reorganization promotes the basic objectives of education?

15. Will our legislative and educational leaders have courage and foresight enough to require that prior to the expenditure of large sums of money for equalization programs, ineffective local school units be eliminated through redistricting? Will they, at the same time, make it clear that local autonomy in educational matters will continue?

16. Will we, as we must if our education is to be really good, expand greatly the study of child nature and development, both on the grand scale and by every classroom teacher?

17. Will we correct the common error in school supervision which emphasizes aids and techniques without conducting fundamental studies to find out whether or not they actually result in better learning?

18. Will teacher-education institutions be willing to revise their programs so that students in preparation for teaching can experience the kind of learning and instruction they should promote in their own future classrooms?

19. Will vision and leadership in the education profession be adequate in the future to keep the profession alerted to its goals and mission, united around its clear purposes, and free from entangling alliances with groups that would suppress its voice and modify its procedures?

20. As our school enrolments continue to increase, will we secure for the children the facilities necessary for their good education? When shortages in building materials occur, will we give school buildings at least equal chance with amusement places in the allocation of such materials as are available?

21. Will we continue our historical characteristic of evolving educational institutions and programs to meet new situations and needs? Will we, for example, provide an appropriate educational program for the 22,000,000 persons over sixty-five who will be with us in 1980?

The above challenges, of course, arise from the discussions presented in this book. They could go on at great length. Let them serve to remind the reader as he takes leave of these pages that he is in the middle of something great and on-going, that here, after all, is the fountainhead of the future.

What of the schools of America? They are your schools and mine; we are they who must understand the great freedoms they serve, their firm commitment to human betterment. They need now our fervent study and support, our best judgments and guidance in the years ahead. If they should fail, as they must not, the cry of the children would ring endless in the land; if they succeed, as they can, the voices of the future will be happy and free.

SELECTED READING REFERENCES

Chapter 1: *Backgrounds to American Education*

Cubberley, Ellwood P. *The History of Education.* Boston: Houghton Mifflin Co., 1920.

Eby, Frederick, and Arrowood, Charles F. *The Development of Modern Education.* New York: Prentice-Hall, Inc., 1934.

Good, H. G. *A History of Western Education.* New York: Macmillan Co., 1950.

Knight, Edgar W. *Twenty Centuries of Education.* Boston: Ginn & Co., 1940.

Monroe, Paul. *Textbook in the History of Education.* New York: Macmillan Co., 1914.

Wilds, Elmer H. *The Foundations of Modern Education* (new and enlarged ed.). New York: Rinehart & Co., Inc., 1942.

Chapter 2: *The Development of Education in America*

Cubberley, Ellwood P. *Public Education in the United States* (revised and enlarged ed.). Boston: Houghton Mifflin Co., 1934.

Educational Policies Commission. *Education and the Peoples' Peace.* Washington, D. C.: National Education Association, May, 1943.

Hawkins, Layton S., Prosser, Charles A., and Wright, John C. *Development of Vocational Education.* Chicago: American Technical Society, 1951.

Johnson, Clifton. *Old-Time Schools and School Books.* New York: Macmillan Co., 1904.

Knight, Edgar W. *Education in the United States.* Boston: Ginn & Co., 1929.

Van Til, William. *Economic Roads for American Democracy.* New York: McGraw-Hill Book Co., Inc., 1947.

Chapter 3: *The American Ideal of Education*

American Association of School Administrators. *Schools for a New World.* (Twenty-Fifth Yearbook.) Washington, D. C.: National Education Association, 1947, chaps. i–iv.

Brubacher, John S. (ed.). *The Public Schools and Spiritual Values.* (Seventh Yearbook of the John Dewey Society.) New York: Harper & Bros., 1944.

Cummings, Howard H. *Improving Human Relations.* (National Council for the Social Studies, Bulletin Number 25.) Washington, D. C.: National Education Association, 1949.

Dewey, John. *Democracy and Education.* New York: Macmillan Co., 1916.

——. *The School and Society.* Chicago: University of Chicago Press, 1900.

Educational Policies Commission. *Learning the Ways of Democracy.* Washington, D. C.: National Education Association, 1940, chap. i.

——. *Moral and Spiritual Values in the Public Schools.* Washington, D. C.: National Education Association, 1951, chaps. i–iii.

——. *The Purposes of Education in American Democracy.* Washington, D. C.: National Education Association, 1938.

HALL-QUEST, ALFRED L. "Three Educational Theories." *School and Society.* LVI (November 14, 1942), 452–59.

HENRY, VIRGIL. *The Place of Religion in Public Schools.* New York: Harper & Bros., 1950.

LEWIN, KURT. *Resolving Social Conflicts.* New York: Harper & Bros., 1948.

MOEHLMAN, CONRAD HENRY. *School and Church: The American Way.* New York: Harper & Bros., 1944.

RAUP, R. BRUCE, AXTELLE, GEORGE E., BENNE, KENNETH D., and SMITH, B. OTHAMEL. *The Improvement of Practical Intelligence.* New York: Harper & Bros., 1950.

THAYER, V. T. *American Education Under Fire.* New York: Harper & Bros., 1944.

CHAPTER 4: *Some Aspects of Education 'Abroad*

ARNDT, CHRISTIAN O., and EVERETT, SAMUEL. *Education for a World Society.* New York: Harper & Bros., 1951.

BOOTH, GEORGE C. *Mexico's School-Made Society.* Stanford: Stanford University Press, 1941.

HALL, ROBERT KING. *Education for a New Japan.* New Haven: Yale University Press, 1949.

RICHTER, WERNER. *Re-Educating Germany.* Chicago: University of Chicago Press, 1945.

U. N. DEPARTMENT OF PUBLIC INFORMATION. *How Peoples Work Together* (revised ed.). The United Nations and the Specialized Agencies. New York: Manhattan Publishing Co., 1951.

"UNESCO'S Work in Education." *The Harvard Educational Review,* XX, No. 3 (summer, 1950), entire issue.

UNITED STATES NATIONAL COMMISSION FOR UNESCO. *UNESCO Today.* Washington, D. C.: United States Government Printing Office, November, 1949.

CHAPTER 5: *The Organization and Administration of American Education*

ALLEN, HOLLIS P. *The Federal Government and Education.* New York: McGraw-Hill Book Co., Inc., 1950.

AMERICAN ASSOCIATION OF SCHOOL ADMINISTRATORS. *Paths to Better Schools.* (Twenty-Third Yearbook.) Washington, D. C.: National Education Association, 1945, chap. vii.

———. *Public Relations for America's Schools.* (Twenty-Eighth Yearbook.) Washington, D. C.: National Education Association, 1950, chaps. iv–vii.

———. *School Boards in Action.* (Twenty-Fourth Yearbook.) Washington, D. C.: National Education Association, 1946.

———. *Schools for a New World.* (Twenty-Fifth Yearbook.) Washington, D. C.: National Education Association, 1947, chaps. ix–xiii.

BENJAMIN, HAROLD (ed.). *Democracy in the Administration of Higher Education.* (Tenth Yearbook of the John Dewey Society.) New York: Harper & Bros., 1950.

DAVIES, DANIEL R., and HOSLER, FRED W. *The Challenge of School Board Membership.* New York: Chartwell House, Inc., 1949.

EDUCATIONAL POLICIES COMMISSION. *Education for All American Youth.* Washington, D. C.: National Education Association, 1944, chap. v.

———. *Education for All American Children.* Washington, D. C.: National Education Association, 1948, chap. v.

———. *Learning the Ways of Democracy.* Washington, D. C.: National Education Association, 1940, chap. vi.

———. *The Structure and Administration of Education in American Democracy.* Washington, D. C.: National Education Association, 1938.

GAUMNITZ, WALTER H., and BLOSE, DAVID T. *The One-Teacher School—Its Mid-century Status.* (Circular No. 318.) Washington, D. C.: United States Office of Education, 1950.

HULBURD, DAVID. *This Happened in Pasadena.* New York: Macmillan Co., 1951.

KEESECKER, WARD W. *State Boards of Education and Chief State School Officers.* (Bulletin 1950, No. 12.) Washington, D. C.: United States Office of Education, 1950.

NATIONAL SOCIETY FOR THE STUDY OF EDUCATION. *Changing Conceptions in Educational Administration.* (Forty-Fifth Yearbook, Part II.) Chicago: University of Chicago Press, 1946.

———. *American Education in the Postwar Period: Structural Reorganization.* (Forty-Fourth Yearbook, Part II.) Chicago: University of Chicago Press, 1945.

REEDER, WARD G. *School Boards and Superintendents.* New York: Macmillan Co., 1945.

REEVES, FLOYD W. *Education for Rural America.* Chicago: University of Chicago Press, 1945.

SCHATZMANN, IMAN ELSIE. *The Country School at Home and Abroad.* Chicago: University of Chicago Press, 1942.

CHAPTER 6: *The Support of Schools in America*

AMERICAN ASSOCIATION OF SCHOOL ADMINISTRATORS. *Paths to Better Schools.* (Twenty-Third Yearbook.) Washington, D. C.: National Education Association, 1945, chap. viii.

———. *The Expanding Role of Education.* (Twenty-Sixth Yearbook.) Washington, D. C.: National Education Association, 1948, chap. xii.

BURKE, ARVID J. *Financing Public Schools in the United States.* New York: Harper & Bros., 1951.

COUNCIL OF STATE GOVERNMENTS. *The Forty-Eight State School Systems.* Chicago: Council of State Governments, 1949.

State and Local Public School Finance Programs 1949–50. Washington, D. C.: Division of School Administration, United States Office of Education in cooperation with State Departments of Education, Council of State Governments, and the University of California, 1950.

Still Unfinished—Our Educational Obligation to America's Children. Washington, D. C.: National Education Association, 1948.

The Stake of Business in Public School Education. (An Address by Frank W. Abrams.) New York: National Citizens Commission for the Public Schools, 1951.

CHAPTER 7: *The American Educational Ladder*

AIKIN, WILFORD M. *The Story of the Eight-Year Study.* (*Adventure in American Education,* Vol. I.) New York: Harper & Bros., 1942.

AMERICAN ASSOCIATION OF SCHOOL ADMINISTRATORS. *The Expanding Role of Education.* (Twenty-Sixth Yearbook.) Washington, D. C.: National Education Association, 1948.

BOGUE, JESSE PARKER. *The Community College.* New York: McGraw-Hill Book Co., Inc., 1950.

ELSBREE, WILLARD S. *Pupil Progress in the Elementary School.* (*Practical Suggestions for Teaching,* Bulletin No. 5, Hollis L. Caswell.) New York: Bureau of Publications, Teachers College, Columbia University, 1943.

Higher Education and Society. (A Symposium.) Norman, Oklahoma: University of Oklahoma Press, 1936.

LANDRETH, CATHERINE. *Education of the Young Child.* (A Nursery School Manual.) New York: John Wiley & Sons, Inc., 1942.

THE PRESIDENT'S COMMISSION ON HIGHER EDUCATION. *Higher Education for American Democracy.* New York: Harper & Bros., 1948.

SEXSON, JOHN A., and HARBESON, JOHN W. *The New American College.* New York: Harper & Bros., 1946.

CHAPTER 8: *The American School Population and Related Problems*

AMERICAN ASSOCIATION OF SCHOOL ADMINISTRATORS. *Paths to Better Schools.* (Twenty-Third Yearbook.) Washington, D. C.: National Education Association, 1945, chap. i.

EDUCATIONAL POLICIES COMMISSION. *Education of the Gifted.* Washington, D. C.: National Education Association, 1950.

HECK, ARCH O. *The Education of Exceptional Children.* New York: McGraw-Hill Book Co., Inc., 1940.

KEMPFER, HOMER. *Education for a Long and Useful Life.* (Bulletin 1950, No. 6.) Washington, D. C.: United States Office of Education.

NATIONAL SOCIETY FOR THE STUDY OF EDUCATION. *Early Childhood Education.* (Forty-Sixth Yearbook, Part II.) Chicago: University of Chicago Press, 1947.

———. *The Education of Exceptional Children.* (Forty-Ninth Yearbook, Part II.) Chicago: University of Chicago Press, 1950.

OLSON, WILLARD C. *Child Development.* Boston: D. C. Heath & Co., 1949.

TORGERSON, THEODORE L. *Studying Children.* New York: Dryden Press, 1947.

CHAPTER 9: *The Educational Offering*

AMERICAN ASSOCIATION OF SCHOOL ADMINISTRATORS. *The Expanding Role of Education.* (Twenty-Sixth Yearbook.) Washington, D. C.: National Education Association, 1948, chaps. i-x.

ASSOCIATION FOR SUPERVISION AND CURRICULUM DEVELOPMENT. *Action for Curriculum Improvement.* (1951 Yearbook.) Washington, D. C.: National Education Association.

BATHURST, EFFIE G. *Where Children Live Affects Curriculum.* (Bulletin 1950, No. 7) Washington, D. C.: United States Office of Education.

COLLIER, PAUL D. *The Redirection, Reorganization, and Retooling of Secondary Education.* (Bulletin 37, revised March 1948.) Hartford: Connecticut State Department of Education, 1948.

COMMITTEE ON INTERNATIONAL RELATIONS. *Education for International Understanding in American Schools.* Washington, D. C.: National Education Association, 1948.

CUMMINGS, HOWARD H., LUDINGTON, JOHN R., and ANDERSON, HOWARD R. *Developing Life Adjustment Education in a Local School.* (Circular No. 253, revised June 1951.) Washington, D. C.: United States Office of Education.

DEPARTMENT OF SUPERVISION AND CURRICULUM DEVELOPMENT. *Toward a New Curriculum.* (1944 Yearbook.) Washington, D. C.: National Education Association.

DOUGLASS, HARL R. *Education for Life Adjustment.* New York: Ronald Press Co., 1950.

EDUCATIONAL POLICIES COMMISSION. *Education for All American Children.* Washington, D. C.: National Education Association, 1948, chap. iii.

———. *Education for All American Youth.* Washington, D. C.: National Education Association, 1944, chaps. ii-iv.

———. *Moral and Spiritual Values in the Public Schools.* Washington, D. C.: National Education Association, 1951, chap. iv.

FAUNCE, ROLAND C., and BOSSING, NELSON L. *Developing the Core Curriculum.* New York: Prentice-Hall, Inc., 1951.

FEATHERSTONE, WILLIAM B. *A Functional Curriculum for Youth.* New York: American Book Co., 1951.

GWYNN, J. MINOR. *Curriculum Principles and Social Trends.* New York: Macmillan Co., 1943.

HARAP, HENRY. *The Changing Curriculum.* New York: Appleton-Century-Crofts Inc., 1937.

KILPATRICK, W. H., VAN TIL, WILLIAM, and OTHERS. *Intercultural Attitudes in the Making.* (Ninth Yearbook of the John Dewey Society.) New York: Harper & Bros., 1947.

LEE, J. MURRAY, and LEE, DORRIS MAY. *The Child and His Curriculum.* (2d ed.) New York: Appleton-Century-Crofts, Inc., 1950.

NATIONAL SOCIETY FOR THE STUDY OF EDUCATION. *Curriculum Reconstruction.* (Forty-Fourth Yearbook, Part I.) Chicago: The University of Chicago Press, 1945.

———. *Audio-visual Materials of Instruction.* (Forty-Eighth Yearbook, Part I.) Chicago: University of Chicago Press, 1949.

PITKIN, VICTOR E. *The Task of Citizenship Education.* (Bulletin 50.) Hartford: Connecticut State Department of Education, 1951.

PROSSER, CHARLES A., and QUIGLEY, THOMAS H. *Vocational Education in a Democracy.* Chicago: American Technical Society, 1949.

SANFORD, CHARLES W., HAND, HAROLD C., and SPAULDING, WILLARD B. *The Schools and National Security.* New York: McGraw-Hill Book Co., Inc., 1951.

SPEARS, HAROLD. *The High School for Today.* New York: American Book Co., 1950.

STRATEMEYER, FLORENCE B., FORKNER, HAMDEN L., McKIM, MARGARET G., and OTHERS. *Developing a Curriculum for Modern Living.* New York: Bureau of Publications, Teachers College, Columbia University, 1947.

STRUCK, F. THEODORE. *Vocational Education for a Changing World.* New York: John Wiley & Sons, Inc., 1945.

Vitalizing Secondary Education. (Bulletin 1951, No. 3.) Washington, D. C.: United States Office of Education.

CHAPTER 10: *Counseling in the School*

BAER, MAX F., and ROEBER, EDWARD C. *Occupational Information.* Chicago: Science Research Associates, Inc., 1951.

ERICKSON, CLIFFORD E., and HAPP, MARION C. *Guidance Practices at Work.* New York: McGraw-Hill Book Co., Inc., 1946.

GINSBURG, ELI, GINSBURG, SOL W., AXELROD, SIDNEY, and HERMA, JOHN L. *Occupational Choice.* New York: Columbia University Press, 1951.

HAVINGHURST, ROBERT J., and TABA, HILDA. *Adolescent Character and Personality.* New York: John Wiley & Sons, Inc., 1949.

JENKINS, GLADYS G., SHACTER, HELEN, and BAUER, WILLIAM W. *These Are Your Children.* New York: Scott, Foresman and Co., 1949.

KITSON, HARRY DEXTER. *I Find My Vocation.* (3d ed.) New York: McGraw-Hill Book Co., Inc., 1947,

RUCH, FLOYD L., MACKENZIE, GORDON N., and McCLEAN, MARGARET. *People Are Important.* New York: Scott, Foresman, and Co., 1941.

SEGEL, DAVID. *Frustration in Adolescent Youth.* (Bulletin 1951, No. 1.) Washington, D. C.: United States Office of Education.

SMITH, GLENN E. *Principles and Practices of the Guidance Program.* New York: Macmillan Co., 1951.

STRANG, RUTH. *Educational Guidance: Its Principles and Practices.* New York: Macmillan Co., 1947.

WILLIAMS, BERYL. *People Are Our Business.* Philadelphia: J. B. Lippincott Co., 1947.

CHAPTER 11: *The Learning-Teaching Relationship*

AMERICAN ASSOCIATION OF SCHOOL ADMINISTRATORS. *Paths to Better Schools.* (Twenty-Third Yearbook.) Washington, D. C.: National Education Association, 1945, chap. v.

ASSOCIATION FOR SUPERVISION AND CURRICULUM DEVELOPMENT. *Organizing the Elementary School for Living and Learning.* (1947 Yearbook.) Washington, D. C.: National Education Association, 1947.

———. *Toward Better Teaching.* (1949 Yearbook.) Washington, D. C.: National Education Association.

COMMISSION ON TEACHER EDUCATION. *Helping Teachers Understand Children.* Washington, D. C.: American Council on Education, 1945.

DEPARTMENT OF SUPERVISION AND CURRICULUM DEVELOPMENT. *Group Planning in Education.* (1945 Yearbook.) Washington, D. C.: National Education Association.

EDUCATIONAL POLICIES COMMISSION. *Learning the Ways of Democracy.* Washington, D. C.: National Education Association, 1940, chap. iii.

HUGGETT, ALBERT J., and MILLARD, CECIL U. *Growth and Learning in the Elementary School.* Boston: D. C. Heath & Co., 1946.

KINGSLEY, HOWARD L. *The Nature and Conditions of Learning.* New York: Prentice-Hall, Inc., 1946.

KITSON, HARRY D. *How to Use Your Mind.* (4th ed). Philadelphia: J. B. Lippincott Co., 1951.

NATIONAL SOCIETY FOR THE STUDY OF EDUCATION. *Learning and Instruction.* (Yearbook XLIX, Part I.) Chicago: University of Chicago Press, 1950.

NOAR, GERTRUDE. *Freedom to Live and Learn.* Philadelphia: Franklin Publishing & Supply Co., 1948.

SPEARS, HAROLD. *Some Principles of Teaching.* New York: Prentice-Hall, Inc., 1949.

SUPERVISORS AND DIRECTORS OF INSTRUCTION. *Mental Health in the Classroom.* (Thirteenth Yearbook.) Washington, D. C.: National Education Association, 1941.

WEBER, JULIA. *My Country School Diary.* New York: Harper & Bros., 1946.

CHAPTER 12: *The Improvement of Education and the Evaluation of Its Outcomes*

AMERICAN ASSOCIATION OF SCHOOL ADMINISTRATORS. *Public Relations for America's Schools.* (Twenty-Eighth Yearbook.) Washington, D. C.: National Education Association, 1950, chap. xi.

EDUCATONAL POLICIES COMMISSION. *Learning the Ways of Democracy.* Washington, D. C.: National Education Association, 1940, chap. vii.

GREENE, H. A., JORGENSEN, A. N., and GERBERICH, J. R. *Measurement and Evaluation in the Elementary School.* New York: Longmans, Green & Co., 1942.
——. *Measurement and Evaluation in the Secondary School.* New York: Longmans, Green & Co., 1943.
NATIONAL SOCIETY FOR THE STUDY OF EDUCATION. *The Measurement of Understanding.* (Yearbook XLV, Part I.) Chicago: University of Chicago Press, 1946.
STRANG, RUTH. *Reporting to Parents.* (*Practical Suggestions for Teaching,* Bulletin No. 10, Hollis L. Caswell.) New York: Bureau of Publications, Teachers College, Columbia University, 1947.
WRINKLE, WILLIAM L. *Improving Marking and Reporting Practices in Elementary and Secondary Schools.* New York: Rinehart & Co., Inc., 1947.

CHAPTER 13: *School and Community Interrelationships*

ALDRICH, JULIAN C., and MARKERT, MARLOW A. *We, the Citizens.* New York: Inor Publishing Co., Inc., 1948.
AMERICAN ASSOCIATION OF SCHOOL ADMINISTRATORS. *Paths to Better Schools.* (Twenty-Third Yearbook.) Washington, D. C.: National Education Association, 1945, chap. ix.
——. *Public Relations for America's Schools.* (Twenty-Eighth Yearbook.) Washington, D. C.: National Education Association, 1950, chaps. i, ii, and xii.
——. *The Expanding Role of Education.* (Twenty-Sixth Yearbook.) Washington, D. C.: National Education Association, 1948, chap. xiii.
BRUNNER, EDMUND DE S. *Community Organization and Adult Education.* (A Five-Year Experiment.) Chapel Hill: The University of North Carolina Press, 1942.
DIEKHOFF, JOHN S. *Democracy's College.* New York: Harper & Bros., 1950.
EDUCATIONAL POLICIES COMMISSION. *Citizens and Educational Policies.* Washington, D. C.: National Education Association, 1951.
——. *Education for All American Children.* Washington, D. C.: National Education Association, 1948, chap. vi.
——. *Learning the Ways of Democracy.* Washington, D. C.: National Education Association, 1940, chap. v.
——. *Moral and Spiritual Values in the Public Schools.* Washington, D. C.: National Education Association, 1951, chap. v.
GOVERNOR'S FACT-FINDING COMMISSION ON EDUCATION. *Do Citizens and Education Mix?* Norwalk, Conn.: O'Brien Suburban Press, 1950.
HULBURD, DAVID. *This Happened in Pasadena.* New York: Macmillan Co., 1951.
IVINS, WILSON H., and RUNGE, WILLIAM B. *Work Experience in High School.* New York: Ronald Press Co., 1951.
LANE, BESS B. *Your Part in Your Child's Education.* New York: E. P. Dutton & Co., Inc., 1948.
MELBY, ERNEST O. *American Education Under Fire.* ("Freedom Pamphlets," Frank N. Trager.) New York: Anti-Defamation League of B'Nai B'Rith, 1951.
What Do We Know About Our Schools? New York: National Citizens Commission for the Public Schools, 1951.
YEAGER, WILLIAM A. *School-Community Relations.* New York: Dryden Press, 1951.

CHAPTER 14: *The Profession of Education*

AMERICAN ASSOCIATION OF SCHOOL ADMINISTRATORS. *Public Relations for America's Schools.* (Twenty-Eighth Yearbook.) Washington, D. C.: National Education Association, 1950, chap. viii.

———. *Paths to Better Schools.* (Twenty-Third Yearbook.) Washington, D. C.: National Education Association, 1945, chap. vi.

COMMISSION ON TEACHER EDUCATION. *Teachers For Our Times.* Washington, D. C.: American Council on Education, 1944.

EDUCATIONAL POLICIES COMMISSION. *Education for All American Children.* Washington, D. C.: National Education Association, 1948, chap. iv.

FRAZIER, BENJAMIN W. *Teaching As A Profession.* (Pamphlet No. 95.) Washington, D. C.: United States Office of Education, 1944.

MAUL, RAY C. *Teacher Supply and Demand in the United States.* (Report of the 1951 National Teachers Supply and Demand Study.) Washington, D. C.: National Education Association, 1951.

PETERSON, HOUSTON. *Great Teachers.* New Brunswick: Rutgers University Press, 1946.

Public-School Retirement at the Half Century. (Research Bulletin, Vol. XXVIII, No. 4, December 1950.) Washington, D. C.: National Education Association.

INDEX OF NAMES

INDEX OF SUBJECTS